THE GREEKS AND THEIR GODS

THE CLASSICAL EXPERIENCE

The Greeks and Their Gods, by W. K. C. Guthrie
Hellas: A Short History of Ancient Greece, by C. E. Robinson
Plato's Thought, by G. M. A. Grube
Alexander the Great, by W. W. Tarn

William Keith Chambers Guthrie, Fellow of Peterhouse. Cambridge University, is Professor of Ancient Philosophy and Public Orator of the University. Between 1929 and 1932 he was a member of three expeditions of the American Society for Archaeological Research in Asia Minor. He served in the British Intelligence Corps during World War II. His books include *The Greek Philosophers and Orpheus* and *Greek Religion;* he is a co-author of *Monumenta Asiae Minoris Antiqua,* as well as editor and translator of Aristotle's *De Caelo* (Loeb Classical Library).

THE GREEKS AND THEIR GODS

by

W. K. C. GUTHRIE

BEACON PRESS · BOSTON

First published by the Beacon Press 1950
(Reprinted, with corrections, 1954)

First Beacon Paperback edition published 1955

Beacon Press books are published under the auspices
of the Unitarian Universalist Association

International Standard Book Number: 0-8070-5793-2

19 18 17 16 15 14 13 12 11 10

To
ARTHUR BERNARD COOK

*δικάζει τἀμπλακήμαθ', ὡς λόγος,
Ζεὺς ἄλλος.*

Published by arrangement with Methuen & Co., Ltd. This edition is for sale within the United States of America only and is not to be imported into any part of the British Empire.

Printed in the United States of America

PREFACE

THE primary aim of this book is to serve as a kind of religious companion to the Greek classics. It does not so much set out to interest specialists as to be useful to those who enjoy Greek literature, whether in the original or in translation, and have made the inevitable discovery that almost every branch of it—epic, tragedy, comedy, philosophy, history, and even the life of the political arena and the law-courts as revealed by the orators—is permeated by religion. Those who feel a deeper interest in the subject for its own sake, or are stimulated by these pages themselves to probe it further, will find jumping-off points in the footnotes, in which alone a knowledge of Greek is sometimes demanded for full understanding. The references there given are intended to provide the necessary guidance for further reading which might otherwise have been given in a separate bibliography. So far as possible I have quoted the more accessible works, and this is why I have been so sparing of references to the invaluable first volume of Nilsson's *Geschichte der Griechischen Religion* (Munich, 1941), for it is even now not easily obtainable in this country.

For some years now I have been lecturing on Greek religion at Cambridge, and there is naturally a connexion between the lectures and the book. In case some of those who heard them may wonder what the relationship is, I should like to say that the general arrangement of the most recent lectures has been preserved, since that had been shown by experiment to be a workable order of exposition, but that the book contains nearly twice the amount of matter.

Now that the book is written, I am chiefly conscious of its omissions. In particular I owe an apology to those whom Ovid called the "plebs superum"—

> Fauni Satyrique Laresque
> Fluminaque et Nymphae semideumque genus

—for the scant notice which they receive. Omissions were however inevitable if the double purpose were to be achieved of producing a single volume of a not too alarming size and at the same time giving it an organic unity by following a particular theme rather than attempting a disjointed and cursory survey of the whole field. This second aim was pursued in the hope that the result would be readable.

My grateful thanks are due to Professor E. R. Dodds, who found time to read through the proofs of the first eleven chapters although they came when he was engaged in immediate and absorbing tasks of his own. I owe to him a number of corrections, many additional references, and in several places a salutary change of emphasis or the necessary qualification of an unduly dogmatic statement. It does not of course follow that he would agree with all that remains. I have also had the advantage throughout of the criticism and advice of my wife, and the work owes more than I can well express to her classical training, her clear sense of form, and her immediately unfavourable reaction to obscurity or clumsiness of expression.

Peterhouse
Cambridge
December 1949

W.K.C.G.

CONTENTS

INTRODUCTION

ἐπεί γε ἀπεκρίθη ἐκ παλαιτέρου τοῦ βαρβάρου ἔθνεος τὸ Ἑλληνικόν, ἐὸν καὶ δεξιώτερον καὶ εὐηθίης ἠλιθίου ἀπηλλαγμένον μᾶλλον.

. . . seeing that from old times the Hellenic has ever been distinguished from the foreign stock by its greater cleverness and its freedom from silly foolishness. Herodotus i, 60 (trans. A. D. Godley)

λάβωμεν δὲ ὡς ὅτιπερ ἂν Ἕλληνες βαρβάρων παραλάβωσι, κάλλιον τοῦτο εἰς τέλος ἀπεργάζονται.

We may take it that whatever Greeks inherit from other races, in the end they turn it into something better. Plato, *Epinomis* (987d)

"WHEN I say 'religion', I am instantly obliged to correct myself. It is not religion, it is ritual that absorbs me." The confession is Jane Harrison's, and although her own position was complicated by the reaction from a somewhat narrow evangelical upbringing, it affords a good illustration of the attitude to their subject adopted by many writers of the older generation, especially when taken in conjunction with the explanatory sentence which follows soon after. "Great things in literature, Greek plays for example, I most enjoy when behind their bright splendours I see moving darker and older shapes." Ritual is preferred because it is older, because it takes one beneath the Greek achievement of clear thought and classic art to see the dark soil from which it sprang and the humbler but necessary forms of life which pullulate there. This attitude was the product of the age of anthropological discovery, with its revelations, fascinating and astonishing to a contemporary, of the primitive origins to which even the highest forms of religious belief may be traced. It was an urgent, as well as an absorbing, task to track down such primitive elements surviving, often uncomprehended, in the life of classical Greece, and it cannot be said that the distinctively Greek achievement was thereby obscured, at least for the discerning reader, who when he turned back to Greek literature with the new knowledge in his mind could only stand amazed at the transforming genius there displayed.

Nevertheless there is perhaps room now for a book in English by one whose inclination is to bring out through the study of their religion the distinctive character of the Greek mind and its differences from, rather than its resemblances to, earlier and surrounding cultures from which, in the phrase of Herodotus, it had "become separated off". It was by this separation, this capacity to build a new culture and new, more civilized, modes of thought, that the Greeks were enabled to become the founders of European civilization, and it is this, therefore, which constitutes our justification for bestowing so much time and attention upon them. It is seen to best advantage in the works of their great individual thinkers, an Aeschylus or a Plato, rather than in the average superstitious citizen or countryman, who more closely (though by no means entirely) resembled his counterpart elsewhere. The great writers themselves were products of their age, and cannot be understood except in relation to their historical setting and the social, economic, and psychological surroundings in which they lived. But genius transcends this background, or—should we say? —distils the purest essence of its epoch into vessels perfectly fitted to receive it by the creation of works of art such as none of its contemporaries would have conceived; and it is the genius which in art delights and in thought assists us. "You would never have been famous if you had been born in Seriphos," said an inhabitant of that insignificant islet to Themistocles. "True, nor you if you had been born an Athenian," was the great man's reply. If Plato had been born in Western Europe after the Second World War his political philosophy (though not necessarily his metaphysics) would in some respects have been different; but if, to test the limits of environment as a deciding factor, one puts the converse question, whether any representative citizen of fourth-century Athens, told to write down his political philosophy, would have produced anything remotely resembling Plato's, the answer is no. We must find out what we can about the beliefs of ordinary Greeks, because without that knowledge it is difficult to understand and appreciate their leaders in literature and philosophy. That indeed is the inquiry with which this book will be to a large extent concerned; but it is written on the assumption that it is only a means to an end.

It has been truly remarked by a German worker in this field that "in the study of religion, the general outlook of the researcher plays a more prominent part than in any other branch of knowledge",[1] and the reader may as well be warned of this at the start. In conformity with what I have said, I find that my confession would be the opposite of Jane Harrison's. It is not ritual that absorbs me, it is the state of mind of the people who performed the ritual. It is sometimes objected that ritual at least gives certainty. One can know what people did, but how can we fathom what they thought while they were doing it? I doubt the validity of this objection. According to Clement of Alexandria (note that our witness is a hostile critic who lived some six hundred years later than the contemporaries of Sophocles or Plato), the formula repeated by a candidate for initiation at the Eleusinian mysteries, to show that he had carried out the necessary preliminary ritual, was, literally translated: "I fasted: I drank the *kykeon*:[2] I took from the chest: having performed (or "handled" or "dealt with"; the object is not specified) I put away into the basket and from the basket into the chest." Granted that Clement has accurately learned and transmitted the statement of these ritual acts, I doubt if they teach us anything either so precise or so interesting about the mysteries as the words in the Homeric Hymn to Demeter, written as early as the beginning of the sixth century B.C. in Attica: "Blessed among men who dwell on earth is he who has seen these things; but he who is uninitiated and has no part in the rites has never an equal lot when he has died and passed beneath the dank darkness", or the lines which Plutarch quotes from Sophocles: "Thrice blessed are those mortals who have seen these rites before they come to Hades, for to them alone is granted true life. Everything evil awaits the rest."

The theme which I wish to develop in the following pages may be described in some such words as these: *The relations between man and God (or gods, or divinity) as they appeared to the Greeks of the classical period.* In setting chronological limits I have tried to act, not mechanically, but under the guidance of a ruling idea, namely, to try to discover in what direction lie the distinctively Hellenic contributions to religious thought. It follows that the inquiry must be

[1] Kurt Pfister, "Die Religion der Griechen und Römer" (Bursian's *Jahresbericht über die Fortschritte der Klass. Altertumswissenschaft* (Leipzig), suppl. 229 (1930), 10): "Mehr also als in jeder anderen Wissenschaft, spielt in der Religionswissenschaft die Weltanschauung des Forschers eine Rolle."

[2] A mixture of wine with grain and cheese, drunk in commemoration of the myth of Demeter who was offered it during the course of her distracted wanderings in search of Persephone. The reference to Clement is *Protr.* ii 18.

concentrated on the period when there was such a thing as a distinctively Hellenic civilization. Other periods are relevant only as they help to explain, or to show up by contrast, the peculiar characteristics of this one. This not only limits the amount of attention which we shall pay to primitive origins, but means also that our subject ceases with the breaking-up of the city-state during the fourth century. I hope to show that the most typically Hellenic elements in religion were bound up with the typically Hellenic form of society; and when the military and political achievements of the Macedonians destroyed the one, they dealt a heavy blow at the other also. Herodotus speaks of a time when the Hellenic had separated itself off from the foreign stock by its greater cleverness and freedom from foolish and simple notions. When we delve into what we call the origins of Greek religion, we must remember that we are recalling an age of what appeared to the Greeks themselves as "non-Greek and foolish simplicity", and that one of the most important origins of Greek religion was the superior mentality of the Greek. And just as there was an age of infancy, when τὸ Ἑλληνικόν was not yet free from the swaddling-clothes of εὐηθίη ἠλίθιος, so also there came a later age, sometimes called an age of decline, though in many ways it was anything but that—but an age, at least, when the exclusive character of the Hellenic once again broke down. The Hellene ceased to live for himself. He went abroad in the world and took his culture with him. The world benefited, but the consequences for Hellenism were inevitable. It had to mingle with the general stream, to receive as well as to give. It became watered down, and the days of the *separateness* of Greek culture were over. Herodotus speaks of the opening of an era. We can see its close as well. If what we are seeking is the Greek mind, we must look for it between these limits, where it is easiest to find, that is, where it is purest, in the age when the Hellenic was, in so far as it ever became so, separated off from foreign strains.

Chapter I

OUR PREDECESSORS

WHEN a subject has had as many books written about it as have been written on the religion of the ancient Greeks, it is important to know where we ourselves stand. We cannot bring to our study of the primary sources a virgin mind, untouched by the opinions of the many generations of writers, scholarly or otherwise, who have gone before us. Their influence may work either directly or inversely. That is to say, we may either follow our predecessors or react from them. In either case it is they who will, to a considerable extent, determine the trend of our thought. We may not like it, but it is inevitable. To be conscious of this, and to have enough knowledge to estimate it correctly, is of varying degrees of importance in different subjects. In the study of Greek religion it is all-important, and I can think of no better way of introducing the subject than by calling attention to a few facts which will help to form this consciousness.

For the beginnings of a scientific interest in Greek religion, if we use that overworked epithet to mean no more than an interest prompted solely by the desire to know and understand, we should have to go back to the ancient Greeks themselves, among whom an intellectual curiosity about the origins and history of their own religious beliefs, rites and customs was by no means lacking. From the results of this curiosity we shall learn much as we proceed, but it will serve the limited and purely practical purpose of the present chapter if we make a somewhat arbitrary beginning in the eighteenth century of our era. It was in the latter part of this century that the literature and art of Greece, as known at the time, were exercising an especial fascination on the creative minds of Germany; but how incomplete and distorted was the view of Greece on which this influence was based has been ably demonstrated by more than one recent writer,[1] and must indeed be

[1] Cf. Humphry Trevelyan, *The Popular Background to Goethe's Hellenism* (London, 1934), and *Goethe and the Greeks* (Cambridge, 1941); E. M. Butler, *The Tyranny of Greece over Germany* (Cambridge, 1935).

obvious to anyone who reflects for a moment on the various sources of information—archaeology, epigraphy, comparative religion and many more—which to-day are as tools in daily use in the investigator's workshop and were then almost completely unknown. In the earlier years of the century, when classical studies in Germany were at a low ebb, and the English were beginning to lay the linguistic and textual foundations for a knowledge of ancient literature, religion meant for most people mythology, and the myths were chiefly thought of in the form in which the ingenuity and taste of Roman poets had cast them. Such mythology it was difficult to connect with religion in any true sense of the word. In the form in which the myths were generally encountered, they had often ceased to have any connexion with religion, and had already become the self-conscious literary and poetic fancies which, in the almost universal opinion of Western Europe, they had always been. It was, to be sure, the age of rationalism, but such was the evidence available that this rationalism could take the form, as it did in the writings of a professor at Halle in the 1730's, of asserting that the Romans were the inventors of polytheism, which they devised for reasons of political expediency.[1]

There was no real knowledge of the Greeks to correct these curious ideas, and as literary ornaments the myths provided useful material for the particular poetic genius of the eighteenth century. The aim of art was pleasure, and the rococo its typical form. This aim it was assumed that the myths had always been intended to serve, and into this form they were successfully moulded.

The reaction which followed, discrediting the aesthetic theories of the age of rationalism, made possible a more realistic approach to the myths and a deeper understanding of their significance. When Herder said that "poets, and none but poets, made the myths and gave them their character", he might be thought to be using the language of rationalism. In fact, however, his words arose from an entirely different conception of the poetic impulse, which he regarded as closely akin to the religious instinct. One might almost say that his answer to the eternal question of the origin of religion was that it sprang from the poetic, or more generally from the artistic instinct in men. Religion arose from the awareness of beauty, and the earliest revelation of the divine

[1] H. Trevelyan, *Popular Background*, p. 28, n. 1. The professor had presumably been misled by Polybius.

was through poetry. Although Herder did not limit this conception to the Greeks, it was of course in them that it was most plainly manifested, and however far from the mark he may have been in trying to account for all religion in this way, he certainly came near the truth when he insisted that the distinctive features of Hellenic religion were inseparable from the eagerness of their response to the beautiful in nature and its representation in literature or art. We may be grateful for his explicit statement that it was art which gave to the religion of the Greeks most of its lasting worth. And if in restoring to its rightful place the artistic element in Greek religion he did a lasting service, by emphasizing conversely the religious element in art he pointed the way to entirely new methods of investigation which have only borne fruit as successive excavations and discoveries on Greek soil have provided the necessary material to put them into practice.

In sharp contrast to the ideas of rationalism, it was an essential part of Herder's aesthetic theory that poetic and artistic creation were not the result of conscious and deliberate thought acting according to the artist's will. Rather they were the outward expression of forces within him over which he had no control, and the forms which this expression took were not consciously chosen by him but imposed themselves as being the only outlet for the tumultuous surge of feeling which would not be denied its passage. Myth was an example of such expression, and the myths were for Herder at the same time the kernel of the Greeks' religion and their highest poetic achievement.

To this circle of ideas belonged naturally another, whose influence for a better understanding of Greek religion has been far greater than could ever have been imagined at the time. The belief that poetry is a wind which bloweth where it listeth, not the creation of individual minds but springing rather from certain fundamental natural instincts which are common to all men alike, brought with it a realization of the undoubted truth that mythological poetry is in its origins popular, a possession of the whole people. The Greek tales were not the graceful invention of some polished Alexandrian or Roman poet. What in its extant form appeared as purely literary fiction had once been folk-poetry, treasured in the hearts of common people, and contained a far-off echo of genuine religious belief.

I have taken the name of Herder to represent the tendency of an age. He was not of course alone in his reaction from the rationalists, and some of his views were not original. It was nevertheless largely due to his enthusiasm and the power of his personality that they gained general currency. This was especially true of the great literary and philosophical figures in the Germany of his time, to whom, rather than to the world of scientific scholarship, Herder himself belonged. Goethe, Schiller and even Kant came directly or indirectly under his influence. From the standpoint of strict scholarship, more was no doubt achieved by his friend and admirer Christian Gottlob Heyne, who though an older man than Herder, lived to assist in the posthumous publication of his works.[1] During his long tenure of the classical chair at Göttingen Heyne made it his especial task to revive the study and appreciation of Greek poetry, in contrast to his predecessors who, largely because their pupils had not the necessary linguistic equipment, had confined themselves to the prose authors. In the execution of this task mythology acquired an outstanding position, and his treatment of it was far ahead of his time. One might say that he took Herder's idea of the myths as relics of a more primitive folk-poetry and gave it the necessary foundation of systematic scholarship which Herder neither cared nor was qualified to supply. He was at pains to distinguish the myth in its popular form (*sermo mythicus*) from the poetic treatment of myth (*sermo poeticus*), deriving the former "ab ingenii humani imbecillitate et a dictionis egestate". He tried to relate myth to cult, though from his own standpoint and with the limited sources of knowledge at his disposal his chances of success seem small to-day. Seeing the origins of religion in superstition and magic, he posited some form of fetishism as its earliest manifestation, and derived from this in their turn animal worship with the worship of trees, mountains and springs, the worship of the heavenly bodies and a more or less personified Nature, and later still the whole pantheon of gods in human form. Fetishism was also put forward as one of the original forms of religion in the theory of the Frenchman Charles de Brosses, whose *Du Culte des Dieux Fétiches* was published in 1760. This theory was not taken up again until the middle years of the nineteenth century. In the intervening period the tendency of religious historians was governed by other discoveries and they worked by other methods, which directed their attention for the time being to more highly developed stages of culture.

This new turn of the wheel was occasioned by advances in the

[1] Herder, 1744–1803; Heyne, 1729–1812.

science of linguistics. It is sometimes said that the history of religion, as a science, was born in the early years of the nineteenth century. This is a partial truth, and we may add to it another partial truth, that comparative philology was its parent. Philology did indeed draw attention to the value of the comparative method for the study of mythology, a method which has kept its place at the centre of the whole science of religious history. The positive lesson which comparative philology taught was that the various names of a number of gods occurring in the myths of different peoples speaking Indo-Germanic tongues could be shown to have a common origin. But if the names of gods in use in various tribes and nations were only different versions of the same name, they must originally have referred to one god, and by comparing the stories told and the beliefs held about them, it must be possible to reconstruct the religion of the original Indo-Europeans. The philological studies on which these conclusions were based were in their early youth. This meant, first, that the actual identifications were sometimes wrong, and secondly that in the first flush of discovery they were regarded as a kind of magic key and forced into locks which they did not really fit.[1] This undue widening of the sphere of application of a new method or theory, just because it is new, is something which will meet us at every stage. We must be prepared to recognize and discount it, not forgetting that without the enthusiastic sense of discovery which lies behind it, neither this science nor any other could probably advance at all.

One identification which has stood the test of time is that which connects the group of names including the Greek Zeus (genitive *Dios*) and his consort Dione, Latin Jupiter (also Diana, Janus and Dianus), Sanskrit Dyauspitar (compare *Ζεὺς Πατήρ*, Father Zeus), Old High German Ziu, old Norse Tyr etc. The common root has the meaning "shine", and from this the proof was built up that the greatest god (the "father-god") of the Indo-European people before they set out on their migrations was the god of the sky and weather. More generally one may say that the Indo-European religion as it appeared to these pioneers was a religion of nature-myths, i.e. one in which the most important powers and phenomena of nature were personified and treated as gods. There was some truth in this, but unfortunately the enthusiasm of its

[1] Cf. especially the later results of Max Müller (said to have reduced mythology to "a disease of language"), the theory that word-endings denoting grammatical gender served as a reason for the personification of the gods, etc.

discoverers was so great that they argued for nature-myths not only as the dominating feature in the original religion of the Indo-European peoples, but also as the original form of *all* religion. In fact, of course, the researches of these early investigators had introduced them to a family of peoples only when it was already living, anthropologically speaking, at a comparatively advanced stage of culture.

This method suffered from the further defect that the myths of the Indo-Germanic peoples as we know them—the myths of Greeks, Romans or Norsemen—are already blended with non-Indo-Germanic elements with which the peoples themselves have become mingled as they wandered, conquered and settled in different parts of the world. The distinctive character of Greek mythology and religion, for example, is very largely due to the blending of Northern and Mediterranean stock, and the differences and relations between the two elements will form a theme to be developed in the present book. But it is obvious that Indo-European philology can tell us nothing of the religion of the Mediterranean race. Nevertheless the value of philology for our subject is by no means exhausted, for of recent years, in conjunction with the other sciences ancillary to a study of Greek religion, it has been doing good service in this very field, that is, in the separation of the Indo-Germanic from the original Mediterranean elements in the Greek religious consciousness.

The myths were now being studied for the kernel of true religion (that is, of a once living belief in the divine) which they contained, and their study was taking on a more scientific colour. Yet although the science of religious history was born, it remained in essence mythology. The meaning of the gods was still sought only in the myths. For Herder, as for Creuzer who at the beginning of the nineteenth century offered his "symbolic" interpretation of myth, religion and mythology were almost identical conceptions. This was natural, for the simple reason that no other source of knowledge was yet available. Before the study of Greek religion could be set on a wider and firmer basis, two other sciences had to be developed which as yet could hardly be said to exist, namely archaeology and anthropology. Apart from the myths, what evidence had these pioneers for the nature of Greek religion? As Wilamowitz has strikingly expressed it, their idea of a Greek deity was the Apollo Belvedere or the Capitoline Venus: we may take ours, for example, from the archaic goddess in the

Berlin museum which was found on Attic soil and dates from the time of Solon. The former are much-restored Roman copies of works which were carved by people in whom all fear of the gods, all sense of their power, was dead. In an original Greek work of the sixth century B.C., however unskilful the artist may have been, one can feel the spirit of a living religion and look on a god who was actually worshipped. To suppose that in a Roman Venus one can see the Aphrodite of whom Sappho spoke is, as Wilamowitz maintained, nothing short of blasphemy.

Let us remind ourselves therefore that most of these objects of genuine cult, these images of gods to whom real worship was once paid, have been brought to light within the last sixty years, and some of them very much more recently. What ruled the field until at least the middle of the nineteenth century was not yet archaeology but anthropology alone. This was the time when scientists first turned their attention to the reports of travellers among the savage races of Africa, Oceania and America, and somewhat later of Australia, whose tribes provided especially valuable examples of some of the most backward cultures known. As the anthropological field was widened, so the religions of these uncivilized peoples came more and more to attract (one might almost say to monopolize) attention. As archaeology also progressed, the two combined to dominate the study of Greek as of all religion, but for some time anthropology (and the comparative method which made it possible to apply the results of anthropology to the religion of a highly developed people like the Greeks) held almost undisputed sway.

Looking back over a century or so of this work, one is inclined to make two comments. The task which the religious historians had set themselves was to find out what might be the central and original impulse behind all religion, that in men's hearts or their surroundings which first brought them to a belief in higher beings to whom their reverence was due, or whose power at least must be acknowledged. Our first observation is that in the series of successive theories which this inquiry called forth, we can see something like the historical succession of religions, only in the reverse order. That is simply because the more highly developed peoples were the more easily accessible and the first to be studied. The progress of the study lay in the discovery of ever more backward races or tribes. The second characteristic which we notice in the theories of the generations immediately preceding our own is their exclusiveness. Fetishism, animism, ancestor-worship, totemism, pre-animism—each had its turn, and each was put forward either by its first supporters or by the less critical of their followers as, purely and simply, "the origin of religion". Another youthful science, psychology, affords an interesting parallel, with its successive theories (sexuality, will to power, race-memory, etc.) of the subconscious sources of our thought and action. Thus in 1913 Jung was pointing out that the theories of Freud and Adler each applied only to one by no means universal type of mind, and added: "The difficult task of elaborating a psychology which should pay equal attention to the two types of mentality belongs to the future." The study of religions has, fortunately for us, now reached the maturer stage where a synthesis is possible, and new theories no longer act as tidal waves swamping the structures which their forerunners have built. Very little of the work of our predecessors is useless if we see it in its proper place as part of a larger whole, and resist the temptation to give universal application to a particular theory, a temptation to which its contemporaries were quite excusably prone. It may well be that "the origin of religion" will for ever elude us. Certainly the more recent works on the subject tend to speak more cautiously (and I think more wisely) of "the origins of religion".[1]

The first theory which we may notice among those sponsored by anthropology is that which taught that the origin of religion lay in fetishism. The word fetish has been much misused, and it is necessary to know in each case what the author of a particular theory meant by it, as well as to determine (for it cannot be dispensed with altogether) what sense we are going to attach to it ourselves. It is a Portuguese word (*feitiço*, from Latin *facticius*), and apparently was first used by Portuguese Catholics of relics or other objects believed to bring luck or protect the owner from

[1] R. Karsten, *The Origins of Religion* (1935), E. O. James, *The Origins of Religion* (1937). The title chosen by Father W. Schmidt, *The Origin and Growth of Religion* (1930), is the exception that proves the rule, for in his advocacy of a primitive ethical monotheism as the earliest of all forms of religion he can, as Dr. James observes, "hardly be exonerated from theological motives", and his language suggests that he can hardly be reckoned among the most scientifically mature of exponents. Compare his claim that his hypothesis is "not one of the many transitory theories which, when their time comes, are replaced by others; it is not one of the many errors, but a permanent conquest, an entire and therefore an enduring truth". After saying this I should like to pay a tribute to his book, which undoubtedly contains much of enduring value, and to draw attention particularly to its admirably clear and succinct outline of the history of the subject. Anyone who reads it will see how much my own account is indebted to Father Schmidt.

harm. From this it was extended to indicate any ordinary object (i.e. one not carved or otherwise worked upon by human craftsmanship) which was believed to contain supernatural power. Such objects of potency were known to be recognized in particular by negroes of West Africa. The sense of an incomprehensible power, which might do great harm but might also, if the proper procedure were discovered and carried out, be forced into the service of mankind, had been thought by de Brosses to have first made itself felt in inanimate objects of this sort. The idea of gods, whose images might be made in human or animal forms, came afterwards. De Brosses, however, wiser than his successors of a century later, did not regard fetishism as the sole primitive form of religion, but assumed that there might be others, e.g. the cult of dead persons, which were equally primitive. The word fetishism was again used as a name for the earliest known stage of religious belief in the history of religion given by Auguste Comte as part of his *Cours de Philosophie Positive* (1830–42). He extended the application of the term to include the sun, moon and earth, and indeed made fetishism synonymous with the worship of nature. It retained this essential characteristic, however, that the worship was supposed to be directed to the natural objects themselves, without any idea that they possessed, or were inhabited by, a living spirit of any sort. Even the most rudimentary ideas of personification belonged, on Comte's theory, to the next phase of development. As late as 1870, when this theory was, to say the least of it, not without a rival in the field, it was still being maintained in an improved form by Lord Avebury (Sir John Lubbock).

In what follows I shall use the word fetishism to denote the habit of paying worship or reverence to inanimate objects such as stones or lumps of wood, which will certainly meet us when we come to consider the religion of the Greeks. It may take its origin in some mysterious circumstance connected with the discovery of the object, or some peculiarity in the object itself which has caused it to attract attention in this way. We shall probably find it attached to the worship of some god, and described perhaps as an image of him (though totally lacking in resemblance to the human form) or as one of his abodes. Its sanctity may go back to a period before the existence of the god, or it may be a comparatively recent discovery to which the power of the most appropriate god has been attached. It would be unwise to suppose that all have a similar explanation, and in our use of the word no assumption of this sort will be implied. It will simply serve to mark off one class of objects of worship from others such as living trees or plants, animals or personal deities.

Two theories now followed each other in quick succession, both based on the premiss that the ever-increasing knowledge of present-day savage life could be used as a source from which to infer the beliefs of man before the dawn of history. These are: the theory of Herbert Spencer about the cult of the dead (first published in volume one of his *Principles of Sociology* in 1876), and the animistic theory of E. B. Tylor (*Primitive Culture*, first edition 1871). Spencer's theory, though given to the world slightly later than Tylor's, belongs more to the past. It had older roots, though now for the first time decked out with the wealth of positive data which anthropological science supplied, and it had less power of survival. Indeed, as a theory of the origin of all religion it was in a measure supplanted by Tylor before it was actually published, for Tylor included ancestor-worship in his own survey, but only as a later development. Spencer sums up his conclusion in these words:[1] "There is no exception then. Using the phrase ancestor-worship in its broadest sense as comprehending all worship of the dead, be they of the same blood or not, we reach the conclusion that ancestor-worship is the root of every religion." From this source he derives all other forms of religion, enumerated as idol-worship and fetish-worship, animal-worship, plant-worship, nature-worship, and finally the worship of deities in the accepted sense. It is a striking revival of the theory of Euhemeros at the end of the fourth century B.C., that the gods were famous men of old, forgotten days; for as Spencer says just before the passage quoted above: "Behind the supernatural being of this order, as behind supernatural beings of all other orders, we thus find that there has in every case been a human personality."

In Tylor we have no universal philosopher, whose views on the origin of religion had to be made to square with a general preconception of society or the world as a whole. He was a specialist, who had trained himself for ethnology and regarded it as his life-work. To a naturally gifted mind he added an indefatigable industry in collecting factual material for his study, and the result is a brilliant synthesis of permanent value, whatever may be the ultimate answer to the question of "the origin of religion". In

[1] Quoted by Schmidt, *Origin and Growth of Religion* (Methuen, 1930), p. 62.

his work religion and animism are identified. That is to say, he claims, as a minimum definition of religion, "the belief in Spiritual Beings", and to the belief in spiritual beings he gives the name of animism. It is true that he makes the cautious assertion that, so far as can be judged from the immense mass of accessible evidence, the lowest races of whom we have knowledge do possess this minimum of religious belief. Yet it is only in a limited sense that any "pre-animistic" hypothesis, if such should be proved, could overthrow his theory, since according to his very reasonable definition, pre-animistic beliefs should not be accounted religious at all. In fact, the "pre-animistic theory" is founded to a large extent on magical practices, of whose existence and significance Tylor himself was well aware.

His view, very briefly, was this. To the primitive mind all the creatures of the world have a dual nature. They are a compound of body and soul. As far as mankind was concerned, the savage based his conviction on two sets of data. There were, first, the phenomena of sleep and death as viewed from outside. To the observer it seemed obvious that although the man lay there to all outward appearance complete, something had gone out of him which was present to animate him when he was alive and awake. It was no part of his body, for no part of that was lacking. Thus there must be a separate spirit or soul, which literally left the body, usually through the mouth, either temporarily in sleep and unconsciousness, or permanently in death. Corroboration of this view was forthcoming in another class of phenomenon, those connected with dreams and visions. To dream of another person was taken to mean that his spirit actually came and visited the dreamer. Now to the savage all nature is akin. There is no hard and fast line such as we draw between men and animals or plants, and still more strongly between living creatures and such things as sticks, stones, weapons, clothing or other objects. The belief in a universal kinship or sympathy which renders such a line faint or non-existent is, after all, the basis and foundation of the practice of magic. Thus the dualism of body and separable spirit is carried on into the (to us) inanimate world. If a man appears to another in a dream clothed and carrying a spear, this, as we have noted, is no figment of the dreamer's imagination, but an actual visit from a spirit; and savage logic goes far enough to insist that if the man is real, the clothes and spear must be real too. Yet they are not the material clothes and spear which are met with in waking life.

Thus "lifeless" objects must have their spiritual doubles as much as human beings.

In such an intellectual atmosphere all sorts of things are possible and intelligible which to us are merely nonsense. "What we call inanimate objects—rivers, stones, trees, weapons and so forth—are treated as living intelligent beings, talked to, propitiated, punished for the harm they do."[1] Since death is not an ending of life, but only a separation of the life-principle from the body, it is obviously wise to pay attention to the needs and desires of the surviving spirit which, generally invisible but by no means powerless, continues to haunt the scenes of its corporeal existence and may exhibit benevolence or the reverse according to the way it is treated. Just as in the body it needed the physical substance of food, clothing and weapons (not to mention servants if the dead were a person of importance), so as a ghost it needs the ghosts of these things, which can be sent to it by burning or otherwise destroying them.

Thus even these few brief examples make plain the remarkable comprehensiveness of Tylor's account, which, supported as it was by an irresistible weight of evidence presented with skill and judgment, embraced in its single hypothesis fetishism, nature-worship, cult of the dead, or whatever else had been successively put forward as the original form of religion.

It was not long after this that the effects of archaeology began to make themselves felt. Among its earlier achievements was the laying bare of the relics of the Babylonian and Assyrian civilizations with their libraries of cuneiform inscriptions, whose secrets were soon made an open book by linguistic researchers. They revealed a mythology which was manifestly rooted in the personification of natural phenomena, and in particular of the heavenly bodies. Now the society to which these documents belonged was of course no primitive one. Their authors were no low, or even higher, savages, but civilized city-dwellers. Consequently to make them the foundation of a new theory of the origin of religion was a notable deviation from the way along which anthropology had hitherto been leading. Such, however, was the intoxicating effect of the new discoveries that that is what happened. Animism had now to face an opposition, that of the astral-myth school and the Panbabylonianists. These maintained that the true origin of religion lay in the personification of natural phenomena, and in

[1] Tylor, *Primitive Culture*, 5th ed., i, 477.

particular of the moon, the sun and certain stars. Probably this departure from strict anthropological method was all the more readily followed because it appeared as a historical confirmation of the first theory of all. In the days when the methods of comparative philology still held the field, a favourite theory had been that of the nature-myth, and particularly the sun-myth, as the origin of all extant mythology and religion whatsoever, and this old view now seemed to receive striking support from the latest discoveries. The Panbabylonianists, who were almost entirely confined to Germany, appear as the extreme wing of the astral-myth school, not all of whom went so far as to claim absolute and universal validity for their theories. The absurdity of Panbabylonianism is shown by the definition of its doctrine as that of "a primal [*uralt*], compact system of religious ideas, which originated in Babylon, whence its influence extended over *the whole of the world* and was exercised upon the religions of *all* peoples at their higher levels".[1] The belief that certain elementary ideas could have arisen independently in different parts of the world owing to the general similarity of human nature and the human mind was explicitly rejected by these people, as it was also by the English "diffusionist" writers G. Elliot Smith and W. J. Perry, who replaced Panbabylonianism with an equally all-embracing Panegyptianism.

Meanwhile the anthropologists had been busy too, and were playing with another phenomenon of primitive belief, that of totemism. This has been defined as the belief current among some of the lowest savage tribes that they are descended from, and related to, certain species of animals, for which in consequence they entertain a religious respect. It was made known to the scientific world, in a somewhat exaggerated form, by J. F. MacLennan in the sixties, and put forward as a candidate for "the origin of religion" by his pupil Robertson Smith. At the centre of Robertson Smith's theory was his view of sacrifice among the Semitic peoples, which he regarded as a ceremonial killing and eating of the totemic animal, identified by the people with their god. On ordinary occasions it would be impious to treat the totem thus, but at certain special festivals the people were gathered together for this very purpose of feasting communally on the

[1] Kurt Pfister, "Die Religion der Griechen und Römer" (Bursian's *Jahresbericht über die Fortschritte der Klass. Altertumswissenschaft*, 229 (1930), 72). (The italics in the translation are mine).

body of the god, thus renewing their connexion with him and absorbing into themselves his vital powers in a primitive communion service. F. B. Jevons (1896), a pupil of Robertson Smith, brought the theory into explicit conflict with Tylor's animism, trying to derive animism from an earlier state of mind which is in reality not religious but pre-religious.

Totemism found a curious ally in Sigmund Freud, who accepted it as the original form of religion and linked it with the Oedipus-complex, though it is doubtful whether his adherence did much to raise its status in the eyes of most historians of religion. Neither did the somewhat uncritical enthusiasm of Salomon Reinach greatly enhance its credibility. It has been criticized on two grounds, first that it is not after all universally found in the lowest layers of culture, secondly that it has nothing to do with religion. By now the enormous industry of Sir James Frazer was at work, indeed both *The Golden Bough* and Robertson Smith's *Religion of the Semites* testify in more than one place to the lasting friendship and fruitful interchange of ideas between the two men. Nevertheless Frazer's consideration of his vast collections of material led him to the conclusion that pure totemism could after all not be regarded as religion or a source of religion, being no more than a certain pre-political organization of society. The totems were not objects of worship. There was among these same totemistic peoples a set of beliefs and practices which might be the forerunner of religion, indeed was declared by Frazer to be so. But this was not their totemism: it was magic. Magic "assumes that in nature one event follows another necessarily and invariably without the intervention of any spiritual or personal agency. Thus its fundamental conception is identical with that of modern science; underlying the whole system is a faith, implicit but real and firm, in the order and uniformity of nature."[1] Animism now, at the beginning of the present century, meets its most serious rival in pre-animism, and the pre-animistic stage is the magical. Its content has been developed and enlarged by researches into

[1] *Golden Bough*, i, 220. It may be noted here that Frazer's loyalty to truth caused him to point out later to the posthumous editor of Robertson Smith's work that he had met with certain cases where the totem is actually the object of cult. The science of religious history had already progressed too far for any serious theory to be completely discarded. The relation between Robertson Smith's and Frazer's views is well and sympathetically summed up by S. A. Cook in his introduction to the third edition of *The Religion of the Semites* (A. & C. Black, 1927), pp. xl ff. It affords a fine illustration of the fellowship of learning on its highest levels.

the conceptions of *mana* and *orenda*, words taken respectively from the language of Melanesian and American Indian peoples and made into terms of world-wide application. Words of similar meaning in other languages have also been collected. They are supposed to denote a mysterious magical power or influence which is attached to certain persons or inanimate objects indiscriminately and is itself entirely non-personal. The man who possesses it will be *felix* and is marked out for distinction among his fellows. If it attaches itself to a thing, the thing becomes a powerful charm. It may also inhere in words or phrases, which thus achieve the binding power of a spell. The kernel of the pre-animistic theory is put thus by Karsten, quoting the words of its advocate T. K. Preuss: "Among many primitive peoples . . . there occur a great many magical and religious rites which are quite independent of animism and have no connexion whatever with the belief in spirits. In these rites it is only a question of an impersonal magical power [*Zauberkraft*] which is present in things and inanimate objects as in plants, animals and men."[1]

The tendency of the present day is to regard any controversy between animism and pre-animism as an indication of undue rigidity in the concepts employed on both sides—undue because the modern distinction between animate and inanimate is not present with the same clarity to the primitive mind. It is beginning to be understood that the process of getting inside the skin of the savage, and looking out at the world through his eyes, is extremely complex and difficult for anyone whose mind runs naturally in the grooves of civilized European thought, and calls for a more delicate and subtle approach than that of earlier researchers. Among others who are trying such an approach, the name of Lucien Lévy-Bruhl may be cited as a leading figure.[2] We are already acquainted with the notion of "sympathy", according to which a peculiarly intimate relationship exists, for example, between a man and any detached part of him like cut hair, nail-parings or excreta, or a personal possession, or again anything intended to be a representation of him. It is this that enables the sorcerer to interfere with the well-being of a fellow-creature by operations performed in his absence on any such personal appur-

[1] Karsten, o.c., p. 32, referring to Preuss, "Der Ursprung der Religion und Kunst", in *Globus*, vols. 86 and 87 (1904 and 1905).

[2] See e.g. his *Primitive Mentality* (London, 1923), and *The "Soul" of the Primitive* (1928), which I mention, though they are not his latest works, as being easily available in English.

tenances. A belief in the efficacy of these practices is only one part of a state of mind in which no clear distinctions exist like those usually drawn to-day, not only between different classes of entities (living or non-living), but also between such notions as identity, similarity, representation and so forth. Lévy-Bruhl, quoting in part the field-anthropologist P. Wirz, notes the "indifferent" character of a concept similar to that of *mana* among Papuans, and continues: "Ce qu'il désigne n'est ni personnel ni non plus impersonnel formellement, mais souvent à la fois l'un et l'autre", and again of fetishes and similar objects: "A la grande surprise des observateurs, ce qu'ils 'représentent' semble n'être que très vaguement défini dans l'ésprit des primitifs." "Il n'est pas nécessaire de savoir ce que sont ces puissances—très mal définies dans l'ésprit des indigènes, incapables de dire s'ils les conçoivent comme personnelles ou impersonnelles—ni de saisir un rapport intelligible entre elles et leurs symboles."[1] On the other hand certain stones may quite definitely "represent" the spirits of the human dead.

The theories which we have so far considered have obviously been produced in the atmosphere of the nineteenth-century philosophy of progressive evolution. In the background is always the presumption, explicit or implicit, that the further back we penetrate into primitive life the less developed (as nineteenth-century European civilization chose to understand the term) will be the religious beliefs. There are of course some grounds for this presumption in the fact that religion is not to be divorced at any stage from the organization of society and the general conditions of life. This should be recalled here, since it is a point which for the sake of brevity has not been emphasized in the rapid enumeration of theories hitherto given. In speaking of fetishism, totemism, ancestor-worship and the rest I have not paused to consider how each is related to the kind of life lived by those who practise them, whether for instance they get their food by hunting or fishing, or are nomadic breeders of cattle or settled agricultural peoples. In fact one of the most fruitful developments of twentieth-century anthropology has been a growing awareness that religion is a function of the whole personality, and that the personality is

[1] *La Mythologie Primitive* (Paris, 1935), xxxi, *L'expérience Mystique et les Symboles chez les Primitifs* (1938), 195, 197. The author is a follower of Émile Durkheim, and in drawing attention to the above facts I do not mean to commend "collective representations", "pre-logical mentality", and all the tenets of the French sociological school.

intimately bound up with the contemporary organization of society. The way to this has been led in particular by Émile Durkheim and his followers in the French sociological school of anthropology. These went so far as to hold that religion arose at first from the "collective representations" imposed on all the individuals of a social group, the group being conceived as an entity over and above the individuals of whom it is composed, and related to them almost as a Platonic "Idea" to its particulars. The group is the unit, not the individual, who has no separate existence over against society, but exists only as immersed in one continuous social mentality. According to Durkheim, the "origin of religion" was to be sought in totemism, in which the totemic animal or plant embodied the collective personality of family or clan. One may agree with the criticism of Dr. James: "Now while it is true that religion has emerged within society, that it functions as an integral aspect of its structure, and makes its own life and characteristics explicit through a social medium, it is very much more than the evaluation and personification of the organization of the community".[1] But the general lesson has been learned that any religious phenomenon must be studied in the context of the particular culture in which it is observed, and is being applied to-day both in England and in America. It is of course by no means necessarily bound up with the evolutionary hypothesis in its nineteenth-century form, the *a priori* assumption that because religion is so integral a part of life, the simplest and most primitive societies must necessarily exhibit the religious beliefs and practices furthest removed from our own. As an extreme reaction from that assumption, one might cite the theory of the so-called "primitive high gods", first propounded by Andrew Lang and upheld to-day by the Austrian Catholic school of Father W. Schmidt. This school professes to find in the beliefs of the most primitive peoples (e.g. the Pygmies) nothing less than an ethical monotheism coupled with the belief in divine creation.[2] In general however we may say that the special characteristic of present-day research on this subject is a linking-up of anthropology with both sociology and psychology in an attempt to understand

[1] *The Origins of Religion*, 21. The theories of the French school were criticized at length by C. C. J. Webb in *Group Theories of Religion* as early as 1916. The validity of Durkheim's whole method is impugned by George Simpson in *Émile Durkheim on the Division of Labour in Society* (New York, 1933).

[2] For criticisms see James, o.c., 122 ff., and in detail A. J. Festugière in *Rev. Ét. Gr.* lvii (1944), 252 ff.

the primitive mind as a whole, and so to get a truer view of primitive religion as an integral part of that mind, instead of taking religious phenomena alone and criticizing them from the point of view of a mentality largely alien. How far success can be achieved it is still early to say, but at least the task is being approached with greater sympathy and a fuller understanding of its difficulties.

At this point it is to be hoped that the reader will be asking himself a question in some such terms as this. The picture which has been given of anthropological historians striving to roll back the mists of the primitive ever a little further in order to disclose the primal and original form in which the religious instinct first emerged on earth may be in itself extremely interesting; but what possible relevance has it to a study of religion among the classical Greeks, whom it is surely right to regard not as savages, whether primary or secondary or at whatever other stages may be recognized in these barbaric cultures, but as a highly civilized people? This is the question from which I myself started, being by nature suspicious of the "beastly devices of the heathen" (to borrow a phrase which we shall see in other contexts very soon) and finding them occupying a prominent place in the writings of the greatest authorities on Greek religion in recent times. It did not of course take long to find the necessary intellectual link, which can be summed up in the one word "survivals". Among the Greeks, civilization was a mushroom growth. In contrast to the societies of the present day, it had sprung at a bound from darkness into light. The result was that, in spite of any veneer of civilized thought or habit which they might have acquired in their religion, the primitive was always lying just beneath the surface. In any case, it is a universal truth that it is in his religion that man is at his most conservative. He may have completely forgotten the reason for the ritual acts which he performs, but he is loth to cease performing them. The wealth of primitive custom which forms the illustrative material of *The Golden Bough* is by no means all drawn from savage, or even from ancient, societies. Much of it was observed in the more rural parts of nineteenth-century Europe.

This intellectual justification is a real one, and in pointing out the parallels between Greek customs and beliefs and those of savage tribes to-day, our immediate predecessors rendered invaluable service. Yet two comments may without unfairness be made. First, these comparative methods tend to emphasize the lower at the expense of the higher, to concentrate attention on the potential rather than the actual, the seed rather than the flower. From their point of view Dikaiopolis, the average Athenian citizen (who, as we know, was in all things somewhat superstitious), or even Strepsiades, who lived and worked far off in the fields, is of more importance than Plato. Secondly, it is perhaps permissible to point to the emotional stimulus under which these scholars worked. A new light seemed to have dawned, and new life to have been given to the study of the classics. Thus a tremendous fascination was exerted over the minds of the greatest of them by the "beastly devices of the heathen". I quote this phrase because it is one which they use themselves in half-humorous deprecation of their own enthusiasm. Here are two passages in which it occurs, from the works of two honoured leaders of the movement, Gilbert Murray and Jane Harrison.

"First there is the primitive *Euetheia* or age of ignorance . . . a stage to which our anthropologists and explorers have found parallels in every part of the world. . . . There is certainly some repulsiveness, but I confess that to me there is also an element of fascination in the study of these 'beastly devices of the heathen', at any rate as they appear in early Greece, where each single 'beastly device' as it passes is somehow touched with beauty and transformed by some spirit of upward striving."[1]

No doubt the feeling behind these measured terms is scarcely less than that expressed by the infectious exuberance of Miss Harrison. Perhaps it may be agreed that her own introduction of the "beastly devices" is a little disingenuous as compared with Professor Murray's.

"We Hellenists were in truth at that time a 'people who sat in darkness', but we were soon to see a great light, two great lights —archaeology and anthropology. Classics were turning in their long sleep. Old men began to see visions, young men to dream dreams. I had just left Cambridge when Schliemann began to dig at Troy. Among my own contemporaries was J. G. Frazer, soon to light the dark world of savage superstition with a gleam from *The Golden Bough*. The happy title of that great book . . . made it arrest the attention of scholars. They saw in comparative anthropology a serious subject actually capable of elucidating a Greek or Latin text. Tylor had written and spoken; Robertson

[1] Murray, *Five Stages of Greek Religion*, p. 16.

Smith, exiled for heresy, had seen the Star in the East; in vain; we classical deaf-adders stopped our ears and closed our eyes; but at the mere sound of the magical words 'Golden Bough' the scales fell—we heard and understood. Then Arthur Evans set sail for his new Atlantis and telegraphed news of the Minotaur from his own Labyrinth; perforce we saw that this was a serious matter, it affected the 'Homeric Question'."

This is a rare and precious glimpse of the spirit in which it was given to an older generation to work. If we can ever come near to recapturing it, it is in reading words like these. But let us see how she goes on.

"By nature, I am sure, I am not an archaeologist, still less an anthropologist—the 'beastly devices of the heathen' weary and disgust me."

That is a sentence which, I would suggest with all the humility due from one who did not know her personally, is not borne out either by the rest of Miss Harrison's work or by the passage which follows it in this delightful book of reminiscences:

"But, borne along by the irresistible tide of adventure, I dabbled in both archaeology and anthropology, and I am glad I did, for both were needful for my real subject—religion. When I say 'religion', I am instantly obliged to correct myself; it is not religion, it is ritual that absorbs me. . . . I mention these ritual dances, this ritual drama, this bridge between art and life, because it is things like these that I was all my life blindly seeking. A thing has little charm for me unless it has on it the patina of age. Great things in literature, Greek plays for example, I most enjoy when behind their bright splendours I see moving darker and older shapes."[1]

It is difficult not to wonder what these "darker and older shapes" can be, if not the "beastly devices of the heathen" which were so ill spoken of a little while before. In any case we need look no further for the answer to the question why this generation turned with such eagerness to the studies of anthropology and pre-classical archaeology for help in the elucidation of classical problems.

We may, however, take a few simple illustrations to show how easy it was, as each anthropological theory in turn focused attention on its favourite religious manifestation and set scholars happily hunting for instances of it in their chosen field, to find

[1] *Reminiscences of a Student's Life*, pp. 82 ff.

points of contact between the Hellenic mind and whatever was the fashionable definition of the primitive.

Suppose fetishism was the order of the day, that is, the worship of inanimate objects without even advancing to the notion that they possessed a soul. As far back as the eighteenth century, K. A. Böttiger, whose lifetime overlapped that of de Brosses, was explaining the attributes of the gods (Hermes' magic staff, Poseidon's trident and so forth) as originally fetishes, to which personal deities had only been attached as an afterthought. We are not however left to argue back from a known anthropomorphism to a conjectural primitive state. There is a wealth of examples still extant in classical Greece. The sacred *omphalos* at Delphi could be regarded as a perfect example of a fetish, nor is it by any means the only sacred stone in Greece. The statues of Hermes which stood before the houses of Athens, human above but ending below in a plain quadrangular pillar of stone, might be pointed out as an intermediate stage in the development. At Thespiae in Boeotia, where Eros was the god chiefly worshipped, Pausanias wrote that side by side with statues of him by the renowned masters Praxiteles and Lysippos "they have a very ancient image of him, consisting of an unwrought stone".[1] It was characteristic of the Greeks that while they honoured the god by ordering statues of him from the greatest of contemporary sculptors, the age-old fetish, which since the introduction of Eros had passed for his image, lost nothing of its sanctity in their eyes.[2]

When ancestor-worship took the place of fetishism, Greece was obviously so full of that, in the form of hero-cults, that it could not be hard to construct a theory reducing all Greek religion in the last resort to this one origin.

But ancestor-worship was speedily dethroned, and for a long time animism held the field. The classical scholar might now find new meaning in the well-known fact that every spring had its nymph and every tree its dryad, while rivers were worshipped by the Greeks as mighty personal powers, and argue that on this theory too the primitive origins of religion were for the Greeks just one step round the corner.

[1] Paus. ix, 27, 1. Similarly at Hyettos, also in Boeotia, there was a temple of Herakles, who "is represented, not by an artificial image, but in the ancient fashion by an unwrought stone". (Id. ix, 24, 3.)

[2] On the relics of fetish-worship in Greece the remarks of Otto Kern (*Die Religion der Griechen*, i (1926), 2 ff.) are valuable.

In a few years, perhaps, his allegiance to animism might fade and he would become converted to totemism. In this case his only trouble in applying the theory to Greece would be an *embarras de richesses*. Since our imaginary scholar is not of the highest and most critical class, we may perhaps be pardoned for supposing him first of all to see traces of the now fashionable phenomenon in anything which points to the worship of animals, or of gods in animal form. If this were so he could find on every hand beings whose attributes or epithets seemed to suggest that they were no more than the recently humanized relics of animal-gods. Many, like Zeus Lykaios, Apollo Lykeios and the hero Lykos, seemed to carry in their titles the root of the word "wolf". Dionysos was addressed by his worshippers as both kid and bull. Poseidon had the epithet Hippios, suggesting that he may once have been a horse. Everyone knows of the variety of animal forms which were adopted by Zeus in the pursuit of his various amours. Homer speaks regularly of Hera as "ox-eyed" (or "ox-faced") and Athena as "owl-eyed" (or "owl-faced"). These epithets might be thought to point back to a time when the goddesses were actually imagined in the form of these animals. Our scholar can however be more strictly totemistic. Were not the Athenians the descendants of grass-hoppers? Did not the girl-priestesses of Brauronian Artemis in Attica call themselves bears, and the goddess whom they served the great She-bear? Among the heroes there was Orpheus, who in the course of his passage through the hands of the religious historians has suffered as many transmigrations as even he, the great preacher of transmigration, could have wished. Ernst Maass called him a god, Robert Eisler a fish, Jane Harrison a man. When totemism was the favourite theory Salomon Reinach duly came forward to maintain that he was a fox, the totem of the Bassarid tribe. *Bassara* certainly seems to mean a fox,[1] and the Thracian maenads who tore Orpheus in pieces called themselves *Bassarids* in Aeschylus' play of that name and no doubt clothed themselves in fox-skins.

There is no need to dwell on the passing popularity of sun-myths or other fashions of the same exclusive character, for we have done enough to show the dangers which for the student of Greek religion lurked in the atmosphere of the late nineteenth and early twentieth centuries. It was an age of discovery, with all its

[1] Farnell (*Cults of the Greek States*, v, 106, n. 1) is a little over-scrupulous when he calls the evidence for this meaning "frail".

attendant excitement, and in spite of the calls for caution which we find reiterated in the actual works of the pioneers themselves—a Robertson Smith, a Frazer or a Tylor—their followers were tempted to hail each theory as universal and allow it to swallow all religion and mythology with little discrimination. To be alive in the world of scholarship then was a thrilling experience, as our quotations from Jane Harrison made abundantly clear. For those of us to whom it has not been given to live in that age, it would be unprofitable to pretend to an enthusiasm which has passed us by. We have missed much, but must take what profit we can from our position as epigoni. The classics live only because each generation sees in them something a little different from the last, and to try to see them through the eyes of the last generation would be unwise even if it were possible. My brief summary of the history of Greek religion as matter for scholarship has brought us down to our own day, and becomes an apologia for a certain reaction from the anthropological and comparative point of view. This does not mean ignoring the solid and lasting work which will always be associated with such names as Rohde, Cornford, Murray and A. B. Cook. I hope I shall not lay myself open to the reproach which Plato was said to have levelled at Aristotle, by acting like the foal which kicks its own mother. It should mean only a shifting of the balance, a change of emphasis, a rearrangement which brings some things to the fore and pushes others a little more into the background. The account may fittingly end with a few illustrations from fairly recent work to indicate that such a rearrangement is in the air, that in many places the tide is already turning, and that to suggest that some shifting of the balance is needed is, as might indeed be guessed, not to propound something daring and original but only to show oneself to be, like most people, under the sway of the spirit which is already abroad in the age.

The pages of the *Journal of Hellenic Studies* in 1933 and 1934 saw an amusing and instructive passage of arms between the late Dr. Farnell and Professor H. D. F. Kitto. The subject was the *Prometheus Vinctus* of Aeschylus. Farnell had written impressively of the play as an insoluble paradox, because by all the analogies of religious history he found it inexplicable. Prometheus was classified as an example of the suffering God, but as such he presents certain unparalleled features, and "the commentators on the play, through their lack of familiarity with Greek or Comparative

Religion,[1] have failed to appreciate this unique phenomenon at its proper magnitude". Professor Kitto's reply, which among other things illustrates the more or less subtle change of idiom and style between the two generations, is summed up in the sentence: "The *Prometheus* is a play, and if you treat it as a document in Comparative Religion it will not work." "One may perhaps be pardoned", he says, "if one feels, in reading his article, that Dr. Farnell both knew and cared more about Zeus-cults than Aeschylus did. . . . Dr. Farnell's criticism is specialist criticism, and I suggest that the major difficulties that make his paradox are directly attributable to this fact." It may be objected that we have here not two ways of looking at Greek religion, but one article on Greek religion and another which maintains that religion should not come into the argument at all, since the work under discussion is a purely literary and dramatic one and religious considerations are irrelevant to its appreciation. This however would be a superficial judgment. Kitto has no quarrel with those who use our knowledge of Greek religion as a means of throwing light upon Greek literature. The difficulty is that sometimes, to use his own words, "this light proceeds from a fixed source, and that, often, the wrong one". In other words, the specialist may actually hinder our appreciation of a tragedy by importing from outside, that is, from his studies in Greek or comparative religion, ideas which did not happen to be in the mind of the poet when he was writing his play. A scholar who has chosen among the rich fields of classical antiquity a particular corner for intensive cultivation has, to change the metaphor, a choice of two backgrounds against which to see his subject. He may look at it against the background of its time, that is, as a part of classical study. If it be the Greek language, he will regard it as the verbal expression of the Greek people and their civilization at a particular stage of their evolution. On the other hand, instead of seeing it as a part of classical study, he may see it as a part of philology or linguistic. He will not relate the language to contemporary Greek life, thought and literature so much as to its Indo-Germanic predecessors and contemporaries, and to its successors in the *koine* of the Roman Empire, and so through Byzantine to modern Greek. Similarly with our researches into Greek religion, we may either regard ourselves as historians of religion with Greece as our field of specialization, or as classical scholars whose aim is to understand the Greeks. Our

[1] The capitals are Farnell's.

background then is not primarily made up of comparative religion. That will have its uses, but our primary task is to see the religion of Greece in the historical setting of Greek modes of thought and expression, the life of the city-state or the Boeotian farm, religion as it was affected by the Persian invasion or the Peloponnesian war, above all religion in a small, mountainous, sea-girt country with an East Mediterranean climate.

The following is from Gilbert Murray: "The things that have misled us moderns in our efforts towards understanding the primitive stage in Greek religion have been first the . . . error of treating Homer as primitive, and more generally our unconscious insistence on starting with the notion of 'gods'." Now Wilamowitz, though he was over eighty when he died in 1931, was one who stood aloof from some of the tendencies of his age and was never attracted by the anthropological approach to the Greeks. At the end of his life he felt it necessary to enter a strong protest against it, and did so in his last, great work, *Der Glaube der Hellenen*. In the first volume, published in 1931, we read these sentences, which may be contrasted with the words of Murray: "The gods are present. To know and to recognize that for the Greeks this is a given fact, a datum, is the first and necessary condition for an understanding of their belief and their cult."[1] The work contains other similarly forthright remarks. For example: "I don't understand the languages from which are borrowed the words so beloved by the present day, *tabu* and *totem*, *mana* and *orenda*, but I consider it a safe procedure to stick to the Greeks, and in what concerns Greece to think in Greek." (p. 10.) "In reading the historians of religion, one gets all too often the impression that what their *historie* leads to is the disappearance of religion." What takes its place, he goes on, is magic, and religion turns out to be based on fear. "If that is so, then certainly it is a creation of primeval folly [*Urdummheit*], an expression which Gilbert Murray borrowed from the German scholar Preuss, and perhaps I may seem to be a κρονόληρος if I side with Humboldt and say with Welcker, 'Even in the most primitive manifestations which do duty for religion, the human soul betrays its awareness of gods [*Gottessinn*]'." (p. 9.)

With greater moderation Otto Kern admits that we cannot altogether do without the contribution of anthropological know-

[1] p. 17. "Die Götter sind da. Dass wir dies als gegebene Tatsache mit den Griechen erkennen und anerkennen, ist die erste Bedingung für das Verstandnis ihres Glaubens und ihres Kultus."

ledge. But he feels bound to put in a caveat against the uncritical way in which much of the mass of material was collected, which now serves as the basis of the anthropologist's deductions, consisting as it often does of the accounts of untrained travellers and missionaries, who were often ill acquainted even with the language of the people of whom they wrote. "All conclusions must be drawn with the utmost caution, and this growth must never be allowed to run riot over our representation of the religion of ancient peoples. It will always be safest if the researcher can explain Greek customs by Greek words."[1]

Finally one of the greatest historians of Greek religion, Otto Gruppe, wrote in 1920 a history of the subject as a supplement to Roscher's *Lexicon of Greek and Roman Mythology*. It is a monument of learning some 240 pages long, and in closing this inadequate summary I cannot do better than quote the sober words with which he ends it.

"The truth is this. The mythologies of savages have certainly sharpened the eyes of the classical mythologist for possibilities which had hitherto been undreamed of; but the positive harvest of unquestionably correctly interpreted myths and cults is so far scanty. As in all earlier times so in the present, all real progress in the knowledge of classical religious phenomena has been discovered by means of classical studies themselves, and moreover their investigations have always been all the more fruitful the more they relied on the ancient evidence and refused to borrow from the methods of other sciences, building rather on the distinctive character of their own particular sources of knowledge."

[1] *Die Religion der Griechen*, i (1926), 13.

Chapter II

THE DIVINE FAMILY

While the higher forms of religious faith pass away like clouds, the lower stand firm and indestructible like rocks.

Frazer, *Adonis, &c.* (*G.B.*), i, 109

I. Origins: Preliminary Remarks

AFTER what I have said, both by way of preface and in the last chapter, no one will expect to find this book predominantly concerned with questions of origin. The gods of the Greeks were complex characters, with both Northern and Mediterranean strains in their ancestry, and there is something to be said for taking them as we find them. It is interesting, and not always difficult, to separate the strands that have been interwoven in their making. If we are to attempt it, however, we must remember two things which there is a danger of forgetting. The first is that the whole is in this case greater than the sum of its parts. In the judgment of many scholars the Apollo of the *Iliad* is what he is because the Greeks took over and hellenized a native Asiatic deity. But though this may be true, the result is not a clumsy dual personality. Such a character could never have inspired generations of poets and artists. He is a single, living god, and a very great one. Since that is what he is to the Greeks, nothing else matters very much. This leads to the second point, that the more we investigate the complicated origins of the great Greek gods, the less we are looking at them as they appeared to Aeschylus or Sophocles. The new picture of them which we are forming is not the same, and it will be as well to retire sometimes from the heat of the historical chase, and, if Apollo be our quarry, stop for a while to pray with Electra, as the awful moment approaches for which she has waited through eight weary years of captivity embittered by daily taunts, insults and hardships:

O Lord Apollo, graciously hear their prayer, and hear me also, who so oft have come before thine altar with such gifts as my devout hand could bring. And now, O Lycean Apollo, with all my strength I beseech thee—I fall before thee—I implore thee: be thou provident in aiding these our counsels, and show unto men the rewards of the wicked, how they are dealt by the gods.[1]

Sophocles, in fact, can tell us more about the meaning of *eusebeia* than the comparative study of religion.

Having made this point of view clear (and my only fear is that I may have laboured it unduly), I should be able to continue for the present to discuss matters which I regard as introductory without encouraging anyone to exaggerate their undoubted interest and importance. One of the most remarkable things about the Greek genius, at least as manifested in religion, is the way in which it preserved the old alongside of the new. Not only was it capable of astonishingly rapid development to some of the highest forms of religious experience; it was also loth to let even the oldest and crudest forms of worship disappear without trace. This is the fact which the researches of anthropologists have put beyond doubt, and for which they have provided a wealth of authentic examples.

To speak of the Greek religious genius, and say that "it" does this or that, is of course to be guilty of a misleading generalization. To say that "it was loth to let even the oldest elements disappear without trace" means only that in fact the oldest elements have not so disappeared. There is no one thing, "the Greek genius", which like a single person accepts the new without relinquishing the old. I make a point of this correction here because I want not only to call to mind this coexistence of diverse elements, but also to attempt to explain it. The explanation lies in this very fact, that the Greek genius was not something single and simple, but complex. Before the history of Greece begins, before the Greeks as we know them existed, a series of invading peoples from north or east had successively overrun and possessed themselves of the peninsula. These waves of invasion cannot be dated with precision, but they probably occupied most of the second millennium

[1] Soph. *El.* 1376 ff.

ἄναξ Ἄπολλον, ἵλεως αὐτοῖν κλύε,
ἐμοῦ δὲ πρὸς τούτοισιν, ἥ σε πολλὰ δὴ
ἀφ' ὧν ἔχοιμι λιπαρεῖ προὔστην χερί.
νῦν δ', ὦ Λύκει' Ἄπολλον, ἐξ οἵων ἔχω
αἰτῶ, προπίπτω, λίσσομαι, γένου πρόφρων
ἡμῖν ἄρωγος τῶνδε τῶν βουλευμάτων
καὶ δεῖξον ἀνθρώποισι τἀπιτίμια
τῆς δυσσεβείας, οἷα δωροῦνται θεοί.

B.C., and the last-comers, the Dorians, entered Greece about 1100. To an ethnologist the Greeks are represented by certain of these invading waves of people, and it is their language which, with a few additions from the indigenous Mediterranean tongues, became the language of Greece. But the civilization which arose from this state of affairs was by no means Greek in this exclusive sense. A conquering race does not wipe out all trace of the conquered. More often it is the indigenous stock which displays the greater vitality and stronger powers of survival. To take an example which touches our present subject, an invading race does not, at this early stage of civilization, seek to stamp out the gods of the invaded. On the contrary, their conduct is guided by a strong belief in the attachment of gods to the soil of the country. In these strange lands their own gods may well be less powerful to help them, if indeed they are present at all, and it is of great importance to get the new gods on their side. Every wanderer knew this. When the Argonauts arrived at Colchis and anchored in the Phasis, the first thing that happened, as the story is told by Apollonius Rhodius, was that "Jason himself with a goblet of gold poured sweet libations of unmixed wine to the river, and for the Earth and the native gods and the souls of dead heroes, and prayed that they would do them no harm, but be kindly helpers and receive their ship propitiously". Professor Nilsson has drawn attention to the scholiast on this passage, who comments: "Jason's offerings are in accordance with ancient custom, which is that those who have arrived in a strange land make offering to the gods of the locality [τοῖς ἐγχωρίοις θεοῖς]. Alexander himself is said to have done this."[1]

When the period of conquest and migration was over, the various cultures continued to make their contribution to the civilization of classical Greece, whether in conflict or reconciled with one another. In religion, two widely different strains seem to call for notice, which we may accord them without in any way committing ourselves to the over-simple view that there were only two, or that these two are wholly or mainly explicable by a difference of race, the one being characteristic of a "Nordic" people and the other of a "Mediterranean race" with which they

[1] Ap. Rhod. ii, 1271 ff., Nilsson, *Minoan-Mycenean Religion*, p. 2, n. 2. Cf. the advice which the King of Argos gives to the maidens from Egypt who have arrived as strangers and suppliants in his land: πρὸς ταῦτα μίμνε καὶ θεοὺς ἐγχωρίους λιταῖς παραιτοῦ. (Aesch. *Suppl.* 520 f.).

fused. This indeed accounts for much, but to adopt it as the whole explanation would lead to difficulties which would soon prove us to be wrong. In view of the uncertainty which still prevails concerning both the identity of the various peoples who at different times before the classical age had entered the Greek peninsula and the dates of their arrival, the attempt to explain Greek religion on racial lines cannot, anyhow at present, be completely satisfactory or conclusive.

The two main types of religion which appear among the classical Greeks, and so often give an air of paradox to their expressed beliefs, are represented by the Olympians of Homer on the one hand, and on the other, by the kind of cult of which we have an example, considerably modified by official Athenian sentiment, in the Eleusinian mysteries. These were celebrated in honour of Demeter, the Mother of life, whose worship in the lands of the eastern Mediterranean goes (to quote Sir John Myres) "as far back as either records or monuments carry us". "Wherever that culture penetrates", he writes, speaking of the ancient, pre-Indo-European culture of Anatolia, "there seem to go intimately associated with it those gross female figurines which express the kind of nature-worship which finds classical expression in the cults of the 'Great Mother of Asia', in completest contrast with the father-gods who are central in all unsophisticated forms of the Indo-European religion."[1] Those who have visited Mediterranean countries know something of this element, for it is eternal, and in some of the local practices of Orthodox or Roman Catholic communities it is not hard to see the survival of religious phenomena that are indigenous to the Mediterranean world and have known a history far longer than that of Christianity. A striking example is quoted by D. G. Hogarth in his attractive book *A Wandering Scholar in the Levant*. "In honour of the Maid of Bethlehem the peasants of Kuklia (in Cyprus) anointed lately, and probably still anoint each year, the great corner stones of the ruined temple of the Paphian Goddess. As Aphrodite was supplicated once with cryptic rites, so is Mary entreated still by Moslems as well as Christians, with incantations and passings through perforated stones, to remove the curse of barrenness from Cypriote women, or increase the manhood of Cypriote men."[2]

[1] In *European Civilization*, ed. Eyre (Oxford, 1935), pp. 150, 241.

[2] Frazer notes that continuity is here preserved even in the name, and the Virgin is worshipped under the title of Panaghia Aphroditessa (*Adonis, Attis, Osiris*, i, 36).

The Mother-goddess is the embodiment of the fruitful earth, giver of life and fertility to plants, animals and men. Her cult takes certain forms, involving at least the more elementary kinds of mysticism, that is, the belief in the possibility of a union between the worshipper and the object of his worship. Thus the rites may take the form of adoption as her son or of sexual communion. Orgiastic elements appear, as in the passionate, clashing music and frenzied dancing employed by the followers of Rhea or Kybele. The feelings of the initiate may be worked on by sudden contrasts of darkness and dazzling light. All this must be considered in detail later, but at the moment I am concerned to point out what an essentially different atmosphere we are in from that of the religion of the Achaean heroes described by Homer. There we are in clear daylight, in a world where the gods are simply more powerful persons who might fight for or against one, with whom one made bargains or contracts. The Achaean warrior did not seek to be born again from the bosom of Hera. He was indeed the reverse of a mystic by temperament.

Sharp as the contrast is, both these conceptions of worship and of the relation between man and god persisted in historical Greece, and the place and significance of each is a theme which I hope to develop and illustrate as we proceed. The immediate object of this preliminary statement is to give a reason for the continued existence of some of the most primitive elements in Greek religion beside certain other manifestations which appeared during the rapid progress of the Greek mind in historical times. To seek to explain them as following the lines of a racial cleavage between Mediterranean and Northern peoples would be rash, as a single example will at once make clear. Dionysiac religion, though known to Homer, had no place in the society which he describes. It descended upon Greece from Thrace in post-Homeric times as a foreign intrusion, and was met with considerable hostility. It was an orgiastic religion involving a belief in possession by the god whereby for a fleeting instant, under the influence of torches, wine, heady music and dancing, the worshipper felt lifted out of himself and exalted to the plane of the divine. Its natural affinities seem to be all with the fertility-cults of the Mediterranean basin, and have nothing in common with the prosaic Achaean religion. Yet Dionysos is the god of a Northern people, the Thracians, speaking an Indo-European tongue, and whatever accretions his cult may have acquired from the lands through which it spread, ecstasy and immortality are the gifts of the native Thracian religion.[1]

This outstanding exception we shall deal with in due course. Having noted it, I will still make bold to say that in most cases the dark and orgiastic phenomena in Greek religion, connected with fertility and showing an interest in the soul of man as a potentially divine entity, are to be associated with the religious life of the pre-Achaean inhabitants of the land. They belong to a stage which the newcomers had left behind and forgotten long before the period of their overlordship as depicted in the Homeric poems. Thus the old and the new are often in conflict, and associated with different strata of the population. The religion of the ruling classes is often widely different from that of the humbler and sometimes oppressed sections of Greek society. Often on the other hand there is a reconciliation. Even then the originally diverse elements have not always disappeared, and it may remain possible to see where a fusion has been effected.

This is not to say that the devotees of the more primitive cults (to use that misleading epithet for the moment) were necessarily autochthonous, non-Greek inhabitants of the Aegean lands. The history of the Indo-European migrations thither is obscure, and Homer's Achaeans were not the first to arrive. On the other hand, the dark-haired, olive-skinned people of the Mediterranean have a habit of imposing both their physical type and their culture upon their successive invaders. They assimilate and they survive, as no one who knows those regions to-day would deny. Homer's Achaeans were newcomers, still living by battle and violence. They may well have found that their kinsmen by race, who had been settled in the land perhaps for centuries, bore a greater resemblance in their manners and beliefs, and even in

[1] The statement that Dionysos came from the North is challenged by Nilsson (*Min.-Myc. Rel.* 492 ff.) on the ground that he is a composite figure including both Thracian and Phrygian elements. The Phrygians were originally a Thracian tribe, but they migrated early, probably about 1200 B.C., to Asia Minor. Hence, Nilsson maintains, the distinction is a real one, since the god of the Phrygians had absorbed elements of the native Asiatic religion. The Greeks themselves spoke of Dionysos as Phrygian as well as Thracian, and certain aspects of him including his character as a god of vegetation are to be attributed to Phrygia and are of native Asiatic origin. The correctness of this dichotomy does not affect the statement about ecstasy and immortality in the text, nor my general contention that the social character and way of life of a community do more to form its religion than its often problematic racial origins. On this cf. pp. 34 f., 53, 302 f. below.

their appearance, to the Mediterranean stock than to themselves.[1]

Before we turn to the individual gods, a warning is necessary against a facile use of the terms "primitive" and "developed". An example may help. In his chapter on the origins of religious life in the Aegean lands,[2] Otto Kern describes a stage between fetishism (or animism) and complete anthropomorphism when the gods are already imagined in human shape, but their worshippers apparently do not dare to represent them in the visible form of statues and images wrought by human hands. To this stage he would assign two prehistoric phenomena widespread in the region, the cult of the double-axe and the cult of thrones. The occurrence of both these objects in a religious context puts beyond doubt the fact that the worship was directed to beings with human attributes, for how else could they wield an axe or sit in regal state upon a throne? In later representations we are actually shown the man-like god of the thunder and lightning shouldering his axe, just as in later times the sculptured figure of Zeus takes its seat upon the throne; but at first the axe is set up by itself, and the thrones are empty. The cult of the axe is familiar to all from Crete, where it was set up in positions which put beyond doubt that it was an object of worship, but it is found also in widely separated parts of the Aegean region. The throne too is a familiar sight in the same countries, at least to those who have the energy to climb to the tops of hills and mountains, for it is on crags and summits that the thrones are found. The god dwelt on the mountain-tops, as Zeus later on Olympus, no doubt because he was already conceived as the cloud-gatherer, the sender of rain and thunder from on high. Sometimes there is one throne, sometimes a pair for god and goddess. Always they are empty, and hewn, sometimes only roughly, from the rock of the mountain itself. Names and legends grew about them later. Thus the one on the hills above Megara became known as the throne of

[1] Speaking of the England of Henry II, Trevelyan wrote: "The feudal system had established a class of warriors living at the expense of the cultivators of the soil." It is very like a description of Homeric society, and here too the lords represented very largely the latest wave of invaders. But if we knew as little of the composition of the serf and villein classes as we know of their counterparts in Homeric Greece, it is easy to guess what a poor effort we should make at reconstructing that amalgam of Celt, Anglo-Saxon and Dane. A parallel like this, from an entirely different historical situation, is a slippery foundation for positive conclusions, but a salutary incitement to caution in cases where our ignorance is deeper.

[2] *Die Rel. der Gr.*, i, ch. 3.

Xerxes, and one on Mount Sipylus in Asia Minor as the throne of Pelops.

The ubiquity of these symbols is indelibly impressed on my own mind by coming across both quite casually in a remote part of Phrygia during the course of a journey whose primary object was to look for other things. The double-axe was carved on a piece of architrave from a temple. Though the actual building was of post-classical date, the worship was directed to a native god whose ancient, un-Greek name survived, and in whose cult, as inscriptions recorded, curious practices were observed which had little in common with Hellenic or Roman ideas. It was indeed a place to which Greek or Roman influence had scarcely penetrated. The throne, a double one, was rudely but unmistakably carved from the rock on the summit of an isolated hill which I climbed out of curiosity, though without much expectation of finding anything there. These casual finds brought home even more than the numerous published examples how widespread were both forms of cult.

Now chronologically it is true that empty thrones came before sculptured gods, and that orgiastic rites like those of Dionysos or the Great Mother are older than the Olympian religion of Homer. If that is all that we mean, we may call them more primitive, but it does not follow that there was progress from one to the other. That depends on what our criterion of progress is. If it is the growth of spiritual insight, there is much to be said for the view that the man who carves a stone seat and leaves it for the god to occupy when he will, asking only to see him with the eye of the imagination, is at a higher stage of religious development than the man who demands to see the god in physical form, carved by the hand of a Pheidias. Similarly the Dionysiac idea of communion and identification with the god, or the belief of the worshipper of the Mother-goddess that he could be adopted into the family of his deity, together with the other mystical forms of religion practised from time immemorial in Aegean lands, contained, despite their crudeness, possibilities of spiritual development which were lacking to the religion of Homer.

Apart from the subjective bias which inevitably enters into them, the terms "primitive" and "developed" are unsatisfactory because in themselves they contain no hint of an explanation why one form of religion is different from another. In the present case it is more profitable to remember that an invading people has no roots in the soil. During its migrations and for some time after, while it constitutes a ruling class, it is living by its sword, its horses and its wits, as were the Achaeans at Troy. The gods of this race of mobile warriors are likely to be different from those of the people who live by tilling the same soil on which their ancestors have dwelt for untold generations. To see the contrast as one between a folk whose interest is in the maintenance of uninterrupted fertility and another which is absorbed in battle, conquest and dominion is more helpful than to talk of primitive and advanced cultures. Finally let us remember that in no historical document are we likely to find evidence of either of these types of religion existing in unadulterated purity.

We should now be able to turn with profit to the main task of this chapter, which is to take some of the most important Greek deities individually and briefly discuss the origins of each, at least in so far as these have determined, and therefore throw light on, their character in historical times.

II. Zeus

Greek literature begins with Homer, and from Homer the Greeks took their portraits of the gods. In Homer they already appear as fully formed, clear-cut characters, and these divine characters were inherited by the classical Greeks. Hesiod also contributed, as Herodotus remarked, but the Homeric poems were the prevailing influence and it was their clear and vivid pictures that impressed themselves indelibly on the mind of later Greece. Mainly out of Homer, and certainly in Ionia at an early date, there took shape the circle of the Twelve Gods, which formed a kind of canon for the Greeks of succeeding centuries. Some are more important than others, and when we reach the last two or three places we find a certain amount of disagreement and competition for the favour of inclusion. In particular districts a deity who has been for centuries an object of superstitious awe to the local inhabitants will not yield his place easily to the conquering Olympians.[1] Suppose however we take some of the most important and universally acknowledged of these gods, and introduce ourselves to them with a brief sketch of what and where they are likely to have been before they set up house together on

[1] For further details about the Twelve, see Appendix.

Olympus. In the earliest Greek literature that we know, they appear as a number of strongly individual personalities already united in the bonds of a settled, if somewhat quarrelsome, family life, under the paternal aegis of Zeus. But in fact they are a heterogeneous collection whose settlement as one family on Olympus has something about it of a *tour de force*. Who really are Zeus, Hera, Apollo, Poseidon, Artemis, Athena, and where do they come from? The question is worth asking, if only for the glimpse it will give of the complex world which existed around the shores of the Aegean before the Homeric poems were written. To be reminded that there was such a world is important, but the reader should be warned that the inquiry will lead us into regions of doubt and controversy, from which nothing pre-Homeric is free. Into such regions it will not serve our present purpose to follow it far.

The complexity which went to make the Olympians of Homer is well described in a paragraph from H. J. Rose's *Handbook of Greek Mythology*, which will serve as a good starting-point for our own observations:

"The imagination of the Greeks had peopled every part of the world they knew with divine beings who were not all of one origin. Some few had been brought with them by the Greek-speaking peoples when they entered the countries they occupied in historical times; some no doubt belonged to the Minoan-Mycenean civilization which they found there when they entered, or perhaps helped to create; others again, especially little local deities, had been there since the days of savagery, many centuries in the past. Moreover, the invading Hellenes were not all one political unit, and never attained unity, and it is highly likely that various divisions of them were variously blended with the pre-Greek population. Hence almost from the time when first the Greek speech was heard in Greece, there was a vast assemblage of all manner of cults and all sorts of deities, great and small, savage and civilized, credited with functions connected in various ways with the processes of nature and the life of man. No people of lively imagination, least of all the ancestors of European philosophy, could have refrained from asking what connexion there was between these different gods, and also between them and the world in which they and their worshippers lived. Thus it is that we find, not indeed a single orthodox account of how the universe and its divine and human inhabitants came into being, but a general agreement in outline, the fruit of early and imaginative speculation, as regards these matters. In Homer the gods are already organized on the model of a human clan, with Zeus at its head; Hesiod preserves the earliest account of how this state of things came about."[1]

Our concern just now is not with the speculations of the Greeks about the origins of their gods, but rather with our own. I use the quotation to illustrate the vast complexity that had existed before Homer, and the selection, by Homer and his unknown predecessors, and organization of this divine material into a small and compact family of clearly defined persons.

'Eκ Διὸς ἀρχώμεσθα—we must follow the poet's advice and begin with Zeus. "Frankly stated", wrote Martin Nilsson, "our knowledge of the invading Greeks amounts almost to one word only, but this one word is very important—the name Zeus." Since however the object of this study is not so much to explain the origin of a purely Hellenic deity as to account for the character that he acquired in the eyes of that very mixed people, the classical Greeks, I wish in this section to point out that Zeus as, say, Euripides knew him is a composite figure in which among others two main strands are entwined. This can be done quite simply, and moreover the disentangling of these two strands is of the utmost importance for the understanding of Greek religion.

First and foremost he is the god of the sky and weather whom all Indo-European peoples acknowledged under names variously derived from the same root. This root originally meant "to shine", but the limitations of this meaning seem soon to have been forgotten, and it is probable that even the parent word of the undivided Indo-European language was itself extended to mean the sky in general, whether by day or by night, in sunshine or in storm. So much the philological school of mythologists have had to teach, and in this case there is no possibility of doubting their results. As such Zeus is, as Nilsson says, purely Hellenic, a part of the inheritance which the Greeks brought with them when they broke off from the common stock and started the migrations which finally settled them around the shores of the Aegean. In this aspect Zeus is known to everyone, and there is no need to spend much time in multiplying examples to illustrate the fact that for the Greeks Zeus was primarily the god of sky and weather. "The

[1] *Handbook*, pp. 18 f.

portion of Zeus is the broad heaven, in brightness and in cloud alike."[1] His constant epithet in Homer is the Cloud-Gatherer. He sends the rain, the lightning, the thunderbolt and the thunder. In this last and most terrifying capacity, as god of the thunder and thunderbolt, he naturally impressed himself particularly strongly on the imaginations of his worshippers, and it gave rise to a magnificent series of sonorous epithets.[2] In visual representations the thunderbolt is his constant attribute. In Greek houses altars have been found dedicated to Zeus Kataibates, Zeus who Descends, an epithet under which he was worshipped as the god of lightning. Sacrifices were made on these altars to appease the god and avert the stroke of lightning from the house. They served the purpose of the lightning-conductor on a modern building.[3]

From Homer onwards Zeus dwells in the sky, and is also spoken of as being the sky itself. From the way in which this latter notion appears in Greek literature, one might suppose it to be a late, poetical and semi-philosophical conception, and there will be more to say about it later on. But as the etymology and other considerations suggest, it is probably a return to the oldest belief of all, "the primary and yet age-long conception of the animate sky".[4] In a well-known line Theocritus says that Zeus sometimes shines brightly and sometimes rains.[5] In a purely prosaic passage Aristotle, criticizing the views of materialist and mechanistic philosophers, attributes to them the opinion that "Zeus does not rain in order to make the crops grow, but from necessity" (*Phys.* ii, 198b18). Euripides, who is fond of speaking of the bright *aither*, or heaven, as the home of Zeus, also speaks of it as "that which men call Zeus" (fr. 877). For the Greeks of the classical period

[1] *Ζεὺς δ' ἔλαχ' οὐρανὸν εὐρὺν ἐν αἰθέρι καὶ νεφέλῃσιν.* (*Il.* xv, 192.)

[2] Homer, Pindar and Aristophanes between them give us the following: *βαρύγδουπος, βαρύκτυπος, ἐριβρεμέτης, ἐρίγδουπος, κεραυνοβρόντης, μεγαβρόντης, ὑψιβρεμέτης, ἐγχεικέραυνος, τερπικέραυνος, ἀργικέραυνος.* As the rain-giver he is *ὄμβριος* (Lykophron 160, Plut. *Sept. Sap. Conv.* 158 e, and see other reff. in Cook, *Zeus*, iii, 525 ff.) and *ὑέτιος* (Ditt. Syll. 1107, inscr. of *c.* 200 B.C. from Kos, Cook, *Zeus*, iii, 561 ff.). As god of lightning, besides *καταιβάτης* Homer and Pindar call him *ἀστεροπητής, στεροπηγερέτα* and *φοινικοστερόπας.* The roll of the thunder itself is in Hesiod's line *τοῦ καὶ ὑπὸ βροντῆς πελεμίζεται εὐρεῖα χθών*, and Pindar's *ἐλατὴρ ὑπέρτατε βροντᾶς ἀκαμαντόποδος.*

[3] For Zeus Kataibates, see Cook, *Zeus*, ii, 13 ff., Nilsson, *Greek Popular Religion* (1940), p. 67. Aeschylus calls the thunderbolt *Ζηνὸς ἄγρυπνον βέλος, καταιβάτης κεραυνός* (*P.V.* 358 f.), and Zeus Kataibates himself is punned on in Aristoph. *Peace*, 42. These and later reff. will be found in Cook, l.c.

[4] That this is so is the conclusion of Professor Cook's great work *Zeus*, from which the quotation is taken.

[5] iv, 43: *χὠ Ζεὺς ἄλλοκα μὲν πέλει αἴθριος, ἄλλοκα δ' ὕει.*

the universal belief is that Zeus is either the sky itself or, more usually, the being who lives in the sky, from which he sends and controls the weather.

Now a god like this, naturally enough, was for the people who believed in him the supreme deity. Consequently it was natural for them to think of him as having always been what he is now, the venerable and majestic figure of a ruler. His existence and greatness tend to be taken for granted. Myth-makers may produce stories of his parentage, but in the popular belief there will be no emphasis on them. The primary thought in men's minds is that he is the ruler and the father. (The two go naturally together since in the headship of a human clan they are normally combined.) This is the position of Zeus in the *Iliad*. Son of Kronos is his conventional title, but Kronos himself is scarcely mentioned. He is known to have been banished by Zeus at some time in the dim past, but there are no reminiscences of the struggle for power which that fact implies. Zeus is "Father of gods and men"; he "rules among all the immortals". That is his essence, and it is solely as father and ruler that he is imagined. There is a further point about a god of this sort which at present may seem platitudinous, but will gain significance as we go on and are able to develop it later. Before him, man stands helpless as a creature of a lower order altogether. He is immortal, man is mortal; he is all-powerful, man is weak. He is a being entirely external to man, and to get into right relationship with him it is necessary to proceed accordingly, acknowledging his supremacy and placating him with offerings and worship. He is simply a ruler who will brook no rivals. Even another god, should he set himself up against Zeus, could expect no better treatment than to be seized by the leg and hove out from Olympus, to suffer in his fall the nearest to death that an immortal god can suffer.[1] How much worse would be the fate of a mortal who had thoughts above his station and in any way questioned Zeus' supremacy. His case is certainly not helped because from the moral point of view Zeus may stand no higher than the lowliest of his human subjects. The two planes have nothing to do with morality, but are planes of power. It is in fact a class-distinction which separates the man from his god, like that which separated the human king or chieftain from the common people.

The god of sky and weather has not always or everywhere been

[1] *Il.* i, 590 ff.

conceived like this. This is the character with which he was endowed by a particular society, a feudal society where war and hunting, sport and feasting were the favourite and most honoured occupations, and where loyalty to a powerful baron was the most necessary and desirable virtue. We know of this society from Homer, and to Homeric society and its religion we shall return again. Enough has been said to explain the first of the two most sharply contrasting threads from which, as I said, the Zeus of classical Greece was woven.

From the Olympian of Homer we turn to a different Zeus, whose legends form the second of these strands. Homer makes no mention of the birth of Zeus. True, it had little to do with his story, and might have been left out on those grounds alone. But we have seen enough of the Olympian Zeus to know that, his nature being what it was, birth-legends if applied to him would seem out of place. They would scarcely be applicable to one whose essence it is to be the father and lord of all. The Olympian of Homer was not thought of as a baby. Yet the conception of Zeus as a baby was by no means unfamiliar to the Greeks of post-Homeric times. The story of his birth, which we know first of all from Hesiod,[1] takes us to Crete, the island home of a civilization older than that of the Homeric princes. Before the present generation of the gods was the generation of the Titans, sons and daughters of Earth and Heaven (Gaia and Uranos). Among these the most important were Kronos and Rhea, who were united—

> in Saturn's reign
> Such mixture was not held a stain—

and had several children. Kronos however had received a prophecy from his parents that it was fated for him to be overthrown by his own son, and to prevent this he swallowed the children as soon as they were born. This grieved Rhea, and she went to her parents for advice. Gaia and Uranos had no objection to becoming the instruments of the fate which they themselves had prophesied, and when Rhea was about to bear another child they sent her to Crete. Here she bore Zeus, and he was hidden in a cave on a mountain to which Hesiod gives the name Aigaion, which may be a reference to the legend that he was suckled by a goat. Elsewhere in ancient tradition the mountain is said to have been

[1] *Theog.* 453 ff.

either Mount Ida or Mount Dikte.[1] Gaia herself (in Hesiod's version) became the baby's nurse, and devised a stratagem to deceive the simple-minded Kronos. She gave him a stone wrapped in swaddling-clothes, which he, all unsuspecting, swallowed under the impression that it was his latest-born son. The stone served a double purpose, for it did not agree with the god, who later was compelled to disgorge it, and with it the rest of his children whom he had previously engulfed. To this circumstance a number of the other gods of Zeus' generation, including Hera, Poseidon and Hades, owed their continued existence. The relation of these crude stories will have served a purpose if they help to show to what a different religious climate we have been transported from that of the Homeric pantheon.

The safety of the infant Zeus was ensured in another way also, and by another class of divine creatures who are of some interest for our theme. In order that his first cries might not be heard by his father, certain *daimones* of Crete called Kuretes danced around him their war-dance, clashing their shields and spears together. This is not mentioned by Hesiod, but is clearly referred to by the maenads of Euripides' *Bacchae*, who in the wildly mingled strains of one of their choruses sing (lines 119–125):

> O lair of the Kuretes, holy haunts of Crete that saw the birth of Zeus, where in thy caves the triple-crested Korybantes invented this my circle of stretched hide.[2]

Callimachus in his Hymn to Zeus (lines 52 ff.) is more explicit:

> About thee the Kuretes danced continuously their war-dance, striking upon their arms, that Kronos might hear the clash of the shield and not thy infant cries.

The story is repeated in later writers both Greek and Roman, and depicted on monuments, especially coins, of the Hellenistic and Roman ages. There were naturally variations, and also additions from the common stock of folk-lore, to which the myth of Zeus' birth already owed several features, for example the prophecy to the father that his son would overthrow him, the consequent perils of the baby, and the episode of the swallowing

[1] Archaeological evidence has shown that there were sanctuaries of the god on both these mountains, and the finds suggest that the one on Mt. Dikte is the older, and the other only came into use when the Dictaean cave was deserted. (J. D. S. Pendlebury, *Archaeology of Crete* (Methuen, 1939), p. 327.)

[2] For the Korybantes, here identified with the Kuretes, see below, p. 154.

of the stone. Later writers tell how the babe was suckled by a goat or other animal, or by a nymph, or fed by bees.

In this story we are transported to another world from that of the Homeric Achaeans. This is no Indo-European sky-god. His affinities are rather with the chthonian cults of the Aegean basin, which had been carried on there for countless centuries before the arrival of the Achaeans or any other Greeks on the scene. Whatever his original name may have been, it was certainly not Zeus. That was the name that he acquired when he had become identified, as such an important god of the land was bound to be, with the supreme god of the conquerors from the north.

Let us briefly run over the most important characteristics of this Cretan god, for in the two aspects of Zeus that I am bringing forward here we have an example of a contrast which meets us everywhere in Greek religion. It is the contrast between the virile, clear-cut and prosaic religion which the Achaeans brought with them and the dark and orgiastic and in some ways far more primitive cults which were certainly in Greece before the Achaeans and which it is natural to connect with the original inhabitants who possessed the land before the arrival of any Greek tribes at all. These cults combined with those of the Achaeans, which were stamped indelibly on their own minds and on those of their successors by the greatness of the Homeric poems, and went far to make Greek religion what it was and to explain many of its seeming inconsistencies.

We can scarcely do better than start from the Kuretes, since amid the many elements of this strange story which have crept in from the common stock of folklore or *Märchen*, they stand out as in the first place bringing us into contact with a real religious cult, and in the second place belonging especially to Crete.[1] The subject of the Kuretes is complex, and its complexity can be succinctly illustrated by a passage from Strabo, the great geographer of the Augustan age (x. 466). He has been led to speak of them during his discussion of Aetolia and Acarnania in Western Greece, for Homer mentions an ancient human tribe called Kuretes living in those parts. Strabo rightly regards these as

[1] Cf. the opinion of Nilsson (*Min.-Myc. Rel.* 472): "The Couretes belong to Crete; in all other districts and places they are introduced later, or else their name denotes a people", and the reff. ad loc. For a detailed study of the Kuretes, see especially J. Poerner, *de Curetibus et Corybantibus*, diss. philol. Halenses, 1913.

having originally nothing to do with the daemonic protectors of the infant Zeus, but says that "since owing to the identity of name historians have confused these different things, I have no objection to making a digression in order to explain them more fully". This is how he begins the subject:

I turn to what is remote from my theme, but has been brought into connexion with it by historians owing to the identity of name, being known as Kuretic or concerned with the Kuretes as if it had to do with the former inhabitants of Aetolia and Acarnania. In fact these Kuretes are different, and what is known about them suggests rather the Satyrs and Sileni and Bacchi and Tityri. For according to writers on Cretan and Phrygian lore, the Kuretes are similar daemons or attendants upon gods, and are mixed up with certain sacred rites, both mystic and other, concerned with the rearing of the child Zeus in Crete and the orgiastic worship of the Mother of the Gods in Phrygia and around Mount Ida in the Troad. There is much confusion in these accounts. Some declare that the Korybantes and Kabiri and Idaean Daktyls and Telchines are the same as the Kuretes, others pronounce them related and distinguish certain small differences between them, but agree that in general terms, and to name their prevailing characteristics, all alike are enthusiastic and Bacchic types, who in the guise of acolytes, by dances in arms with tumult, noise, cymbals, tympana and weapons, also with the music of flutes and shouting, arouse the passions in the course of religious ceremonies. Thus the rites also become common property, both those of the Kuretes and those performed in Samothrace[1] and in Lemnos[2] and many others, because the attendant daemons were identified.

Strabo next describes the nature of orgiastic rites and their value in exalting the hearts of men so as to turn them away from everyday affairs towards the divine, and enumerates the various gods in whose honour such rites are performed by the Greeks. He then proceeds:

Now in Crete, besides these, the cult of Zeus used to be carried out in a particular way, with orgiastic rites and attendants similar to the Satyrs of Dionysos. These they called Kuretes, and they were youths who executed armed movements and dances, enacting the myth of Zeus' birth.

There follows an account of the myth, with the part played by the

[1] The mysteries of the Kabiri.

[2] The orgiastic rites of the Thracian goddess Bendis, also called the Great Goddess, a goddess of the fruits of the earth identified by the Greeks with Artemis, Persephone and Hekate.

Kuretes in deceiving Kronos "with tympana and other similar noises and armed dancing and general tumult".

These extracts from the account of a scholarly Greek of the Augustan age—he was in fact a native of Asia Minor, which by no means diminishes his authority—are fortunately confirmed by earlier references, some of which we have seen already. We may note in passing how common throughout the Greek world was the phenomenon of a deity worshipped with orgiastic rites and provided with a train of attendants of whom the Satyrs of Dionysos are the best-known example. The similarities were so great that as civilization advanced and communications improved, and the devotees of these cults in different parts became known to each other, the daemons connected with each became confused and identified, and we may assume that in their nature the various cults were identical, though originally separated locally and therefore furnished with separate, local names.

To delve further into their relationships would not be to our present purpose. The thing to notice here is that this noisy dance of armed youths, mythically explained as a device to save the life of the infant Zeus, is no mere fairy-tale but takes us immediately into the sphere of mystic or orgiastic religion, in which such dances were actually carried out by the young men of the neighbourhood. *Kouros* or *koures* (the latter form occurs in Homer) is simply, as Strabo rightly saw, the Greek for a youth, especially a young warrior.[1] This part of the story of Zeus is in fact one of the clearest cases of an aetiological myth, that is, one which has arisen to provide a basis for an existing ritual whose real origin is lost in the mists of a savage past. At this point let us take two other testimonies to the nature of this Cretan ritual, which may enlarge our acquaintance with its features.

The first is the fragment of Euripides' play *The Cretans*, quoted by the Neoplatonist Porphyrios, who says that it describes the practices of the inspired worshippers of Zeus in Crete.[2] The words are spoken to King Minos by a chorus of these worshippers, and may be rendered thus:

[1] The most exact equivalent in sense is probably provided by modern words from the same area, where a similar ideal of manhood has persisted—the modern Greek *παλληκάρι* or the Turkish *delikanli*.

[2] *τοὺς ἐν Κρήτῃ τοῦ Διὸς προφήτας*, Porph. *de abst.* iv, 19. In Euripides' *Bacchae* (551) the maenads call themselves the *προφῆται* of Dionysos. I have treated the fragment in my *Orpheus and Greek Religion* (Methuen, 1935). See esp. pp. 111, 199 and notes thereto. See also Jane Harrison, *Prolegomena*,[3] 479, and Nilsson, *Min.-Myc. Rel.* 506 f.

Son of the Phoenician princess, child of Tyrian Europa and great Zeus, ruler over hundred-fortressed Crete—here am I, come from the sanctity of temples roofed with cut beam of our native wood, its true joints of cypress welded together with Chalybean axe and bull's-hide glue. Living a pure life from the day when I became an initiate of Idaean Zeus and herdsman of night-wandering Zagreus, and having accomplished the feasts of raw flesh and held aloft torches to the Mountain Mother, torches of the Kuretes, I was raised to the holy estate and named Bacchos. Clothed in raiment all white, I shun the birth of men nor touch the coffins of the dead, and keep myself from the eating of food which has had life.

This is not the time to go into all the interesting points which this important passage raises. Euripides describes a cult which existed in the fifth century B.C., and, warned by Strabo, we shall not be surprised to find it uniting originally diverse elements, so that, for example, the initiate of the Cretan Zeus, connected with the Kuretes, takes the name of Bacchos. The origin of the name Zagreus is uncertain, but it, or a less Hellenized form of the name, may possibly have been the original name of the Cretan deity who became identified with the Greek Zeus.[1] The word "herdsman" is due to a modern correction in the manuscripts of Porphyrios. If right, it refers to a class of priests in the service of gods conceived in the form of bulls, most commonly Dionysos or his Thracian equivalent Sabazios.[2]

What we may take as certain is that the original cult of the Cretan god, to be capable of such syncretism, was of a mystic character. It is of the essence of a mystery-cult that, by means of such stimulants to the emotions as Strabo describes, the worshipper felt the god enter into his own being and could, while the ecstasy lasted, call himself, the follower, by the name of the god he worshipped. The culminating point of the rite was often the eating of a newly slain animal who was thought to embody the god. By imbibing the fresh life-blood, the visible, physical form or symbol of deity, the worshipper believed himself to acquire the spirit, strength, holiness or whatever of the divine characteristics was most desired. Hence the reference to "feasts of raw flesh" as necessary for the initiate, a feature which meets us again in the *Bacchae* (line 139). In Crete the animal which embodied the god was a bull. The actual statement that the Cretans in their rites "tore a live bull with their teeth" we owe to the somewhat dubious

[1] *O. and Gr. Rel.* 113. [2] Ib., p. 260 and n. 11.

testimony of the Christian writer Firmicus Maternus,[1] but we need not doubt it on that score. The *Cretans* fragment, with its mention of "raw feasts", opens by reminding us that Minos was the son of Zeus and Europa, and everyone knows in what form Zeus wooed Europa and carried her away to Crete. The Cretan myths of Pasiphae and the Minotaur tell the same tale.[2] The bull was one of the forms of Dionysos' epiphany also, and since it cannot have been borrowed from him by the god of Crete, this only adds confirmation. Both were gods of the same type.[3] The words in our fragment "I was raised to the holy estate and called Bacchos" give us the aim of the rites, namely communion or identification with the god, even though the name itself be a result of later syncretism. Some of the injunctions and prohibitions in the rest of the fragment are very primitive, and common to the devotees of many mystery-cults. We may be sure that the warlike, excited dances formed part of the rites, though in this passage we have only the bare mention of the name Kuretes to go on. We come nearer to them in the very interesting document to which we turn as our second testimony.

Its interest lies particularly in this, that it was found as an inscription and is clearly intended to be used in the actual cult. It is not a mere literary creation. That is excluded by its purpose, even if in the form in which it has come down to us it was commissioned from a poet of the fifth or fourth century B.C. Its elements are far older. It is a hymn to Zeus, addressed as "Greatest Kuros", and was found inscribed in stone at Palaikastro at the eastern end of Crete, "one of the great centres of Minoan civilization".[4] The actual lettering is of about A.D. 200 and the language of the hymn suggests the fourth century B.C.[5] In the following translation, the words in brackets represent supplements or partial supplements by the editors, where the Greek words are entirely or partly obliterated on the stone.

Io! Greatest Kuros, I give thee hail, Son of Kronos, all-powerful and bright one. Thou hast stepped forth at the head of thy daemons. To Dikte for the year O come, and rejoice in the notes which we strike for

[1] Ch. vi, p. 15, Ziegler = Kern, *Orph. Fr.* p. 234. Cf. *O. and Gr. Rel.* p. 109.

[2] Cf. also *O. and Gr. Rel.* ch. iv, n. 35.

[3] And possibly of a common origin. But that is ἄλλος λόγος.

[4] Pendlebury, *Archaeology of Crete* (Methuen, 1939), p. 9.

[5] So the editors and first commentators. See *Annual of Brit. Sch. at Athens* (1908–9). For the significance of the hymn cf. also Nilsson, *Min.-Myc. Rel.* 475 ff., Ch. Picard, *Éphèse et Claros* (1922), 424 ff.

thee on the strings and blend with our flutes, as we stand and sing about thy well-fenced altar. For there the shield [-bearing nurturers] took thee, a babe immortal, from Rhea, and [with beat of] foot [hid thee away] . . . [three and a half lines missing] . . . of fair dawn. [And the seasons swelled with increase] year by year, and mortals were swayed by justice, and peace, that consorteth with prosperity, [attended all] creatures.

[Leap for us, for our wine-jars], and leap for fleecy [flocks], and leap [for our fields] of crops, and for [hives that bring] full increase. [Leap also for] our cities, and our sea-faring ships, and leap for [the young citizens], and leap for [fair] law-abidingness.

Here we have a chorus standing about the altar of a son of Kronos who is called Kuros (Youth), and inviting him with music and song to come back to the scene of his birth-place "for the year". They explicitly say that the reason, or justification, for their actions is the procedure of his armed guardians at the time of his actual birth. ("For there" etc.) Doubtless therefore their *molpe* included dance as well as song. They also make clear the purpose of their performance. The connexion between mystic and orgiastic cults and the promotion of fertility is so regular that we might have inferred the one from the other, but we are not left to do so The god is called upon to "leap" in the first place that the flocks and the crops may have increase, and secondly to bring prosperity, peace and law-abiding ways to the cities, cherish their youth, and speed their ships and trade upon the sea. This word "leap" has a double meaning. It is used also for the action of the male in covering and impregnating the female, and the word translated "for" means rather "to" or "upon", a translation difficult to retain when in its present metaphorical use it is applied to cities, ships and law. This secondary sense would undoubtedly be present in the minds of the singers, though probably they thought also of the way in which they wished the crops to leap up high as the result of the god's blessing, and by a common kind of sympathetic magic would themselves leap in the air (like the Kuretes whose action they believed themselves to be commemorating) at each repetition of the word.

We can now, without troubling to collect the further scraps of evidence which undoubtedly exist, though they mostly require us to argue back from testimony of Hellenistic or Roman date, sum up the essential nature of this cult and of the god for whom it was performed. The young warriors, the Kuroi or Kuretes of Crete, performed at regular intervals—probably once a year—a war-like dance. It was a primitive rite, whose true origin was unknown to the performers, and remains unknown to us. Most probably, as the Palaikastro hymn suggests, it was a fertility charm, but the extent of our ignorance is well shown by the variety of the explanations which have been suggested. It has been interpreted by various scholars as rain magic, apotropaic magic (weapons may be used to scare evil spirits), initiation ceremony, greeting to the morning sun, and (surely a counsel of despair) sheer joy in bodily movement and noise. The connexion of the ceremony described in the first stanzas of the Palaikastro hymn with the story of the Kuretes is so clearly and explicitly stated that I do not think we need worry unduly because there is no mention of arms in the action of the human chorus, and the music of song, strings and flutes seems to have no obvious connexion with the din raised by the mythical Kuretes. The shields of the latter are mentioned when they themselves are referred to, and this may have been deemed sufficient in a later age when the music of instruments had proved a more suitable means to excite the emotions to the required pitch. The flute at least was in classical times a regular accompaniment of mystic or orgiastic ritual.

By means of their dances and singing, these young warriors believed that they were summoning into their midst the god of their society, whom also, since he was addressed as "the greatest of the Kuroi", they themselves in some way *represented.* We are here introducing ourselves to an idea which is familiar in Greek religion, yet difficult to express in our own terms, since our civilization has removed us so far from it. It was noticeable how easily Strabo, in the passages quoted, slipped from the notion of the Kuretes as *daimones*, or as we should say mythical or semi-divine beings, to speaking of them as human youths, who by their movements enacted or represented the behaviour of their prototypes. To us, three distinct orders seem to be involved: the god, whom the Greeks called Zeus; the divine warriors who, according to the myth, in those strange far-off days before the dawn of history saved his life by their antics; and the human worshippers of historical times who reproduced the story in a kind of mummers' play or country dance. No such clear-cut distinctions were in the minds of those to whom all this was part of a living religion. By letting themselves be caught up in the spirit of the orgiastic ritual, which involved abandoning their everyday, human personalities, they not only represented, but *were* the Kuretes, and the god himself was the leader of their band. To find the priests of a god calling themselves by the god's own name is by no means uncommon. The *Bacchoi* and *Bacchai* of Bacchos or Dionysos are the best known.[1] But it is only possible within a certain circle of beliefs, for it rests on the possibility of obliterating the line between human and divine, and, whether for a long period or for a brief moment of ecstasy, blending the two natures in one.

This primitive communion was achieved by consuming the flesh and blood of the god in his animal form, a culmination which we have seen referred to by Euripides. We cannot say for certain how many of these ritual elements belonged to one and the same occasion, but analogies suggest that the raw feast was the final act of the drama, for which the dances, flute-playing, shouting and any other features (there was probably a procession in which sacred objects were displayed[2]) were a very necessary psychological preparation.

Finally we have seen clear evidence that the god of this cult was a spirit of fertility, whose presence would ensure abundant crops and healthy flocks and herds. In this he shows himself to be a single example of a very large class. Such spirits were worshipped all over the lands around the Aegean and in the Near East, not only in Crete but in Asia Minor, Egypt and Greece itself.[3] Indeed, to confine them to any particular area of the earth's surface is

[1] Other examples are quoted by Ch. Picard, *Éphèse et Claros* (Paris, 1922), p. 231 with n. 4, 279.

[2] This is suggested by the late syncretistic account of Firmicus (*O. and Gr. Rel.* p. 109) and the analogy of other mysteries. The Eleusinian and other mysteries were sufficiently like those of Idaean Zeus for the Cretans to claim in later days that they had been the teachers of the Greeks in all such matters. (Diodorus v, 77, quoted in *O. and Gr. Rel.* 110 f.)

[3] It is surely significant of a natural affinity of cult when we find that the Kuretes were taken up into the legend of the birth of Artemis at Ortygia at the foot of Mt. Solmissos near Ephesus. The purpose of their armed dance here was to distract the attention of the jealous Hera so that she should not observe the birth-pangs of Leto. In commemoration of this there was, as in Crete, a human fraternity of Kuretes who, among other functions, carried out "sacrifices of a mystical character". The evidence for all this goes back only to Hellenistic times. The sole literary authority is Strabo (xiv, 640), who is supported by inscriptions. See Ch. Picard, *Éphèse et Claros* (1922), pp. 277 ff., 423 ff. Of Picard's conclusions, we may quote here (p. 298): "Nous avons indiqué les rapports de la danse des armes avec les cérémonies de la rénovation vernale. Cette danse magique, au jour principal des mystères de Solmissos, formait l'élément essentiel du drama sacré. Le mythe qui le justifiait, et qui fut d'ailleurs emprunté de toutes pieces, lors de la constitution de la légende sacrée éphesienne, aux traditions crétoises sur la naissance de Zeus, ne laisse point oublier cette antique origine."

probably to circumscribe them too much. They belong as a class not to any particular locality but rather to a stage of culture. Our subject is the Greeks, and for us therefore it is sufficient to notice that they existed on every hand in the Aegean basin when the Greeks arrived there. Their character may be generally described as that of a male spirit of fertility who by his virility will impregnate the earth that is to bear the crops and give fecundity to the animals. In this way his life entered into them, their life was his own, and so by an easy transference (for we are speaking of days before the development of nice logical distinctions) he was identified with them. We have seen that he was imagined in the forms both of a bull[1] and of a young man. He was also (as may be more plainly seen in the case of his famous Egyptian counterpart Osiris and others) identified with the life of the crops.

To return to Zeus and the god of Crete, we now have a general idea of the elements indigenous to the Cretan religion which the imaginative Hellenes discovered when they came to inherit the ruins of its ancient civilization. With this religion they had to come to terms, and one result of this was the legend of Zeus' birth in Crete, in a cave on Mount Ida or Mount Dikte. Both caves have been excavated and show signs of having been sacred places long before the arrival of the Greeks.[2] To the deity of this ancient cult Zeus gave his name. Another feature, besides the story of his birth, which resulted from the identification, was his embodiment sometimes in the form of a bull, sometimes in that of a child. The armed dance of the Cretan Kuroi, a rite whose real origin was lost in the mists of antiquity, comes to be interpreted as a commemoration of the saving of Zeus from his unnatural father. Again, with gods of the type to which the Cretan belonged, and which was common in the religion of the Near Eastern peoples, an essential feature of their mythology was their death. The explanation of this as due to their association with the annual life and death of the crops, though not entirely free from difficulty, is no doubt the true one. Hence it came about that the grave of Zeus was to be found in Crete. This sort of inconsistency, the attribution of a grave to an immortal, does not trouble his worshippers so long as his religion is a living thing. The age of doubt

[1] For the significance of the bull as a fertilizing agent of singular potency, see e.g. Cook, *Zeus*, i, 633–5. In Crete it was identified with the sun, ib., 468, and cf. the myth of Talos, ib., 719 ff.

[2] p. 41, n. 1.

and questioning comes later, and the grave of Zeus was a thing for Alexandrian poets to play with, and caused misgivings among the first to attempt a science of mythology. Thus Callimachus the Alexandrian wrote, in his Hymn to Zeus (lines 8 ff.):

The Cretans were ever liars. They even fabricated a tomb for thee, O Lord. But thou didst not die, for thou livest for ever.

All this obtained acceptance as part of the canon of Greek mythology, however little it may have affected the actual cult of the god on the mainland of Greece. It is scarcely necessary to emphasize how unsuitable it is to the Olympian Zeus of Homer, to the conception of an august father and ruler, jealous of his powers, which was brought with them by the invading Achaeans. Who could imagine the idea of human communion with the divine in connexion with the Homeric father of gods and men? Yet once the Cretan god is called Zeus, this idea has to be admitted. The performers of the ritual dance were called Kuroi or Kuretes, and Zeus himself is addressed as "Greatest of the Kuroi", just as in the religion of Dionysos, the best example of a religion of communion or *enthusiasmos* in Greece, the god was called Bacchos, and his worshippers, as through participation in the rites they came to feel themselves one with him, took the title of *Bacchoi*.

Zeus, then, is originally the god of sky and weather belonging to the peoples who, speaking the Indo-European language which we call Greek, invaded and settled in the country which we call Greece. He was also the supreme head of their pantheon and in that capacity had taken on a number of functions outside the sphere of his original nature as sky-god. But the country to which they came already possessed its own forms of worship and belief, which for the most part were fundamentally different from those of the invaders. The objects of this worship were in many places dispossessed by Zeus, a process whose most important result we have already seen. The indigenous deity took the name of Zeus, but remained essentially what he had been before. Then we find the name of Zeus applied to ancient Mediterranean spirits of fertility whose worship is involved in rites and ideas utterly foreign to those of the supreme god of the Greeks. An invading race may change the names, but the tenacious roots of an ancient religion are not so easily dug out and thrown away.

There are other features of Greek religion which in the earlier days of its study were differently explained, but now that the usurpation of Zeus is established find a more satisfactory explanation there. Among these is the tradition, related in Hesiod's *Theogony*, that before he came to power Zeus had to overthrow an earlier race of gods, the Titans, one of whom, Kronos, was his own father. According to the most probable explanation, the Titans were indeed of an older generation in Greece, and their defeat reflects the fruitless opposition offered by the older religion to that of the newcomers. This view of the matter has certainly relegated to a deserved obscurity the old interpretation of the Titanomachy as a symbolic representation of the struggle between the forces of nature, the powers of storm and darkness pitted against those of sunshine and light in the unending struggle which makes the weather. The present explanation must perhaps remain a hypothesis, but it is not to be so lightly overthrown, for it rests on at least some positive evidence, and not merely on a preconceived notion to which, indeed, the evidence offers but little support.[1]

In describing the dual character of the historic Zeus, it became clear that the contrast between Aegean and Homeric cults was, generally speaking, a contrast between a religion of the soil, a worship of the fertility of the earth not unmixed with magical practices to secure its continuance, and a religion of the sky, whose

[1] The historical explanation has been supported by most modern scholars, though not necessarily as a certainty. Nilsson for example (*Min.-Myc. Rel.* pp. 3 f.) speaks of "guessing", and writes, "this however must remain as yet a more or less problematical suggestion". Kern on the other hand accepts the idea of a historical conflict without argument, as an established fact. (*Die Rel. der Gr.* i, 254 f. "In der Sage von der Titanomachie lebt die erinnerung an den alten Religionskrieg fort, an die heftigen geistigen Kämpfe, die es gekostet hat, ehe das olympische Göttersystem zum Siege kam.") More recently still, evidence has been adduced to suggest that the form of the myths concerned owes much to borrowings from the East. Fragments of the epic of Kumarbi, discovered in the Hittite library at Bogaz-Köy but Hurrian and Babylonian in origin, show strong resemblances to the Hesiodic story of Zeus' conflicts with Kronos and the other Titans. (See R. D. Barnett in *Journ. Hell. Stud.* lxv (1945), 100.) These include the motifs of castration and of the substitution of stone for baby. A similar significance had already been attached by Cornford to similarities noted in Babylonian mythology (in a paper called *A Ritual Basis for Hesiod's Theogony*, now being printed in *The Unwritten Philosophy and other essays* by the Cambridge Press). It is not yet clear to me whether these borrowings, if proved, must invalidate the "historical supersession" view. The Greeks were adepts at turning old or foreign mythological material to account in explaining a new or Hellenic situation, and these tales learned from the Orient may only be the mould of expression into which they cast the memories of their own history. In their original home they formed the mythical basis of an elaborate ritual for which there is no evidence among the Greeks, and the question therefore remains: Why did the Greeks borrow them?

chief god was the sender of thunder and lightning upon those who displeased him.[1] His connexion with fertility, which as the rain-provider he must certainly have once possessed, had sunk to an insignificant place among his functions. It is easy to see why the spirits of the earth and of vegetation should have retained their importance among the original inhabitants of the land and lost it among the invaders. For the invaders were by that very fact a wandering people, living by the sword rather than the plough. They had left their native soil far behind them, and when they settled as conquerors could demand that their new subjects should continue to till the ground for their benefit as well as their own, leaving the masters free for the aristocratic occupations of fighting, riding, games and hunting. To the people whom they had conquered, the soil on which and by which they lived belonged as it had to their ancestors. Its tilth and pasture were their means of life. It is therefore relevant to the explanation of the Titans as the ancient gods of the land, displaced by Zeus, that they were known as sons of Gaïa, the Earth. The scanty remains of actual cult of Kronos which have lingered on into historical times point in the same direction, for they suggest that he had been a god of the harvest.[2]

The foregoing account involves certain difficulties. To resolve them, in so far as the means to resolve them are available, it is necessary to say something of the *Sacred Marriage*. The various amours and marriages of Zeus are certainly not all to be put down to poetic fancy. Some at least have a religious basis, though all do not admit of the same explanation. The sacred marriage (in

[1] Cf. Hom. *Il.* xvi, 384 ff.

[2] The best upholder both of the "historical conflict" explanation of the Titanomachy and of the character of Kronos as a god of the harvest is Pohlenz. See his article "Kronos und die Titanen" in *Neue Jahrbücher*, xxxvii (1915), pp. 549–94, and for Kronos also Pauly-Wissowa-Kroll, *Realenc.* xi, 1987 f. In English cf. Farnell, *Cults of the Greek States*, vol. i, ch. 3. A hypothesis too attractive to pass over, but in view of its uncertainty best relegated to a footnote, is that which sees further evidence for Kronos being a god of the conquered race in the fact that at his festival slaves are related to have sat down to feast on an equality with their masters. The slaves would originally be the members of the conquered race, and it was fitting that on the feast-day of their own god they should claim and be allowed to remember their freedom under his protection. The suggestion is made by Farnell, but Pohlenz will have none of it (PWK xi, 1984). It was, he says, a simple harvest-festival, which it was natural for masters and men to celebrate together. The evidence for the cult of Kronos is too scanty to provide certainty.

Greek ἱερὸς γάμος[1]), in which a god is paired with a goddess, is a feature not only of myth but of ancient belief and cult among the Greeks, and some of Zeus' unions are instances of the belief in the union of Heaven and Earth whereby the earth is fertilized. The process has from a very early stage of human culture been imagined in terms of human life, the earth being the feminine principle and the sky the masculine, whose seed is represented by the rain. The classical expression of this belief is in a fragment of Aeschylus' play the *Danaids*:[2]

"The pure Sky longs passionately to pierce the Earth, and passion seizes the Earth to win her marriage. Rain falling from the bridegroom sky makes pregnant[3] the Earth. Then brings she forth for mortals pasture of flocks and corn, Demeter's gift, and the fruitfulness of trees is brought to completion by the dew of their marriage.[4] Of these things am I part-cause." (The speaker is Aphrodite.)

A very primitive formula involving this belief appears to be preserved by the Neoplatonist Proclus (fifth century A.D.), who states that at the Eleusinian rites the Athenians "looked up to the sky and shouted ὕε! ('Rain!'), then down to the earth and shouted κύε! ('Conceive!')". It is quoted also in the polemics of the Christian apologist Hippolytus against the pagans as "the great and unspeakable mystery of the Eleusinia".[5]

[1] The convenient phrase does not itself occur in extant Greek literature before the Alexandrian period, since as used by Plato (*Laws*, 841d) it refers to human marriage and is not directly relevant. Cf. Theocritus, xvii, 131: ὧδε καὶ ἀθανάτων ἱερὸς γάμος ἐξετελέσθη, and Menander: *Μέθη*, *Fr. Com. Gr.* iv, 162 Meineke. It is used by the Byzantine lexicographers, who speak of it as the name of a real festival at Athens also called *Theogamia* (Cook, *Zeus*, iii, 1047). Passages are conveniently collected by Farnell, *Cults*, i, 244 ff. Cook, *Zeus*, iii, app. R, deals exhaustively with the marriage of Zeus to Hera. A. Klinz, *Hieros Gamos* (Halle, 1933), covers a wider field. See also other reff. in *Zeus*, iii, 1026, n. 7.

[2] *Tragg. Graec. Frr.* ed. Nauck² 44. Cf. Euripides fr. 898.7 ff.; Cook, *Zeus*, iii, 452 ff.

[3] ἔκυσε mss., altered to ἔδευσε by B. Heath, whose conjecture Nauck adopts, presumably out of mistrust for the causal sense. L. and S.⁹ however retain the mss. reading and quote it as a transitive use of κύω.

[4] Retaining the mss. reading ἐκ νοτίζοντος γάμου. γάμους Gomperz.

[5] Procl. *in Plat. Tim.* iii, 176.26 ff., Diehl, Hippol. *Ref.* 5.7, p. 146, Duncker-Schneidewin. See Cook, *Zeus*, iii, 299, 454. I agree that the formula sounds primitive, but the varying opinions of scholars bring home to one the wisdom of using such late sources, unsupported by earlier evidence, as little as possible. Compare Cook's "The words have at once the directness of primitive thought and the jingle of primitive magic" and Farnell's "This genuine ore of an old religious stratum sparkles all the more for being found in a waste deposit of neo-Platonic metaphysic" with Wilamowitz (*Der Glaube der Hellenen*, i, 212, n. 1): "How Proclus knew that Attic law ordained Οὐρανῷ καὶ Γαίᾳ προτελεῖν τοὺς γάμους ('that the preliminary marriage-sacrifice should be offered to Sky and Earth'), and what it is supposed to mean, is very doubtful. Immediately afterwards follows the *suspicious* υεκυε (Rain—Conceive)." (My italics.) However, the arguments of W. to which this note refers are not particularly convincing.

Zeus for the Greeks was the masculine sky-god, and the above-mentioned belief explains therefore a number of his unions, e.g. those with Demeter, Semele and Persephone, all of whom are demonstrably goddesses embodying the fruitful earth. It is also the likeliest explanation of his union with Hera, though the evidence for her having been originally an earth-goddess is not so abundant or unchallenged.[1] These earth-goddesses with different names would at first be the goddesses of different, isolated localities. Argos would believe that Hera was the consort of Zeus, Eleusis that she was Demeter, Thebes that she was Semele.[2] This led to difficulties however as soon as any attempt was made to correlate the various local legends. Either Zeus had wives rather according to oriental than European custom, or if he had only one legitimate wife, he was hopelessly unfaithful. As it happened, the latter idea was less repugnant to the Greeks than the former. They were a monogamous people, in the sense that they believed in having only one lawful wife. But they were tolerant of irregularities, and no stigma attached to the children born from them.[3] Therefore, as the legends fused and hardened into an amalgam (a process brilliantly achieved by the unparalleled epic poetry of the Greeks), one goddess was singled out as being the wife of Zeus, and the others were accounted his mistresses. This was of course a situation which offered limitless possibilities to later myth-makers and poets, and an extraordinary amount of fancy and ingenuity was expended on inventing variations of the stories which have little or no connexion with anything but literature. Besides literary imagination, there existed also the motive of family pride, which is undoubtedly at the bottom of many of the stories of Zeus' intrigues with mortal women. For a Greek, the equivalent of having ancestors who came over with the Conqueror was to trace his descent back to an Olympian god, preferably Zeus. In this way, as Professor Rose has put it, many families sought "to provide themselves with an

[1] Cf. the section on Hera, below pp. 66 ff.

[2] This is not to say that we necessarily know these local divinities by their original names. Semele is fairly certainly a name taken from Thraco-Phrygian religion, being related to the Phrygian Ζεμελω, the earth. If so, she must have been introduced at Thebes contemporaneously with the worship of Dionysos. Similarly Dione, the consort of Zeus in the strange oracular cult at Dodona, whose name is simply a feminine form of Zeus-Dios itself, must, one would think, have ousted a pre-Greek earth-goddess on the spot. Cf. the remarks of H. J. Rose, *Hbk. Gr. Mythol.* (Methuen, 1928), p. 53, where references to other literature will be found.

[3] Rose, *Hbk. Gr. Mythol.* 49 f.

illustrious ancestry at the price of a bend sinister many generations back".[1]

Yet even some of the mortal women with whom Zeus consorted were not originally such, but divinities themselves. Even Semele, the mother of Dionysos, was made into a woman by the Thebans and called the daughter of Kadmos, though her original character as an earth-goddess is transparently evident. In spite of the pretensions of the aristocracy and other false scents, the religious idea can be traced, vouched for by the undoubtedly genuine belief in the *Hieros Gamos* as the root from which the whole many-branched tree first sprang.

We have now to face a difficulty inherent, as it seems to me, in the suggested explanations of the marriages of Zeus. We have spoken of them as arising out of the belief in a union of the goddess of the earth with a god whom we have so far called the sky. Coupled with this belief we may assume an ancient ritual in which this marriage was enacted or symbolized by human participants, with the object of achieving by sympathetic magic the production of fertility, especially that of the soil. Though extinct in Europe, such primitive practices are still carried on in other parts of the world, where the union of the human sexes on the actual ground where the crops are to grow, either at seed-time or before the maturity of the plants, is considered to promote fruitfulness.[2] It is a safe inference that they were performed at an early date in Greece, and doubtless lingered long in the less civilized parts. The union, real or simulated, of the priest and priestess at the Eleusinian mysteries is attested by Christian writers, and though their evidence is suspect,[3] it obtains some support from analogy. The Greeks themselves could not of course be expected to tell us the nature of the central act of their most secret mysteries. A clear example of the *Hieros Gamos* in ritual is furnished by the union of Dionysos with the wife of the Archon-Basileus at Athens (for which see p. 177 below). In myth we have e.g. the reference of Homer

[1] The previous paragraph is largely dependent on Rose, *Hbk. Gr. Mythol.* (1928), pp. 49 f.

[2] See Frazer, *Golden Bough: The Magic Art*, vol. ii, ch. 11, "The Sexes and Vegetation". To quote one out of Frazer's many examples: "In some parts of Java, at the season when the bloom will soon be on the rice, the husbandman and his wife visit their fields by night and there engage in sexual intercourse for the purpose of promoting the growth of the crop."

[3] A. B. Cook says cautiously that the procedure "has some claim to be regarded as fact" (*Zeus*, iii, 301, where the evidence is collected), but Nilsson argues strongly against it (*Gesch. Gr. Rel.* i, iii f., 627).

to the union of Demeter and Iasion "in the thrice-ploughed field".[1] Aetiological stories naturally grew up around the rites, and just as the dance of the young Cretan warriors was lifted on to the theological plane and regarded as a commemorative representation of the protection of the infant Zeus by divine Kuretes, so the fertility-ritual was frequently explained as commemorating the nuptials of Zeus and Hera, or sometimes of Zeus and other goddesses.

Now in reading the explanations of modern scholars, one gets the impression that they tend to amalgamate two theories about the *Hieroi Gamoi* without sufficiently making clear their relation to one another and to the probable truth. It will be obvious from what I have said so far that there is a general tendency to replace the favourite nineteenth-century explanations of myth on the basis of nature-symbolism by theories based on the historical fact of the supersession of aboriginal cults by those of the invading peoples. The *Hieros Gamos* however is a phenomenon for which the explanation as nature-symbolism cannot be given up. There is too much positive evidence to vouch for it. It is still generally held, therefore, that the myth of a *Hieros Gamos* symbolizes the fertilizing of the earth by moisture from the sky, and that it is enacted in ritual in order to ensure, by a common kind of sympathetic magic, that this fertilization will in fact take place. The marriage of Zeus and Hera is the marriage of Sky and Earth as described in the lines of Aeschylus' *Danaids*.

At the same time the historical explanation is not given up. It is pointed out that among the aboriginal peoples of Greece and the neighbouring lands around the Aegean the most important deity was the Great Mother, who represented the teeming life of the earth and was the mistress of all that it produces, both vegetable and animal. The goddess who appears, often accompanied by obsequious animals, on many Minoan engraved gems and gold rings, is to-day a familiar example of the class. This fact can scarcely be called in question. It is also noted, and is even less open to question, that the invading warriors worshipped as their supreme deity a male god who was originally a personification of the sky and still retained many of his functions as a rain- and weather-maker. When therefore they are describing the ways in which the religion of the invaders came to terms with that of the original inhabitants, religious historians say that the marriage of

[1] *Od.* v, 125 ff.

Zeus to the ancient earth-goddesses of the various localities is one of the devices employed for the purpose. The two explanations are to be found in different parts of the same book without, so far as I can see, an adequate attempt to correlate them. Yet to the layman at least, it looks a little like trying to have it both ways. If the sacred marriage is to be explained as the accommodation of the new cult of Zeus to the old worship of the Earth-Mother, did the Mother have no consort until the Greeks appeared to give her one? If on the other hand she had a consort already, how did Zeus fit into the scheme?

I have therefore tried to think out this problem independently and set forth a possible solution, which I do with all the humility due from one writing a few pages on a subject to which more learned writers have devoted volumes of considerable length. Reference to some of these may be found in the notes to this chapter, and fuller documentation might obscure my primary aim, which is, by covering a fairly wide field, to interest others in the subject of Greek religion and to suggest ideas which may bear more fruit in other minds and which will at least not be misleading or contain more contradictions or obscurities than are inherent in the nature of the subject. I would also reiterate my conviction that in trying to penetrate the fog of pre-literary antiquity we are dealing with a subject where certainty on many things is impossible, and probability or improbability is the most that we can allege. There will always be those to whom this very fact is an enticement to further inquiry. I trust that these pages will prove no discouragement to them, but for myself regard it as a reason for passing as quickly as possible out of the fog into clearer air.

This, then, appears to me to be the most likely sequence of events. Where there is an agricultural people whose religion, like their life, is bound up with the fecundity of the earth, we do undoubtedly find the human analogy. That is to say, the earth is worshipped in the likeness of a mother, and her fertility is thought of as being achieved in the same way as it is for a woman.[1] Indeed, it is doubtless wrong to confine this notion to agricultural peoples. The Great Mother not only bears the crops for the husbandman, but also the flocks and herds for pastoral peoples and even the wild creatures whose abundance is necessary for men at a still earlier stage of culture, who live by hunting and fishing. She may

[1] Cf. the remark in the *Menexenos* of Plato (238a): *οὐ γὰρ γῆ γυναῖκα μεμίμηται κυήσει καὶ γεννήσει, ἀλλὰ γυνὴ γῆν.*

in fact be one of the oldest religious representations of all, and her presence an indication that the idea of personal divinity has been in man's mind for as long as we can trace his history, and at least as long as belief in the efficacy of magic or in a vague animism, such as have often been thought to precede the religious conception of deity. This is indeed the case if there is anything in the attractive suggestion of Professor Cook[1] for explaining the remarkable series of cave-paintings in Spain and Southern France. These paintings, which belong to palaeolithic times, represent, as is well known, the animals most hunted by man. They have generally been thought to have a practical, that is a magical, purpose, and much perplexity has been caused by the fact that they are depicted in the innermost, most inaccessible and darkest parts of the caves. Professor Cook suggests that these artists already had at least a vaguely anthropomorphic conception of the earth, and that their motive was to implant in her very womb the animals which it was hoped she would bring forth abundantly for the feeding of mankind.

This is to venture far indeed into the fog. But it is certain that the idea of the goddess of fertility, the Great Mother Earth, goes very far back. To look no further afield, it is abundantly proved by Frazer's examples in the *Golden Bough*,[2] which show her to have been the author and protector of all life, both vegetable and animal. The character of the Greek Artemis, the Mistress of Wild Animals in Homer,[3] owed much to this earlier conception, which persisted before the eyes of the Greeks above all in the cult of Kybele, the great mother of Phrygia, and other Asiatic cults.

If then for an agricultural or pastoral people the earth is a mother, who if she is to be fruitful must be impregnated like others, they do believe in the existence of a consort for her. But he is felt to be little more than a necessary adjunct. For a settled agricultural people particularly, it is the earth on which they live, and from which they draw the means of living—it is she whom they primarily love and worship, just as it is she to whom they must devote their labour and their attention if they are to enjoy the fruits of her fertility. The male consort plays a minor part. This sounds as if it were mere *a priori* speculation about the mental

[1] Unpublished, and communicated to me verbally by Professor Cook. The case for taking the cult of the Earth-Mother back to palaeolithic times has been best put by Miss G. R. Levy in *The Gate of Horn* (London, 1948). In the necessary absence of literary evidence, much must remain hypothetical.

[2] See especially *The Magic Art*, vol. ii.

[3] For Artemis see pp. 99 ff. below.

processes of peoples of whom in fact we know little or nothing. We do know, however, that, whatever the reason, a characteristic of Mediterranean religion was the supremacy of the female principle in nature, the earth-mother. The reason may be what I have suggested, or lie in a state of society when in human relationships too the mother occupied the chief place, or be something as yet undiscovered.[1] Whether or not we know the reason, the fact remains. Male spirits of fertility existed, but they were subordinate figures, satellites of the mother and no more. Fortunately we know much about the cults of Asia Minor, where the ancient religions were preserved and in some parts the influence of the Greeks was little felt. And in the figures of Kybele and Attis we can see surviving into classical times the sort of pair which may have existed in Greece and the islands also before Zeus appeared on the scene. Kybele is the dominating figure, and Attis is by no means on a level with her. He is only a youthful attendant who is passionately devoted to her service. Though a divinity, he is her servant and high priest rather than her compeer. The Cretan Kuros or Kures sounds like a similar figure, and we have already seen adequate reason to describe him as a male spirit of fertility. Some difficulty seems to have been felt in connecting him with Attis, apparently on the ground that, as the story of the birth of Zeus in Crete indicates, he was conceived of as an infant as well as a youth. I cannot understand this difficulty. Professor Nilsson wrote:[2] "On the strength of the comparison with Magna Mater, at whose side her youthful lover Attis stands, it is generally believed that the Minoan Nature-goddess too had a youthful paramour. But certain indications seem to me to point to quite another and a peculiar idea." These indications are provided by the "especially Cretan" myth of the birth of Zeus, of which "an outstanding feature is that the child is not nursed by its mother". The child, he says, is "the year-god . . . the spirit of fertility, the new life of spring". With this we may agree, adding that it is strongly suggested by the Palaikastro hymn, in which however the Cretan spirit appears not as a child but as a youthful figure like Attis. What is more difficult to understand is how this constitutes any

[1] Frazer derives the comparative unimportance of the male partner in a fertility-cult from a primitive state of mind when the actual fact of paternity was unknown. The connexion of the sexual act with conception and birth was simply not realized. (*G.B.: Adonis, Attis, Osiris*, i, 282.) I do not see that any of these suggestions can be more than conjectures.

[2] *Hist. Gr. Rel.* (Oxford, 1925, 2nd ed. 1949), p. 31.

objection to supposing that the Cretan god is, like Attis, a youthful lover of the Nature-goddess. No contradiction was involved in imagining the spirit now as a babe and now as a virile youth.[1] Owing to his connexion with the cycle of vegetation, the fertility-spirit must be born, grow to maturity and die within a single year, and it is natural therefore that his development should proceed with miraculous speed. Dionysos, the most famous god of vegetation among the Greeks, was said by Homer to have had "nurses", and Plutarch speaks of a rite in which his female votaries, the Thyiades, awaken the Liknites, the child in the *liknon* or winnowing-basket which served him as a cradle. His tomb was shown at Delphi as that of Zeus in Crete.[2] There are many stories of heroes who grew with miraculous rapidity from babyhood to manhood, or, like Herakles and the infant Hermes, performed adult prodigies of strength when only a few days, or hours, old. They doubtless attached themselves, in the shifting tradition of folk-tale, to figures who had no connexion with fertility. The motive may be traced in lands remote from Greece, for example in the Babylonian hero Marduk, also a bringer of fertility, who grew up quickly and was given to procreation from the beginning. Thus Dionysos, though worshipped as a babe, was most commonly imagined in the form of the beautiful youth, in the first bloom of manhood, whom we meet in the *Bacchae* of Euripides.

Although we are now familiar with the conception of the fertilization of the mother Earth by moisture from the father Sky, which found classical expression in the lines of Aeschylus, fertility-spirits of the class which we have just been considering were not necessarily, or even probably, regarded as celestial. Let us turn again to Frazer:[3] "But Zeus was not always the sky-god, nor did he always marry the corn-goddess.[4] If in antiquity a traveller, quitting Eleusis and passing through miles of olive-groves and cornfields, had climbed the pine-clad mountains of Cithaeron and

[1] Nor do I find the two conceptions regarded as contradictory in Professor Nilsson's masterly analysis of the myth of the birth of Zeus in ch. xvi of *Minoan-Mycenean Religion*, where Dionysos is cited as another example of the divine child to set beside the Cretan Zeus.

[2] Hom. *Il.* vi, 132, Plut. *Is. et Os.* xxxv, 365a (Nilsson, *Min.-Myc. Rel.* 493). On Dionysos see ch. vi below.

[3] *Golden Bough: The Magic Art*, ii, 140.

[4] Frazer has been speaking of the marriage of Zeus with Demeter at Eleusis as signifying to the Athenians the marriage of sky-god with corn-goddess "to make the fields wave with yellow corn".

descended through the forest on their northern slope to Plataea, he might have chanced to find the people of that little Boeotian town celebrating a different marriage of the great god to a different goddess." He goes on to describe from the antiquarian guide-book of Pausanias a local festival in which the Greek god Zeus has obviously taken over the functions of a local deity. The central act is the cutting-down of an oak-tree and dressing and treating it as a bride. Illustrating his conclusion with parallels from the spring and midsummer festivals of modern Europe, Frazer shows that this festival "represented the marriage of the powers of vegetation —the union of the oak-god with the oak-goddess. . . . All such ceremonies, it must be remembered, are not, or at least were not originally, mere spectacular or dramatic exhibitions. They are magical rites designed to produce the effect which they dramatically set forth." It is therefore highly relevant to recall that in the ceremonies of mourning carried out for the Phrygian Attis, the body of the god was represented by a fir-tree, which was wrapped in grave-clothes and decked with wreaths. Similarly Dionysos was known as δενδρίτης, the tree-god, and ἔνδενδρος, the god in the tree. We possess the inscription recording the introduction of the cult of Dionysos at Magnesia on the Maeander in the third or second century B.C. A plane-tree in the city had been blown down by a storm, and an image of the god was found inside it. The citizens sent envoys to Delphi to ask the meaning of the portent. There follows the metrical text of the oracle's reply. It bids them build a temple to Dionysos and fetch three maenads from Thebes to instruct them in the rites of the god and found *thiasoi* of worshippers in the city.[1] Finally, the prevalence of the tree-cult in Crete has been demonstrated from the archaeological evidence by Sir Arthur Evans.[2]

These tree-gods embody the life of the vegetation. They are in turn child, consort, and again child of the Earth, for she bears them and brings them forth from her bosom, and they in turn as

[1] Dionysos δενδρίτης, Plut. *Quaest. Conv.* iii, 675 f. For the Magnesian inscription see W. Quandt, *de Baccho ab Alexandri Aetate in Asia Minore Culto* (diss. Halle, 1913), pp. 162 ff., 165 ff. Zeus was locally given a similar title, if we may believe Hesychius (s.v. *Ἔνδενδρος· παρὰ Ῥοδίοις Ζεύς· καὶ Διόνυσος ἐν Βοιωτίᾳ.*) On the whole question of Zeus as the oak-god see A. B. Cook, "Zeus, Jupiter and the Oak", *Class. Rev.* xvii (1906). The cult of Zeus at Dodona is of course of the highest importance in this connexion.

[2] *Mycenean Tree and Pillar Cult and its Mediterranean Relations* (Macmillan, 1901). Cf. Nilsson, *Min.-Myc. Rel.* ch. viii.

they grow to maturity produce their seed which she receives into her womb again.[1]

Cults of this sort, of which many, with numberless individual variations, were to be found all over Greece, existed before the coming of the Achaeans. Among the invaders, as we have noted already, conditions were reversed. They had detached themselves from the soil and no longer lived a settled life or depended directly on the earth for livelihood. Their chief deity was masculine, fitter object of worship for a community of rulers and warriors. Among them he had achieved a position of unassailable supremacy. If they had ever, in the dim past, paid supreme honour to Mother Earth in their northern home, the tradition was forgotten. Zeus of Olympus, the Father of Gods and Men, and no lesser personage, was the god who had to be accommodated to the religion of the conquered southern lands.

Perhaps it may now be seen how the two aspects of the sacred marriage can be fitted together. I do not think it should be doubted that the tradition of the marriage of Zeus with ancient earth-goddesses preserves in many cases the memory of a linking of new cults with old. It reflects a historical fusion. Nor do I think it should be doubted that it was regarded by the people as a marriage of the male and female principles in nature to produce fertility in the latter. The effect of Zeus' introduction has been that whereas in times past the goddess was the unquestioned mistress, who more or less commanded the services of a youthful and obsequious consort, the union has now become a solemn marriage between two mighty deities in which Zeus plays the leading part. In Homer indeed he is the King, and Hera no more than his consort, who must bow to his will, albeit sometimes with reluctance and anger. It has a certain minor interest that when for once Hera does get her own way, which, since she is the less powerful, she can only do by a successful piece of deceit, the story contains a far-off, poetic echo of the days when the marriage of god and goddess was linked with the fertility of the earth.[2]

To judge then from Homer, one would say that the masculine god of the invaders had succeeded completely in imposing himself as the dominant partner. So no doubt he had in the circles of the Achaean nobility, and among the aristocratic societies which

[1] Cf. Aesch. *Cho.* 127 f. *καὶ γαίαν αὐτὴν, ἣ τὰ πάντα τίκτεται,*
θρέψασά τ' αὖθις τῶνδε κῦμα λαμβάνει.

[2] *Il.* xiv, 346 ff. See below, pp. 68, 69 n. 2.

followed them in the cities of Greece. But where Zeus has been introduced as partner into the ancient fertility-cults of the common people, we sometimes find a different story. The traces of the Earth-mother's majesty and independence are by no means obliterated.

This subject could be discussed endlessly. The variations of local cult are infinite, and my own brief account itself contains unanswered questions and perhaps latent inconsistencies. It gives the impression, for instance, that pre-Greek fertility spirits were always spirits of vegetation rather than celestial. Doubtless this was not so. The two aspects may even have been united at some periods in the same spirit. Frazer has discussed the possibility that Attis may have been regarded as a sky-god or heavenly father like Zeus, though he concluded: "However, the evidence for the celestial aspect of Attis is too slight to allow us to speak with any confidence on this subject."[1] Again, I have spoken of the union of a tree- or vegetation-spirit with the Earth-mother. The Plataean rite as described by Frazer represented the marriage of two vegetation-spirits—"the union of the oak-god with the oak-goddess". Was the bride-tree in this rite regarded as identical with the Earth-mother? It could be argued that she was, but I do not intend to go into the question here, partly for reasons of space, but partly also because I am not so much afraid of leaving unnecessary inconsistencies in my account as I am of wiping out inconsistencies which were inherent in the historical situation that we are trying to recover. It would be strange indeed if there were no confusion in the minds of these rustic worshippers, and without making it an excuse for slipshod thinking, we may well be on our guard against introducing out of our own heads a non-existent order and self-consciousness.

It can obviously be no part of my plan to attempt a comprehensive account of Zeus. I have tried to bring out briefly the two most sharply contrasted elements in his nature, which are, as it happens, the most relevant to my central theme, that is, the relations between man and god in Greek religion. Even within this field one might go much further. In speaking of Zeus as a baby, I told the story of his birth in Crete. But Crete was not alone in claiming the honour of being his birth-place. Many places in Asia

[1] *Golden Bough: Adonis, Attis, Osiris*, i, 281–4. Cf. the identification of the Cretan fertility-spirit with the sun, p. 50, n. 1 above.

Minor boasted the same distinction, as on the mainland of Greece did Thebes, Messenia, and above all Arcadia.[1] This is not surprising, for we know that the baby-god was one of a type, and our justification for singling out the Cretan myth is a sound one, namely that the Greeks did the same.

Of course, Zeus is far more than a blend of these two elements only, Indo-European sky-god and Cretan babe or Kuros or bull (that is, Cretan fertility-spirit). To the Greeks he is throughout their history the supreme god of all, and we may say of him, adapting words used by Aristotle in a different connexion, that he is *καθόλου οὕτως ὅτι πρῶτος*—that supremacy carries with it universality. There is scarcely a department either of nature or of human life with which he was not connected by his worshippers. This is reflected by the titles and epithets which they heaped upon him, and which include almost everything that a Greek held sacred. In a dozen different names they call him king and lord. He is Zeus of the clan and of the ancestors, Zeus who guards the home, who minds the storehouse, the protector of suppliants, the god of hospitality to strangers, of the sanctity of the oath, the bringer of justice, guardian of the city—and there are countless others, too well known to need enumeration. Let us only note before we leave him that the Greeks carried the notion of a universal god considerably further than anyone had ever done before, and very nearly as far as anyone has carried it since. So firmly were his supremacy and universality established that his name came to be used by poets and philosophers almost as the name of God might be used by a Christian or that of Allah by a Moslem. Aeschylus felt no incongruity in applying it to the great moral power which was his conception of God, and in the second century A.D., in the deeply philosophical writings of a Marcus Aurelius, we find that the sublime Stoic belief in the brotherhood of man can be fitly expressed by calling the world the City of Zeus.

Wilamowitz made a good remark which shows the Greeks to have been the teachers of some modern nations in this respect. If he had written it a few years later, and if its mild irony had been observed (which is unlikely), it might have been frowned on by some of his own countrymen. It is simply this: "From the point of view of nationalism, the Greeks suffered from a disadvantage, in that they recognized the universal god too early."

[1] Cook, *Zeus*, i, 151–4.

III. Hera

Hera to the Greeks had two main aspects: she was the one legitimate wife of Zeus, and she was the patron and guardian of the institution of marriage. In origin she may have been neither, but in that case the question of her origin need not detain us long, since her character must have been greatly transformed by classical times.[1] This question of her origin has been much disputed. All use the same counters, but arrange them in different ways. That is to say, Hera appears in several guises, or performs several functions, upon which all are agreed, and which are naturally connected. It is possible therefore to choose any one of them as primary, and derive the others from it, by arguments which are neither completely convincing, nor yet easily to be refuted by the exponent of a rival view. There are three main claimants: her authority over marriage was part of a wider interest in the life of women in general, certain indications seem to connect her with the moon, and others suggest that she may herself have been a form of the earth-goddess.

That Hera was originally a moon-goddess was the view of W. H. Roscher. It has not found much support, nor are his arguments convincing. Many of the facts which he adduces are either susceptible of another explanation or else false or doubtful in themselves. Thus he asserts that she was depicted with a rayed crown, but investigation shows that no certain or even probable instance of this can be found. He makes much of her connexion with the life of women, pointing to the menstrual periods and the belief that certain phases of the moon were particularly favourable or unfavourable to child-birth. But here the relation of cause and effect may be more plausibly reversed. Similarly she may surely have ridden in a chariot and at one place (Lebadeia in Boeotia) have been addressed as the Charioteer, without being the moon, even though the moon, like the sun, was thought to ride in a chariot.[2]

[1] For the theory that Hera was originally the goddess of a matriarchal tribe, with Herakles as her consort, and Zeus the god of a patriarchal tribe, with his female counterpart Dione or Dia as consort, and that the cult of Zeus and Hera as husband and wife resulted from the amalgamation of these two tribes, see A. B. Cook, "Who was the Wife of Zeus?" in *Class. Rev.* xx (1906).

[2] Roscher, *Lexikon*, I, ii (1886–90), 2087 ff. For a criticism, see Farnell, *Cults*, i, 180 f. For Hera *Henioche* at Lebadeia, Paus. ix, 39, 5. Rose (*Hbk. Gr. Myth.* 102) calls Roscher's view "a sort of reversed image of the truth".

Professor Rose shuffles the counters in a more satisfactory way, deriving the goddess's other characteristics from a primary and essential connexion with the life of women. Since the moon is supposed to influence the life of women, it is natural for a goddess of women to take on certain lunar characteristics. If the Stymphalians in Arcadia knew of her by the three titles of Maid, Wife and Widow,[1] this is simply to identify her with her worshippers, for "all women, whatever their condition, worshipped her".[2] She is above all the goddess of marriage, "guarding the keys of wedlock" as Aristophanes says.[3] She also attended women in child-birth, and the regular goddess or goddesses of child-birth, Eileithyia or the Eileithyiai, were called her daughters as early as Homer (*Il.* xi, 270 f., cf. Hes. *Theog.* 921 f.). At Argos, her double character as virgin and wedded was accepted literally, for it was believed there that by bathing in the spring Kanathos at Nauplia she renewed her virginity every year.[4]

Being pre-eminently the goddess of marriage and child-birth, Hera is, of course, in the words of Professor Rose, "much concerned with fecundity". "It is, however," he continues, "that of women, not of plants, which she governs." The question whether Hera's connexion with fecundity is limited to that of women, or extends to the propagation of all life including that of plants, brings us to the third explanation of her nature, which sees her as originally a manifestation of the Earth-mother whom we were brought to consider in speaking of Zeus. The idea that Hera was originally an earth-goddess was put forward nearly a century ago by

[1] Paus. viii, 22, 2. The unconvincing aetiological myth related by Pausanias explains the last epithet (*Χήρα*) as = "deserted", and refers it to a quarrel with Zeus after their marriage, which caused Hera to return to Stymphalos. The meaning is a possible though rare one. Rose's explanation of the threefold character repeats Farnell, whose view of Hera is very similar (*Cults*, i, 191).

[2] Rose, *Hbk. Gr. Rel.* 103. It is worth noting however that the story of the quarrel (see previous note) recalls the aetiological myth which was told to explain the festival of the *Daedala* at Plataea. This is the festival of the marriage of the oak-tree bride referred to above (pp. 61 f.), about which the Boeotians said that Hera had quarrelled with Zeus and left him. Zeus thereupon pretended that he was going to marry again, and had an image of wood dressed up as a bride. Hera's jealousy brought her back, and tearing off the dress of her supposed supplanter she discovered the trick and was reconciled. Agreeing that the legend has grown out of the rite, Rose says of the rite itself that "its exact significance is obscure". (o.c., 104.) Yet its connexion with fertility (and not that of women) is, to say the least of it, extremely probable.

[3] *Thesm.* 973. The title of *Τελεία* here given to her, as also by Aeschylus (*Eum.* 214) and in cult, refers to the same function. For other evidence of H. as goddess of marriage see Farnell, *Cults*, i, 244 ff. It is emphasized by other cult-epithets also.

[4] p. 103 below.

Welcker,[1] and is rejected by Rose as it was by Farnell. Yet we have seen reason to believe that the Sacred Marriage of a god and goddess was not only the divine prototype of human marriage—though in the case of Zeus and Hera it was certainly that—but also went back to the belief in a union of two great spirits of fertility which was re-enacted in ritual to ensure the abundance of the crops. Strangely enough, on the same page as his restriction of Hera's connexion with fertility to that of women, Rose writes:[2] "But all manner of local rites existed involving a marriage between two deities, a holy marriage (*ἱερὸς γάμος*) as it was technically called. Very often these were explained as the marriage of Zeus and Hera. Like the union of Demeter with Iasion, such weddings had for their object the production of fertility, especially perhaps that of the soil; and it is not without reason that a reminiscence of this is found in the famous passage of the *Iliad* in which all manner of flowers and also thick soft grass spring up to make a marriage-bed for Zeus and Hera on Mount Ida."

Have we not here a guide to the most likely order for the counters which we have to arrange? Farnell, who disagrees with Welcker's view, notes that we have record, direct or indirect, of the Sacred Marriage of Hera, either in myth or rite, at the following places: Plataea, Euboea, Athens, Hermione, Argos, Arcadia, Samos, Crete, and Falerii in Italy, and adds: "We may believe that it existed in other sites of the Hera-worship than these." But he regards it as "rather the reflection of human life than of the life of nature", and points out (though he has to go to Photius for the statement) that it was performed as a rite by the bridal pair at an ordinary marriage.[3] But is it likely that the Greeks themselves drew this sharp distinction between the life of men and that of the rest of nature? (I say "the rest of nature", for Farnell's own distinction between "human life" and "the life of nature" is of course a false one.) Speaking of the annual ceremony at Samos in which the image of Hera was taken from its temple secretly, and hidden near the shore,[4] Farnell sees in it only an allusion to the early custom of the bridegroom secretly abducting his bride. Rose

[1] *Die Griechische Götterlehre*, in three volumes published between 1857 and 1863.

[2] o.c., 103, referring to *Il.* xiv, 346 ff.

[3] If one wished to be argumentative on the strength of late sources, one might suggest that the words in Photius *οἱ γαμοῦντες ποιοῦσι τῷ Διὶ καὶ τῇ Ἥρᾳ ἱεροὺς γάμους* (Farnell; *Cults*, i, 245, n. 171), should be brought into relation with those of Proclus *Οὐρανῷ καὶ Γαίᾳ προτελεῖν τοὺς γάμους* (quoted above, p. 54, n. 5).

[4] *Athenaeus*, 672.

adopts the same interpretation, yet the rite has some resemblance also to the Boeotian myth of Hera hiding herself away from Zeus, and this myth formed the *aition* for the festival of the Daedala, the connexion of which with general fertility-magic it is difficult indeed to give up. That there may be a connexion with human marriage-customs as well I should be the last to deny, for I do not think that the Greeks saw any reason to distinguish human fecundity from any other kind, so that a confusion between the two types of custom or ceremony was almost bound to occur. There are not two entities, "man" and "nature". Man is a part of nature—at least until the age of the Sophists.

There is evidence from Menander and later writers that the festival of the Sacred Marriage was celebrated at Athens. The names ἱερὸς γάμος and θεογαμία are recorded, and it seems certain that it was held in the Attic month Gamelion, which means "Marriage-month" and moreover was said to be sacred to Hera. This was the month which corresponded to our January. It was the month most favoured for marriages, hence presided over by Hera as the goddess of marriage, and on this occasion no doubt, as Farnell says, the Sacred Marriage was thought of first and foremost as the pattern for the human one. But the primary purpose of the union of the sexes was procreation. "In Southern Europe" wrote August Mommsen, "the warm season is less favourable for the engendering of offspring; the right time is the winter." Whether true or not, this opinion was certainly shared by the Greeks, and Aristotle wrote of marriage in the *Politics*: "The season of the year should also be considered. According to our present custom, people generally limit marriage to the season of winter, and they are right."[1] If Hera was the goddess of marriage, it was because of a more fundamental character as a goddess of fecundity. To limit this fecundity to that of human beings is, I should say, to make an arbitrary and un-Greek distinction. Yet if it is not so limited, it is difficult to resist the conclusion that in the dim past she had been worshipped as an embodiment of the fruitful earth. At Athens in historical times it was human marriage that was in question, but the month following the winter solstice is (*pace* Farnell) no bad season for the union of spirits of fertility, if such they originally were.[2]

[1] A. Mommsen, *Feste der Stadt Athen* (Leipzig, 1898), p. 382; Arist. *Pol.* 1335a36.

[2] Farnell (*Cults*, i, 185) thinks that such a union would have to take place at time of the spring flowers, as the account of the bridal bed in *Iliad*, xiv, 346 ff., sug

Some details may be mentioned which perhaps support, and have largely been used to support, the connexion of Hera with the fertile earth. They do not provide conclusive arguments, since some are open to a different interpretation and it may always be urged by those who prefer a different arrangement of the counters that it is unfair to seize on these particular details and insist upon them to the exclusion of others. According to late witnesses, who were probably recording genuine tradition, at Argos she was worshipped as "goddess of the yoke" (*Ζευξιδία*) and "Rich in oxen". The island of the same name, Euboea, was held sacred to her and was full of her legends, e.g. when she quarrelled with Zeus she was said to have fled there, and her marriage with Zeus was localized on one of its mountains. This connexion with cattle reminds us that sacred herds of cows were kept at the Heraion of Argos, and that many votive images of cows have been found there. There were myths of her transformation into a cow, like the cow-maiden Io whose own story brought the two into close contact. In the *Iliad* Hera is "ox-eyed". All this was otherwise interpreted by those to whom Hera was the horned moon, but the connexion is a natural one for a goddess of flocks and herds (the goat was also sacred to her), and we remember the significance of oxen as agents of fertility.[1]

The Byzantine *Etymologicum Magnum*, which told us of Hera's worship at Argos as "Goddess of the yoke", says also that at the same place ears of corn were called the flowers of Hera. Pausanias saw at Argos a temple of Hera of the Flowers (*Ἥρα Ἀνθεία*), and she was said to delight particularly in the lily. When the milk

---

I have always thought it a mistake to use this particular passage as an illustration of any genuine religious belief. It seems so obviously a creation of poetic fancy. To indulge further in subjective criticism, I should say that a comparison with the fragment of Aeschylus' *Danaids* quoted above (p. 54) serves to point the contrast.

In any case, Farnell's point would be a mere gnat to the camel which all of us who believe in fertility-spirits and the year-god have to swallow. The festivals of the death and resurrection of the latter are said to represent the dying and renewal of the crops. Whether "dying" means the reaping, or the burial of the seed in the ground at sowing-time, is not always made clear by the authorities, but in either case one would expect there to be two festivals separated by an interval of months. In fact the death and resurrection are usually represented as taking place within a week-end. I do not think this destroys a well-attested theory, for it is easy to imagine thought-processes to account for it, or to imagine it as taking place without much thought. But if we demand that the chronology of nature should be reproduced in one case we should expect it in another.

[1] Above, p. 50, n. 1. For the evidence for Hera's connexion with cows, see Farnell, *Cults*, i, 181 f., Cook, *Zeus*, i, 444 ff.

of Hera caused the creation of the Milky Way (the subject of Tintoretto's famous picture in the National Gallery), some drops of it fell to the ground, and lilies sprang up where they dropped. Our sources for these statements are of the Christian era, but we are brought back to classical times by fifth-century coins of Elis and Argos, on which the crown which the goddess is wearing is clearly made of fleurs-de-lys.[1] Certain flowers were held sacred to her because they were believed to possess medicinal powers of peculiar interest to women, to regulate the flow of the menses or as a cure for sterility.[2] This has been held to weaken the argument that her connexion with flowers has anything to do with her character as an earth-goddess, but in fact it is an excellent illustration of her fertilizing power in one of its aspects.

Again, Hera was said to be the mother of strange monsters, such as Typhoeus and the Lernean Hydra, of a kind which elsewhere are said, like the whole race of the Giants, to have sprung from the Earth. Indeed, Hesiod makes the Earth (Ge) the mother of Typhoeus, whereas Stesichoros and the author of the Homeric Hymn to Apollo call him son of Hera.

It is perhaps worth mentioning that Hera shares the character of goddess of child-birth with Artemis, who in Plato's words (*Theaet.* 149b) "though childless herself has child-birth for her province". She was worshipped under the title *Locheia* and even identified with Eileithyia. Yet Farnell, who in Hera's case will have none of the idea, sums up his review of the evidence about Artemis with the statement: "it seems reasonable to conclude that Artemis in the earliest Greek religion was an earth-goddess, associated essentially and chiefly with the wild life and growth of the field, and with human birth".[3]

"Hera is from time immemorial the great goddess of Argos." So Professor Rose, and indeed all the evidence points to Argos as having been her original home. She is "Argive Hera" in the *Iliad*, and is made to say that the dearest of all cities to her are the three in the Peloponnese, Argos and Mycenae and Sparta. Pindar bids sing of "Argos, city of Danaos and the fifty bright-throned maidens, the home of Hera". To Samos, after Argos the greatest

[1] *κρίνῳ δὲ ἥδεσθαι τὴν Ἥραν φασίν*, Clem. Al. *Paed.* 2, 8, 72, 4, p. 201, 24 Stählin. For other references see Farnell, *Cults*, i, 242, n. 13a, 250, n. 38, Cook, *Zeus*. i, 624 f. (and 622 f. for the lily as a symbol of fertility). Relevant coins are most accessibly illustrated in Farnell, *Cults*, i, coin-plate A, 17 and 18, and Head, *Hist. Num.*[2] p. 422, fig. 231.

[2] Roscher, *Lexikon*, 1, i, 2090.

[3] *Cults*, ii, 456. For Artemis cf. p. 103 below.

centre of her cult, legend said that she had been brought by the Argonauts, who carried her image from Argos and founded her temple there.[1] The safest thing to say about her origin is simply this, that she was the goddess of Argos, whence her cult was taken to other parts of Greece and she was ultimately promoted to her high place in the Panhellenic Olympian circle. It is of course possible that she, or at least her name,[2] was brought there by an early wave of Greek invaders, but overwhelmingly likely that the Greeks found there a powerful goddess of the original inhabitants and recognized her greatness by uniting her with their own chief god, respecting here as elsewhere the power and rights of the native deities (ἐγχώριοι θεοί). Her universal acceptance as the wife of Zeus owes much to the dominating influence of the Homeric poems, and it may be relevant to her position in the *Iliad* to recall, as Rose does, that the chief heroes in the poem are the great kings of Argos and Mycenae and their vassals.

This last consideration favours, so far as it goes, the opinion here expressed that Hera was originally a local form of the Earth-mother, promoting the fertility of all her creatures and identifying herself with their life, marrying and upholding marriage, taking the herds under her protection and herself occasionally appearing in bovine form, creating and adorning herself with the lilies of the field: for analogy suggests that such a goddess was worshipped under different names all over the lands bordering the Aegean before the arrival of the Greeks.[3]

Let us end as we began. If what I have suggested is true, then the original nature of Hera is unimportant, so much had the Greeks transformed her. Of her original functions only her authority over marriage was widely recognized. Obscure local cult-practices might perpetuate the memory of the rest, but in general, Homer, here as in so much else, had set the tone for succeeding generations. She was the Olympian wife of Zeus, with scarcely a trace of chthonian associations, as Farnell was quick to point out. Moreover, for a goddess who could promote fecundity in others, her own marriage with Zeus was surprisingly unfruitful. The great majority of the numerous offspring of Zeus were got in other ways. According to Hesiod, Hera gave him three children, Hebe, Ares and Eileithyia, besides producing Hephaistos on her

[1] Hom. *Il.* v, 908 and iv, 51; Pindar *Nem.* x, 1 f.; Paus. vii, 4, 4.

[2] Wilamowitz regarded it as a feminine form of ἥρως, and equivalent in meaning to δέσποινα, "Our Lady" (*Glaube*, i, 237).

[3] Cf. p. 55 above.

own account without the aid of a male partner; but Professor Cook at least will have it that not even the three have a good claim to be regarded as originally the offspring of the royal pair.[1]

IV. Apollo

Apollo presents us with a curious state of affairs. He is the very embodiment of the Hellenic spirit. Everything that marks off the Greek outlook from that of other peoples, and in particular from the barbarians who surrounded them—beauty of every sort, whether of art, music, poetry or youth, sanity and moderation—all are summed up in Apollo. Yet there seems little doubt that in origin he is not Hellenic. No one has been able to derive his name convincingly from a Greek etymology.[2] At the very centre and heart of his worship in Greece, at Delphi, he was remembered by the Greeks themselves as a late-comer, who had succeeded generations of earlier tenants of the shrine. Other indications will emerge as we proceed. It may be said that religious historians to-day are generally agreed in seeking his origin outside the Greek peoples. When we ask where exactly it is to be sought, we find no such unanimity. Before discussing individual opinions, it

[1] A. B. Cook, "Who was the wife of Zeus?", *Class. Rev.* xx (1906), 365 ff.

[2] Endless etymologies have of course been proffered, both in ancient and modern times. But the only notable modern scholar still bold enough to derive both racial origin and essential nature of Apollo from a single word is Otto Kern (*Rel. d. Gr.* i, 110 ff.). The word ἀπέλλαι is known only from Hesychius and a Laconian inscription of the first century B.C. The gloss in Hesychius runs: ἀπέλλαι · σηκοί, ἐκκλησίαι, telling us that the word meant (*a*) sheepfolds, (*b*) public meetings. On this evidence Kern (following C. Robert) decides that the name of Apollo is derived from this word and shows him to have been in origin a simple god of herdsmen (ursprunglich nichts anders als ein schlichter Hirtengott). "Apellon" is a widespread local variation of the name. This however is to choose arbitrarily between the two meanings given by Hesychius, of which in fact only the other seems to be attested. In the Laconian inscription mentioned above, the word means "meetings", and Plutarch cites the verb ἀπελλάζω as Laconian for ἐκκλησιάζω. (See L. and S. s.v.) If then this little-known word must be hailed as the eponym of the most striking of all the Greek gods, there is as much to be said for the view which Farnell thinks "worth mentioning" (*Cults*, iv, 98 f.), according to which (for it ignores σηκοί as completely as Kern ignores ἐκκλησίαι) Apollo or Apello was originally the Dorian deity of the political meeting. (For the origin from ἀπελλα see also S. Solders in *Arch. f. Religionswiss*, xxxii (1935), 142 ff).

Professor A. B. Cook also suggests a Greek etymology for the name, deriving it from ἀπελλόν, a black-poplar tree, a word whose interpretation we also owe to Hesychius (*Zeus*, ii, 484). He does not pretend however that if this etymology is correct it explains the whole original nature of the god. Cf. o.c., p. 500: "With regard to Apollon's original character we are still lamentably ignorant. . . . *Apollon* appears to be merely a cult-epithet, 'he of the Black-Poplars'. The full name of the god is possibly preserved in the Homeric designation Phoibos *Apollon*."

will be as well to recall the warning expressed by K. Wernicke in his article on Apollo in Pauly-Wissowa's Encyclopaedia, that any view which seeks to derive the manifold aspects of the historic Apollo from one original source is probably wrong. It is more likely that a great Panhellenic god such as Apollo became in historical times had absorbed into himself deities, or religious elements, of widely different origin.

We cannot here trace the history of Apollo-theories. It must suffice to discuss briefly the weightiest of those in favour at the present day. And it should perhaps be mentioned at the outset that the popular view of Apollo as a sun-god (last upheld by Roscher) has been fairly conclusively shown to be without foundation as an explanation of his original and essential nature. There are nowadays two main schools of thought. The one believes that Apollo is in origin Asiatic, the god of some non-Greek people of inner Asia Minor, the other, relying mainly on the tradition which connects him with the Hyperboreans, holds that he comes from somewhere in the north, where in the course of their southward migrations the Greeks found and adopted him and so brought him down into Greece. The champion of the Asiatic theory was Wilamowitz, and he has found a distinguished successor in Professor Nilsson. The northern origin is most stoutly defended by Professor A. B. Cook and Professor Rose.[1]

Apollo's connexions with the Hyperboreans are strong, both in myth and cult. The earliest literary reference which has been preserved is to a Delphic myth. It is from a poem of Alcaeus (*c.* 600 B.C.), though unfortunately what we have is not the poem itself but a prose paraphrase of it in the works of Himerius, a rhetorician of the fourth century A.D.[2] When Apollo was born, Zeus intended him to go to Delphi to dispense law to the Hellenes. Instead, he made use of the swan-chariot with which he had been provided to fly to the land of the Hyperboreans, where he re-

[1] None of the rival champions show signs of shaking hands over a compromise such as that proposed by Gilbert Murray (*Five Stages of Greek Religion* (1925), p. 71): Apollo is on one side clearly a Northman, but on the other side (which, we may say, is his mother's side), "reaches back to an Aegean matriarchal Kouros". This more complex view of his origin may well be the true one, but it is not to the author's purpose in *Five Stages* to argue the point or marshal the evidence.

I have picked out the most strongly contrasting views and their most able exponents in recent times. For an excellent short summary of the different phases of the controversy, mentioning the opinions of Wernicke, Farnell, Zielinski, Wilamowitz, Nilsson, Gruppe, Aly, E. Mayer, A. L. Frothingham and Murray, see A. B. Cook, *Zeus*, ii, 453–9.

[2] Himer. *Or.* xiv, 10.

mained for a whole year before turning back to Delphi in response to the paean, song and dances of the young men with which the Delphians had been invoking him. It was midsummer when he came back, and Himerius, in commenting on the poem, generalizes this in the words: "And hence when the god is in the land the lyre too brightens into a summer strain concerning him." No doubt, as he here hints, the mention of the season, as well as of the paean, song and dances of the young men "about the tripod", indicate that the myth served as *aition* for an actual rite, though it is difficult to decide which of the Delphic festivals is in question. Certainly Apollo was believed to desert Delphi for the winter months, which he spent among the Hyperboreans, but it seems that the period of his absence was only three months, and he must surely have returned before midsummer.

Pindar in his tenth Pythian ode does nothing to make the Hyperboreans seem less mythical. "Neither by ship nor on foot", he says, "couldst thou find the wondrous way to the assembly of the Hyperboreans." Yet Perseus went there, and found them sacrificing hecatombs of asses to Apollo.[1] They are a blessed throng,[2] a sacred race who know not disease or old age, but spend their whole time in dancing, playing the lyre and flute, and feasting happily with crowns of bay on their heads. They are beyond the reach of Nemesis, and live a life free from toil and battle. The description makes the country sound like a sort of Islands of the Blest for the souls of departed heroes and heroines. According to Strabo[3] Pindar also said of the Hyperboreans, as did Simonides and other writers, that they lived for a thousand years. Bacchylides strengthens our impression of the land as a home for the souls of the blessed by the ending which he provides for the well-known story of Croesus on the pyre. Apollo, he says, transported Croesus and his daughters to the Hyperboreans on account of their piety.[4] Pindar makes mention again of this mysterious country in the third Olympian, where one feature of the account seems to promise a more precise earthly location for them. When Herakles was pursuing the hind with the golden horns, he came to "that

[1] Pind. *Pyth.* x, 29 ff. The asses may suggest a custom of earthly tribes. Strabo (xv, 727) says the Carmanians sacrificed them to Ares, other late writers (and, according to Clement, Callimachus) attribute ass-sacrifice to the Scythians. See Cook, *Journ. Hell. Stud.* xiv (1894), 86, 88, and *Zeus* ii, 464. But for such sacrifices in Greece cf. the warning of G. Daux in *Rev. Ét. Gr.* liii (1940), 98 f.

[2] ἀνδρῶν μακάρων ὅμιλον, line 46. [3] xv, 711, Pindar ed. Bowra (O.C.T.) fr. 272.

[4] *Bacchylides* iii, 58 f.

land beyond the blasts of the cold North Wind" (Boreas—the common Greek interpretation of the name Hyperborean was that it meant "beyond the North Wind"). The trees that he saw there filled him with wonder, and he was seized with a desire to plant them at the end of the race-course at Olympia. As a result he persuaded the Hyperborean folk who serve Apollo, and brought back (the climax contains two surprises) the grey olive from the shady springs of the Istros (Danube). This mention of the Istros has been said to bring the Hyperboreans down to earth and give them a local habitation in the Balkans, but when one considers, first, their alternative location "beyond the cold North Wind", and secondly the improbability of a story which makes someone bring to Greece, the land of the olive, olive-trees from a northern country where they would be scarce or non-existent, it cannot be said that Pindar helps us to make much progress in the realm of fact as opposed to fancy.[1]

Herodotus gives us at least some contact with fact. Writing of the Hyperboreans in his fourth book, he says that the fullest account of them is given by the Delians. These told him that certain unspecified sacred objects wrapped in wheat-straw are taken by the Hyperboreans to the confines of their land and handed to their neighbours, who duly hand them on so that they pass from hand to hand and land to land until they reach Delos. Once long ago they sent two of their own maidens, Hyperoche and Laodike, all the way with the offerings, together with an escort of five men for their safety. But since these did not return they were indignant, and ever afterwards have employed the method described instead of sending envoys of their own. The maidens died and were buried in Delos, where Herodotus saw their tombs. Of the men, he simply says that they are now called Perpherees and highly honoured in Delos. In memory of the maidens, the girls and youths of Delos make offerings of their hair at the tomb. The tradition of the maidens existed in a double form, for Herodotus was also told by the Delians that before the time of Hyperoche and Laodike, in fact "together with the gods themselves", two

[1] Professor Cook, with his usual wealth of learning, shows that the road to the Hyperboreans, in their mythical aspect as a concourse of the Blessed, was conceived as the Milky Way. That was the route traversed by Apollo in his airy chariot, and described by Pindar as a wondrous road neither on sea nor land. But taking Pindar's mention of the Istros together with the evidence of the offerings brought to Delos (to which we are now coming), he would give them a double existence, supposing them also to be a real human tribe living in northern Europe at the far end of the trade-route by which amber reached Greece. (*Zeus*, ii, 459–501.)

other maidens, Arge and Opis, came from the Hyperboreans and are also buried in Delos and receive honours from the Delian women, who call upon them in a hymn composed by "Olen, a man of Lycia".[1]

Presumably we may take it as fact that sacred offerings wrapped in straw and destined for the shrine of Apollo and Artemis did arrive at Delos in Herodotus' time and were believed by the Delians to have originated in that far-off land of the blessed folk beloved by Apollo, the Hyperboreans. But no living Delian had ever seen a Hyperborean. Owing to an unfortunate incident in the past, the Hyperboreans no longer sent envoys to Delos, but entrusted the offerings to their neighbours with instructions to pass them on. And as the commentators How and Wells justly remark, the Greek stages of their journey are given carefully, but the northern ones are unknown. The ultimate source of the offerings has been the subject of many conjectures, to which I do not propose to add. I would only say that I cannot see anything in the account of Herodotus to alter the impression which we have already received of the Hyperboreans as a mythical concourse of semi-divine beings. Herodotus himself, who went to Delos and examined the evidence with care, remained sceptical, in spite of having been shown the tombs of both pairs of Hyperborean maidens, the situation of which he described with such accuracy that they were discovered by the French excavators exactly where he had told them to look. But the discovery only confirmed the soundness of his instinct towards scepticism. For, as Mr. C. T. Seltman has said in a most interesting article on the Hyperboreans, "the discovery of these tombs . . . has finally dissolved any shadow of reality that the maidens could ever have claimed. Both groups of burials were of the bronze age, and contained Cycladic, Middle-Minoan II–III and Late Minoan II pottery. As Nilsson has pointed out, the primitive tombs had a cult attached to them in the Cycladic and Mycenean age. The inhabitants of the tombs were forgotten, the sanctity of the tomb remained, and later on degraded deities or imaginary heroines were associated with the spot".[2]

To do justice to Herodotus' account, we should take note of the passages at the beginning and end which betray his own attitude. His first mention of the Hyperboreans is in ch. 13, where in his account of the northern lands he states that Aristeas of Prokonnesos claimed to have travelled as far as the Issedones, and wrote

[1] Hdt. iv, 32–5.

[2] *Class Quart.* xxii (1928), p. 156. See Ch. Picard, *Les Religions Préhélleniques* (Paris, 1948), p. 271 for other examples of 'hero-cult' attached to Mycenean graves in historical Greece.

that beyond them live the one-eyed Arimaspi, beyond them the gold-guarding griffins, and beyond them again the Hyperboreans. This hardly puts the last-named in a matter-of-fact setting, and by his own admission Aristeas did not know of them from any nearer source than the Issedones, on whose word he was relying (ch. 16). Having disposed of sundry other matters, Herodotus returns to the Hyperboreans in these words: "As for Hyperboreans, neither the Scythians nor any others living in those parts say anything about them, unless indeed it be the Issedones. But in my opinion, they have nothing to say either. Otherwise the Scythians would have spoken of them, as they do about the one-eyed race. Yet Hyperboreans are mentioned by Hesiod, and by Homer in the *Epigoni*, if that poem is indeed by Homer. It is the Delians who have by far the most to say about them. . . ."

That is the beginning of the account. He ends it as follows: "So much for the Hyperboreans. I refrain from citing the story of Abaris, who is supposed to have been a Hyperborean—how he carried the arrow[1] about all over the earth and never touched food. But if there are any hyperborean men, there are presumably hypernotian as well."[2]

The interpretation of Hyperborean as meaning "Beyond the North Wind" was without a rival among the ancients. But modern etymologists could hardly be expected to leave such a problem-folk to enjoy unmolested their blissful northern calm, and we must mention their conjectures, which do much to weaken belief in the northern origin of Apollo's servants, and hence of the god himself.[3] One is that the name contains the root not of "northern" but of a pre-Greek Balkan word for "mountain", and that Boreas is not the North Wind but the wind from the mountain. Bora is the name of a mountain in Macedonia, which is compared with Slavonic *gora* (cf. Crnagora=Montenegro). The Hyperboreans then are either the people who live *beyond* Bora (if you are one of those who believe in their earthly existence) or *above* Bora, i.e. in the sky (if you prefer to think of them as divine).[4]

[1] Symbol of Apollo.

[2] i.e. if there is an Extreme-Northern race, why not an Extreme-Southern as well, beyond the South Wind? The one tale is as likely as the other. I take it to be a somewhat contemptuous dismissal of the whole business.

[3] For a full discussion of them, and attribution to their authors, see Cook, *Zeus*, ii, 494 ff. with n. 6 to p. 495.

[4] Stanley Casson wickedly remarked (*Class. Rev.* xxxiv, 1920) that this afforded equally good etymological grounds for placing the Hyperboreans in Southern Spain, since there was a town of Bora there. Considering the resemblance of their country to

The second modern suggestion is that, just as the initial Greek and Latin sound in φέρω *fero* has become *b* in modern northern tongues (cf. English "bear"), a transposition which also took place in northern Greece in ancient times, so in this case *Hyperboreioi* comes from the root *fer-* and means simply "Carriers-over" in Macedonian or some allied tongue of north Greece. The escort of the Hyperborean maidens, who according to Herodotus were known at Delos as the Perpherees, would have the same name in an easy variant. If this is true, the Hyperboreans were originally only known by their gifts, and hence given no other name than "those who hand over", a title whose significance was completely lost before the time of our earliest authorities.[1]

It is noteworthy that, in spite of the traditional derivation of the name, the accounts of ancient geographers seem to have agreed in relegating the Hyperboreans rather to the north-east, to Asia, than to the far north of Europe. Pausanias, though he gives a different route for the carrying of the sacred offerings from the Hyperboreans to Delos, agrees with Herodotus (or rather Aristeas) in saying that the Hyperboreans themselves lived beyond the Arimaspi who lived beyond the Issedones.[2] Now the Issedones, as Herrmann says, form one of the most remarkable problems of ancient geography.[3] Yet no one has seen any evidence for putting them elsewhere than far to the east, as well as to the north, of Greece. I quote from the introductory paragraph of Herrmann's article. "Antiquity ascribed them to the most varied localities, north of the Black Sea, north-east of the Caspian, at the southern foot of the Caucasus and finally in the farthest East, in the land of the Seres. Our own research has held for preference to the last-named view." Herrmann himself, who thinks that a critical examination of the sources leads to yet another view, propounds

---

the Islands of the Blest it is indeed surprising that no one has thought of locating them in the West. But although they have been detected in places as far apart as China and Britain, no one, so far as I am aware, has transferred them to the lands of the sunset.

[1] περφερέες might rather mean "carriers-*round*", as it was said of Abaris the Hyperborean that he τὸν ὀϊστὸν περιέφερε. (But see end of note.) I do not see that this is an objection to the theory as Daebritz claims (PWK *Realenc*. ix, 261, quoted in *Zeus*, ii, 496, n. o), nor do his other philological objections seem final. The theory was favoured by Farnell (*Cults*, iv, 102 f.), and Rose does not appear to reject it, though it does not weaken his conviction that the Hyperboreans, and therefore Apollo himself, came originally from the North. The most damning evidence against it is that cited by Cook (l.c.) in the shape of two dedications from Thessaly to Zeus Perpheretas, where the epithet fairly clearly means "who excels, or surpasses".

[2] Paus. i, 31, 2.

[3] PWK *Realenc*. ix, 2235.

his own as follows: "The Issedones appear as an Indo-Germanic race of nomads whose home was east of the Urals in the basins of the rivers Iset (which obviously preserves their name) and the lower Tobol." Sir Ellis Minns put them much further to the south-east, considering them to have been Tibetan tribes in the Tarim and Bulunggir basins.[1] And these are the near neighbours of the Hyperboreans, upon whose location (for there is little other evidence) is based the theory that Apollo became known to the Greeks in a north-European home!

There is little other evidence, but the Delphic festival called the Stepterion, or Festival of the Wreaths, should be mentioned in this connexion, since some have seen in it a reflection of the god's original arrival from the North. The festival can be reconstructed in some detail from passages in Plutarch, Aelian and Strabo.[2] Like the festivals called Herois and Charila, it was held at intervals of eight years. It seems to have consisted of two parts, whose exact relation is not made clear by the incomplete accounts which have come down to us, and which may in fact have been originally distinct and never organically connected, though made artificially into parts of the same festival with a comprehensive mythical explanation to unite them. At Delphi itself a structure was set up on a threshing-floor, and supposed to represent the lair of the dragon which guarded the oracle in the days when it belonged to Earth, and which was slain by Apollo on his arrival. Plutarch says however that it looked more like a king's palace than a dragon's lair. A company of women approach this house in silence, bearing lighted torches and conducting a boy. They set fire to the house, "overturn the table", and without looking round flee "through the doors of the Temple". The boy, says Plutarch, then undertakes "wanderings and servitude", which we may perhaps compare to the time that Apollo was supposed to have spent in servitude to King Admetos of Pherae, since the actions of the boy were explained as a representation of the wanderings of Apollo in search of purification.[3] The wanderings ended in the Vale of

[1] E. H. Minns, *Scythians and Greeks* (Cambridge, 1913), p. 110.

[2] Plut. *Quaest. Graec.* 12, 293c, *Def. Orac.* 14, 418a, *De Mus.* 1136b; Aelian *Var. Hist.* iii, 1; Strabo, ix, 422. The Greek is extensively quoted in Farnell, *Cults*, iv, 425 f., n. 264 e,g. For translations see Frazer, Paus. iii, 53 f. Besides Farnell's and Frazer's accounts, see especially Nilsson, *Griech. Feste* (Leipzig, 1906), 150 ff. Other reff. to modern literature in Cook, *Zeus*, ii, 240, n. 1.

[3] Apollo's servitude to Admetos was a punishment for killing, though according to the myth, for the death of the Kyklopes, not of the Python.

Tempe, where purification was administered. This part of the story is told by Plutarch rather as a series of asides than a connected narrative. From Aelian we learn that the journey to Tempe was one of festal pomp carried out by the young nobility of Delphi with one of their number as processional leader. (The "servitude" was no doubt symbolic only. It is not mentioned by Aelian.) On arrival in Tempe they carried out a "grand" sacrifice and wove themselves crowns (hence the name of the festival) from the very laurel of Tempe from which Apollo himself had crowned his head before making his way to Delphi after his own purification on the same spot. Then, still following the example of the god, they returned to Delphi. A flute-player accompanied them (Plutarch), and the inhabitants of the states through which they passed sent them on their way with due honours and reverence (Aelian). Aelian adds that it is from this laurel brought from Tempe that the victors in the Pythian contests were crowned.

Believers in the northern origin of Apollo are impressed by this festal train of youths, one of whose number certainly represents the god himself as they retrace in his honour the very route by which he came to Delphi from the North. The same thought was not of course in the mind of the Greeks, since the myth which for them represented the *aition* of the proceedings required that Apollo should already have been in Delphi and slain the Python, making, for the sake of purification, the double journey to Tempe from Delphi and back exactly as his youthful worshippers did. They did not therefore connect it with his original arrival at Delphi from the land of the Hyperboreans (p. 75 above), though it may be significant—and it is something which I have not seen commented on in this connexion—that in describing it both Plutarch and Aelian are *reminded* of the Hyperboreans. "The youth who brings back the laurel of Tempe to Delphi", says Plutarch, "is accompanied by a flute-player; and they say that in olden times the sacred gifts of the Hyperboreans were sent to Delos with flutes and pipes and the lyre." Aelian writes that the states through which the procession passes pay to it "as much reverence and honour as is accorded to those who bring to the same god the sacred gifts from the land of the Hyperboreans".

That is as far as the Stepterion takes us. Although certain features of it remind Plutarch and Aelian vaguely of the way in which the Hyperborean offerings were brought to Delos, it takes us no further than Tempe, that is, than Thessaly. Nilsson expresses the opinion that the procession from Delphi to Tempe had originally nothing to do with the myth of the slaying of the Python and Apollo's need for purification. He approves the conclusion of K. O. Müller that it was from Tempe that the cult of Apollo originally reached Delphi, and that the sacred embassy to Tempe represents a recognition of the priority of the cult there. Yet he is the strongest modern upholder of the theory that Apollo came to the Greeks from Asia Minor. He clearly sees in the Stepterion no evidence to shake that theory, and neither need we.

At the same time it would be foolish to deny the possibility that a god of northern Europe may have played some part in the formation of the Apollo of classical Greece. In arguing for this, A. H. Krappe has echoed the wisdom of Wernicke in the words: "Many of the most bitter controversies concerning the nature and origin of Apollon could have been avoided, had it been realized that the Apollon of the classical epoch is as much of a compound as was the Hellenic nation itself." From his connexion not only with the Hyperboreans but also with (a) singing swans and (b) amber, Krappe considers that Apollo had certainly absorbed something of a god from the Frisian North Sea coast.[1] Possibly the Greeks of the archaic age identified such a god with their Apollo, but the Apollo of Homer is more likelv to have come from the East alone.

What then of the Asiatic side? Its champions start from Apollo's ancient epithet Lykios or Lykeios, which they say means Lycian, of Lycia in Asia Minor. The alternative is to interpret it as = "Wolf-god", which was the interpretation of the Greeks themselves.[2] Rose himself describes this as "falling back on" the meaning "wolf-god", which does not sound as if it expressed great satisfaction, and he accepts the theory according to which Apollo was originally a deity of shepherds. To shepherds one of the chief concerns of life is the presence or absence of wolves, and their god was the one who could protect from their depredations, or bring them on if he were angry. He is a musician, because playing and singing have always been favourite activities of shepherds in the Mediterranean area.[3]

[1] See Krappe's discussion in *Class. Phil.* xxxvii (1942), 353 ff.

[2] e.g. Aesch. *Sept.* 145, Soph. *El.* 6.

[3] Rose, *Hbk. Gr. Myth.* 136. These are not of course the only possible alternative interpretations, though after reading the arguments of the modern protagonists it is quite a surprise to turn to Jebb's commentary on the *Electra* and find (on line 7): "*Λύκειος* must ultimately be traced to the root *λυκ*, *lux*, as designating the god of

One can at least say that Lycian is a very natural meaning for Lykios or Lykeios, and I would add that one would hardly expect the Greeks themselves to emphasize it after they had not only adopted Apollo into the Olympian pantheon but made him into their most typical representative. The chief arguments of the Anatolian school of thought are briefly these.[1] In the *Iliad* Apollo is on the side of the Trojans, and Pandaros, instructed by Athena, prays to him as Apollo Lykegenes. Since Pandaros is himself a Lycian, the invocation presumably meant that Apollo was a native of his own country. True, he is invoked by the Greeks along with Zeus and Athena, but it is sufficient to suppose, as Wilamowitz remarks (justly, in view of other evidence for the habit; cf. p. 29 above), that the Greeks had learned to revere an originally hostile god, whom they found on all sides in the country to which they had come. Next, he is commonly called Letoides, after his mother, and Herodotus (i, 173) says of the Lycians: "They have one peculiar custom in which they agree with no other men: they call themselves after their mothers, not their fathers." This is striking, though it must be admitted that Hermes, who has no such connexions, is equally commonly called Son of Maia.[2] For the name of Apollo's mother Leto, Wilamowitz

light. But it was popularly connected with λύκος." The derivation from light is not perhaps dead, but certainly seems to have gone out of favour with the sun-myth. In this connexion it would be pertinent to take account of Zeus Lykaios as well, for whose etymology (wolf-god versus light-god) see Cook, *Zeus*, i, 63 ff. Various combinations are of course possible. One can see the root "light" in the name of Lycia itself, as in the theory of Zielinski (1899, quoted by Cook, *Zeus*, ii, 453) that "Apollon and his sister Artemis, a pair of light-divinities, came from the Troad, where behind the rocks of Mount Ide lay *Lykia*, a blissful 'Land of Light' inhabited by the pious Hyperboreans." (Lycia, Light-god and Hyperboreans all reconciled in a single theory! One would have thought that was generous enough to satisfy anybody, but scholars are hard to please.) It is also possible to turn the tables, and speak with Farnell of "Apollo Lykeios who gave his name to Lycia", i.e. was brought there by the Greeks, but I think we may agree with Professor Cook in regarding it as "highly improbable" that Lycia was named after Apollo Lykeios. (Farnell, *Cults*, iv, 112, Cook, *Zeus*, ii, 458, n. 2.) It was, however, already the view of Wernicke (PWK *Realenc.* ii, 59 f.), who points to the very strong and apparently ancient traditions connecting the title with the Peloponnese, where also Zeus Lykaios was at home.

[1] First put forward by Wilamowitz in *Hermes*, xxxviii (1903), 575–86. See also his *Der Glaube der Hellenen*, i (1931), 324 ff., ii (1932), 28 ff., and, in English, his lecture on *Apollo* translated by Gilbert Murray (Oxford, 1908). Nilsson has summarized his views in *Min.-Myc. Rel.* 443, n. 1.

[2] So Rose. Yet though Hermes is referred to as *Μαίης υἱός*, he has no matronymic appellation corresponding to *Λητοΐδης*. The other example quoted by Rose, Dionysos, is surely unfortunate, in view of this god's connexion with Phrygia. In spite of Herodotus, the emphasis on the mother is rather an Anatolian than a peculiarly Lycian characteristic, and for this particular point to support the Anatolian origin of Apollo is enough.

accepts its identity with that of the Lycian goddess Lada.[1] Leto and her twin children, Apollo and Artemis, are spoken of in the *Iliad* (v, 445–8) as united in one sanctuary in Troy, and Wilamowitz argues that in spite of the general recognition afterwards accorded to the trio in Greece, there are signs that it originated in Asia Minor, and the myth of the birth of the twins was first found in Lycia. Delian tradition spoke usually of the birth of Apollo alone, whereas that of Artemis was located in Ephesus. Leto in Greece is very much in the background, and never became one of the Olympian pantheon. Then again, Olen, who as we saw (p. 77 above) composed the hymns for the Delians which were their authority for honouring the memory of the Hyperborean maidens, was a Lycian, a point which Herodotus repeats, saying a few lines further on that he "came from Lycia". Pausanias calls him in one place (v, 7, 8) a Lycian, saying at the same time that he was the first to affirm the existence of Hyperboreans, and in another (x, 5, 4) a Hyperborean himself. In discussing the Hyperboreans we saw how they tended to shift towards the East, and in the mysterious figure of Olen we actually seem to have a contact between the Hyperboreans and Lycia, though admittedly it only seems to be achieved by means of contradictory statements on the part of our authorities.

Support for the Asiatic origin of Apollo is found in the fact that at most of his great cult-centres on the mainland of Greece he appears as an intruder. At Delphi the Greeks recognized this themselves, at other places there is clear evidence that he has taken over the worship previously paid to another god. (See below, pp. 86 f.) This in itself is no indication of where he came from, but whereas his festivals are altogether comparatively rare in Greece, they are much more frequent on the islands and in Asia Minor. Some of his greatest holy places are on Asiatic soil, sites of sanctuaries which gave rise to epithets of the god that became commonplaces. Patara is in Lycia itself. Didyma (Branchidae), the site of a famous oracle of the god, is in Caria, some two hours' ride south of Miletos. Somewhat further north, in Ionia, was the equally famous Klaros, and further north still, in Aeolia, the oracle-shrine of Gryneion. All these sites were of

[1] This name is simply the Lycian word for woman. Sir William Ramsay (*Cities and Bishoprics of Phrygia*, i (1895), 91, n. 2) is inclined to give up this derivation for Leto in favour of Robertson-Smith's identification of her with the Semitic Al-lat or Alilat (see Herodotus, i, 131, iii, 8). For references to other suggestions, see Cook, *Zeus*, ii, 1042, n. 5.

course on the hellenized western fringe of the great peninsula. A god who was not worshipped in lands where the Greeks settled could hardly have been taken over by them. Nevertheless the same fact makes possible the objection of an unbeliever like Professor Rose that "worship in Asia Minor need mean no more than that the Ionian Greeks brought Apollo there". This was not the opinion of Pausanias, who bears express testimony to the great antiquity of the shrines at both Didyma and Klaros.[1] Perhaps no single piece of evidence can be completely convincing in a case like this. It is only by cumulative effect that the testimonies of one or the other theory can prevail, and the cumulative effect in the matter of an Anatolian origin for Apollo seems to me to be strong. Moreover there is a little more to be said on this particular question of the distribution of Apollo-worship in Asia Minor. The shrines which gained most fame among the Greeks were indeed those situated where Greek settlement was earliest and most permanent. I do not see how it could well have been otherwise. But the worship of Apollo was not confined to those coastal regions. "To strengthen the proof that Apollo was an immigrant into Europe," wrote Wilamowitz, "an expert on inner Asia Minor could show from the inscriptions that he was one of the gods most worshipped not only in the hellenized coastal belt but deep into the peninsula."[2] "Ich kann das nicht", he continues modestly, and quotes from Sir William Ramsay, an expert on inner Anatolia if ever there was one, a definite statement to this effect. Though far from being a "Kenner", I have myself at least penetrated as far on to the central plateau as Iconium and Synnada, and can testify to the abundance of inscriptions up and down the countryside which express devotion both to Apollo and to Leto. Most of our evidence for the cults of inner Anatolia comes from inscriptions which are themselves of Graeco-Roman date, but their value lies in the fact that those remote parts were little affected by Greek ideas or even language. Had Greek settlement penetrated as far in early days, who knows that the indubitably native shrine of Apollo Lairbenos, to take an example from the upper waters of the Maeander, with its belief in impurity and temporal punishment sent by the god, and its strange, un-Hellenic practice of written confession, might not have become as famous as the holy places of Klaros or Didyma?

This god, said Wilamowitz, must have had many different names among the different peoples who worshipped him from the

[1] Paus. vii, 2.4 and vii, 3.1.

[2] *Der Glaube*, i, 328.

Troad to Lycia. At one place the Greeks must have heard him called Apollo or something similar, and recognizing in him the same god at other places too, they, being one people with one language, perpetuated the name that they heard first or found most widespread. "Where they heard the name Apollo", he continues, "will perhaps some day come to light. At present it is impossible to say." Doubtless we shall never know the exact spot at which the Greeks first heard the name. But it is just possible that since Wilamowitz died in 1931, we have discovered both what the name was and to what people it belonged. In 1936 the Hungarian scholar B. Hrozný published the inscriptions found on four Hittite altars at sites in Anatolia near two villages called Emri Gazi and Eski Kişla. "Among other gods"—I quote from Nilsson—"there is mentioned one whose name is read *Apulunas*. He is a god of the gates. If this be so, then the oriental origin of Apollo, which has often been asserted but which has also been vehemently contested, is proved beyond doubt. This Oriental Apollo was the protector of the gates; so was the Apollo of classical Greece."[1]

Our discussion of Apollo's origin has been practically confined to his geographical origin. His original nature cannot be discussed with profit, since it is too deeply wrapped in obscurity. Wherever we meet him his greatness is already so universally acknowledged that he has taken a wide variety of the aspects of human life under his wing, and it would be hard to say whether any single one of them reflects his original character. No doubt, as Wernicke suggested (p. 74 above), widely differing religious elements and minor deities had already been attracted into his orbit in a period to which our records do not reach. The most indubitable instance of Apollo having taken the place of a pre-Greek deity is provided by the festival of the Hyakinthia at Amyklai in Lakonia. The festival was a joint one in honour of Apollo and Hyakinthos, who

[1] *Archiv Orientalní* viii (1936), 171, Nilsson, *Greek Popular Religion* (Columbia U.P., 1940), 79. N. is referring to the cult of Apollo *Agyieus*, who in the form of an aniconic pillar stood in front of Greek houses to ward off evil from the doors. (R. D. Barnett however, in *Journ. Hell. Stud.* 1950, p. 104, says that this is based on a false reading of the Hittite text).

[2] This is perhaps a convenient place to mention the other supplementary arguments produced by Nilsson in support of the thesis of Wilamowitz. They are of a somewhat technical nature, concerned with the day of the month on which his festivals were held. I quote from the summary in *Zeus*, ii, where references will be found. "N. further notes that the first day of the month was sacred to Apollon as *Noumenios* and that the twentieth was sacred to him as *Eikadios*, but that his festivals regularly fell on the seventh of the month. Hence we are to infer that Apollon was essentially connected with the lunisolar calendar and its sacred sabbath, that his worship originated in Babylonia, and that it spread through Asia Minor to Greece." In carrying the story to Babylonia, N. is of course going further afield than Wilamowitz.

was supposed by the Greeks to have been a youth beloved by the god but killed by him through an unlucky throw with the discus. His name is betrayed as pre-Greek by the suffix *nth*, universally agreed among philologists to belong to names and words of the language spoken by the original inhabitants of the country, and according to Pausanias his cult-statue was not that of a youth at all, but of a bearded man. Other indications also go to show that this festival of mourning for a dead god was an aboriginal vegetation-cult which Apollo had taken over.[1] He became an agrarian god as he became a god of shepherds and many others.

On the question of his character and functions we shall have something to say in a later chapter. Above all he is the Averter of Evil (*Apotropaios*) (whether physical as of disease or exerting a less tangible influence), the god of purification (*Katharsios*) and the god of prophecy. Some of these characteristics, in so far as they seem essential to him, may throw light on the question hitherto under discussion, of the peoples or lands from whom the Greeks took him over. It will be well to suspend judgment on this question not only because the arguments so far mentioned are weighty on both sides, but because the character of the god, to which we have not yet paid attention, may prove relevant. In the foregoing exposition, the arguments for an Anatolian origin may have seemed to tip the scale. But we have yet to consider, for instance, the possible bearing on this of the ecstatic possession by the god of the Pythia and others of his servants. A resemblance has been noted between the behaviour of Aristeas, Abaris, and their kind, and that of the Shamans of northern Asia, which opens up a new line of thought about the possible origins of the god. Such considerations must wait for the present.

V. Hermes

It is tiring to be always treading the mazes of controversy. In turning to Hermes, let us allow ourselves the luxury of leaving them, and, to refresh our spirits, follow one path only, which, in the present state of Hermes-lore, we are justified in doing. Nemesis must first be placated, so we shall listen attentively to the warning of Professor Rose: "We must not forget the possibility that the

[1] For the Hyakinthia see Farnell, *Cults*, iv, 125, 264. The most recent study is that of Miss M. J. Mellink, *Hyakinthos* (Utrecht, 1943). Other festivals which probably or certainly show the same order of events are the Attic Thargelia, the Laconian Karneia, the Theban Daphnephoria and the honours paid to Skephros at Tegea (Nilsson, *Gr. Feste* (1906) 102).

Arkadians found him in Arkadia when they arrived there, and that his name is not Greek at all." There will be more to say about this, but for the present we need only note that it is not beyond the bounds of possibility for the Greeks to have found and adopted an ancient indigenous god and given him a title of their own. Let us even note the opinion of Boisacq, that "l'étymologie de *Hermes* est inconnue". But having made these necessary offerings, we shall align ourselves firmly with Professor Nilsson when he declares, "The name is one of the few that are etymologically transparent and means 'he of the stone-heap'."[1] Hermes then is an ancient god of the countryside, named by the Greeks from the ἕρμα, also called ἑρμαῖον, which was a cairn or heap of stones. These cairns served as landmarks, and can already be seen as such in Homer, where Eumaios, describing to Telemachos how he has seen a ship, indicates his position by saying, "I had reached that point above the city where there is a ἑρμαῖος λόφος.[2] "A hill of Hermes"? Yes, but also "a mound in the form of a cairn". The *Etymologicum Magnum* defines ἑρμαῖον as "heap of stones, and in general stones by the wayside", and the scholiast on the passage in the *Odyssey* explains the ἑρμαῖος λόφος in the same way, and adds that the same name was given to Roman milestones.[3] To explain the connexion of Hermes with the cairns, the Greeks characteristically invented an aetiological myth. When Hermes killed Argos, he was brought to trial by the gods. They acquitted him, and in doing so each threw his voting-pebble (ψῆφος) at his feet. Thus a heap of stones grew up around him.[4] In fact he must simply have been the daemon or spirit of the stone-heaps themselves, about which there were several more or less superstitious beliefs. Even now, in the mountainous parts of our own country, the wayfarer who wishes for good luck will add a stone to the cairn which he finds on the hilltop, and this custom prevailed in ancient times too.[5]

[1] Rose, *Hbk. Gr. Myth.* 146, Boisacq, *Dict. Etym. de la Langue Grecque*, 282, n. 3, Nilsson, *Hist. Gr. Rel.* 109. See also J. Chittenden in *Hesperia*, xvi (1947), 94, 95, to whom further reference will be made.

[2] *Od.* xvi, 471. [3] Text in Farnell, *Cults*, v, 67. [4] *Etym. Magn.* s.v. ἑρμαῖον.

[5] Schol. *Od.* xvi, 471, Cornutus *Theol.* xvi, 24, Lang. The origin of the custom has been variously explained. According to Frazer (*G.B.*: *The Scapegoat*, ix, 8 ff.) it was a magical act whereby the traveller transferred his tiredness to the stone and threw it away at a particular spot where his fathers had done so before him. It had no religious significance, since neither the act nor the words which sometimes accompanied it were addressed to any spiritual being. Haddon on the other hand (quoted by Farnell, *Cults*, v, 18, n. b) regarded it as "an act of ceremonial union with the immanent spirit".

To speak more accurately, the *hermaia*, as the aetiological story suggests, consisted of an upright monumental stone with a heap of stones around its base. Gradually the god, and the pillar which represented him, became more and more anthropomorphic in conception. He was given a phallus to promote fertility, and finally emerged as a fully human figure.[1] Yet even the herms which stood in front of Athenian houses in the fifth century had not thrown off all traces of their origin, but were no more than half-human in shape. Since the pillar-and-cairn were set by the wayside to serve as landmarks, the commonest function of Hermes was to be the guide of wayfarers and god of roads.[2] Sometimes the stones would mark graves, which of course were commonly by the roadside in ancient times, and perhaps for this reason, perhaps simply by a natural extension of his function as guide, he became the spirit who led the souls of the dead down to Hades, *psychopompos*. One of these explanations is likely since he does not seem to have had any essential connexion with the deities of the underworld. Orestes addresses him as *Chthonios* in the impressive prayer for aid in which he invokes both Hermes and his dead father at the beginning of the *Choephoroi* of Aeschylus. He is standing, as he says, actually "at the funeral mound" of his father, and it is this that gives the invocation its point. Hermes is present at the grave-mound, and may help Agamemnon to rise from the shades and assist his children.[3]

Another purpose of the cairns was to mark the boundaries of estates, and Hermes was set up for this purpose too. He is thus in

[1] See for example the illustration from a red-figured vase reproduced by Nilsson, *Gr. Pop. Rel.* (1940), fig. 3, and J. Chittenden, *Hesperia*, xvi (1947), pl. xv f., where the hunter Kephalos offers libation to a Hermes, who, fully human at least to the waist, is clearly seen set in his heap of smaller stones.

[2] διάκτορος, πομπαῖος, ὅδιος, ἐνόδιος.

[3] It is interesting to note that the custom of throwing stones on cairns applies also to graves. F. W. Hasluck (*Christianity and Islam under the Sultans* (Oxford, 1929), p. 413), speaking of the reputed grave of a Moslem saint, Yusuf Dede, at Smyrna, says that the precinct contains "as yet no formal tomb, only a heap of stones". In a footnote he gives references attesting the custom of throwing stones on graves in Asia Minor, in Herzegovina, among the Arabs of Syria and among the Yuruks (a nomad people of Anatolia). The practice is evidently widespread and might repay further study. Cf. the following from Villani's *Chronicles* (bk. vii, ch. 9, trans. Selfe) about the burial of Manfred: "Since he was excommunicated, [the king] would not have him laid in holy ground but at the foot of the bridge of Benivento. And each of the host threw a stone upon the grave, so that there arose a great heap of stones at the spot." Here the motive was perhaps to keep down the naturally unquiet spirit of one who died beyond the pale of the Church. As other random examples (for I have made no systematic search), Joshua vii, 26, and 2 Sam. xviii, 17, are perhaps also relevant.

one aspect the equivalent of the Roman Terminus, another figure who was both boundary-stone and tutelary daemon. A clear example, of late date and out-of-the-way provenance, is a marble basis found at the site of Synnada in Asia Minor and bearing the inscription "No. 1 Hermes of Ankira", that is, the first boundary-mark of the estate of Ankira. Here the name Hermes is used practically as a common noun.[1] This stone, which is dated, belongs to the third century A.D. A monument which from its date and provenance is of incomparably greater interest may have served the same purpose. In 1877 the Germans H. Dresel and A. Milchhöfer published an account of a find in Laconia. In the house of a villager some three hours south of Sparta they were shown a relief representing offerings being brought to a seated god and goddess. According to the finder's "thoroughly trust-worthy" account, it had stood upright in a tumulus-like heap of earth and stones with bigger boulders underneath. At the place where it had been found, a few feet away among other heaped-up stones, was an unwrought slab with the single word HERMANOS incised on it in letters of the sixth century B.C. The word is the genitive of Ἑρμάν, the Laconian form of Hermes, and E. S. Roberts translates the inscription as *Mercurii hic fundus*. It is surely a boundary-stone, a counterpart of the one which was set up on the fringes of the Greek world eight centuries later.[2] The boundary-stone was put there to warn off intruders, so it was natural that the spirit inhabiting it should be regarded as a sort of watch-dog or protector of the owner's property. It was in this capacity that Hermes stood outside the houses of Athens, in a form, as we have noted, which still showed evidence of his origin as a stone pillar.[3]

Where art made him into a fully anthropomorphic figure, it is most commonly as the divine wayfarer that he appears, with wings, generally but not always on his sandals, staff in hand and broad-brimmed traveller's hat. He is never a violent god. It is his part to appear suddenly beside the traveller and help and

[1] α ἑρμῖς Ἀγκίρας, *Mon. As. Min. Ant.* iv, ed. Buckler, Calder, Guthrie (Manchester, 1933), no. 71.

[2] Dresel and Milchhöfer, *Ath. Mitt.* ii (1877) 303. See also J. Chittenden, *Hesperia* (1947), p. 94. (I owe my knowledge of the monument to Mrs. Chittenden's article.) The inscription is illustrated by Dresel and Milchhöfer and again by Mrs. Chittenden, pl. xv d. The reference to Roberts is to *Intro. to Gr. Epigraphy* (1887), p. 251. It seemed proper to mention the relief also, though the connexion, if any, between it and the Hermes-stone is hardly clear.

[3] ἡ τετράγωνος ἐργασία, Thuc. vi, 27.

guide him with good advice. Thus we see him employed in the earliest Greek literature of all. Sent by Zeus, he guides the aged Priam safely into the tent of Achilles, and he gives Odysseus the magic plant that is to keep him from harm, and instructs him how to use it.[1] His sudden and unobtrusive comings and goings are illustrated by the Greek saying used when a sudden silence fell on a company. We say that an angel has passed by: they said that Hermes had entered the room.[2] His virtue lay in his speed and his wits, not in his strength. It was natural that he should become "cleverest of the gods" and even "crafty", a thief and patron of thieves, as well as the averter of evil and the giver of good things.[3] It was good luck to meet him, and a piece of good luck was called a gift from Hermes.[4] Among the gods he is not great, but rather their clever servant, used by Zeus to run his errands and take his messages to mankind. The embittered Prometheus of Aeschylus refers to him as Zeus' lackey and errand-boy.[5] He was essentially the god of simple people, and that is perhaps sufficient reason why shepherds took him as their own and made him *nomios*, the protector of their flocks. His worship flourished particularly, and from a very early date, in Arcadia, land of shepherds—which may have been either cause or effect. There is little indeed to support those who see in his connexion with flocks and herds evidence for an original connexion with fertility. He is also the god of the market-place or assemblies of men, *agoraios*. This could be explained by his patronage of the common man, or by his astuteness which made him a particularly helpful ally in the driving of a bargain by Levantine methods. It is simpler, however, to account for it by nothing more than his visible presence, which need not originally have had anything to do with buying and selling. Where we have our market crosses, the Greek *agora* had its Herm,

[1] *Il.* xxiv, 331 ff. *Od.* x, 275 ff.

[2] ὅταν ἐν συλλόγῳ τινὶ σιωπὴ γένηται, τὸν Ἑρμῆν ἐπεισεληλυθέναι λέγουσιν (Plutarch, *de garrulitate*, 502 f.). Since Hermes was the messenger (*angelos*) of the gods, no great change has taken place in the saying.

[3] σοφώτατος θεῶν, Ar. *Peace* 428. The other epithets referred to are δόλιος, ἀλεξίκακος and ἐριούνιος. It is hardly necessary to recount his precocious exploit of carrying off Apollo's cattle, and the same Homeric Hymn illustrates his inventiveness in the making of the first lyre.

[4] Ἑρμαῖον. Nilsson suggests that the name may have arisen from the practice of laying an offering on the cairn which might benefit the next hungry traveller who passed that way and be ascribed by the finder to the grace of the god. (*Gr. Pop. Rel.* 8.) We know at any rate on the authority of Cornutus (first century A.D.) that anything picked up on the road was likely to be appropriated by the finder with the saying κοινὸς Ἑρμῆς. (*Theol.* xvi, 24, Lang.)

[5] *P.V.* 941 f.

and we are back again at our primeval upright stone from which so much of Hermes' nature seems to have taken its origin.

One problem remains. If the name Hermes is derived from the Greek word for a cairn, was he then a god of the immigrant Greeks, unknown to the land of Greece until their arrival? This problem has been recently, and most successfully, tackled by Jacqueline Chittenden.[1] There can be no question here of doing justice to her treatment of it, but we may attempt a summary of her conclusions. It is of course on the face of it unlikely that so primitive a custom as the worship or placation of the spirit in the stone-heap should have waited for the arrival of the Greeks. to become so embedded in the traditions of the land as we find it to be. Farnell had already noted certain things about the cult of Hermes which seemed to him to suggest a non-Hellenic origin, e.g. his aniconic form, the fact that his worship was most powerful in districts like Attica and Arcadia with deeply rooted Pelasgian traditions, his connexion with the earliest Arcadian genealogies, the Saturnalia-like practice at the Cretan Hermaia where masters and slaves changed places. Mrs. Chittenden adds his subordinate place among the Olympians, his thievishness, his connexion with early legendary characters like Odysseus, Perseus, Autolykos, his share in divine conflicts involving racial collisions (e.g. the clash with Apollo which ended in reconciliation), and the unwavering devotion to him of the common people. Moreover a connexion with Minoan religious customs is suggested by his cult in caves and on mountain tops (as on Mount Kyllene in Arcadia, near Patsos in Crete, on Mount Juktas in Crete and elsewhere), by his connexion with stone and pillar-cult (by no means confined to him among the Greek gods, but especially marked), and a certain connexion with tree-cults. In illustrating this Mrs. Chittenden shows that his famous staff, the caduceus, was in all probability originally of wood, and is sometimes depicted as having leaves and therefore living.[2] She adds also his power of winged flight, claiming that it antedates his function as the divine messenger and suggests an origin in Minoan bird-epiphanies. Proceeding to concrete monumental evidence from the Bronze Age, she is able to show that a number of representations from both Mycenae and

[1] See at present her article "The Master of Animals" in *Hesperia*, xvi (1947), 89 ff. Fuller details will be available in her forthcoming book.

[2] *Hesperia*, l.c., pl. xx a. Illustrations of other monuments referred to will be found among pls. xv to xxi.

Crete depict heaps of stones which have a clear religious significance. We may refer here to a glass plaque from a rock-cut tomb at Mycenae on which two animal-headed daemons hold libation-jugs over a large rough stone set on the top of a heap of smaller stones. The parallel with the Greek *hermaion* is exact, and a comparison with other representations from Minoan Crete makes it clear that the idea expressed belongs to the pre-Greek stratum.

The god of the stone-heaps, then, existed in Greece before the coming of the Greeks. But was he conceived of as similar in character to the Greek Hermes? Mrs. Chittenden says yes, on the following grounds. The outstanding characteristic of Hermes is his *protectiveness*, seen alike in his guidance and help to wayfarers and in his guardianship of the flocks. (With this we must certainly agree.) Now the chief danger incurred by both wayfarers and flocks in early Greece was from wild beasts. If Hermes could protect from these, he must have been believed to have some control over them, and this in fact he has, as we see from literature as early as the Homeric Hymn to Hermes, where it is said that he was not only enjoined by Apollo to tend the horned oxen that dwell in the fields, the horses and labouring mules, but was given dominion over fierce lions and sharp-tusked boars and dogs and flocks and all cattle that the wide earth nurtures.[1] There is moreover considerable evidence to connect him with hunters. We have noted already that on the red-figured vase showing Hermes standing upright in his heap of stones, a libation is being offered to him by Kephalos, who is doubtless soliciting his favour in the hunt. In front of him stands Artemis, dressed for the chase with two spears in her hand. This connexion of the god of the stone-heaps with wild animals is to be traced also in Minoan art. We see two wild goats with their forefeet on the cairn, also two lions with their forefeet on it, standing in heraldic attitudes. Moreover the same animal-headed daemons which were to be seen bringing libations to the "*hermaion*" also appear carrying the carcases of wild animals or showing their authority over them by placing their hands upon their heads. Finally the same scheme is repeated with a male human figure as the centre-piece, and in the subordinate positions either wild animals or the animal-headed daemons themselves. On one gem he places his hands on the heads of two of the daemons who carry libation-jugs. On another he actually holds

[1] Hom. Hymn Hermes, 567 ff.

them by their tongues. Again, he holds two lions, one by the throat and another by the hind leg, or places his hands on their heads.

The conclusion is that the male deity is a Master of Animals, corresponding in this to the goddess prominent in Minoan art who appears to have been a Mistress of Animals. The strange animal-headed daemons are his especial minions, in virtue of which they themselves have power over the beasts as he does. He is moreover the spirit of the stone-heaps, to which we see the same daemons offering libation, in its anthropomorphic form. This Minoan god combines the character of a spirit of the stone-heaps and a lord of the wild beasts. Hermes among the Greeks, and Hermes alone, does the same.

The interpretation of Minoan religion is difficult, owing to the exclusively archaeological nature of the evidence. In particular one would like to know what was the relationship between the Mistress and the Master of Animals, whether for instance it was anything like that suggested in the explanation of the *hieros gamos* offered earlier in this chapter. But as far as the origin of Hermes is concerned, it is difficult not to be convinced by this account.

What then of Hermes' Greek name? I have never been able to see any difficulty in the supposition that the Greeks, finding and paying homage to a friendly and helpful spirit of the country to which they had come, gave him their own title or nickname, which in this case Mrs. Chittenden translates as "Old Heapy". The suggestion as she puts it, like the rest of her argument, must be read in the light of her own reasoning and full presentation of the evidence, but on the question of name the position adopted surely does not need elaborate defence.

VI. Poseidon

Poseidon is a god who is generally supposed to be Greek in origin, though as to the meaning of his name there is truth in the remark of Roscher which may be rendered, "they have multiplied the interpretations but not increased the certainty".[1] There is however much to be said for the view maintained by Wilamowitz

[1] "Die Deutungen des Namens nehmen fortwährend an Zahl zu, aber nicht an sicherheit", *Lex. der Myth.* iii, 2789. On Poseidon cf. now F. Schachermeyr, *Poseidon und die Entstehung des griechischen Götterglaubens* (Bern, 1950).

that it means "consort of the Earth".[1] This is not in itself inconsistent with supposing him a god of water, since it is water that fertilizes the earth, but that is not the line that Wilamowitz took. Before we speak of his original nature, let us enumerate the chief of the functions which he seems to possess in historical times. First and foremost he is the god of the sea. In the division of the Universe between the three great brother-gods, as described in the *Iliad*, the sea was allotted to Poseidon, as the sky to Zeus and the underworld to Hades.[2] From Homer onwards the sea is his unchallenged domain, and his symbol the trident, or three-pronged fish-spear.[3] Those who displease him are at his mercy if they have to venture out in ships, as Odysseus found to his cost. Every sailor and fisherman therefore does his best to placate him, and to make him due offering after a safe voyage. And when the toils of life are over, it is in Poseidon's temple that the weary fisher hangs up his net and trident as he prays for a peaceful old age. Secondly he is the Earth-shaker, *Enosichthon*, *Ennosigaios*, and all earthquakes are his work. Thirdly he is *Hippios*, a god of horses, and himself at one time equine in shape. As such he was worshipped in many parts of Greece, particularly in Arcadia, where the story was told of how he met Demeter when she was wandering in search of Persephone. He pursued her, and to escape him she turned herself into a mare. He replied by turning himself into a stallion, and in that form caught her. This story was supposed to explain both Poseidon's epithet *Hippios* and the fact that at Phigaleia in Arcadia the ancient wooden image of Demeter had been in the shape of a woman with a horse's head.[4] He is lord of fresh water as well as salt, and many springs were attributed to a blow from his trident. The most famous is of course that which he struck from the rock of the Akropolis at Athens. Earlier still, in all probability, it was not a blow from the trident, but a stamp of his hoof, which caused them to gush forth. Many springs contain that suggestion in their names—Hippokrene, Aganippe, Hippe. According to tradition, it was the hoof of the winged horse Pegasos that was responsible for

[1] *Glaube*, i, 212 (*Πόσις Δᾶς*). The suggestion was originally made by Fick, supported by P. Kretschmer in 1909 (*Glotta*, i, 27 f. See discussion in Cook, *Zeus*, ii, 583 ff). It is supported by O. Kern in *Rel. d. Gr.* i, 44, and has, I think, the unusual distinction of not having been attacked on philological grounds. Those who disagree do so because they think the character and functions of the god can be more plausibly explained by another origin.

[2] Hom. *Il.* xv, 190 f.

[3] Aeschylus calls it an *ἰχθυβόλος μαχανά* (*Sept.* 131).

[4] Paus. viii, 25, 4; 42, 1.

Hippokrene, the fount of the Muses on Mount Helikon, but the universality of these "Hippo-" names makes it certain that this was not the original story, and we remember that as early as the *Iliad* Poseidon bears the name of Helikonios. Pegasos, whom Homer does not mention although he tells the story of Bellerophon, is in any case said by Hesiod to have been Poseidon's son.[1]

Now seeing that in historical times Poseidon's command of the sea completely overshadows his other characteristics, it used generally to be thought that it reflected his original nature; but it certainly leaves much unexplained. For his connexion with horses, some have suggested the metaphor whereby the waves are called "white horses". But not only is this figure nowhere used in extant Greek literature, it is very unlikely to have been a common one among a people whose sea was the Aegean.[2] It is the metaphor of northern peoples, who are more used to the rough, foam-capped waves of North Sea or Atlantic. Again, he is very emphatically the god of earthquakes. These may, it is true, be caused by inundation or erosion of the sea, but they are not true earthquakes, neither does it seem natural for a people in a land subject to earthquakes to attribute them generally to a sea-god. It is far commoner, as well as more mysterious and therefore divine, for them to come apparently from some hidden power within the earth.[3]

For reasons like these Wilamowitz put forth his view that the "husband of Earth", the *posis Das*, known to the Greeks as Poseidon or Poseidan (as well as in other dialectal forms), was originally a male spirit of fertility who dwells in the earth. At Troezen and Athens he was worshipped as *Phytalmios*, he who

[1] Hom. *Il.* xx, 404; vi, 155 ff., Hes. *Th.* 278 ff. Two examples in classical literature of P. as god of fresh-water springs: Aesch. *Sept.* 309: *ὕδωρ τε Διρκαῖον εὐτρεφέστατον πωμάτων ὅσων ἵησιν Ποσειδῶν ὁ γαιάοχος Τηθύος τε παῖδες*, and Plato *Critias* 113e (P. provides springs of water on the island of Atlantis). It has been argued that the cult of P. Helikonios refers not to Boeotian Helikon but to Achaean Helike, but this question has been satisfactorily dealt with by Farnell, *Cults*, iv, 28 f.

[2] As Rose has pointed out, *Hbk. Gr. Myth.* 63.

[3] Nilsson points out that river-spirits appear in the shape of horses, e.g. in Sweden and Scotland. He would explain thus both the equine nature of P. and his connexion with earthquakes, which he says may be caused by the habit that Greek rivers have of sinking into the ground and flowing in subterranean channels for long distances before breaking forth again. (*Hist. Gr. Rel.* 120, *Gr. Pop. Rel.* 11.) It is interesting to note that in modern Greece earthquakes are ascribed to "the god below" (*τὸν κάτω θεό*, J. C. Lawson, *Mod. Gr. Folklore and Anc. Gr. Rel.* (1910), p. 50). Lawson's informant said that in her island at least (Thera) this god no longer sent up water, though he used to. It is obviously difficult, and probably wrong, to distinguish between a spirit of fertility who dwells beneath the earth and a god of rivers, since the rivers both spring from underground and fertilize the fields.

makes the plants grow, and the story of his pursuit of and union with Demeter in Arcadia seems to point in the same direction. In discussing this story Rose admits the probability that it is "a very old tale indeed, in which a female and a male power of fertility unite and have offspring". These old powers were imagined in the form of horses. On Rose's supposition, these fertility-powers were pre-Greek, and the male became identified with Poseidon the sea-god because for other reasons Poseidon was already called Hippios. Of the epithet itself, he will only say that it is rather to be explained "as the result of the god's worship, we cannot now say from what causes, by horse-breeding peoples in northern Greece, probably Thessaly".[1]

One thing we can say, that if Poseidon was, as is generally agreed, a purely Hellenic god, if, that is to say, he did not originate in the peninsula of Greece but was brought there by immigrant Greek-speaking tribes, it is not likely that he was a sea-god from the start. Those who say that he is, and that the other aspects of his character were originally alien to him, tend to emphasize his Hellenic origin and the strong contrast which he presents to the gods of the original inhabitants of Greece. Yet it is unlikely that among peoples living high up in the Balkans or further north the sea and its god should occupy so outstanding a position as that of Poseidon, brother of Zeus. Wilamowitz goes on to point out (and he has the support of no less a philologist than A. Meillet) that the Greek language had originally no word for *sea*, corresponding to the Latin *mare* and its group of related words.[2] *Thalassa* is foreign. Confronted with the Mediterranean, the Greeks called it "the salt element" (ἅλς), "the flat expanse" (πέλαγος, equivalent in meaning to the Latin *aequor*), or "the way across" (πόντος, cf. πόρος and Latin *pons*).

Poseidon, then, if we may follow the lead of Wilamowitz, was *Gaiaochos* because he lived in the earth, from which he sent up springs and rivers of water to fertilize the land. In origin he will have been a figure similar to his brother Hades or Pluto, who was also, and remained, lord of the underworld, and resembled Poseidon again in being famous for his horses (*Klytopolos*). Besides horses, bulls were regularly sacrificed to Poseidon in some places,[3]

[1] *Hbk. Gr. Myth.* 63. For a full discussion of the epithet, which comes to much the same conclusion, see Farnell, *Cults*, iv, 14.

[2] Cf. A. Meillet, *Aperçu d'une Histoire de la Langue Grecque* (4th ed. 1935 or later), p. 12. Meillet, speaking purely as a philologist, makes the same point.

[3] See reff. in Farnell, *Cults*, iv, 95, n. 112.

and we have already noted the connexion of the bull with fertility.[1] Just as the horse suggests a connexion in the mind of the worshipper between spirits of fertility and of rivers,[2] so also does the bull, for river-spirits were commonly imagined by the Greeks in this form. To cite one well-known example out of many, it was in this shape that the river Acheloos wooed Deianeira and was overcome on her behalf by Herakles.[3] As a male spirit of fertility, the original Poseidon is a consort of the Earth, Ge or Da or Demeter. Farnell has noted that Demeter and Poseidon are often associated in cult, so that Plutarch went so far as to call Poseidon the sharer of Demeter's temple.[4] I have suggested (pp. 59 f. above) that such consorts, though necessary, had a minor part to play, and this is perhaps implied by his title, since on this hypothesis he had, properly speaking, no name of his own, but was simply known as "the spouse of Earth". He only became a great god when his original nature, and doubtless also the origin of his name, were forgotten, when he was assigned lordship over the new element that had entered into the life of the Hellenes and was to be for them, during the period when they were "separated off from the barbarians", their means of access to other lands, for some their livelihood, and to all an ever-present force that filled them with fascination and dread. The male fertility-spirits whom we have so far discussed have of course belonged to the Mediterranean precursors of the Greeks. Poseidon, we must note, was, on the suggestion here made, a figure in some ways similar but appearing in Indo-European lore. It is no wonder if his original nature was forgotten in the changed conditions under which the Hellenes lived during and after their migrations. Zeus himself had a connexion with fertility, which lingered through historical times in his character as a rain-bringer, but when his people left their native soil for a career of wandering and conquest, he, as their chief god, assumed functions more proper to their needs.

Once more we are groping in the fog, and putting forth conjectures, not free from objection. It may be that those are right who see in the first element of Poseidon's name a root meaning "moisture", or that contained in the first syllable of *potamos*, "river"; or Professor Cook, who adopts the interpretation "Lord

[1] p. 50, n. 1 above. [2] p. 96, n. 3 above.

[3] Soph. *Trach.* 9 ff. and 508: ὁ μὲν ἦν ποταμοῦ σθένος, ὑψικέρω τετραόρου φάσμα ταύρου, Ἀχελῷος.

[4] For examples of the association, see Farnell, *Cults*, iv, 6 f. Plutarch's words (*Quaest. Conv.* 668e) are διὸ καὶ Δήμητρος σύνναος ὁ Ποσειδῶν.

Zeus" and argues for an original identity of Zeus and Poseidon. (*Posis* meant "husband" because it originally meant "master", as its feminine form *potnia* continued to mean "mistress".) Both the uncertainty and the fact that most of the interpretations lead us far from the conception of Poseidon held by the Greeks whom we know, bring home once more the lesson that the study of origins can afford only a strictly limited assistance towards the understanding of the Greek religious mind.

VII. Artemis

I close this series of examples with two great goddesses, Artemis and Athena. In the history of Artemis we can see a change of character at least as complete as that of her brother Apollo from the non-Hellenic to the Hellenic. Her name does not appear to be Greek, and the goddess who bears it was first and foremost, and from a very early date, the πότνια θηρῶν as Homer calls her[1]—the Mistress of Wild Animals, who was one of the greatest, if not the greatest, of the deities worshipped by the inhabitants of pre-Hellenic Greece, of Western Asia Minor and of Minoan Crete. Flanked by wild beasts, she appears on a number of monuments, of which the earliest is the now well-known Cretan seal.[2] She must have had many names, for she was worshipped over a wide area by peoples who spoke different languages. In Phrygia she was Kybele, who yoked the lions to her car, and it is lions which stand beside the goddess both on the Cretan seal and the Boeotian vase. In Cappadocia she bore the expressive name of Ma, in Crete perhaps the name which the Greeks hellenized into Britomartis.[3] Where she was first called Artemis, it is difficult to say. Perhaps the Ephesian Artemis preserved her original name, just as in spite of

[1] *Il.* xxi, 470 f. τὸν δὲ κασιγνήτη μάλα νείκεσε, πότνια θηρῶν, Ἄρτεμις ἀγροτέρη.

[2] First published by Evans, *Ann. Brit. Sch. Ath.* vii (1900–1), 28 ff., fig .9. Conveniently illustrated by Jane Harrison, *Prolegomena to Gr. Rel.* (3rd ed. 1922) 497. Other early and interesting monuments of the Mistress of Wild Animals are a Boeotian vase, probably of the eighth century B.C., first published by P. Wolters in *Eph. Arch.* (1892), p. 212, pl. 10, 1, and reproduced by O. Kern in *Mitth. Deutsch. Arch. Inst. Ath.* 50 (1925), p. 160, fig. 1, and Farnell, *Cults*, ii, 522, pl. xxix, and an ivory relief of about the same date, said to have been found in or near Smyrna, published by Kern, o.c., pl. vii and pp. 162 f., and on a much smaller scale by Nilsson, *Gr. Pop. Rel.* fig. 5. Kern's article, in which he compares these representations in art with the description of Hekate in Hes. *Theog.* 411-52, is of considerable interest. (Nilsson now thinks the Smyrna relief may be a forgery, *Gesch. gr. Rel.* ii, corrections on p. 714).

[3] pp. 105 f. below.

the Greeks she retained much of her un-Greek character. But in the centre of Greece also, in Arcadia, the cult of the old goddess under that name seems to go back a very long way.

In this aspect Artemis had the epithet Agrotera, She of the Wild, used in Greek literature from Homer onwards. In particular she took the young of all creatures under her protection, as all readers of Greek poetry know from the passage in the *Agamemnon* describing her wrath at the sight of the two eagles cruelly devouring a hare with its unborn young in the womb: "The goddess out of her pity is angry with the winged hounds of the Father who slay the poor hare with her young before she is brought to labour." Similarly she is addressed as "thou who art gracious to the tender cubs of lions, and all the suckling young of roving beasts".[1]

As protectress of wild animals, she was also the patron goddess of hunters. This is not so contradictory as it sounds. The huntsman never regards himself as the enemy of the creatures he hunts. The fox is supposed to enjoy the chase, the owner of estates speaks of "preserving" game and likes to visit with heavy penalties those who disturb it at the wrong time or in the wrong way. Their sanction is now the law, but in ancient times it was religion. Perhaps the earliest example of a game preserve is the grove of Artemis where Agamemnon slew the deer and was visited by the wrath of the divine gamekeeper. Whatever the logic behind it, Artemis was the ancient St. Hubert, and, as with the saint, a stag was one of her most constant attributes. The huntsman has his own code of chivalry, and were Artemis worshipped to-day, her wrath would be invoked upon the man who shot a fox or a sitting bird. Xenophon actually notes, in his work on hunting, that hares below a certain age are left alone as sacred to the goddess.[2]

If Artemis protected the young of all species, including mankind,[3] it was for a very good reason, namely that she had originally been their mother. In Asia this aspect of her was especially

[1] Aesch. *Ag.* 134 ff.

[2] Xen. *Ven.* v, 14: *τὰ μὲν οὖν λίαν νεογνὰ (sc. τῶν λαγίων) οἱ φιλοκυνηγέται ἀφιᾶσι τῇ θεῷ (sc. Ἀρτέμιδι).* (Quoted by Farnell, *Cults*, ii, 563, n. 26k.)

[3] The cult-epithets *Παιδοτρόφος*, *Κουροτρόφος*, *Φιλομεῖραξ* vouched for by Pausanias and Diodorus (reff. in Gruppe, *Gr. Myth. und Religionsgesch.* ii, 1271, n. 0), are doubtless old. Kern (*Mitth. Deutsch. Arch. Inst. Ath.* (1925), p. 159), notes that she shares the epithet *Κουροτρόφος* with Demeter, Ge and Leto, as well as Hekate, Eirene and Hestia.

prominent, as we should expect, for we know that there the Olympian religion impressed on Greece by Homer had less power to suppress the more ancient forms of worship. The cult-images themselves of the Ephesian Artemis leave no doubt of it. The signs of her motherhood are so multiplied as to make her into a grotesque. Wherever worshipped, and under whatever name, she was the same goddess, the All-mother. We can trace this in Greece as well, where in Arcadia, the oldest centre of her worship, she was closely associated in cult with Demeter and Persephone. Herodotus says that Aeschylus actually called Artemis the daughter of Demeter, thus identifying her with Persephone the corn-goddess.[1] Vegetable as well as animal life was in her province. With less evidence than we now possess, Farnell concluded "that Artemis was in the earliest Greek religion an earth-goddess, associated essentially and chiefly with the wild life and growth of the field, and with human birth". Later research has tended to modify his view that she was originally Greek, but not to shake this account of her original function and character.

This was a goddess whom the Greeks must have found on every hand when they came to occupy Greece, Crete and parts of Asia Minor. It was useless to try to ignore her or to abolish her worship: she was far too powerful and her cult too deeply rooted. Yet this cult must in many ways have shocked them, since it involved ideas and practices contrasting sharply with the beliefs and customs that they brought with them. The contrast is well summed up by Gilbert Murray, in a sentence where he speaks of "the tradition of a Northern conquering race, organized on a patriarchal monogamous system vehemently distinct from the matrilinear customs of the Aegean and Hittite races, with their polygamy and polyandry, their agricultural rites, sex-emblems and fertility-goddesses".[2]

What then happened? The Greek genius for adaptation asserted

[1] Hdt. ii, 156. For this and other reff. see Farnell, *Cults*, ii, 572, n. 55.

[2] *Five Stages of Greek Religion* (1925), 80. It is interesting to note in passing, with Rose (*Hbk. Gr. Myth.* 113), the humiliations and indignities to which Artemis is subjected in Homer. Hera whips her with her own bow and sends her off the field weeping bitterly, which may reflect the feeling of a time when Hera was fully naturalized as an Olympian but Artemis not yet. We may add that the poet displays much the same lack of respect for Aphrodite, since Diomedes is allowed to wound her and make her beat an ignominious and tearful retreat. The reason is probably the same. I do not wish to extend this chapter to include her but she is doubtless in origin an Oriental mother-goddess.

itself, and though the name remained, the goddess whose primary characteristic had been her ever-fertile motherhood became the beautiful figure of the virgin huntress whose highest expression we see in the *Hippolytus* of Euripides. More probably the process was one of identification. That is to say, the Greek tribes may have worshipped a virgin huntress whom they identified with the more thoroughly female deities of the Aegean lands, seeing perhaps a connexion in the fact that both were powers of the world of wild nature and mistresses of the beasts. Alternatively they may have found already in Greece a Mistress of Animals in whom these Amazonian traits were more prominent, and the maternal less so, than in the Asiatic deities whom they assimilated to her. The surviving monuments of Minoan cult show no trace of maternal or sexual symbolism, though this by no means proves that (as has been suggested) the goddess was not regarded as a mother. In the Artemis-worship of Arcadia and neighbouring parts of the Peloponnese, which certainly goes back to pre-Homeric times and may or may not be actually pre-Greek, her character as a goddess of fertility is certainly indicated by sexual elements in the ritual.[1] Huntress Artemis doubtless was before the appearance of the Greeks. As mistress as well as mother of the beasts, she had to keep them in order. Kybele yoked the lions to her car, and on the Cretan seal the goddess who dominates the lions holds something in her hand which is doubtless no mere ceremonial staff of office but a genuinely useful weapon. She may even have been *parthenos*, the Greek word which is usually translated "virgin". This could happen in more than one way. In the first place, there is some evidence that the word did not always nor of necessity have that meaning. It might mean no more than unmarried, not tied by any bonds to a male who must be acknowledged as master. There were priestesses as well as deities in pre-Greek and Oriental cults who lived like that, but without preserving their virginity. Indeed, to sacrifice her virginity might be part of a priestess's service, but she did not sacrifice her freedom to a male nor become his property, as marriage in early times would imply.[2] Another possibility is also worth mentioning, to show that the distinction between pure maiden and mother, which seems to us a logical necessity,[3] was no stumbling-block to the Greeks. It was quite

[1] Nilsson, *Gesch. Gr. Rel.*, i (1941), 467.

[2] See e.g. Farnell, *Cults*, ii, 448 f., and the story of Atalanta on p. 443.

[3] Save with regard to the Christian belief in the Virgin Mother: this is another conception which was by no means foreign to pre-Christian antiquity.

commonly believed that virginity could be renewed periodically by a process of lustration. Pausanias[1] records this of Hera in the belief of the people of Nauplia and Argos. There was a spring at Nauplia called Kanathos, and the Argives said that every year Hera recovered her virginity by bathing in it. Pausanias adds that the story is taken from a mystery which they celebrate in Hera's honour. That is, the myth was based on a rite, which reminds us of the festival of the Plynteria at Athens, where the women took the old wooden image of the city's goddess and washed it in the sea. At Argos the same thing was done, the image of Athena being dipped in Inachos. This is a rite which has found a fine reflection in Greek literature, for so I think we may fairly designate the hymn of Callimachus *For the Bath of Pallas.*

There is perhaps no decisive evidence to say which of these possibilities represents the early feeling about the *parthenia* of Artemis, but if we are to judge by countless analogies—Kybele and Attis, Aphrodite and Adonis, Demeter and Triptolemos, Selene and Endymion on Latmos (which brings us near to Artemis herself)—she was probably thought of originally as having a youthful attendant and lover but no husband and lord such as Zeus became to Hera. Later, as the more Hellenic notion of strict virginity prevailed, the attendant remained, but like Hippolytus, was vowed to chastity as was the goddess herself. Whichever explanation of her original motherhood be correct, the fact itself sets her in strong contrast to the Artemis of classical Greece. Artemis was childless, as Plato says. She was however, as he goes on to say, a goddess of child-birth like Hera,[2] and she was worshipped by the title Locheia (*lochos*=child-birth) and identified with Eileithyia the goddess of child-birth herself. This is a strong indication that her own childlessness is not original, but that she was once, like Hera, a patron of women's life in all its phases and was therefore supposed to have experienced them all herself. Her own connexion with the moon, far stronger in later times than Hera's, may also find its explanation here.

For of course the traces of the Mother-goddess were not obliterated in the Artemis of the Greeks. At Ephesus her cult was carried on right through classical times in the old way. In Greece the memory of the past was preserved in particular in one interesting

[1] ii, 38, 2. See Cook, *Zeus*, iii, 224, n. 3 and reff. to modern literature there.

[2] *Theaet.* 149b: ἄλοχος οὖσα τὴν λοχείαν εἴληχε. Many other passages could be quoted, e.g. Aesch. *Suppl.* 676, Ἄρτεμιν ἑκάταν γυναικῶν λόχους ἐφορεύειν.

way, by attaching to her, among the nymphs who were her regular companions, some who themselves had amorous adventures which sometimes resulted in their becoming mothers. These myths, as might be expected, have no prominent place in literature, but are closely connected with cult and belong to particular localities. Thus in Arcadia, where the worship of Artemis seems to have been indigenous, we have the story of Kallisto, a young comrade of Artemis who wore the same dress and shared the hunt with her. As Pausanias tells the story, she was seduced by Zeus and turned into a bear by the jealous Hera, who then incited Artemis to shoot the bear. In another version it was Artemis herself who transformed her, in anger at the discovery that her follower had been unchaste. Zeus saved their son, who was Arkas, the ancestor of the Arcadian people. Euripides also alludes to the story.[1] Now in a later chapter of his book on Arcadia Pausanias describes the grave of Kallisto, a high mound with trees growing on it, and adds that on the summit there stood a sanctuary of Artemis surnamed *Kalliste*.[2] This epithet for Artemis occurs not only in literature but again in cult at Athens,[3] and together with the myth makes it clear enough that Kallisto was once the goddess herself. Further confirmation comes from the worship of Artemis *Brauronia* (from Brauron in Attica). In the *Lysistrata* of Aristophanes the chorus-leader, recounting the state-ceremonies in which she had participated as a girl, mentions the occasion when "wearing the saffron robe I was a bear at the Brauronian festival". The scholiast explains that it was the custom for selected young girls, in doing sacrifice to Artemis Brauronia, to mimic bears, clothed in the saffron robe mentioned.[4] The priestesses, or maiden worshippers of the goddess, are, in the words of Professor Cook, "regarded as the goddess incarnate and bearing the name of the animal specially connected with her divinity". "Such titles imply that the deity worshipped was originally believed to appear in animal form, and that the worshipper . . . pretends to be the animal in question."[5]

[1] Paus. viii, 3, 3; Eur. *Hel.* 375 ff.

[2] i.e. "The Fairest", Paus. viii, 35, 7. If Artemis was originally a bear-goddess, the epithet may well have arisen as a propitiatory euphemism, as A. B. Cook suggests (*Zeus*, ii, 1114, n. 0 (6)).

[3] Eur. *Hipp.* 66, 70–71; Paus. i, 29, 2.

[4] Ar. *Lys.* 645 with schol. quoted Farnell, *Cults*, ii, 564 f., n. 32. For the interpretation of such customs cf. Cook, *Zeus*, ii, 228, n. 4.

[5] *Zeus*, ii, 228, n. 4; i, 444. For reff. to modern literature on the cult of Kallisto see *Zeus*. ii, 1114, n. 0 (6).

Another of these female companions of Artemis was Britomartis, who, significantly, was Cretan, and had Minos for her suitor. Callimachus in his Hymn to Artemis tells of this nymph of Gortyna in Crete who was a huntress, and whom Artemis loved above the others. Minos pursued her for nine whole months, at the end of which, when almost in his clutches, she leaped off a cliff into the sea but was caught in some fishermen's nets and so saved. After this adventure the Cretans gave her the title of Diktynna (*diktys* =net), and, adds Callimachus, called the height off which she leaped Diktaion. In fact the Diktaean mountain is far inland in Crete. Now the identification of Artemis with Diktynna goes back to the time of Euripides and Aristophanes. A chorus of the *Iphigeneia in Tauris* prays to the "daughter of Leto, Diktynna of the mountains", and in the parody of a Euripidean monody which Aeschylus sings in the *Frogs* his heroine appeals for help to "Ye Cretans, children of Ida—come with your bows to the rescue, bestir yourselves, surround the house; and let Diktynna come, the fair maid Artemis with her pack of bitches".[1] The connexion of Diktynna with Mount Dikte is doubtless original, but has nothing to do with the fantastic and geographically impossible aetiological myth which the Greeks drew from a mistaken etymology. The Mother was a mountain-goddess, called after the most striking peak in her country, as Kybele was *Dea domina Dindymei* from the mountain of her Asiatic home. Diktynna in fact was a Cretan mother-goddess as also originally was Britomartis. Clear traces remain of the independent cult of both before they became attached to Artemis either as attendants or simply as alternative names for Artemis herself. After the syncretistic hymn of Callimachus it is difficult to separate the two, but it seems probable that Britomartis belonged originally to the east and Diktynna to the west of the island.[2] Herodotus mentions a temple of Diktynna in the town of Kydonia. There was also a promontory named Diktynnaion in the west of the island which recalls the story of Britomartis-Diktynna's leap and may have been its original location, confused by Callimachus with Mount Dikte in the east. The two place-names can hardly be unconnected however either with each other or with the goddess, and there is little profit here in probing further into Diktynna's home beyond the fact that it was in Crete.

[1] Eur. *I.T.* 126, Ar. *Frogs*, 1356 ff.

[2] PWK *Realenc.* s.v. Britomartis, iii, 880. For ancient testimonies to the cult o Diktynna and Britomartis see also Cook, *Zeus*, i, 541 f. with notes.

It is interesting to note, before we leave the pair, that both Diktynna and Britomartis were associated, at least in later times, with the Cretan Zeus.[1]

If there are inconsistencies in the character of Artemis as her Greek worshippers saw her, this should no longer appear inexplicable or merely foolish now that we are able to form some idea of the components from which that character grew. The worshippers were for the most part simple people, no philosophers of religion. How was it, one might ask, that the goddess who was devoted to complete chastity, and punished any breach of it in her followers with death, could yet find it in her heart to give kindly aid to women in child-birth? Contradictions like this show up the double nature of the tradition, but there is no need to suppose that they worried the Greeks so long as Hellenic religion remained a living and effective force.

VIII. Athena

As for Athena, Nilsson's description of her as a pre-Greek goddess who was the patron of Minoan or Mycenean princes has found general acceptance, which there is every reason to consider justified.[2] No Greek etymology suggests itself for her name. Nilsson sees her in a painting from Mycenae representing a goddess carrying a shield. She was the household goddess of Mycenean princes in their fortress-palaces, which would explain her connexion with handicrafts both of men and women, and in particular with weaving and spinning. Thus she is not primarily a warlike figure, but in her character as protector of the household naturally took on a martial aspect in a society of warlike and predatory barons. So at Athens she lived on the citadel (formerly, be it noted, the site of a Mycenean palace) and was the protector of the *polis*, saluted as such by the titles *Polias* and *Poliuchos*. For the Greeks too she retained her warlike aspect, her spear and shield. Among the few things that one can assert with confidence about Minoan religion, for which our evidence is entirely archaeological, are the worship of a snake-goddess and the prominence of tree-cults. These features seem to survive in Athena, whose constant companion was the snake and who had her sacred olive-

[1] Cook, *Zeus*, i, 541 f.

[2] Nilsson, *Hist. Gr. Rel.* 26, *Min.-Myc. Rel.* 417 ff.

tree on the Acropolis which was burned down by the Persians and grew again in a single night.

I cannot refrain from mentioning also the view of Professor A. B. Cook, which accounts for Athena's various attributes in a temptingly economical way, and acquires a certain probability by bringing an acknowledged pre-Greek goddess into line with what we know from elsewhere about the nature of pre-Greek religion in the Aegean. While it would be rash to say that all goddesses of the early Aegean peoples were local manifestations of the mountain-mother, it is nevertheless true—and we have had occasion to mention a number of examples already—that what we might call the Kybele or Dea Dindymene type was widespread, as is only natural among uncivilized people whose lives and thoughts revolve around the fertility of crops, beasts and men. I will quote Professor Cook's own words, omitting footnotes. "My own opinion —if I may be allowed to state it with dogmatic brevity—is this. The Akropolis at Athens was originally called *Athene*, a place-name comparable with the pre-Greek *Mykene*, *Pallene*, *Mitylene*, *Priene* etc. The old singular *Athene*, thanks to its locative form *Athenai*, gave rise to the new plural *Athenai*, just as *Mykene* came to be replaced by *Mykenai* or *Thebe* (*Thebaigenes*) by *Thebai*. The goddess was named *Athene* like the rock, because at the outset she *was* the rock, a mountain-mother of the usual Anatolian sort. In classical times her motherhood, perhaps comparable with renewed virginity, had passed into perpetual maidenhood."[1] "I take it then that Athena was the pre-Greek mountain-mother of the Akropolis rock. As such she would stand in specially close relation to the rock-products, whether vegetable or animal. Any life issuing from crevices or holes in the rock would be *her* life. The flora and fauna of the place would be venerated as divine manifestations of herself."[2] This, it is suggested, accounts for the attribution to her of the olive, the snake and the owl, all denizens of the Akropolis. This view of Cook's preserves much of the character given to the goddess by Nilsson. She is still pre-Greek, still the protector of the palace of a Mycenean lord. All would admit that the history of Athena is inextricably interwoven with that of her beloved Athens. By calling the goddess after the place instead of the place

[1] *Zeus*, iii, 224. For the singular form of Athens, cf. Hom. *Od.* vii, 80: *ἵκετο δ'εἰς Μαραθῶνα καὶ εὐρυάγυιαν 'Αθήνην*. The subject is Athena, and the sentence therefore states that *Athene* came to *Athene*! For the possibility of renewed virginity, see pp. 102 f. above.

[2] Ib., 749.

after the goddess, Cook simply gives her, in addition to her other characteristics, a specific local habitation from the first. He also emphasizes the likelihood, suggested by analogy, that a pre-Greek local goddess would be of the mountain-mother type.[1]

An interesting possibility is opened up by the name Pallas. Pallas Athene is so familiar a title of the goddess from Homer onwards that this second name seems to acquire more than the quality of an epithet. The one is her name as much as the other, and the priest in Sophocles' *Oedipus Tyrannus* speaks of "the two temples of Pallas" in Thebes.[2] It was an independent name, and the image of the goddess which fell miraculously from heaven was called the Palladion. *Pallas* is in all probability a Greek word meaning a girl. Classical Greek shows the forms *pallake* and *pallakis*, which were current in the sense of "concubine". As *pallax* it occurs with the meanings of both "girl" and "boy", the latter sense being preserved in the modern Greek *pallikari*.[3] This makes it likely that the invading Greeks themselves had a maiden-goddess, who considering their way of life may well have been a martial, Valkyrie-like figure, and that they identified her with the ancient and powerful native goddess when Hellenic and aboriginal civilizations came into contact. Possibly this may account for the transformation of Athena, if like others she was originally a mother-goddess, into the virgin of classical times who turned away in disgust from love and marriage. On this assumption the name *Pallas* would be the equivalent of those other titles, *Kore* and *Parthenos*, by which she was also known.

This has been no exhaustive study of origins. That was not its aim. I hope only that it has been a not uninteresting introduction to the subject, and sufficient to make clear three related points. First, we should be in a better position to estimate the tremendous achievement of the Greek epic bards, those unknown singers whose lays culiminated in the Homeric poems as we have them to-day, in creating the brilliant personalities of the Olympian family out of this welter of ill-defined deities or spirits who as one traces them back almost seem to merge into one another. Secondly, for all the uncertainties that remain, I have found that

[1] Nilsson however will not have it that Athena was ever a mother-goddess (*Gesch. Gr. Rel.* i (1941), 415).

[2] Line 20.

[3] For this etymology see Dümmler in PWK *Realenc.* ii, 2007. It is favoured by Liddell and Scott (9th ed. s.v. *Παλλάς*).

as I wrote about each deity in succession a fairly clear picture was gradually forming itself in my mind of the type of religion that must have existed in Greece before the coming of the Greeks, and I hope that a reading of the account may have produced the same result. Always one is brought back to the immense importance of the fertility of the soil, the dominance over men's lives of powerful Mother Earth and the spirits of plant and animal life. There is little or no conception of the Earth as a whole; the Mother who broods over the scene is the Mother of each man's village or *pays*. He must serve her constantly and understand, in order to further them, the processes by which she is impregnated and made fertile—processes imagined in the light of a belief that both earth and fertilizing force are personal beings sexually differentiated. We have seen also how this worship of the powers of fertility in both animal and vegetable kingdoms leads to the germs of a mystical conception of the relation between gods and men, so that by such means as dancing, cries and other stimulating sounds, and the sacrificial eating of the animal which embodies the *numen*, human youths can take to themselves its powers and call themselves by its name. The third point, closely connected with the first, is the large amount of truth in Herodotus' claim about the Greeks "separating themselves off" from what they regarded as the "foolish simplicity" of their predecessors. The reader can judge for himself how different are the spirits which modern research has recalled out of limbo from the divine creatures who stalk or flit through the pages of Greek poetry: Zeus at whose nod Olympus trembles but who himself can be caught nodding sometimes, the quarrelsome and jealous Hera, the calm majesty of Athena, the grace and frailty of Aphrodite, the terrible wrath of Poseidon, the beauty and cold, pitiless purity of Artemis, the friendly humanity of Hermes. The study of origins serves only to heighten our sense of the Greek achievement, though whether this achievement should properly be called religious, or rather an achievement in the intellectual or artistic field, it is too early in our exposition to say.

Appendix to Chapter II

The Twelve Gods

A German writer speaks of the schoolboy learning about the Twelve Gods in the classroom. Since this hardly applies to England to-day, a note on them may not be superfluous. The fullest account is that of O. Weinreich in Roscher's *Lexikon der Gr. und Röm. Mythologie*, s.v. *Zwölfgötter* (1936).

That the Twelve Gods (οἱ δώδεκα θεοί or simply οἱ δώδεκα) were conceived in classical times as a kind of corporate body is shown in several ways, for example in the erection of a single altar to them and in the oath "By the Twelve!" which we find in Aristophanes (*Knights*, 235). Thucydides (vi, 54) and Herodotus (vi, 108; ii, 7) both mention the altar to the Twelve at Athens, which according to Thucydides was set up in the agora by Peisistratos (grandson of the tyrant) and later enlarged by the Athenian people. From Herodotus we learn that distances were measured from it, as from Charing Cross or the Royal Exchange in London, and that it was a sanctuary for suppliants. Altars to them also existed at Olympia, where Pindar (*Ol.* x, 50 ff.) says that their cult was founded by Herakles. In this case there were six altars, each dedicated to a pair of gods.

The above are the earliest references to them in extant literature. There is no need here to go into the widespread applications of the number twelve, or the question whether an original sacredness attaching to the number was the reason why it was chosen to limit the divine canon. Weinreich, who discusses this fully, supposes their number to be a reflection of human corporate organization and concludes that they arose out of the foundation of the Ionian dodecapolis, that is, the twelve Ionian cities along the western fringe of Asia Minor, not later than the seventh century. It must, one would think, have been earlier, as the phrase of Wilamowitz (*Der Glaube*, i, 329), that the Twelve were united "in Ionia at a very early date", also seems to suggest.

The opinion of Carl Robert (*Archæologische Hermeneutik* (1919), p. 22), that the Twelve were known by their number because they were, even in the fifth and fourth centuries, "fearful daemons" without names, has found little support and is indeed ridiculous. Considering the shape of the Athenian altar (which from what

Thucydides says must have been oblong, not round), Weinreich conjectures that the gods were actually sculptured on it, and thinks it safe to assume that it was the Peisistratean Twelve who became the canonical, as we find them enumerated by later writers, e.g. Eudoxos the pupil of Plato, who assigned each one to a sign of the Zodiac. These twelve are: Zeus, Hera, Poseidon, Demeter, Apollo, Artemis, Ares, Aphrodite, Hermes, Athena, Hephaestus, Hestia. Plato himself in the *Laws* (828) proposed to connect each of the Twelve with a particular month, but he nowhere enumerates them all, presumably because their names could be taken for granted. A passage in the *Phaedrus* (246e f.) also seems to connect the twelve gods with the Zodiac. If so, this is something which Plato learned from Eudoxos.[1]

An actual representation of twelve gods was to be seen in the fifth century not very far from the altar of Peisistratos. This was the famous group which looked on at the Panathenaic festival from the east frieze of the Parthenon. They are the same as the list in Eudoxos with one exception. Dionysos replaces Hestia. Dionysos, a late intruder and hardly of Olympian stature, missed a place in the regular circle, but could not well be refused one on the Akropolis above his own theatre, at the time of the finest flowering of Attic drama. Hestia probably made way without much fuss, for as her name suggests, she was accustomed to stay at home when the other gods went out on holiday. This is just what we find her described as doing by Plato, in a passage which makes her a member of the Twelve and shows that for Plato at any rate they were no nameless daemons. Describing the procession of the gods across the heavens, led by Zeus in his winged chariot, he writes (*Phaedrus*, 246e): "Following on Zeus comes a host of gods and daemons, arranged in eleven companies; for Hestia remains alone in the house of the gods. The others are led by those who, as chiefs, are counted in the number of the Twelve, each in the rank assigned to him."

In classical times, as the example of the Parthenon frieze suggests, individual members, even if the list of Eudoxos was the canonical one, could vary from place to place. Many gods and daemons retained throughout the classical period a particular attachment to certain localities, and this loyalty to the local cult

[1] See A. J. Festugière, *Rev. de Phil.* xxi (1947), 17, 24. Festugière's article is noteworthy for the sober way in which it treats the question of Chaldean influence on Plato. Cf. also W. Koster, *Le Mythe de Platon, de Zarathustra et des Chaldéens* (Leiden, 1951) ch. 2: *Le Phèdre, les doctrines astrales.*

might lead to the ousting of one of the regular Twelve at a particular spot. Thus at Olympia the Titans Kronos and Rhea—elsewhere supplanted by the gods of the younger generation—and the river-god Alpheios took the places of Hephaistos, Demeter and Hestia. (Wilamowitz (*Der Glaube*, i, 329 n.) argues, from the evidence of Pindar and Herodotus, that this change was made between 470 and 400 B.C.) A philosophic writer like Plato, aiming at a reform of political and social organization, would also feel free to make modifications. He assigns the twelfth month to Pluto, in order to have a month devoted to the festivals of the underworld gods, who, he says, must be separated from the heavenly. This suggests that the introduction of Pluto was his own idea. Indeed he seems to think it needs some defence, for he goes on: "True warriors must cherish no repugnancy for such a deity of death, but venerate him as the constant benefactor of mankind, for union of soul with body, as I would assure you in all earnest, is in no way better than dissolution"[1]—a truly Platonic train of thought.

Despite such minor modifications, it is clear that the corporate conception of the Twelve retained its significance throughout and beyond the classical period, so that this collective expression called up definite associations in the mind of a Greek. With Zeus at their head and the clearly marked character which each possessed, they doubtless represented between them, as Weinreich suggests, all that was most typical in Hellenic religious, political and social ideas. We have only to think of the music of Apollo, the wisdom and guardianship of Athena, the war-like spirit of Ares, the sense of physical beauty in Aphrodite, Poseidon the patron of seafarers and Demeter of agricultural life, Hestia watching over the sanctity of family life and the common hearth of the city. To mark his championship of Hellenic ideals Alexander built an altar to the Twelve in India, at the furthest eastward point of his advance (Diodorus 17.95.1, quoted by Weinreich). The compactness and definite character of the Twelve probably had its origin in the conscious work of archaic priests and legislators. They mean more to the official and corporate life of a city than to the religious needs of the individual. It should hardly need emphasis that their embodiment of the Hellenic spirit in classical times has no bearing on the question of the origin and primal home of each one.

[1] *Laws* 828d (Taylor's translation.)

Chapter III

A CENTRAL PROBLEM

I HAVE said[1] that my theme might be described as an investigation into Greek views of the relations between man and god. What has gone before I regard as preliminary, and now in approaching the main theme I should like to draw attention to a curious contrast of which no reader of Greek literature can long be unaware. To explain the existence of this contrast would be to solve one of the most fundamental problems presented by Greek religious thought. There are other problems, and our survey here will of course be only partial. But an account of Greek religion which confines itself to the limits of a single volume, if it is to be of any value or interest, needs to be given unity by being built on the foundation of a definite question or questions to be answered, rather than attempting a diffuse and superficial survey of the whole field. At this point, then, I wish simply to state the underlying problem, which would easily be lost sight of in the detailed inquiry which must follow. One cannot always be making explicit reference to it, yet its solution will continue to be the goal, and the inquiry will only have point and coherence so long as it is borne in mind.

There seem to be two ways of regarding the relationship between man and god which at first sight are diametrically opposed, yet are both strongly represented in the Greek tradition. We become aware of the problem if we try to answer the question: Did the Greeks think it possible or desirable for man to emulate the gods? We probably think first of the many warnings against the folly of setting oneself up to vie with heaven, of "thinking high thoughts" and forgetting that, as Herodotus said, "the divine is jealous", a maxim which the whole of his history and many Greek myths seem designed to illustrate. Above all one would think of the attitude of Pindar, who drives home the same lesson in several places. "Seek not to become Zeus," he says. "For mortals a mortal lot is right." And again "Mortal minds must

[1] Introduction, p. xiii.

seek what is fitting at the hands of the gods, knowing what lies at our feet, and to what portion we are born. Strive not, my soul, for an immortal life, but use to the full the resources that are at thy command."[1] Tragedy offers plenty of examples, and the chorus in Euripides' *Bacchae* are repeating a commonplace when they utter words which may be paraphrased as "The cleverness of men is no real wisdom if it means forgetting their mortality".[2] This however is not the only attitude which has to be taken into account. What are we to say to the conception of man's religious duty which we find in Plato, namely that his aim should be "the completest possible assimilation to god", and the downright statement of his pupil Aristotle that man's chief end is "to put off mortality as far as possible"?[3] These philosophers lived a century and more after Pindar, but Empedocles, a contemporary from Sicily (an island not unknown to the Theban poet), greeted his fellow-citizens with the exultant cry: "All hail! I go about among you an immortal god, no longer a mortal!"[4] Pindar may even have read these words. How did he reconcile their fine abandon with his own prudent counsel?

Which idea, then, are we to take as the more truly representative of the Greek religious mind: that there was a great gulf between mortal and immortal, between man and god, and that for man to attempt to bridge it was *hybris* and could only end in disaster, or that there was a kinship between human and divine, and that it was the duty of man to live a life which would emphasize this kinship and make it as close as possible? Undoubtedly both ideas are strongly represented. It might be argued that Plato and Aristotle were philosophers, and that the immortality or divinity which they set before their hearers as the goal, signifying as it did the development of man's highest spiritual and intellectual potentialities, was something different from the competition with heaven against which the advocates of "mortal thoughts" sought to warn their fellows. But apart from Empedocles, we shall find other evidence that aspirations to divine status were by no means

[1] *Isth.* v, 14: *μὴ μάτευε Ζεὺς γενέσθαι . . . θνατὰ θνατοῖσι πρέπει.* *Pyth.* iii, 59: *χρὴ τὰ ἐοικότα παρ δαιμόνων μαστευέμεν θνατοῖς φρασὶν γνόντα τὸ παρ ποδός, οἵας εἰμὲν αἴσας· μή, φίλα ψυχά, βίον ἀθάνατον σπεῦδε, τὰν δ' ἔμπρακτον ἄντλει μαχανάν.*

[2] *Bacchae* 395 f. *τὸ σοφὸν δ' οὐ σοφία*
τό τε μὴ θνατὰ φρονεῖν.

[3] *Theaet.* 176b: *ὁμοίωσις θεῷ κατὰ τὸ δυνατόν,* *Eth. Nic.* x, 1177b, 33: *ἐφ' ὅσον ἐνδέχεται ἀθανατίζειν.*

[4] Fr. 112, 4 Diels.

foreign to the Greeks, that it was in fact their Hellenic background, the existence of such conceptions in the religious life of their age and country, which caused the philosophers to cast their exhortations in that particular form. In the religious thought of the classical period of Greek culture—say from the sixth to the fourth century B.C.—these two threads appear side by side, sometimes even interwoven. Yet they would appear to be the outcome of two fundamentally different types of religious consciousness. Where do they come from, and what were the influences acting on the poets and thinkers of Greece to make them take now one, now the other point of view? Can we disentangle them, or at least discover how far they can and should be disentangled? That is the question that I shall have in mind as I go on to examine some of the strains which made up the complex religion of classical Greece.

To say that two such apparently conflicting conceptions reflect two fundamentally different types of religious consciousness is to look back at them with the analytic gaze of a religious historian. We must beware of assuming too hastily that they appeared conflicting or fundamentally different to those who experienced them as living, and therefore as constantly shifting and changing modes of thought, and who were probably aware of all sorts of fine shades of belief which it is difficult or impossible to recapture at this distance. We may be certain that many things which seem inconsistent to us conveyed no consciousness of inconsistency to the people for whom they were living articles of faith or at least a part of their traditional religious heritage.

There is one more observation to be made at this stage, namely that we shall treat the concepts *god* or *divinity* and *immortal* as equivalents, because they were so for the Greeks. Gods may have other characteristics, but primarily and essentially they are the immortals, and it is their immortality which differentiates them from men. To say *gods* and *men*, the Greek might use the words *theoi* and *anthropoi*, but he might equally well use the words *athanatoi* and *thnetoi*. *Athanatos* (immortal) is an adjective, and may therefore be used in conjunction with *theos*. But it may equally well stand alone, and its meaning then is unambiguous: it means *god* and nothing else, just as *theos* does. It follows that to believe the soul to be immortal is to believe it to be divine. If man is immortal, then he is god. This is universal in Greek, and it is perhaps worth while drawing attention to it, seeing that we ourselves think differently. We also discuss the immortality of the soul. Some believe in it and some do not. But neither side is accustomed to regard the question as one of equating man with god. To the Greek the two were indissolubly bound together. Yet in glibly asking the question: "Did the Greeks believe in the immortality of the soul?", we are apt to forget the peculiar difficulties with which such a conception was for them bound up. To believe in the immortality of the soul was the same as saying: "Man is a kind of god." There were indeed Greeks who did not shrink from saying that, but let us first of all be clear in our minds about all that was involved in the statement.[1]

[1] As was Erwin Rohde (*Psyche*, Eng. trans., p. 253). I feel strongly the essential truth of the point made above, even though, so far as Homeric religion is concerned, it may seem to differ radically from the opinion of a scholar who commands respect. E. Ehnmark (*The Idea of God in Homer* (Uppsala, 1935), ch. 1), arguing that the essential attribute of the gods is power, writes: "For the believer the immortality of the gods cannot have been of very great importance. It mattered very little whether the god was immortal or not, whereas his power often manifested itself in a very tangible way." I am sure that it mattered a great deal, as the linguistic habit mentioned above is itself sufficient to show. In particular I cannot agree with Ehnmark's description of immortality as "a mere prolongation of life, which is in itself no quality". Examples adduced here and elsewhere in this book should suffice to show that for the Greek mortality and immortality differed in kind; the one is no more a mere indefinite prolongation of the other than eternity for the Platonist or Christian is a mere prolongation of time. The fact that, in Homeric belief, the shade of a man continues to exist after his death, serves only to emphasize this point. Men were not *athanatoi* on that account. In a footnote Ehnmark refers to the case of Menelaos, who, he says, "did not become a god when he was exempted from death". I shall have something to say about this case at a later stage (Ch. X, pp. 290 f. below). Here the conclusion may be briefly stated that (*a*) in the Homeric world the fate of Menelaos is peculiar; it is a prolongation of life *on earth*, granted explicitly by reason of his acquired kinship with the gods, and (*b*) this special case was seized on in a later and religiously maturer age and pressed into service as an argument for the potential immortality *and divinity* of man.

Chapter IV

GODS AND MEN IN HOMER

ἐξ ἀρχῆς καθ' Ὅμηρον ἐπεὶ μεμεθήκασι πάντες.

Since all men's thoughts have been shaped by Homer from the beginning.

Xenophanes

"TO the Homeric Greeks the state was not yet the centre of life. . . . On the other hand, Homer not only provided the foundation on which the Polis and the people of the Polis stood; he was their companion, always present to them, always alive with them, exerting a continuous and strong influence upon them."[1]

With these words no one could well disagree, and they must be my excuse for saying something on an already overworked subject about which I have little or nothing that is new to offer. So great was the authority of Homer that much in later Greek belief is either in fact a development of Homeric teaching[2] or was believed to be so by the Greeks. The latter circumstance is not irrelevant, since it meant that the reasons for following a certain religious practice, that is, the current belief behind it, might suffer considerable distortion in Greek minds owing to their sincere belief that it was not contrary to anything in Homer and their desire to respect his authority, although in fact the practice in question might have its origin in a different world from Homer's and have sprung from feelings incompatible with those of his heroes. It is true therefore, even though in a somewhat peculiar sense, that a great deal in later Greek religion is only a development of Homeric ideas. Owing to the existence of other strong influences, the development might go so far that the last stage was radically different from the first, but even so it rarely happened

[1] V. Ehrenberg, inaugural lecture at Prague, 1929, reprinted in *Aspects of the Ancient World* (1946), p. 4.

[2] If the Homeric poems were composed by people quite unconscious of being teachers and innocent of the intention, this does not make the use of the word any less appropriate. We are dealing with the effect of the poems, not the intentions of the bards.

that all traces of Homeric origin were lost. Often it is that which gives the key to something which would otherwise seem a curious and inconsequent series of ideas. It is true in the sense that the Greeks believed themselves to be following Homer and in that belief modified considerably certain parts of their religious inheritance from other sources. I shall suggest later that the Eleusinian mysteries show a striking example of this adaptation in the beliefs held about the different fates which awaited the souls of the initiated and the uninitiated.[1]

Our theme, then, demands some reference to the relations between gods and men in Homer, but the familiarity of Homeric religion may allow us to deal with it shortly. Professor Rose has shown convincingly that the key to its understanding lies in the organization of Homeric society. It is of course the religion of the chieftains and heroes which we learn of in the poems. Little or nothing is said of the religion of common people, which may have been very different. In the eyes of the warlike aristocracy gods and men together formed one society, organized on a basis of strongly marked class-distinctions as was the human society itself. The highest class of aristocrats were the gods, their relation to the whole of mankind is much the same as that of the king or chieftain (*basileus*) to the lower orders, and the analogy between the two—*basileis* and gods—is helpful in considering questions of mutual relationships and obligations, and of morality.[2]

That gods and goddesses were thought of in this way, as Agamemnon or Achilles, Helen or Arete raised to an even higher degree, brings them in one way closer to mankind, but in another way emphasizes the distance between them. They are closer to mankind in character. Certain faults are unsuited to the nobility, mainly because they detract from its dignity, but from all faults they are certainly not expected to be free. It is the same with the gods. They have a certain, though by our standards a rather crude, code of conduct. On the whole they will be expected to deal fairly, since petty fraud at least is beneath their dignity, but they will not hesitate to stoop to unfairness or deceit on occasion if it suits their purpose. Again, in the sphere of sexual morality, a person of the rank of Agamemnon or Achilles felt at liberty to take any woman whom he fancied from the lower orders. It was his

[1] Ch. X. VI below.

[2] See especially H. J. Rose, *Modern Methods in Classical Mythology* (St. Andrews, 1930), pp. 13 ff.

right, as one of kingly line, and indeed to be thus singled out was to be regarded as an honour by the recipient of his favours. There was certainly no stain on the character of either. The loves of gods for mortals form a parallel to this. Cruelty, provided again it be not too petty, is thought little of, either in the dealings of one of the kings with the people under his sway or in the behaviour of the gods towards their subjects, mankind as a whole. It is quite natural for Menelaos to speak of "clearing out a city" for Odysseus when he offers him a home in the Peloponnese. No one would question his right to do so, nor would they question any more the right of a god to act as he pleased towards men.[1] Since however the society was a courtly one, showing in fact a strong resemblance to the knightly chivalry of the Middle Ages, we find that side by side with cruelty or caprice in action goes a marked preference for the *suaviter in modo*. This does not indeed hold good, any more than it held good in medieval chivalry, between the upper class and the common men, but just as the *basileis* expected it from each other (save in exceptional outbursts of uncontrollable temper), so they had quite a high enough opinion of their own standing to expect it from the gods, for in spite of the difference of level they belonged to the same aristocratic circle. The conversation between Achilles and Athena at the beginning of the *Iliad* is instructive.[2] In his anger against Agamemnon Achilles was drawing his sword from its scabbard to strike him down, when Athena appeared, at Hera's bidding, to see that these two heroes did each other no harm. She stood behind him and took him by his fair hair, appearing to him alone. Achilles turned round in astonishment and recognized her at once, and he was the first to speak, asking her why she had come. Was it to witness the insolence of Agamemnon? "Then let me tell you," he went on, "that his arrogance will soon cost him his life." And the goddess replies, "I came to turn aside your wrath, if you will hearken to me", and goes on to promise him a threefold reward of rich gifts if he will put up with Agamemnon's provocation now. "I must needs respect your word and Hera's," answers Achilles, "bitter though my anger be.

[1] *Od.* iv, 63; Rose, o.c., p. 14.

[2] I owe this point to the book of Professor Bruno Snell of Hamburg, *Die Entdeckung des Geistes* (Hamburg, 1946). Snell's choice of words in commenting on the passage seems exactly right: "Welch vornehme Liebenswürdigkeit liegt in diesen drei kurzen Worten [*εἴ κε πίθηαι*, line 207]. Solche Sprechen setzt aristokratische Gesellschaftsformen voraus: höflich und ritterlich nimmt einer Rücksicht auf den anderen und zügelt die eigenen Ansprüche."

It is better thus. He who obeys the gods is hearkened to by them."

"If you will hearken to me", says Athena, and the hero replies that he will, for he knows it is better to do so, and if he does he may hope for something from the gods in return. He speaks as a free agent, almost as an equal, and the courtesies are preserved throughout. It may have been a polite fiction, for there was indeed little hope for one who set himself up against an immortal god, unless his case caused a split in the ranks of the immortals themselves so that he had a more powerful god on his side. Zeus' thunderbolts or the storms of Poseidon were weapons which no mortal could counter, but for the most part they were in the background and it was not good form to mention them in a conversation between a god and a man.

Gods, then, come near to men in having a moral character beset by many of the same frailties. In another way too they appear simply as the highest stratum of one complex society—and this no doubt goes far to account for the courtesies of intercourse and the fiction of equality which we have noticed—namely that men may be related to them by blood. The gods were captivated by mortal beauty. They mated with fair women and had offspring, and these offspring were the kings among men, with the titles "god-born" or "god-nurtured". Of the royal pair in Phaeacia, Alcinous was the grandson of Poseidon, and Arete his great-granddaughter: Achilles was the son of an immortal mother, the sea-goddess Thetis, by a mortal father; and so forth. Yet the children of these mixed marriages remained mortal. They had blood, not ichor, in their veins. Curiously enough, this conception of the gods, linking them morally and physically so closely to mankind, is the one which bars the way most effectively to any aspirations after divinity in man. It emphasizes rather than blurs the absolute division between the *thneton* and the *athanaton*. A more spiritual notion of divinity, such as later came to the surface in Greek religion, may make the division more shadowy, and hold out hopes of a different sort of relationship whose consummation is the merging of the two together.

There is no hint of this in Homer, nor is the reason far to seek. What made the gods approach our level was an element of human nature in them, not a hint of the divine in us. The parallel between god and earthly *basileus* holds good. Morally the kings or barons may share their failings with the lower orders, but in any matter affecting their prestige it goes ill with the unlucky being who tries to set himself up against them or do them any hurt. Treason, or disloyalty to the lord, is the unforgivable crime. Only one person in Homer is represented as being tortured. It is the serf Melanthios, the goatherd, because he tried to betray Odysseus his master, and the fate of the women of Penelope's household, who had committed the same offence against their lord, is likewise unparalleled.[1] Similarly when men are punished by the gods, it is not usually on moral grounds, because they have sinned in our sense of the word. They are punished for personal offences against the gods. The few who are condemned to eternal torment—Ixion, Tityos, Tantalos, Sisyphos—had personally affronted Zeus. Ixion had assaulted Hera. The only immorality involved was an infringement of Zeus' prerogative. The offence of Sisyphos was actually to have given away the secret of one of Zeus' own intrigues.[2] The myth of Prometheus, though first told for us in Hesiod, is an outstanding example of the same motive for divine punishment. His crime was that he tried to place in the hands of men powers which had been reserved for the gods. The resentment of Zeus was aroused because he feared for the continuance of his tyranny. As the story of Sisyphos shows, it is not for men to criticize or interfere with the actions of the gods, be they good or bad. The gods may criticize each other, and do so freely. Similarly Achilles may tell Agamemnon his opinion of him in no measured terms; but let Thersites, one of lower rank, try to do the same, and his ears are ignominiously boxed. It is not suggested that Agamemnon did not deserve the criticism, but it was not for such as Thersites to give it.

It is in this matter of rank, prestige and power that gods and men are so sharply divided. Herodotus makes Solon say: "I know that deity is full of envy and unstableness",[3] and the words carry no suggestion of impiety. They are a statement of a fact that was generally recognized. The surest way to arouse the jealousy of the gods was μὴ θνητὰ φρονεῖν, to forget your mortality. In this unbridgeable gulf between the mortal and the immortal lay the difference which gave the gods the right to act as cruelly and capriciously as they cared. They are the "easy livers" (ῥεῖα ζῴοντες) who never know death. Man is the creature of a season. It is in Homer that we first meet that pathetic simile to describe his

[1] *Od.* xxii, 169 ff., 465 ff. See Rose, o.c., 13.
[2] Rose l.c. and *Hbk. Gr. Myth.* 80 ff.
[3] i, 32, trans. Rose.

ephemeral nature, which found such a ready echo in the elegiac poets of Ionia: "Even as are the generations of leaves, so also are those of men. The leaves of this year the wind strows upon the earth, but the forest burgeoneth and putteth forth more. So of the generations of men one putteth forth and another ceaseth."[1] The attitude of the Homeric heroes to the possibility of a future life was one of complete pessimism. They were wealthy aristocrats who had won their position by physical prowess. The body was the source of their joy in life, for they had a full and zestful appreciation of its pleasures—sport, meat and drink, and love—and most of their life was spent in the enjoyment of these, or in war which was the means whereby they secured them. Consequently a robust physical frame was the *sine qua non* of happiness. Old age was a grievous evil no less than death, which in their eyes was the separation of the life of man, his *psyche*, from the body. It was not extinction, but meant dragging on an existence deprived of all that made life worth living. Hence the Homeric conception of the dead as strengthless, miserable wraiths, and hence the outburst of Achilles to Odysseus that he would rather be a labourer working for a poor man on earth than rule as a king among the dead.[2] It is safe to say that this statement was based on very little knowledge of what the life of a poor man's servant on earth was like.

This view of the Homeric gods, which explains their nature by an analogy, drawn in the minds of their worshippers, with the contemporary pattern of an earthly ruler, is shared by Nilsson, who writes that the model of the Homeric pantheon "is found solely in the feudal Mycenean kingship of which Homer has preserved traces easily recognizable", and that "the divine community is a copy of the conditions of the age of chivalry".[3] Whereas however we have here, following Rose, used this analogy to account in particular for their peculiar moral character, and the way in which, in their relations with mankind, most of the emphasis is laid on power and little on righteousness or justice, Nilsson on this point adopts a different explanation. He prefers to account for it

[1] *Il.* vi, 146 ff. οἵη περ φύλλων γενεή, τοίη δὲ καὶ ἀνδρῶν.
φύλλα τὰ μέν τ' ἄνεμος χαμάδις χέει, ἄλλα δέ θ' ὕλη
τηλεθόωσα φύει, ἔαρος δ' ἐπιγίγνεται ὥρη.
ὣς ἀνδρῶν γενεὴ ἣ μὲν φύει ἣ δ' ἀπολήγει.

[2] *Od.* xi, 489 ff.

[3] *Mycenean and Homeric Religion* (a lecture delivered in Cambridge and Manchester, 1936, and published in *Beitr. zur Religionswiss. der religionswiss. Ges. zu Stockholm*), p. 85; *Hist. Gr. Rel.* 146.

as something left over from their origin as nature-spirits. "Of all the numerous characteristics which the gods carried with them from their primitive origin on their journey towards a higher religious plane, characteristics to which the Homeric anthropomorphism gave such clearness and prominence, none was more fateful than the lack of any connexion with morality. . . . The power of the gods, and not its limitations, was present to the religious consciousness. The absence of morality preyed on the vital nerve of religious feeling. In proportion as the gods are Nature-gods, they have nothing to do with morals. The rain falls alike upon the just and the unjust. Animism implants in the gods human will and feeling, passions and caprices."[1] The contrast between the two explanations is instructive (and this is why I have thought it worth while to quote them both) because of their difference in kind. One scholar seeks to explain a phenomenon of a certain age by reference to a remote and misty past, whose reconstruction depends to a large extent on inference and analogy, the other relies on known characteristics of contemporary thought and society. My own preference should be clear by now, and perhaps a little more may be said in justification of it.

In Homer the will of a great man is his law. He does not so much do things because they are right. Rather, since he is an irresponsible aristocrat, they are right because he does them.[2] This can be illustrated very simply by the change in meaning undergone by one of the commonest of Greek words, the word *dike*. We translate it "justice", and something akin to that meaning it acquired very early. But whether or not its etymology connects it, as is probable, with the meaning "direction" or "way", the earliest sense of which we have record is that of the "customary behaviour" of any particular class. In this sense it is commonly used with a dependent genitive. This first example shows how far removed it was in the mind of the writer from any sense of "justice". The men of Ithaca have forgotten, complains Penelope, during the long absence of Odysseus, what an unusual king he was. "He never did nor said anything unfair among the people, though

[1] *Hist. Gr. Rel.* 152.

[2] That this was the once prevailing view about the gods, which was only with difficulty superseded in a more philosophic age by a different conception, is well illustrated by the question seriously debated in the *Euthyphro* of Plato, whether righteous acts are righteous because the gods love them or the gods love them because they are righteous.

that is the *dike* (the usual way) of god-like kings: one man will they hate, and favour another." In the following we may be sure that the meaning intended was the same, though they show how easily the word could slip from signifying no more than what was customary to indicating what was right and just. [Eumaios the swineherd to Odysseus:] "What I have to give is little, though gladly given; for that is the *dike* of (the way with) servants, who live in constant fear when young men are their lords." [The mother of Odysseus, when he tries to embrace her and finds that she is a mere bodiless shade:] "Nay this is the *dike* of (what happens to) mortals, when one of us dies." [Odysseus, in disguise, to Penelope, who has asked him who he is:] "Thou layest upon me fresh grief in addition to that which I already bear: for that is *dike* (for so it is) when a man is parted from his homeland so long as I now have been." A pleasant example is furnished by the meeting of Odysseus with his old father, whom he finds working in the fields like a common labourer. Odysseus congratulates him on his husbandry but suggests that he does not look the sort of man who should be doing this work. He should rather be in a position to enjoy his bath and his meal and then go comfortably off to sleep. "For that is the *dike* of old men." Here the word may indicate a habit or a right. No doubt Odysseus had both in mind and *dike* can easily mean both together.[1]

Justice, then, for the Greeks consisted first of all in doing what custom alone had established as being suitable for a particular station in life, whether that of serf *(dmos)*, king or even god. The gods, however, being the highest class, are also the most free. The slave does not dictate to his lord, nor a mortal to a god. The king dictates to his people, and gods to men. Hence *dike* for us is what the gods will. It is right because they will it, not vice versa. Nevertheless, as we have observed, one cannot help having a certain idea of how a king ought to behave. Neither cruelty nor a hot temper nor a roving eye for women is outside the *dike* of king or god, but certain types of baseness or pettiness are. It can hardly be called a high conception of divine morality, but it contained the seeds of an ethical religion. The word *dike* itself early acquired the thoroughly moral colouring which it has in Aeschylus, and when Euripides makes a character cry, "If the gods do aught

[1] *Od.* iv, 689 ff.; xiv, 58 ff.; xi, 218; xix, 167; xxiv, 254 f. The old sense was of course preserved in the later adverbial use of the accusative to mean "like", "after the manner of".

ugly,[1] they are no gods!", he could easily have maintained that his teaching was only that of Homer, who sang of gods who acted according to *dike*. If it seems important to make it clear that Homer and Euripides had different qualities in mind, it is no less important to understand how easy it was for a Greek to ignore the distinction. Both would profess their belief that the gods, if true gods, must follow *dike*, and though we may be aware that the word had radically changed its meaning, this cannot have been so obvious to those who used it.

It is not of course true that the only meaning of *dike* in Homer is what I have called the earlier one, and that all moral developments of the word must be sought in post-Homeric literature. This is perhaps a good place to remind ourselves of the inadequacy of throwing (as Wilamowitz put it) everything Homeric into the same pot. His reasoning was that if one passage seemed to show a more advanced morality than another, then that passage was later, and in this and other ways the great poems were chopped up. It is possible to be grateful to him for drawing our attention to the differences without following him in his explanation of their origin. Without denying that there are earlier and later elements in the Homeric poems, we may doubt whether this matter of moral "advance" provides a satisfactory criterion for distinguishing them. Even the general belief that the *Odyssey* is a later poem than the *Iliad*, which is doubtless right, could be as easily refuted as supported by arguments drawn from the moral atmosphere. Wilamowitz quotes in one place the joyful cry of Laertes when Odysseus announces his victory: "There are still gods on Olympus, if the suitors have really paid the penalty for their *hybris*."[2] Anything like this, he says, would be unthinkable in the *Iliad*. Yet all my examples of the earlier, non-moral sense of *dike* have been drawn from the *Odyssey*, simply because they were easier to find there,[3] and there is a passage, admittedly unique, in the *Iliad* which depicts Zeus as eager to punish wrongdoing. It describes, for the purposes of a simile, how Zeus sends a storm on an autumn day. The whole black earth is oppressed by it, and

[1] Or "low". The word may have been αἰσχρόν or φαῦλον. The line is fr. 292, 7 Nauck, from the *Bellerophontes*.

[2] *Od.* xxiv, 351 f.

[3] It would not however have been difficult to quote passages from the *Odyssey* illustrating the "higher" morality also. Nilsson has done so (*Hist. Gr. Rel.* 153), and adds: "But it is significant that these passages occur in the *Odyssey*." In my view there is no significance in this at all.

Zeus pours down a furious rain, because "he is heavy with anger against men, who in the assembly pass crooked judgments by force, and drive out justice [*dike*], heeding not the vengeance of the gods".[1] Since the vengeance of Zeus here takes the form of showing his powers as a nature-god, the passage does not altogether support Nilsson's view, just quoted, that "in proportion as the gods are nature-gods, they have nothing to do with morals". This criticism surely has force, even if it be right to say, as he does, that the passage "occurs in a simile and therefore in one of the newest parts".[2] We need not go into the vexed question of early and late elements in Homer, for if our interpretation of the divine morality is right, chronological considerations have little to do with it, and I have tried to show that they break down when applied to it. It is in fact perfectly possible for the various conceptions of right that we have mentioned to coexist in the same society at the same time, and their coexistence is very naturally explained in the way here suggested, namely by supposing that to the people of whom Homer wrote the analogy between their kings and their gods was a close one. This needs no lengthy repetition. In general the will of a king, or a god, is his law. Neither is above human passions, they indulge in jealousy and favouritism and sometimes use dubious means to secure the safety of their favourites. Yet they uphold the chivalrous code of their society, which includes for example the duty of hospitality and the sanctity of the oath, and there will always be certain things which are outside their *dike* on grounds of *noblesse oblige.* Once the notion of obligation is introduced, however, its extension is easy and inevitable, and will vary according to individual preference. If the Homeric gods exhibit a mixture, to us almost incomprehensible, of irresponsible power and crude moral ideas, there is no need to separate the passages which emphasize the one or the other and assign them to different periods. The mixture was there all the time, and only serves to strengthen their resemblance to the Homeric *basileus*, for in him alone is that peculiar combination repeated.

NOTE. An addendum to the discussion of the word *dike* may be of interest. Plato wrote his greatest work ostensibly for no other purpose than to discover what it (or its close correlative *dikaiosyne*) meant. Are we sometimes disappointed at the mouse-like

[1] *Il.* xvi, 384 ff.

[2] *Hist. Gr. Rel.* 153. Leaf, we must admit, argued that lines 387–8 are an interpolation by "a poet of the Hesiodean school". See his note ad loc.

result which finally emerges after his mountains of discussion? It is nothing more than τὰ ἑαυτοῦ πράττειν, to act in the way that is properly your own and not another's. The conclusion has a certain added interest when it appears that what Plato has done is to reject the meanings of the word which were current in his own day, and from which we have taken our translation of it as *justice*, and, with a historical sense that was doubtless unconscious, to go back to its original sense. It is rooted in the old Homeric idea of strict class-distinctions, and class-distinctions were the mainstay of Plato's aristocratic state.

For *dike* cf. now L. R. Palmer, *The Indo-European Origins of Greek Justice*, *Trans. Philol. Soc.* 1950, pp. 149-168.

Chapter V

THE CONTRIBUTION OF IONIA

Then said he unto me, Prophesy unto the wind, prophesy, son of man, and say to the wind, Thus saith the Lord God; Come from the four winds, O breath, and breathe upon these slain, that they may live. So I prophesied as he commanded me, and the breath came into them, and they lived.

Ezekiel xxxvii, 9, 10

I. The Poets

NEXT to Homer among the remains of Greek literature come, in strict chronology, the poems of Hesiod. Being the champion of the poor peasants of Boeotia, he naturally developes and upholds the conception of *dike* as justice, the rights of the weak against the strong. He also goes behind Homer in telling the genealogies of the gods and in the details which he gives of a time before the supremacy of Zeus, which in Homer is always an accomplished fact. Moreover he more than hints at a condition of the dead different from that to which they are condemned in Homer and reflecting an older stratum of belief. Some of his ideas will find their place later in this exposition. For the present let us turn to a literature and a society which, though they may be later than Hesiod, are far closer in spirit to the world of Homer which we have just left. This is the society of the Ionian Greeks who colonized part of the coast of Asia Minor or lived on the islands between that coast and Greece itself. It has left us some literary remains of the seventh and sixth centuries B.C. which, though scanty, reflect a fairly definite and consistent attitude to life. This legacy is twofold, and at first sight there seems to be little connexion between its two sides, which are, first, the poets of elegy and iambus, and secondly the earliest natural philosophers, who wrote in prose. Both have come down to us in sorry fragments, which should make one chary of generalizing from them, but they seem to have represented well enough the general tendency of the times they lived in. The seventh century in Ionia was the heyday of the aristocracy, to which the poets of the age belonged, enjoying the wealth, luxury and leisure consequent on commercial expansion and the fruits of colonization, and overshadowed by frequent raids, and threats of worse, from the growing power of Lydia. In conformity with this, the poetry is practically confined to two themes, reflecting either the joy of battle and the glory that attends the good fighter, or else a thorough appreciation of material pleasures and good living. This delight in martial prowess or in the joys of food, wine and love makes the present life alone worth caring for. The one shadow on the poet's enjoyment is the inevitable creeping on of old age and death, both of which he regards with feelings of unmixed horror. As for the gods, they did not give us these joys. We won them for ourselves. One thing they could have done for us: they could have given us the power to enjoy the sweets of youth for ever. This they have not done. Hence either the gods are careless and neglectful of mankind, or they appear solely in the light of tormentors. That at least seems to be the conclusion of Mimnermos. Others stress, like Homer, the pitiable impotence of man in face of the immortals.

Mimnermos of Kolophon, who was writing in the second half of the seventh century, is perhaps the best representative of this spirit. In him it finds expression thus:

> What life is there, what pleasure, without golden Aphrodite? May I die, as soon as I have no part in her ways. Stealthy wooing, lovers' gifts and lovers' union—these alone are flowers of youth worth plucking for man or woman. Once let old age come on, making a man evil and ugly at once, and heavy cares gnaw at the heart continually. No joy has he in seeing the sun's light, unhonoured by the young and despised by womankind. Thus bitter is old age, as the god hath willed.
>
> Like are we to the leaves that flowery springtime bears, when swiftly they wax strong beneath the rays of the sun. Like them we enjoy for a span the flowers of youth, knowing from the gods neither good nor evil. But the black fates stand by, and one holds in her hand the goal of bitter old age, the other that of death. Brief is the fruit of youth, no longer than the daily spread of the sunshine over the earth; but when once that springtime of life is past, then verily to die is better than life, for many are the ills that invade the heart.

Mimnermos goes on to catalogue these ills of later life—poverty, disease, childlessness. Other fragments harp on the same theme, which acquires the character of an obsession. "Aforetime fair, but when the prime of life is past, honoured neither as a father nor as a friend." "To Tithonos Zeus gave never-ending sorrow, for he gave him old age, more to be dreaded even than bitter death." "Shortlived as a dream is precious youth, and at once old age, bitter, shapeless, hangs overhead. Hateful and without honour is it, for it descends on a man and makes him of no account, striking his eyes and his wits."[1]

"Like are we to the leaves. . . ." It is the old Homeric simile. Another elegiac writer fits Homer's own hexameter into his verse, with the comment: "This was the best thing the Chian poet said."[2]

This joy in the delights of a fair and healthy body finds expression also, naturally enough, in the glorification of the warrior, exemplified in the verses of Kallinos of Ephesus, another elegiac poet of the middle of the seventh century. Glory is to be sought for the same fundamental reasons that moved Mimnermos to choose the life of pleasure, namely a deep-rooted fatalism and pessimism about the final outcome of existence. In Homer himself we find the belief in an awful power of Fate or Destiny (Moira), against which even the gods cannot stand. In the *Odyssey* it is said that not even the gods can save a man, though they love him, when the dread fate of death lays hold on him. In the *Iliad* no less a god than Zeus falls to lamenting because it is fate that his own son Sarpedon, dearest to him of mortals, must die by the hand of Patroklos.[3] Yet in the epics the providence of the gods for men is everywhere apparent. In these seventh-century poets the providence of the gods has disappeared, and men's lives seem dominated entirely by the black shadow of the Moirai. Thus Kallinos:

Honourable it is and glorious for a man to fight with foes for his country, his children and his wedded wife. As for death, it will come whenever the Fates with their spindle decide. . . . For in no way is it decreed that a man may escape death, though he have the Immortals themselves for forebears. He may retire and shun the fray and the javelin's blow, but in his house the Fate of death finds him out. Then

[1] Mimnermos, frr. 1-5 Diehl.

[2] Semonides of Amorgos fr. 29 Diehl. But there is some doubt whether Semonides is the author.

[3] *Od.* iii, 236; *Il.* xvi, 433. *Moira* means the portion or share allotted to a man. Much has been written on this important conception, e.g. by Cornford, *From Religion to Philosophy* (Arnold, 1912), especially chapters 1 and 2, Nilsson, *Hist. Gr. Rel.* (1925), 168 f. and most recently *Greek Piety* (1948), 52. For a full study see William C. Greene, *Moira: Fate, Good and Evil in Greek Thought* (Harvard, 1944). The Greeks personified and then pluralized it.

is he less loved and less regretted by the people, but the warrior if aught befall him is mourned by low and high, and in life is the equal of the demi-gods.

The iambics of Semonides, whose date also falls most probably within the seventh century and who may have been born on Samos, tell the same tale:

> My son, the end of all things is in the hand of Zeus the heavy thunderer. There is no wit in man. Creatures of a day, we live like cattle, knowing nothing of how the god will bring each one to his end. Hope and self-persuasion are the nourishment of us all as we seek the unattainable. [One man, he continues, is caught up by old age before he reaches his goal, others have wasting diseases, are taken off by war or shipwreck or commit suicide; and so it goes on.] Thus evil is with everything. Yea ten thousand dooms, woes and grief beyond speaking are the lot of mankind.

Simonides of Keos, born in the middle of the sixth century and surviving through the Persian Wars, travelled and cosmopolitan, knowing life at Athens and the courts of Thessalian and Sicilian princes, was a greater and more many-sided genius than these others. Quoted with lively interest by Aristophanes, Plato and Xenophon, he was in his own talents, as Croiset said of him, "presque un Athénien". Yet the same strain is noticeable in his lines, as indeed it ran like a black thread through Greek literature down to the late elegists of the Anthology.

> Men? Small is their strength, fruitless their cares, brief their life, toil upon toil. Death unescapable hangs over all alike, dealing impartially with good and bad.
>
> All wisdom is with God. In mortal life nothing is free from woe.

There is remarkably little of Greek poetry that can be called secular, but one is tempted to apply the epithet to the voluptuous melancholy of Mimnermos and the fatalism of some of his fellow Ionians. They affirm a belief in higher powers only to put forward an entirely negative view of their relation to human life.[1]

II. The Philosophers

Sixth-century Miletus, treated with especial consideration by the Persians when they became masters of Ionia, provided a somewhat similar soil for the growth of ideas. Under the Tyrants it

[1] Kallinos, fr. 1, lines 6 ff., Semonides, fr. 1, lines 1-22, Simonides, frr. 9, 10 Diehl.

was, says Herodotus, the pride and glory of Ionia, a city of immense commercial prosperity though disturbed during part of the century by periods of internal strife. Shipping, trade and industry combined to give it flourishing connexions from the Black Sea in the north and Egypt in the south to southern Italy in the west. This typically Ionian community produced in the intellectual sphere a phenomenon which seems very different from the poetry from which I have been quoting, and yet, curiously enough, was an equally typical product of the same race and circumstances. This was the Milesian or Ionian school of philosophers. At first sight there is little in common between the poetry of Mimnermos and the thought of men like Thales, Anaximander and Anaximenes, the founders of European natural philosophy. Yet both are typical products of the same general state of society, presupposing alike intellectual freedom, a high material standard of life, and abundant leisure. The spirit of their age and class was materialistic. Their interests lay in this world, they had not much faith in another, and seeing no reason to suppose that the gods had men's interests at heart, they felt at liberty to leave them alone. Poet and philosopher shared this outlook, though the one looked inward to the microcosm, mourned his ephemeral nature and took refuge in the consolations of love and wine, whereas for the other an interest in this world took the form of a consuming curiosity about the macrocosm. The gods had been politely shelved, and divine explanations of the origin and nature of the world were no longer tolerable. The question was raised, and raised for the first time, whether man's intellect could solve these problems without recourse to myth.

It looks perhaps as if the society and the writers among which we now find ourselves are, so far as that is possible, men without religion, and it may be wondered what contribution they can make to our subject, the Greek conception of the divine and its relation to human beings. Yet they have not taken us so far from it as might be thought, and we can bring ourselves back with a brief glance at some of the ideas of the Ionian philosophers.[1] For,

[1] It is emphatically brief, and written from one point of view only. If accounts of Milesian philosophy are wanted, they should be sought in Burnet's *Early Greek Philosophy* (A. & C. Black, 4th ed. 1930) or in the short but illuminating expositions of Cornford, *C.A.H.* iv, 538 ff., and *Before and After Socrates* (Cambridge, 1932) ch. I. For their contribution to religious thought, we have now Werner Jaeger's *Theology of the Early Greek Philosophers* (Oxford, 1947), which appeared after this chapter was written.

from our present point of view, the interesting thing about them is that they did not deny the existence of divinity—of *theoi* or a *theos*—or even ignore it. They made use of the word, but had their own conception of what they meant by it, a conception by no means without influence on the later religious thought of Greece, and it is worth pausing to consider what this conception may have been. Whatever it was, we must remember throughout that in their own opinion at least the Ionians were purely rationalistic; to them it was the result of reasoned argument and not of faith.

The problem to be solved presented itself to these pioneers simply in the form, What is the world made of? The first step was to seek "that simplification whereby the human mind flatters itself that, by reaching something it can clearly imagine, it has surprised the stronghold of reality in a wilderness of appearances far too multifarious for its comprehension".[1] They felt convinced that the apparently manifold variety of substances perceived in the world around us was in fact reducible to one single, primary substance which for some reason manifested itself to our senses in different forms, and they set themselves to discover what this primary substance was. Philosophy of course rests on the conviction that beneath apparent chaos there exists an underlying stability, hidden perhaps from sense but discernible to the reason. Somewhere there must be permanence. This applies to all philosophy, and a modern description of the philosophic mind might have been written especially for the Milesians:

"There seems to be a deep-rooted tendency in the human mind to seek what is identical, in the sense of something that persists through change. Consequently, the desire for explanation seems to be satisfied only by the discovery that what appears to be new and different was there all the time. Hence the search for an *underlying* identity, a persistent stuff, a substance that is conserved in spite of qualitative changes and in terms of which these changes can be explained."[2] At this early stage of thought it seemed as if the riddle of the Universe would be solved if the single "persistent stuff" could be discovered. There is a further question, which troubled Aristotle and seems a natural one to ask, namely, why

[1] F. M. Cornford, from an unpublished lecture.

[2] L. S. Stebbing, *A Modern Introduction to Logic* (Methuen, 1st ed. 1930, 2nd ed. 1933), p. 404. The italics are Miss Stebbing's, and draw attention to the close similarity of phraseology in Aristotle's repeated statement of the need for a *ὑποκείμενον* which *ὑπομένει* while its qualities *(πάθη, ἐναντία) μεταβάλλει*.

does this single stuff adopt these diverse forms? If a single stuff, why not a dead static world? What was the motive force which caused it to evolve and develope in this way, or as the Greek word for the process is usually translated, to become? This question was not yet raised explicitly. The early thinkers saw no need to postulate what the language of religion calls a creator and that of philosophy a first cause. They set themselves to discover the single, primary substance underlying everything in the changing world, but they did not see any necessity for an external cause by whose operation that substance underwent its changes. If they had already held the conception of dead, inert matter which became popular in later ages, and which it is difficult not to read back into their theories, this would argue an inexcusable blindness, and their rationalism would not be much to boast of. In fact however they were fully aware of the element of change and motion, and if they seem to be silent about it, making no reference to the need for an external agent, this is because they tacitly assumed the only possible alternative, namely that the primary stuff contained within itself the source of its own motion and change. When their choice fell upon one of the substances perceived by the senses, it was to water or air or fire that they looked for their primary principle. Aristotle remarks that none of the early monists made earth the primary substance,[1] though he sees no special significance in the fact. In accepting one of these elements as the sole fount of being, they had in mind its mobility. One thought of the ceaseless tossing of the sea, another of the rushing of the wind, another of the leaping and flickering of flame. They doubtless had subtler reasons too. In commenting on Thales' choice of water as the first principle, Aristotle suggests that "he got the notion perhaps from seeing that the nutriment of all things is moist, and that heat itself[2] is generated by the moist and kept alive by it . . . and that the seed of all creatures has a moist nature, and water is the origin of the nature of moist things".

These reasons are, as Aristotle makes clear, a matter of conjecture, but there is no need to reject them, as Burnet did, on the grounds that an interest in physiology only developed after Thales' time. No great interest in physiology is implied by the explana-

[1] *Metaph.* 989a4.

[2] Considered here as a necessary attribute of life. The connexion between heat and life, which is an obvious fact of experience in the animal world, was insisted on as essential and causative by the Greeks.

tion suggested. The reason why considerations of this sort are likely to have influenced Thales lies in his assumption that the primary substance contained within itself the power of initiating movement. The only known natural substances which contain such a power are organic substances, possessed of life. To say of something that it contains within itself the principle of change, growth and motion is tantamount to saying that it is alive. In Greek eyes it was always the primary and essential characteristic of life or soul (*psyche*) that it was the source of motion. Throughout the history of Greek philosophy it retained this as its essence,[1] and in so far as we know anything about Thales (whose own writings were already lost in the time of Aristotle) it was so described by him. "It appears from what is recorded about him", wrote Aristotle, "that Thales too conceived the *psyche* to be a motive force."[2] It is Aristotle also who says of Thales that he believed all things to be "full of gods", and connects it with the statement of "certain thinkers" that "soul is mingled in the whole".[3]

On these ostensibly rational grounds, therefore, that the primary substance, as the sole fount of being, must be the principle of change as well as providing the material substratum of the world, the Ionians believed that it must have life (hence the term hylozoists, "life-in-matter philosophers", which has been coined to describe them), and moreover, since the world is not ephemeral like the animals in it, eternal life. It was to denote this that they described it as *theos*, and these were the restrictions by which their use of the term was surrounded. It must have been in this sense that Thales said that everything was full of gods, as it was in this sense that Anaximander gave the name *theos* to the boundless and undifferentiated substance which in his view once filled the universe and was the matrix in which our world was formed. In the view of Anaximenes, the primary substance was air, and he therefore is represented as having said that air was *theos*. This doctrine was taken up and developed at Athens in the fifth century by his follower Diogenes of Apollonia, who emphasized in particular the point that air was not only the one original and eternal substance but also in its purest form the substance of all *psyche* in the universe, and hence had especial affinities with the soul in animals and human beings. His works have not survived entire, but Simplicius possessed his book *On Nature* and gives excerpts from it, in which the following passages occur:

[1] Cf. especially Plato, *Phaedrus*, 245e. [2] *De An.* i, 405a19. [3] Ibid. 411a7.

Mankind and the other animals live on air, by breathing; and it is to them both soul and mind.

The soul of all animals is the same, namely air which is warmer than the air outside, in which we live, though much colder than that near the sun.

In my opinion that which has intelligence is what men call air, and by it everything is directed, and it has power over all things; for it is just this substance which I hold to be God.

Theophrastus ascribes to him the doctrine which is a logical consequence of these statements, that "the air within us is a small portion of the god".[1]

Diogenes in particular seems to have exercised a great influence on his contemporaries. The doctrines just described do not sound as if they had much connexion with a living religion. The *theos* which they affirm seems no more than an abstraction of rudimentary physics, a useful scientific hypothesis. In all probability that is all that the Ionian philosophers intended it to be. Their motive seems to have been simple scientific curiosity, though perhaps our knowledge of their opinions is too fragmentary to enable us to pronounce this with certainty. We may never know exactly what was in Thales' mind when he said that all things were full of gods. But the evidence, which in the case of his successors is less tenuous, does not suggest that they had any use for the religious consciousness or any interest in satisfying it. On the other hand, unpromising as their ideas of divinity were, they seem to have been clutched at by people who in an age of doubt were seeking a faith to live by and a god to pray to. This is a phenomenon which can be seen in many ages, and not least in our own. Science makes itself felt, and demands that unreasoning faith shall give place to beliefs which have the sanction of the intellect. The effect of its impact is that some people are moved to give up all belief in higher powers. Others see no need for this, but modify their faith in conformity with the discoveries of science. Is the universe turning out to be nothing more than a series of mathematical formulas? Then, say some, there is no god: man is lord of the universe. Not at all, say others. It is only that we are always learning more about God's nature. Now we know that he is a mathematician. Similarly in Greece in the late fifth century, the new scientific theories were making the old belief in anthropomorphic

[1] Diog. Apoll. *ap.* Simpl. *Phys.* 152, 11; 152, 21. Theophr. *de Sens.* 42 = Ritter and Preller 210, 211, 210a = Diels-Kranz *Vors.*[5] ii, 59–61 (B.4 and 5) and p. 56 (A.19).

gods impossible for the educated and intelligent. Its whole roots seemed to be cut away. Some therefore declared themselves agnostic or even atheistic. Others adopted the alternative solution, and turned the new scientific conceptions into objects of worship. After all, it could be argued, the scientists themselves, who had discovered that everything came from air, and depended on air for its existence, called that air *theos*, and declared that it had eternal life and even consciousness and intellect. They held moreover that in its purest form it was that which gave life to the animals and ourselves, and constituted the thinking part of us. Of the popularity of this last theory we may perhaps judge from the parody of it in the *Clouds* of Aristophanes, where Socrates, asked why it is necessary for him to conduct his investigations while swinging aloft in a basket, replies: "I could never find out the truth about the phenomena of the heavens, if I did not hang up my mind and mingle my fine wit with the kindred air."[1] In one form or another, this opinion was shared by several of the early philosophers, but this passage probably owes its inspiration to Diogenes of Apollonia.

There was a further reason why these superficially materialistic theories could be seized upon and impressed into the service of religion. So far I have been writing as if the earliest physicists simply set themselves a question and proceeded to answer it out of their own heads, by a combination of observation and reasoned inference, with no preconceived notions save the one assumption common to all scientific thinkers that the apparent chaos of phenomena is capable of simplification. There must be one primary substance, and since there is motion in the world, it must be the originator of motion. Therefore it must be alive, and since the motion is everlasting, its life must be eternal. This is equivalent to saying that it must be divine. Now air is extremely subtle, mobile and frequently invisible,[2] and obviously of all known substances the best fitted to perform this part. Air must be the primary substance, therefore air is divine. Moreover as we live by breathing in air, no doubt the substance of our souls—that which gives life to us—is identical. Some such train of argument we have ascribed to them, and in so far as their reasoning was conscious it is clear that it followed these lines.

In fact however they were far from having arrived at their conclusions by the unaided light of reason, nor was the connexion

[1] *Clouds*, 227–30. [2] Not always, for the Greek word ἀήρ covers mist as well as air.

of air with *psyche* an invention of their own. No philosopher thinks in a vacuum,[1] least of all the first Europeans to attempt scientific thought. Without underestimating their achievement of stripping cosmology of its mythical dress and subjecting it to the examination of sceptical intellects, we may be sure that they could not at one bound free themselves from the mass of traditional ideas, some enshrined in poetry and others absorbed less perceptibly from popular lore, amid which they had grown up. The connexion of life with breath, and so with air, seemed obvious to the simplest and most primitive minds, and we meet it in contexts which were far from philosophic or even from the suspicion of philosophic influence. The Latin word for soul, *anima*, means both air and breath, and the history of the Greek *psyche* is the same.[2] The connexion is natural and inevitable, and was the basis of a number of popular superstitions. Among philosophers themselves, it is noteworthy how many different schools, with different theories and outlooks, find room for the same belief, which suggests that it was the invention of none of them but a presupposition common to all. We have already seen it exemplified in Anaximenes and Diogenes of Apollonia. It was probably shared by Herakleitos, though the passage in which it is attributed to him is not a direct quotation and the language may have taken on a Stoic colour. It runs: "This divine reason we draw in by respiration, as Herakleitos says, and thus become thinking creatures."[3] We find it also in the earliest atomists, for if, as in Aristotle's account, Demokritos distinguished the soul-particles in the air from the air itself with

[1] Cf. Cornford, *The Laws of Motion in Ancient Thought* (Inaugural Lecture, Cambridge, 1931), p. 12: "If we look beneath the surface of philosophic discussion, we find that its course is largely governed by assumptions that are seldom or never mentioned. I mean that groundwork of current conceptions shared by all men of any given culture and never mentioned because it is taken for granted." Also Whitehead, *Science and the Modern World* (1925), p. 71: "When you are criticizing the philosophy of an epoch, do not chiefly direct your attention to those intellectual positions which its exponents feel it necessary explicitly to defend. There will be some fundamental assumptions which adherents of all the various systems within the epoch unconsciously presuppose." (Quoted by Cornford, l.c.).

[2] For parallels in other languages see Tylor, *Primitive Culture*, I, 433; Karsten, *Origins of Religion*, 53. Anthropological literature does not suggest that the notion of the soul as breath or air was so distinctly conceived and isolated from other ideas (soul as shadow, soul in heart, etc.) by other peoples as it was among the Greeks, although the other views existed among them as well.

[3] Sext. Math. vii, 129 (Ritter and Preller, 41): *τοῦτον δὴ τὸν θεῖον λόγον καθ' Ἡράκλειτον δι' ἀναπνοῆς σπασάμενοι νοεροὶ γινόμεθα.* But cf. also Aristotle *de An.* I, 405a25. Respiration (*Ἀναπνοή*) was one of the new gods of the advanced thinkers of the fifth century B.C., by which the comic Socrates is made to swear in the *Clouds* (627).

which we breathed them in, this is not so important as that he subscribed to the general notion that it is by breathing in air that we acquire the life-principle, which he of course, above all others, regarded as material. The passage in Aristotle runs: "For in the air there are many of those particles which he [Demokritos] calls mind and soul. Hence, when we breathe and the air enters, these enter along with it, and by their action cancel the pressure [*sc.* of the surrounding atmosphere which presses them *out* of our bodies], thus preventing the expulsion of the soul which resides in the animal. This explains why life and death are bound up with the taking in and letting out of breath; for death occurs when the compression by the surrounding air gains the upper hand, and, the animal being unable to respire, the air from outside can no longer enter and counteract the compression."[1]

The connexion of these theories with popular belief may be illustrated from Plato's *Phaedo*, where Kebes mentions the fears of the ordinary man that the soul may not be immortal, but that when a man dies and it leaves his body "it goes forth like breath or smoke and is scattered, gone, vanished, and no longer exists anywhere". Socrates rallies him and Simmias for being influenced by "the fear that children have, lest it be true that when the soul leaves the body the wind blows it away and scatters it, especially if one happens to die not on a calm day but in a gale!"[2]

The connexion of the soul with air and wind was evidently not thought by everyone to be a bar to its immortality, and it is interesting to see the same idea put forward by two schools of thought so far apart as the atomists and the Orphics, the one purely scientific, denying the existence of a purpose in nature and any interference by divine powers in human life, denying above all things the possibility of an immortal soul, and the other preaching a mystical form of religion, of which the immortality of the soul, and the striving after its union with the divine, formed the very heart and core. One would have thought they could have nothing in common, yet we are told, again on the authority of Aristotle, that "the account in the Orphic verses, as they are called, says that the soul comes in from space as we breathe, borne by the winds".[3]

[1] *de resp.* 472a8, trans. G. R. T. Ross.

[2] *Phaedo* 69e–70a, 77d,e. The comparison of the *psyche* to smoke (*καπνός*) occurs in Homer.

[3] *de an.* i, 410b28: *τοῦτο δὲ πέπονθε καὶ ὁ ἐν τοῖς Ὀρφικοῖς ἔπεσι καλούμενος λόγος· φησὶ γὰρ τὴν ψυχὴν ἐκ τοῦ ὅλου εἰσίεναι ἀναπνεόντων, φερομένην ὑπὸ τῶν ἀνέμων.*

A dogma propounded in the Orphic writings is likely to be shared by the Pythagoreans, and in Diogenes Laertius we find ascribed to Pythagoras the belief that "the faculties of the soul are winds".[1]

Diogenes Laertius is an authority of the Christian era, and if we were so far to forget our primary aim as to be drawn into the Graeco-Roman world, we should find the topic assuming large dimensions indeed. Stoic modifications of the idea would alone provide material for long discussion. Let us withdraw then, after simply noticing its persistence in one of the more amusing examples. Lucian's *Vera Historia* is an account of a wonderful voyage by land, sea and air carried out in a manner reminiscent of the Baron Munchausen. In the course of it his party reach the moon, where among other things they find that children are born in a different way from those on earth. "They are born lifeless, and they bring them to life by laying them out with their mouths open towards the winds."[2] Even in classical Greece, the belief in the kinship of the life-principle in animals with air or wind had already given rise to a number of curious ramifications. There is for instance the complementary notion that a female could be impregnated by the wind. This is suggested as early as Homer, for in the *Iliad* the horses of Achilles were born by their mother Podarge to "the wind Zephyros". The wind-impregnation of mares is elaborated in picturesque detail by Virgil in a well-known passage of the *Georgics.*[3] Wind-impregnation seems to have been taken quite seriously in antiquity, though it was thought that the eggs of birds conceived in this way were sterile. They were called wind-eggs or zephyr-eggs, because, says Aristotle, "in springtime the birds are observed to inhale the breezes", just like Virgil's mares.[4] To des-

[1] D.L. viii, 30: *τοὺς δὲ λόγους ψυχῆς ἀνέμους εἶναι.* The translation "faculties" is R. D. Hicks' (Loeb ed.). D.L. also gives a grotesque example of the doctrine among the Pythagoreans when he connects the ban on eating beans with their general prohibition against eating living creatures, on the grounds of their flatulent effect! (viii, 24.) With *ἐκ τοῦ ὅλου* in Aristotle's account of the Orphic view, cf. Cicero, *N.D.* i, 11, 27 of Pythagoras: "animum esse per naturam rerum omnem intentum et commeantem, ex quo nostri animi carperentur".

[2] *Ver. Hist.* i, 22. Cf. Diogenes of Apollonia A28 (*Vors.*[5] ii, p. 57) *γεννᾶσθαι μὲν τὰ βρέφη ἄψυχα.*

[3] *Il.* xvi, 150: *Ζεφύρῳ ἀνέμῳ* , cf. Virg. *Georg.* iii, 271 ff.

[4] *ὑπηνέμιον, ἀνεμιαῖον,* Arist. *Hist. Anim.* 559b20, 560a6, and see other reff. in note to D'Arcy Thomson's translation (Oxford, 1910), *ad* 559b20. He observes that these eggs manifestly appeared to possess *ψυχή* but only the *θρεπτικὴ ψυχή* of the lowest form of life. The male provides the *αἰσθητικὴ ψυχή* necessary to an animal. More reff. will be found in *Orpheus and Gr. Rel.*, where I have discussed the belief in relation to Orphic literature (pp. 94 f., ch. iv, n. 17). Add Plato, *Theaet.* 151e.

cend to Lucian again, it is interesting to find him describing Hephaistos as a "wind-child", to indicate that Hera bore him without recourse to her husband.[1]

The purpose of this diverse and somewhat arbitrary array of authorities, apart from the intrinsic attraction of their curious subject, is to show that the doctrine that our souls are air, or of a material substance closely akin to air and entering wind-borne into our bodies, was not the property of any single philosophical school, but antedated all philosophical schools whatsoever. It was a common assumption which can be traced back to Homer, and is vaguely paralleled among primitive peoples.[2] They show moreover that the belief could be interpreted and twisted in curiously different ways to serve the needs of violently conflicting philosophical and religious schools. This emerged in particular from the citations of Demokritos on the one hand and the Orphic literature on the other. The atomists we may leave, since it is the religious and not the scientific twist that we wish to follow here. The religious mind, supported by the edifice of theory which the philosophers had erected on the foundations of ancestral belief, could without difficulty find comfort in some such train of thought as this. The air is of kindred substance to our souls, that is, it is alive (ἔμψυχον). At its purest, it must be the highest form of soul or life. Untrammelled by mortal bodies, it is clearly immortal, and the purity which it attains in the upper reaches (so pure and brilliant in the eyes of the sun-blessed Greeks that they called the upper air by a different name, *aither*) is such that it must be a very high and intelligent form of life indeed. What else can one call such life but God? The mystically minded could deduce from these same premisses a satisfying promise of immortality for man, not necessarily a personal immortality, for that is not what the mystic seeks, but union after death with this all-embracing, all-pervading deity.

It seems therefore that the air-god of the Ionian philosophers, with which we started, was not so far removed as might be supposed from the religious aspirations of men whose minds were very different. Aristophanes was a parodist. He took no imaginary tendencies as the subject of his mockery, and there is a genuine ring of solemnity about the opening of the prayer which Socrates

[1] Lucian, *de Sacrif.* 6: *ἄνευ τῆς πρὸς τὸν ἄνδρα ὁμιλίας ὑπηνέμιον αὐτὴν (sc. τὴν Ἥραν) παῖδα γεννῆσαι τὸν Ἥφαιστον.*

[2] Cf. p. 138, n. 2 above.

is made to utter in the *Clouds*, where he plays the part of leader of a religious *thiasos*:

> O Lord and Master, measureless Air, who sustainest the Earth aloft . . .

Euripides in the *Frogs* is made to pray to "*Aither* on whom I pasture", and there is little doubt that the same attempt to convert philosophical speculation into religious faith is behind the prayer which he puts into the mouth of Hecuba in his own play of the *Troades*:

> O thou who at once art prop and stay of the Earth and broodest over it, whosoever thou art, hard to divine or know—Zeus, be thou compelling force of nature or the mind of man, to thee I pray. For treading thy noiseless way thou leadest aright all the things of mortals.[1]

To this utterance Menelaus not unnaturally replies: "What is this? Strange prayers dost thou fashion to the gods." That which props the earth below[2] and is over it as well, which is at the same time the directing force in nature (as Diogenes of Apollonia said) and identical with the reason in man, and whose path is noiseless—what is it but Air, which has for a Euripides usurped the name and dignity of Zeus? The promotion of Air to the position of highest among the gods is more directly vouched for by Philemon, a poet of the New Comedy contemporary with Menander:

> I am he from whom none can hide, in any act which he may do, or be about to do, or have done in the past, be he god or man. Air is my name, but one might also call me Zeus. I, as a god should be, am everywhere—here in Athens, in Patrae, in Sicily, in all cities, in every home, in every one of you. There is no place where is not Air. And he who is present everywhere, because he is everywhere of necessity knows everything.[3]

Not only does the comic poet find no religious disadvantages in the adaptation of scientific theory; he even claims to prove that the gods which it provides possess more of the attributes proper

[1] Ar. *Clouds*, 264, *Frogs*, 892, Eur. *Troades*, 884 ff. With *αἰθήρ* Zeus is explicitly identified in a fragment of Euripides (fr. 877, *αἰθήρ . . . Ζεὺς ὃς ἀνθρώποις ὀνομάζεται*). See Rohde, *Psyche* (Eng. trans. 1925), p. 437. I was glad to find after writing the above, that Professor W. Jaeger agrees with this interpretation of *Troades*, 884 ff. (*Theology of the Early Greek Philosophers* (Oxford, 1947), p. 243.) Cf. the very similar language in fr. 941 (Nauck) of Euripides.

[2] Cf. the doctrine attributed to Anaximenes: *τὴν δὲ γῆν πλατεῖαν εἶναι ἐπ' ἀέρος ὀχουμένην*. The words in the *Troades* are *ὦ γῆς ὄχημα*.

[3] Philemon fr. 91, Kock, ii, 505 = Diels-Kranz *Vors.*[5] ii, 68.

to divinity than the old Homeric pantheon, or at least that they can possess them more easily and credibly. It is a natural and hoped-for characteristic of a god to be everywhere at once, even in the hearts of men, and to know everything. Yet how much easier to believe this of the new Zeus, of the Air, than of the old anthropomorphic Zeus who ruled from his palace on Mount Olympus!

III. Conclusions of Chapters IV and V

Greek conceptions of divinity were made up of many strains. After looking at two, it will be as well to pause before going on to others and recapitulate the data which they provide for our main question of the relation between gods and men. The lesson of Homer is clear, that men must keep their distance and not aspire to higher spheres. The gods go their way and we ours, and the two are essentially different. On the moral side, this religion showed itself capable of considerable development. Even in Homer, some of the meaner vices are not thought to consort well with divinity, and the gods are men's teachers in certain elementary moral virtues, such as the duty of hospitality and the sacredness of the oath, which were especially important to the chivalrous society which the poems describe. On the whole however the *dike* of the gods contained as yet no necessary implication of moral righteousness: it was simply the way they chose to behave. Yet we saw how inevitably and quickly associations of righteousness began to gather round the word, until finally they gave it its almost invariable meaning, and Justice became the companion of Zeus. Such changes in moral and religious outlook were the natural accompaniment of social changes. Between the *dike* of Homer and the *dike* of Aeschylus lies the break-up of the Homeric community of kings and a subsequent period of movement and turmoil in which aristocracies were established in Greek cities, poverty and wealth existed side by side and the discontent of the poor became for the first time vocal as it already is in Hesiod. Colonies were founded and flourished, aristocrats like Theognis hardened and became more violent and oppressive in reaction from the growing restiveness of the unprivileged and met their fate at the hands of tyrants entrusted with power in the name of the people. As the outcome of these struggles the Greek conception of democracy was born. These things may be read of elsewhere. I mention them only as a reminder that Greek ideas of justice and of the gods were not modified and developed by academic theologians but hammered out on an anvil of strife, even of party-strife, from which a Greek writer on religion, and still more the popular Greek mind, was never far removed.

How shall we sum up the other conception of deity, that which received such unexpected impetus from the speculations of the physical philosophers? At first it seems to be no deity at all, or none that could be of any interest to the religious mind. But we saw how it was taken up by thoughtful men who felt the need of a religion in the days when the old despots of Olympus could no longer appeal to an intelligent believer. Once again we are witnessing the birth of religious concepts which, crude and ungainly as they still are, contain remarkable possibilities of development. To pray to the air as supreme god is no doubt a grotesquely materialistic notion which fully deserved the attentions of the comic poets. But take the language alone, even as it is caricatured in the passage of Philemon, and it bears comparison with the Stoicizing language of St. Paul: "In Him we live and move and have our being." The later philosophy of Stoicism was in its physical assumptions a materialistic pantheism, but in its religious language, the prayer of Kleanthes or the meditations of Marcus Aurelius, it approached sublimity. This language was being formed in the fifth and fourth centuries B.C., and its importance should not be underrated. Language can stimulate thought. At the lowest it provides a framework within which the mind can develope, and without which its progress is seriously hampered, even if the higher concepts which were to follow lay far beyond the grasp of those who first expressed in these phrases their early groping after spiritual truths.

Chapter VI

DIONYSOS

THE worship of Dionysos is something which can never be wholly explained. Historical research into his antecedents and the adduction of anthropological parallels have done much, but not all. It is useless to try to account for his nature by an origin in one single functional type, such as that of the vegetation-god, however many characteristics of that type he may display. Always there is something more. From the story of his miraculous birth onwards, there are strange, unique elements in his myths and cult for which it is impossible to find exact analogies. This in itself helps to account for the extraordinary hold that he obtained over men's minds, a hold not relinquished even to-day, so that the task of describing him is made more difficult by the fact that many modern writers have inevitably had their emotions stirred, either to sympathy or to hostility, by this incomprehensible and imperious stranger in the midst. A German scholar affirms that for the finest spirits among his countrymen this god of the Greeks has been "a sacred name and an unfathomable symbol",[1] and no very deep acquaintance with the best German thought and poetry is necessary to vouch for the truth of the claim. Perhaps it is no bad thing to have a definite attitude towards him, provided one is on one's guard. It is in any case certain that either the personal outlook of the writer or the spirit of his age will affect his exposition of the cult, if it be only in his choice of a starting-point, which must inevitably give prominence to some features and relegate others to subordinate places. A glance at the variety and contradictions inherent in the worship of Dionysos will be enough to show that this is unavoidable. It presents us with the spectacle of annual festivals in the towns or

[1] W. F. Otto, preface to *Dionysos* (Frankfurt-a.-M. 1933): "ein heiliger Name und ein unendliches Symbol". Is it harsh to agree with one of his compatriots that, from the scholar's point of view, "wo in der Litteratur diese zwei Begriffe (i.e. das Dionysische und das Apollinische) überhaupt eine Rolle spielen, hat man es fast immer mit Dilettantismus zu tun"? (K. Pfister in Bursian's *Jahresbericht*, suppl. 229 (1930), p. 136.)

fields in spring—and with biennial festivals on the bare mountain-tops in winter; with daylight celebrations and torchlit midnight rovings; it has its joyous and bountiful side and its grim and gruesome side, for the same god is hailed as the giver of all good gifts and feared as the eater of raw flesh and the man-tearer; he has animal incarnations, aniconic forms closely connected with tree-worship, a definite connexion with ships and the sea; he offers ecstasy and spiritual union and wild intoxication in which he himself is the leader, so that he can be called the mad, the raving god; at the same time what disconcerts his adversaries and singles him out from them is an uncanny stillness and calm, and stillness and calm too are among the gifts he bestows on his infatuated worshippers; sexual licence as a feature of his *orgia* is now admitted, now denied; his frenzied women votaries, in the passionate abandonment of his service, take young beasts in their arms and with maternal tenderness give them the breast—the same women who with scarcely conceivable savagery tear the limbs from the young creatures and fasten their teeth on them. So the list might be extended.

Such an astonishing phenomenon has naturally been given its full share of exegesis by the religious historians. For a detailed account of the cult and its various forms in the independent states of Greece, as well as for facts and theories relevant to its origins, both geographical and functional, one has the sober and scholarly survey of Lewis Farnell. Erwin Rohde's *Psyche* is still rightly praised for its insight into the Dionysiac psychology; the bosom-friend of Nietzsche and pupil of Schopenhauer was yet a clear-sighted scholar for whom "das Dionysische" was a historical fact rather than an "eternal symbol". What one may rather call the German attitude is vigorously represented in our own day by W. F. Otto, whose book *Dionysos*, published in 1933, is at the same time a contribution to religious history and (may one say it without unfairness?) itself a document of the Dionysiac cult. On the whole it has been unduly disparaged in this country. Its central thesis, that Dionysos was essentially and from the beginning a god of the Greek people, though supported with no lack of learning, is based ultimately on a preconception of the author's and is undoubtedly wrong. Yet when that is said, and his position as the heir to so much in the thought of his country is taken into account, there is that in many of his observations about "the crazed god" (μαινόμενος Διόνυσος, *Iliad* vi, 132—*der rasende, der wahnsinniger*

Gott) which suggests a deeper understanding of his significance than has always been attained by the scientific historian. In English scholarship the tale is taken up most recently by Professor Dodds in his introduction to the *Bacchae*, and in the observations with which in his commentary he illuminates various details of the cult;[1] and by the valuable study of Professor Winnington-Ingram.

There is then no lack of authorities to whom the reader may be referred for a full account of the god. He must play a part here too, but within strict limits, which it will not be easy to observe. To assist in observing them, we shall be guided by two principles: first, he is being discussed from the point of view of the central question posed in our third chapter, to find out what effect he had on the Greek conception of man's relation to the divine powers; and secondly, the period in which we are primarily interested is that of the finest flower of Greek literary achievement. Adherence to the second principle is made easier because to that period belongs the best and most complete document of the cult which has come down to us, from the hand of a genius supremely fitted to treat of it. Whatever world Dionysos may belong to, it is not the world of prose, and by listening to the inspired utterances of the Bacchants of Euripides, poured out in the swift throbbing measures appropriate to the service of the god of ecstasy, we may learn enough for our purpose, more perhaps than if we listened to the cult-historians and anthropologists to the neglect of the poetry. Our main theme is his effect upon the Greeks.

Literary descriptions and artistic representations[2] are available sufficient to give us an adequate idea of the main features of Dionysiac *orgia* in their most typical, untamed form. Moreover these features have been made so familiar by modern writers that they need only be briefly recapitulated here. They usually took place at night.[3] Participation was not confined to women, but they were the most frequent and characteristic worshippers. "A female throng" is how the chorus describe the god-maddened women of Thebes in the *Bacchae*, and their next words suggest a

[1] E. R. Dodds, *Euripides' Bacchae* (Oxford, 1944). See also the same author's article "Maenadism in the Bacchae", *Harvard Theol. Rev.* xxxiii (1940), pp. 155 ff., and for other reff. to modern literature, *Bacchae*, intro. p. ix, n. 2. R. P. Winnington-Ingram, *Euripides and Dionysus* (Cambridge, 1948).

[2] Especially the magnificent pictures of dancing maenads and of the god himself in ecstasy on vase-paintings of the late sixth and the fifth centuries, some of which are reproduced by Farnell, *Cults*, v, pls. xliv and following.

[3] Eur. *Bacch.* 486: νύκτωρ τὰ πολλά· σεμνότητ' ἔχει σκότος.

reason. The greatest gift of Dionysos was the sense of utter freedom, and in Greece it was the women, with their normally confined and straitened lives, to whom the temptation of release made the strongest appeal. Dionysos, continue the chorus, "pricks them to leave their looms and shuttles". The attitude of the Greek male is summed up by Pentheus in words which it is difficult not to translate colloquially: "It really is beyond the limit if we are to put up with this sort of thing from *women*."[1] They have however a male priest of the god to lead them, a slim, long-haired youth of feminine appearance (the locks were especially cherished in honour of the god: *Bacchae* 494) who while the rites last is filled with the god's own spirit and called by his name (line 115).

Clad in fawnskins and taking in their hands the thyrsos (lines 24–5 etc.), which was a long rod tipped with a bunch of ivy or vine-leaves, the god's own potent emblem, and with ivy-wreaths upon their heads (81, 106), they follow their leader to the wildest parts of the mountains, lost in the bliss of the dance. Many carry snakes, wreathed about them (697–8), twined in their hair (102–4) or grasped in the hand as may be seen on the vase-paintings.[2] Their dance is accompanied, and their passions are roused, by the heavy beat of the tympanum (described as a circle of stretched hide (124)) and the strains of the reed-flute (127–8, 160), as well as their own excited shouts and cries. Nothing is lacking which can serve to increase the sense of exaltation and of shedding the self of everyday existence; to the darkness, the music and the rhythmic dance are added the smoky light of torches (144 ff.) and no doubt the god's especial gift of wine. Some have doubted the maenads' use of this extra stimulant, because the messenger who has seen them resting after their rites says expressly that they were sleeping "soberly, not drunk with the wine-bowl as you

[1] 785 f. οὐ γὰρ ἀλλ' ὑπερβάλλει τάδε
εἰ πρὸς γυναικῶν πεισόμεσθ' ἃ πάσχομεν.

[2] There are many ancient references to snake-handling in ecstatic cults, e.g. Olympias the mother of Alexander the Great is said by Plutarch to have indulged in it "to the dismay of the menfolk" (Plut. *Vit. Alex.* ii). Nor is it by any means unknown in modern times, and only a few weeks before writing the above I saw a notice (in *Time*'s issue of 27 August 1947) of a prosecution in Tennessee under a new law against snake-handling. It was accompanied by a convincing photograph, in which the rapt expressions of the participants were particularly interesting. They refused to stop their rituals because "We take our law from God". Pentheus has not yet conquered, though in a parallel scene to one in the *Bacchae* he was more successful, for the account says that some of these modern maenads hoped that their hymns and prayer would shake down the walls of their prison, but, unlike their Euripidean counterparts, were disappointed.

charge them" (686–8). Since however his report also exonerates them in the same sentence from indulging in the sound of the flute, and since they themselves include wine with milk and honey among the miraculous gifts that the god sends them during their *orgia* (142), praise him for granting to high and low "the pleasures of wine" (421–3), and later (534–5) swear by "the grape-clustered joy of the vine, given of Dionysos", we can hardly suppose them innocent of its virtue. Much the same conclusion must be reached about the question of sexual licence in the *orgia*. It is true that nothing of the sort was observed by the messenger, who in view of the stormy accusations of Pentheus denies that he saw the maenads "seeking Kypris in the woods" (688). Yet male participants were not excluded, and we cannot help being reminded of another play of Euripides, the *Ion*, in which Ion considers it a convincing account of his birth that his reputed father Xuthos came to Delphi at the time in question and took part with a *thiasos* of maenads in the Bacchic festival there. "Were you sober or wined?" he asks, and receiving the answer that Xuthus was "under the pleasant influence of Bacchos", he needs no further assurance, but exclaims: "That indeed was my begetting!"[1] Teiresias has said all that can be said in the god's defence: "Dionysos compels no woman to be chaste. Chastity is a matter of character, and she who is naturally chaste will partake of Bacchic rites without corruption" (314 ff.).

Of wine it may indeed be said that little would be needed, in combination with the other elements, to produce the final state of *ekstasis* (standing outside oneself) and *enthusiasmos* (possession by the god), to which all that had hitherto taken place was preliminary. In this state the worshippers saw visions, and nothing was impossible to them. The ground flowed with milk, wine and honey.[2] Endowed with superhuman strength, they hurl themselves upon animals, wild or tame, and tear them to pieces with their bare hands (735 ff.) for the "joy of the raw feast" (139). Charged with divine power, their thyrsi become deadly weapons that can put armed men to flight (758–64). They carry fire on their heads and are not burned (757–8).

Professor Dodds has been at pains to show[3] that this strange

[1] *Ion*, 554: *τοῦτ' ἐκεῖν' ἵν ἐσπάρημεν.*

[2] 142. As Socrates drily remarks in Plato's *Ion* (534a), the Bacchae draw honey and milk from the rivers when they are possessed, but not when they are in their senses.

[3] Especially in his article "Maenadism in the Bacchae" in *Harv. Theol. Rev.* xxxiii (1940).

performance, right down to a detail of gesture like the backward-tossed head and upturned throat which are referred to repeatedly in the play, was no invention of Euripides' poetic imagination. Not only did it go on in various parts of the Greek world down to and beyond the time of the poet, but it has been repeated in many parts of the world in modern times. Not even the miraculous element—the invulnerability of the maenads to spear-wounds and fire—is without its properly attested parallel in religious ecstasy and in certain cases of hysteria. Nevertheless most people will agree that it all sounds, if not incredible, at least remote and difficult of comprehension when set down in cold blood. This is but natural, since cold blood and Bacchic rites have nothing to say to one another. Here fortune has been kind, in that our one full account of the worship from classical times is by a great poet. The choruses of the *Bacchae* are even more untranslatable than most Greek poetry, and no one who can read them will wish to look at a translation. But it may be better than nothing and give some faint idea of the effect of the maenads' breathless utterance. The situation may first be briefly described. Dionysos, angered at the neglect of his worship by the rulers of Thebes, has come to the city with a band of his maenads from the homeland of orgiastic religion, Asia Minor. He has smitten with his madness the three daughters of the aged king Kadmos, the sisters of his own mother Semele, because they had hitherto scorned him, denying that their sister had had Zeus for lover and had borne a god. Together with the other women of Thebes, they have been driven by his "gad-fly" to the mountains in Bacchic frenzy. He himself, disguised as one of his mortal worshippers, has come to display his power and lead their revels. There is thus a curious double meaning in the references of the chorus to their leader, made possible only by the belief in Dionysiac possession. They address their leader as the Bacchic one and Bromios ("The Thunderer", one of the god's own titles), and this was doubtless usual, since in the Dionysiac ecstasy the spirit of the god was believed to enter such a one and take possession of him. Yet here we may be sure that their words are truer than they know, and that in fact the god himself, who in the prologue has explained his disguise and its purpose, is leading their dances. The following extracts are from the first song of the Asiatic maenads. From its formal opening warning against profane presence and ill-omened utterance, through the gradually quickening pace and increasing frenzy of the following verses, it is full of genuine ritual phraseology, and the metre of the original is one in traditional use for cult-hymns to Dionysos.

From Asia's land
Leaving sacred Tmolos I hasten
To perform for Bromios my sweet task,
My easy labour,
To raise for Bacchos my cry.
Who is here? Who is here on our road?
Let him withdraw close in his house,
Let every mouth be sealed in holy silence.
To Dionysos will I sing
The hymns ordained for ever.

O
Blessed is he who favoured of heaven,
Skilled in the mysteries of the gods,
Makes holy his life,
Gives his soul to the chorus,
As over the mountains he dances to Bacchos
In cleansing service
And observing the rites of Kybele Mother of all,
With quivering thyrsos
And crown of the ivy,
Servant of Dionysos.

On ye Bacchae, on ye Bacchae,
Bringing with you
Bromios, yea Dionysos,
Who is god and son of god,
From the mountains of Phrygia
To the broad highways of Hellas—
Bromios! . . .

O nurse of Semele, city of Thebes,
Be crowned with ivy.
Abound, abound with green
Bright-berried bryony,
Be consecrate with boughs
Of oak or fir,
Deck out your coats of dappled fawnskin
With fleecy tufts of white-tressed wool:
Bear reverently the wands of power and violence.
Straight the whole land shall dance.

Whoso leads our bands is Bromios—
To the hills, to the hills where waits
The women's throng,
From looms and shuttles
Pricked by Dionysos. . . .

Joyful on the mountains—
When from the rushing dancing throng
Sinks he to the ground,
With his holy fawnskin round him,
Pursuing blood, slaughter of goats,
Joy of raw flesh devoured,
Pressing on to the mountains of Phrygia, Lydia,
And the leader is Bromios!
Euoi!
The ground is flowing with milk, flowing with wine,
With the nectar of bees;
While the Leader,
Upraising with scent as of Syrian myrrh,
Flaming, the glow of the pine-torch
Fixed to the wand, leaps madly,
With running and dancing
Rousing his roving followers—
Stirring with cries—
Casting to heaven his flowing hair.
Mid Bacchic shouts he thunders:

"O on ye Bacchae, on ye Bacchae!
In the wealth of Tmolos running with gold
Sing Dionysos
To the tympanum's heavy roar,
Greeting the god of 'Euoi Euoi'
With answering 'Euoi!'
Let the shouting of Phrygian voices be heard
Whene'er the sweet-sounding and god-given reed
Adds its strong note to our god-given play.
At one with his bands to the hills, to the hills!"

Glad then as colt with its mother at grass
Lifts in the dance her nimble foot the Bacchant.

How and when did this wild orgiastic cult of Asia descend upon the strongholds of the Greek mind, with all its preference for "the intelligible, determinate, mensurable, as opposed to the fantastic, vague and shapeless"?[1] That it came from without and was not there from the start might almost be inferred from our chorus alone, and may be taken as proved by the work of the scholars mentioned earlier in this chapter and others to whom they refer. Herodotus' personal notion that Dionysos came to Greece from Egypt is based on the view generally accepted by the Greeks that his rites were "lately introduced", just as Pentheus in the *Bacchae*, using the same word, calls Dionysos "this lately-come god, whoever he be".[2] True, when he had been naturalized by the Greeks, their fertile imagination made his mother Semele into a princess of Thebes, the Boeotian city which, at least in their belief, was the first in Greece to receive his rites. According to the story, not wholly explained, of his birth, Semele when pregnant with him was blasted by the lightning. Some said—and this version is alluded to in the *Bacchae*—that Hera out of jealousy had tempted her to make the fatal mistake of persuading Zeus to let her see him in his true form. Zeus saved his son by snatching him from her womb and thrusting him into his own thigh until the time came for his birth. Thus according to the canons of Greek mythology his arrival in Thebes as narrated by Euripides was strictly speaking a homecoming. How little this corresponds to the true state of affairs is shown up at every turn in the play. No Greek city yet knows his rites, which he has come to introduce, not to re-introduce. As he says himself, "Leaving the lands of Lydia, rich in gold, and of Phrygia . . . I have come first to this city of the Greeks, to set them dancing here and establish my mysteries. . . . Thebes first of this land of Hellas have I made to ring with cries, putting the fawnskin round their limbs and the thyrsos into their hands. . . . When I have made all well here I will depart and show myself in other regions." And turning to his troop of maenads he addresses them thus: "Ye who have come from Tmolos the bulwark of Lydia, my sacred band of women, whom I have brought from the barbarians to be my companions and fellow-travellers, raise up your native Phrygian tympana, invention shared by Mother Rhea and myself." The same stress on the Asiatic and non-Greek (*barbaron*) origin of the religion as is seen here and throughout the first chorus pervades in fact the whole play. One more example will suffice. In answer to a question of

[1] E. Fraenkel, *Rome and Greek Culture*, inaugural lecture (Clarendon Press, 1935).

[2] *νεωστὶ ἐσήγμενα*, Hdt. ii, 49, 2, *τὸν νεωστὶ δαίμονα*, Eur. *Bacch.* 219. Similarly Teiresias, the god's apologist, calls him *ὁ δαίμων ὁ νέος* (272).

Pentheus the disguised Dionysos says: "Every barbarian observes these rites and dances". "Yes," replies Pentheus, "for they are far more foolish than the Hellenes." "Nay wiser in this, though their customs are different," retorts the god. Semele herself, when seen in the light of other evidence, appears no longer as a Theban princess but a Phrygian goddess, whose name can be recognized in the *Zemelo* of Phrygian inscriptions and who seems to have been a form of the Anatolian Earth-mother.[1]

Elsewhere than in the *Bacchae* Dionysos is most often represented as a Thracian, and in Thrace his religion was certainly at home. This is no contradiction, for Thracians and Phrygians were of the same race, since some time in the second millennium B.C. there was a movement of tribes from Thrace across the Hellespont to settle in Asia Minor.[2] Thus the religions of Dionysos and of Kybele, the Asiatic Mother-goddess with her young attendant Attis, were of the same orgiastic type, and by historical times had become inextricably mingled, as our chorus showed.[3] Let us pursue for a moment the syncretism as it is revealed in the first chorus of the *Bacchae*.

The Great Mother of Phrygia had a train of attendant daemons called Korybantes, and since from the earliest times of which we have record Thracian and Phrygian religion are closely akin, the Korybantes are brought into relation with Dionysos also, whose home (though we cannot be certain) was probably Thrace. That they were the servants of a cult of ecstatic or orgiastic type is made plain, to take a single example, by the way in which the Greeks formed a verb from their name. "To korybant" (κορυβαντιᾶν) meant to be in a state of divine madness in which hallucinations occurred. It was known to the medical writers of Greece as a pathological condition.

At this point we come to a new element. In our earlier discussion of the birth of the Cretan Zeus, we heard of the Kuretes as

[1] See Dodds' commentary on the *Bacchae*, p. 61, and reff. there. Similarly Dionysos' equally common name Bacchos has been shown by a Sardian inscription to come from Lydia (Dodds, intro. xviii).

[2] The migration is referred to by Herodotus, vii, 73. See also J. Friedrich in PWK *Realenc.* xx, 883 f.

[3] In the *Bacchae* itself, in spite of the wholly Asiatic colouring of the parodos, there is acknowledgment of Thrace also as a land of Dionysos. Compare the lovely second stasimon, especially from line 553 onwards. For Nilsson's view, that Thrace and Phrygia each had a distinct contribution to make to the character of Dionysos as the Greeks knew him, see *Min.-Myc. Rel.* pp. 492 ff. (p. 32, n. 1 above). The dissertation of A. Rupp, *Die Beziehungen des Dionysoskultes zur Thrakien und zur Kleinasien* (Programm, Stuttgart, 1882), is described by Nilsson (in 1927) as "still the best" on the subject.

purely Cretan daemons who according to the legend drowned the infant's cries by their war-like dancing and clashing of arms.[1] For the Greek of Euripides' day, Kuretes and Korybantes are identified, and both are brought into close connexion with the Satyrs, who were the peculiar attendants of Dionysos. Thus Phrygian and Bacchic religion are intermingled with Rhea and the birth of the Cretan Zeus in one gloriously catholic stanza:[2]

O cave of the *Kuretes* and sacred haunts of *Crete*, birth-place of *Zeus*, where the *Korybantes* triple-helmed invented in thy grottoes this my circlet of stretched hide. In *Bacchic* rout they mingled it with the shrill sweet breath of *Phrygian* flutes and gave it into the hands of *Rhea* his mother, fit sound to accompany the cries of *Bacchic* women. And from the Mother Goddess did the frenzied *Satyrs* borrow it, and joined it to the dances of the three-year feasts,[3] in which *Dionysos* rejoices.

Much religious history has been packed into this short song, and since it stretches back beyond the times of which we have record there can be no certainty in our interpretation of it. Yet it is worth reminding ourselves very briefly of the probable course of events, which has already been touched on in a previous chapter. The identification by the Hellenes of the god of Crete with their own Zeus goes back a long way. Hesiod takes it for granted, and we may assume it to have been the first step. The ancient warrior-dance of the Cretan *kuroi* is now given a mythical significance as commemorating the rescue of the infant Zeus. At what date Greece was first swept by the orgiastic worship of Dionysos is uncertain, but we may assume it to have been somewhat later. It is as a Thracian that he is most commonly represented, and no doubt he entered from the North, though there may have been a parallel invasion from Asia Minor by way of the islands.[4] Opposed at first, the new cult has proved irresistible, and all Greece has become acquainted with the emotional experience of its ecstasies and the exaltation of union with the god. Accepted in Greece, the cult reaches Crete, where the Greek devotees of Dionysos find that a religion has been carried on from time immemorial with which their new cult has much closer affinities than with the typical worship of the Olympians whom Homer

[1] p. 41 above. [2] *Bacchae*, 119–34, omitted in the previous translation.

[3] The *trieteris*, the biennial winter festival of orgiastic type, celebrated on Mount Parnassos above Delphi down to the time of Plutarch. See Dodds, intro. xi f., and below, p. 178.

[4] Dodds, intro. xix.

had bequeathed to Greece. Crete too knew a powerful young god of the animal and vegetable creation, and worshipped him, with clamorous dance and sacramental meal of fresh-killed flesh, in the form of a bull. The bull was one of the commonest forms of Dionysos' own epiphany. It is as a bull that he appears to the bemused Pentheus (*Bacchae*, 618, 920–2), and bulls are among the victims of the maenads (743 ff.).[1] Behind this similarity is in all probability an initial prehistoric identity. The racial and religious affinity between Thracians and Phrygians has been commented on already. The young god who stands primarily for "the whole wet element" in nature, as Plutarch describes Dionysos[2]—that is, not only wine, but the life-blood of animals, the male semen which fertilizes the female, the juicy sap of plants—meets us under different names all over the nearer parts of Asia and in Egypt, as well as in Thrace, as Dionysos, Zalmoxis, Sabazios, Attis, Adonis, Thammuz, Osiris and many others. The Cretans were probably of southern Anatolian stock, and had had dealings with Egypt from an early date. Thus the original identity, in a sense of the word which this paragraph should already have made clear, of Dionysos and the Cretan "Zeus", seems certain. Yet if it be a fact, it is a fact which had long been forgotten. For the Greek, Thracian and Cretan were entirely different peoples, the one living to the north of him and the other to the south. When however he found that his bull-god Dionysos, who had come to him from Thrace, was matched in nature and in cult by the bull-god of Crete whom he called Zeus, he was not slow to draw the conclusion that they were one and the same. Since Dionysos had a noisy, dancing train of daemons already, it was easy to guess that these were of the same breed as the Kuretes. Nor was the identity of the Mother-goddess Rhea, associated particularly with Zeus and Crete, and her Phrygian counterpart Kybele more difficult to grasp. Kuretes and Korybantes become one band, as we see them in Euripides, and close relations of the Satyrs. This syncretism may not have been long established in the minds of the Greeks when Euripides wrote his plays, since the worship of Kybele was

[1] Euripides is not of course our only witness. See Dodds, intro. xv ff. with notes. Dionysos had a class of worshippers or priests called "ox-herds" (*βούκολοι*, cf. Guthrie, *Orpheus and Gr. Rel.* p. 260 with notes). At Elis the women called on him to appear *βοέῳ ποδὶ θύων*, and twice invoked him with the cry of *Ἄξιε Ταῦρε* (Plut. *Qu. Gr.* 36, 299b), and so forth.

[2] *Is. et Os.* 35, 365a: *οὐ μόνον τοῦ οἴνου Διόνυσον, ἀλλὰ καὶ πάσης ὑγρας φύσεως Ἕλληνες ἡγοῦνται κύριον καὶ ἀρχηγόν.*

not actually introduced into Greece until some time in the fifth century, but there is no reason to suppose that they were unaware of her existence earlier.

The identity in Greek eyes of the Cretan Zeus and Dionysos is best illustrated by another passage of Euripides, the fragment of the lost *Cretans* which has already been quoted.[1] Here we have the *omophagia* ("eating raw"), of which the chorus in the *Bacchae* also speak (138), performed by a Cretan initiate of Idaean Zeus. It was an original feature of both the Cretan and the Thracian cults, no doubt because an original connexion is to be assumed between the two peoples. But I repeat, for the Greek the similarity must have been a discovery. Having discovered it, he characteristically decides that the two gods are the same, and the initiate of Idaean Zeus becomes a Bacchos.

This attempt to explain the various elements united in Bacchic cult of the fifth century seemed worth while in view of their acceptance in classical literature, so that, in a chorus of the *Bacchae*, Phrygian, Lydian and Cretan are invoked side by side, and names like Satyrs, Kuretes, Korybantes, Dionysos, Bacchos, Mother-goddess, Kybele, Rhea, infant Zeus and Tmolos come tumbling in profusion from the lips of the inspired women. It is probably as good an approach as any to an understanding of the history and nature of Dionysiac worship in Greece. Before passing to other questions, it is worth pausing to note how thoroughly at home in Anatolia is the most characteristic part of the Dionysiac *orgia*, namely the stimulation of music and the vertiginous dance leading to ecstasy, to the sense of union with the divine, and the power of seeing visions, and how often it has erupted through the ages in that particular region. Dionysiac ritual has often been compared with the dancing of the Mevlevi Dervishes, whose order was founded in the thirteenth century A.D. In their services too the music of flutes and the beating of drums are used, and the dancers move round in circles until they drop exhausted to the floor. The belief behind it, in the often-quoted words of their founder, Jelaluddin Rumi, is that "he who knows the power of the dance dwells in God". It has also been pointed out what a contrast is presented by the practices of this unorthodox sect to the orthodox doctrine of Islam, which insists so strongly on the absolute transcendence of God. What is not so often noted is that the sect arose

[1] p. 45 above.

at Konya (Iconium) on the Anatolian plateau, in the centre of modern Turkey, under Seljuk Turkish rule. Now it is a generally accepted belief that the people of these parts have preserved their racial characteristics to a remarkable extent throughout the series of invasions to which they have been subjected.[1] The Turks have never had the reputation of being naturally orthodox Moslems, and perhaps this has had something to do with it. They have hankered after the religion of their Phrygian forefathers. Jelaluddin's innovations naturally aroused the opposition of the stricter Moslems, and his defence of the introduction of music and dancing into their religion is interesting, even if it can hardly be said to represent the whole truth. He said that the "Roman" people[2] were highly esteemed by God, but were lacking in a natural taste for the delights of the spiritual life. He had been sent by God to convert them, and knowing their weakness devised the music and dancing as a means especially calculated to win over to the true faith a people of their particular temperament.[3]

An eruption of the same spirit at a different period can be seen in the activities of Montanism, a heresy which troubled the peace of the Church about A.D. 200, and attracted no less a figure than Tertullian to its ranks. Among the charges brought against them were the following. Their leader Montanus claimed to be the Lord God, because possessed by the Holy Ghost. He chose women as his chief ministrants, ordaining them bishops and elders, who also experienced ecstasy and believed themselves possessed by God. In their services they introduced seven white-clad maidens who carried torches, prophesied and exhibited a kind of *enthusiasmos*. "Publice mysteria celebrant", said one critic. They were even accused of ritual murder (like that carried out under the influence of Dionysos by the daughters of Minyas, who cast lots and slew the son of one of them): "dicunt enim eos de infantis

[1] The modern Turk's claim to be autochthonous in Anatolia is probably more nearly justified than most of such nationalistic ideas. What he does not seem to see is that in arguing for his racial identity with the Hittites and earlier inhabitants he is arguing that the Turk has ceased to exist; for the Turk, who brought the Turkish language to Anatolia, is undoubtedly a very late comer in the series of invaders, whose arrival is no earlier than the middle ages.

[2] i.e. the inhabitants of Asia Minor, known to the Moslem world as the land of Rum (Rome). Jelal himself had come from Persia, and acquired his surname of Rumi by the fact of his settling in Konya.

[3] From *The Acts of the Adepts*, by El Eflaki, a disciple of Chelebi Emir Arif, Jelal's grandson and successor as Head of the Mevlevi (trans. Redhouse, Trubner and Co., 1881).

sanguine in pascha miscere in suum sacrificium". Montanus was said moreover to have advocated the dissolution of the marriage-tie, and his priestesses to have deserted their husbands. This sect grew up around Pepuza, a tiny place in the heart of Phrygia which its adherents believed was destined to be the New Jerusalem, and was commonly known as the "Phrygian Heresy".[1] It is hard indeed to kill the Dionysiac spirit in its native land.[2]

On the chronology and general history of the progress of Dionysiac religion through Greece we can unfortunately say little. Direct evidence is lacking, and we are reduced to inference from mythology, which usually admits of more than one interpretation. A succinct example is provided by the story that the frenzy of Dionysos was due to the anger of Hera, who drove him mad. Why was Hera angry with him? The ancient explanation that jealousy implanted a hatred of her husband's bastard is tacitly rejected by the modern mythologist as superficial. One critic therefore accounts for it by the antagonistic nature of their two cults and what each stood for. Hera is patron of marriage, whereas Dionysos by the licence which his cult bestows on women is a subverter of the marriage-tie. Another sees in it a piece of transmuted history, and points out how natural it is that "the goddess of immemorial supremacy" should be thought "to frown on the intruding deity".[3] More important is the series of myths, to which we shall come shortly, which speak of resistance to the advance of his cult. These stories take the form of cult-myths, that is to say, although they seem to be connected with history by their location in actual cities which could have lain on the line of the god's advance into Greece, the result of the opposition is said to be that Dionysos drives the women of the place mad, and the leader of the resistance falls a victim to their frenzy and is torn in pieces like

[1] ἡ κατὰ Φρύγας αἵρεσις, Eusebius, *Hist. Eccl.* vi, 20. Other passages quoted or referred to in the text are from the same work, book v, 16 and 17, Epiphanius, *Panarion Haer.* xlviii, 11, and Didymus, *De Trinitate*, iii, 41. They are collected in D. N. Bonwetsch, *Texte zur Gesch. des Montanismus* (Bonn, *Kleine Texte*, 1914). Such words as παρέκστασις, κατοχή, and ἐνθουσιασμός are frequent in descriptions of the heresy.

[2] For the moment Pentheus is in the ascendant. Kemal Atatürk suppressed the dancing in Turkey between 1923 and 1929, closed the *tekke* of the Mevlevi at Konya and turned it into a museum. It will be interesting to see how long the suppression lasts.

[3] For the hostility of Hera see Eur. *Cyclops* 3, Plato *Laws*, ii, 672b. Jealousy as the motive is suggested by Apollodorus, iii, 4, 3. The modern views contrasted in the text are those of W. F. Otto (*Dionysos*, p. 161), and Farnell (*Cults*, v. 91).

the victim which was sacrificed in the regular course of Dionysiac *orgia*. In form, then, the myths are plainly aetiological. The question whether they contain a core of historical fact as well is obviously not an easy one to decide.

There is however a more important question than the unanswerable riddle of when Dionysos first entered Greece. It is the question of when, and to what extent, the Greeks gave in to the potent force that he represented, and how far they modified it in accordance with their own different ideas. He represented something foreign, or in their own terminology *barbaron*, and it was their pride, as Pentheus boasted, that the Hellenes stood for something higher and wiser than the *barbaron*. In the Hellenes Dionysos had no easy conquest.

On this more fundamental question there is something to be said. Homer, for example, throws little light on the question of date of entry. He knows of Dionysos but says little about him. This is not however proof that Dionysos was a recent immigrant who was only just becoming known in Greece. It only indicates that to Homer and his society Dionysos was of no importance. He had nothing to say to a race of aristocrats who saw in the Olympians their fit and proper objects of worship. Their lack of interest is clear evidence that he had little hope of conquering the proud Achaean spirit. It would be rash to base on it any theory of how long he had been in the land.

The references to Dionysos in Homer are purely incidental. The most informative is in the sixth book of the *Iliad* (130 ff.). Diomedes the Greek and Glaukos the Trojan have come face to face in the battle. With characteristic good breeding they do not immediately fall upon each other, but Diomedes addresses his foe, expressing a desire to know who he is. He has not seen him before, and yet he has shown himself to be a hero of surpassing courage. If he be a mortal who has thus stood in the path of Diomedes' spear, then, says the Greek with simple pride, unhappiness awaits his parents. If on the other hand he be one of the Immortals come down from Heaven, it would be foolish to fight with him. "Nay, for not even the son of Dryas, mighty Lykurgos, long survived when he strove with the heavenly gods, he that erst chased through the goodly land of Nysa the nurses of frenzied Dionysos, so that all cast their sacred implements upon the ground under the lash of the ox-whip in the hands of murderous Lykurgos; and Dionysos was afraid and plunged beneath the wave of the sea, where Thetis received him cowering in her bosom, for mighty trembling seized him at the threats of this warrior. But thereafter the gods, the easy livers, were angry with Lykurgos, and the son of Kronos struck him blind; nor was he for long, since he was hated of all the immortal gods."

The amount of Dionysiac lore in this passage suggests that the writer was thoroughly familiar with the cult and its aetiological stories. The nymphs or goddesses who acted as nurses to the infant Dionysos are familiar figures of both. They seem to be mentioned in a mutilated fragment of Tyrtaios. The chorus in the *Oedipus Coloneus* speak of Dionysos treading "in the company of his divine nurses". The Homeric Hymn to Dionysos brings out their double function, for the nymphs who in his infancy "received him from his royal father and nursed him in the vales of Nysa" are the same who form his frenzied train when he is grown. When they had brought him to manhood "clad in ivy and bay he roamed his wooded haunts; and the nymphs followed where he led, and the wide forest echoed with their din". All this seems to have been represented in cult, of which no doubt the myths are little more than a reflection. The maenads who roamed the mountains in the train of the youthful leader did so in the character of these nymphs, and we have it on the authority of Plutarch, though his mention of the fact is unfortunately brief and vague, that a part of their ceremonies consisted in "awakening the *Liknites*". *Liknites* (from *liknon*, a winnowing-basket used as a cradle) was the infant Dionysos, as is explained by Servius: "Some affirm that Father Liber is called *Liknites* by the Greeks; for *liknon* is their name for the winnowing-basket, in which he is customarily said to have been placed, after he was taken from his mother's womb."[1] These are late authorities, but Plutarch may be taken as trustworthy. He is speaking of what went on in his own day, and it is not likely to have been a recent innovation. Although the maenads of the *Bacchae* are not expressly called nurses, and Dionysos throughout the play is full-grown, it is striking that one of their acts when they are filled with the divine afflatus is to suckle young animals at the breast. The spirit of Dionysos was embodied in other forms besides the human. The babe in the *liknon* occurs in art,[2] and in certain cults there was an official called the *liknon*-

[1] References: Tyrtaios, fr. i, 25–6 Diehl; Soph. *O.C.* 689 f.; Hom. Hymn, xxvi; Plut. *Is. et Os.* xxxv, 365a; Serv. *ad* Verg. *Georg.* i, 166 (last two in Farnell, *Cults*, v, 305, n. 89). Cf. Hesychius s.v. λικνίτης.

[2] See illustrations in Jane Harrison, *Prolegomena*³, pp. 523 ff.

bearer (*liknophoros*), as appears from Demosthenes' strictures on Aeschines. Finally, though it is rash to assume continuous survival, we may draw attention once again to the curious mummery performed at least until recently in modern Thrace, in the course of which an old woman carries about a child in a basket-shaped cradle still called *likno*.[1]

Of the *thysthla* carried by the nurses in Homer's story (translated "sacred implements" above), and thrown away in their flight, one can only say, with authorities quoted by the scholiast, that it is a general word meaning things connected with the cult. He records guesses that they were boughs, vines or thyrsi. The ox-goad in the hand of the persecutor recalls the bovine form of the god, and may have been a ritual weapon. The scourging of women had its place in cult, being recorded by Pausanias of the biennial Dionysos-festival at Alea in Arcadia.[2] At Orchomenos in Boeotia the maenads were pursued by the priest of Dionysos at the annual festival of the Agrionia, and the element of terror was very real, since if he caught one he put her to death, as happened once, says Plutarch, in his own lifetime. Another feature of this Boeotian rite was that the women searched for Dionysos as if he had run away, and then desisted, "saying that he had fled to the Muses and hidden".[3]

In Homer Dionysos plunges into the sea. That his flight was into water is related in a number of myths, and was shown forth in cult. "Among the Argives Dionysos has the title of Ox-born. And they summon him with trumpets from the water, throwing a lamb into the depths for the Gatekeeper. They conceal the trumpets in thyrsi."[4] The language here carries a suggestion of the world of the dead, which we will not now pursue, our purpose being only to show how many elements of the brief story in Homer seem to be drawn from the world of genuine Dionysiac cult. This contains many indications of an appearance of Dionysos from the

[1] Dem. *de Cor.* 313, R. M. Dawkins in *Journ. Hell. Stud.* 26 (1906). [2] Paus. viii, 23, 1.

[3] Plut. *Qu. Graec.* 38, 299f, *Qu. Conv.* viii, 1, 717a (quoted in Farnell, *Cults*, v, 302, n. 77, and 300, n. 75). Sophocles says that Lykurgos by his attack on Dionysos and his maenads "provoked the Muses", though the connexion with the Muses has not been certainly explained. Note that Plutarch, our authority here, was himself a Boeotian.

[4] Plut. *Is. et Os.* xxxv, 364f, Farnell, *Cults*, v, 305, n. 89. Plutarch writes here in part at second hand, quoting a certain Socrates ἐν τοῖς περὶ ὁσίων. (This Socrates may have lived in the third century B.C., Gudeman in PWK *Realenc.* 2nd series, iii, 805.) For myths of Dionysos driven into water see Farnell, *Cults*, v, 181, and elsewhere.

sea. At the town of Prasiai on the coast of Lakonia he was made the hero of a story similar to that of Perseus and Danae, for it was told that after his birth his mother Semele was put with him into a chest by Kadmos and thrown into the sea. They were washed up near Prasiai. At Patrai there was a cult of Dionysos *Aisymnetes*, in which a sacred chest was carried out of the temple at night by his priest. The story attached to it was that after the sack of Troy the hero Eurypylos received as his share of the booty a chest containing an image of Dionysos. He was himself a Thessalian, but in obedience to an oracle heard at Delphi he let the winds take his ship and was brought over the sea to Patrai, where as a result the natives substituted the cult of Dionysos for that of Artemis, whom they had hitherto worshipped with barbarous rites of human sacrifice.[1] The appearance of a ship at Dionysiac festivals carries the same suggestion. Late literary references speak of this at Smyrna. Thus Philostratos (second–third century A.D.) writes that at that city "in the month of Anthesterion a trireme is brought from the high seas to the market-place, which the priest of Dionysos steers as if he were the helmsman". Similarly the rhetorician Aristides (second century A.D.) says that at the beginning of spring "a trireme sacred to Dionysos is borne in a circle about the market-place". That the practice was early, and not confined to Smyrna, is indicated by a black-figured Athenian vase, found at Akragas and now in the British Museum, on which Dionysos is shown sitting in what looks like a wheeled ship, followed by a procession leading a bull for sacrifice. There is also the well-known and beautiful kylix by the sixth-century artist Exekias, which depicts him reclining in a sailing-boat with dolphins playing around him and a vine growing out of the deck and overshadowing the sails.[2] This does not itself directly suggest ritual, and in this respect forms an artistic parallel to the literary text of the comic poet Hermippos (a contemporary of Pericles) in which he speaks of Dionysos steering his ship over the wine-dark sea and bringing all sorts of good gifts to men in his black ship.[3]

These parallels from later cults could be multiplied, but enough have been cited to make it clear that the story mentioned thus

[1] See Farnell, *Cults*, v, 198 ff. The stories quoted are told by Pausanias, iii, 24, 3, and vii, 19, 3, texts in Farnell, ib., 304, n. 88.

[2] Philostr. *Vit. Soph.* i, 25, 1, Aristid. i, 373, Dind., both quoted by Farnell, *Cults*, v, 331. Cf. ib., 191 f. The vases are illustrated ib., pl. xlii, p. 258, where further reff. will be found. The Exekias vase better illustrated in Buschor, *Greek Vase-painting* (Chatto and Windus, 1921), pl. li, p. 102.

[3] Quoted by Athenaeus, i, 27e.

casually by Diomedes implies a good deal more than appears on the surface, and that it is unlikely that the cult of Dionysos was strange or new to the singer of this part at least of the *Iliad*. Other mentions of the god in the Homeric poems are less informative, and may be briefly enumerated. In making love to Hera, Zeus adopts the questionable method of reciting a list of all his mistresses, in order to protest to her that none of them made on him the deep impression which she herself does at this moment. In the list appears Semele, "who bore Dionysos, a joy to mortals". It has often been noted that there are no direct references in Homer to Dionysos as god of wine, and the inference has been made that this was not a part of his original nature.[1] Certainly Dionysos was very much more than the god of wine. His province, as we have noted, included every type of life-giving moisture. Yet wine, and all that it stands for, seems so essential to his nature that it is difficult to believe that it was only a later accretion, and it would be dangerous to argue from the silence of Homer, who so clearly knew more about the god than his lordly indifference allowed him to say. Perhaps then it was in the poet's mind when in this line he called him a thing to make glad the heart of man.[2]

At the end of the *Odyssey*, the shade of Agamemnon describes the funeral of Achilles. His mother Thetis brought a golden urn for his bones, "and she said it was a gift of Dionysos, wrought by far-famed Hephaistos". Taken in conjunction with the mention of Thetis in the story of Lykurgos, this perhaps strengthens the case for a connexion of Dionysos with the sea and sea-nymphs in the mind of the Homeric bard. There is only one more mention of his name, but it shows that another circle of Dionysiac myths, those which connect him with Ariadne, was known at least to the singer of the descent of Odysseus to the underworld in the eleventh book of the *Odyssey*. "There I saw Phaidra and Prokris and fair Ariadne," says Odysseus, "the daughter of wise Minos, whom once Theseus took from Crete to bring her to the land of sacred Athens, yet had no joy of her; for Artemis first slew her on the testimony of Dionysos."[3] The god is not mentioned again in

[1] The earliest explicit reference to wine as the gift of Dionysos is in Hesiod, *Works and Days*, 614.

[2] *Il.* xiv, 325, χάρμα βροτοῖσιν. See further on this Otto, *Dionysos*, p. 53 f.

[3] *Od.* xxiv, 74 f.; xi, 321 ff. For Ariadne's original nature as a mother-goddess, her identification with Aphrodite, and varying opinions of her relationship to Dionysos, see Nilsson, *Min.-Myc. Rel.* pp. 451 ff., *Hist. Gr. Rel.* pp. 29 f.; Farnell, *Cults*, ii, 631 ff., v, 117, Hero-Cults, pp. 48 f.; Wilamowitz, *Glaube*, i, 409 ff.; also, after reading the other authorities, Otto, *Dionysos*, pp. 168 ff.

either poem, but when Andromache rushes from her palace with beating heart at the thought that harm has befallen Hector, she is said to be "like a maenad" in her frenzy, so it is evident that these wild votaries of the cult must have been familiar to the poet's audience.[1]

From this fairly full discussion of the scanty references to Dionysos in the Homeric poems, we may conclude that his cult was already familiar to the bards, but of little interest. A poet of the common people, had there been such, might have told a different tale. The religious world of the poems, which is that of chieftains boasting their lineage from Zeus or Poseidon and treating with them on human terms, had no place for the mystic ecstasies of the Thraco-Phrygian god. It is a small but significant point that in all later stories of the persecution of Dionysos, the offending mortal is punished by the god whom he has wronged and who appears in power and might to wreak his own vengeance. In Homer, Lykurgos is visited with blindness and death by Zeus and the hatred of the other gods. After all, one can imagine them saying, contemptible weakling as he is, this is a god and Zeus' son, and blood is thicker than water. The only picture of Dionysos himself shows him fleeing in fear and trembling. Contrast the words of Sophocles when he tells the same story: "And the son of Dryas was tamed with bonds, the King of the Edonians swift to wrath: so paid he for his angry taunts, when *by the will of Dionysos* he was shut fast in a rocky prison. There the dread exuberant might of his madness ebbed away. That man learned to know the god, when he attacked him in frenzy with the tongue of mockery."[2]

We must now give some consideration to these stories of persecution, for it has been both affirmed and denied that they illustrate historical facts about the progress of the Dionysiac cult through Greece, and they will in any case help us to understand more thoroughly the nature of the cult and the Greek attitude towards it. They have one almost universal feature, namely that the god's vengeance takes the form of visiting with madness the women of the land where he has been spurned. This usually leads to their tearing a victim in pieces, either the king who has been the god's

[1] *Il.* xxii, 460, μαινάδι ἴση. It is perhaps a matter of opinion whether Wilamowitz (*Glaube*, ii, 60) is right in thinking that this means no more than "a woman with mind deranged", but in view of the evidence for familiarity with Dionysos and his cult which we have already discussed, I am inclined in this to side with Otto (*Dionysos*, p. 53).

[2] *Antigone*, 955 ff.

opponent, or, when the women themselves have been the offenders, one of their own children. The two motives are combined in the Pentheus story, where the king who has forbidden the rites is butchered by his own mother. Madness (*mania*) is of course the word for the ecstasy which actually did take possession of women in their worship, and gave them their name of *mainades*, and the tearing to pieces of a victim was the regular culmination of their rites. It may even be that once in primitive Thrace or Phrygia the victim was a human child, and that some memory of this horror had lingered on.[1] The appearance of these elements of ritual shows that the myths were to that extent aetiological. What is more important, the particular way in which they are introduced reveals the ordinary Greek attitude towards them. They appear as unnatural and dreadful acts only to be accounted for by a visitation of the wrath of an offended deity, not as acts of willing submission to his influence whereby miraculous gifts and unspeakable bliss were to be secured. To the plain man these two sides of one and the same religious experience made no sense. To comprehend the whole needed the unique combination of detachment and full understanding—in other words the poetic genius—which we find in Euripides alone.

By the fifth century Thebes was regarded as the centre of the Dionysiac cult in Greece. Mythology had established it as his birthplace and the burial-place of his mother, and when a city wished to introduce the cult, maenads from Thebes were officially dispatched, with the blessing of the Delphic oracle, to organize it for them.[2] Yet at Thebes the tradition of original opposition was strong. The three daughters of the old king Kadmos, sisters of Dionysos' own mother Semele—ἃς ἥκιστα χρῆν—denied his divinity. Pentheus, the son of one of them, who had succeeded his grandfather Kadmos on the throne, declared the god an impostor and forbade the introduction of his rites. Dionysos in his anger sent his madness upon the three sisters and the other women of Thebes, so that in spite of Pentheus they danced wildly off to the mountains. Disguised as a mortal priest of his own religion, Dionysos was caught and imprisoned by Pentheus, but escaped miraculously. He then began to cast his irresistible influence over the king himself. He persuaded him to go and spy upon the women in their

[1] Cf. *Orpheus and Gr. Rel.*, app. 1 to ch. iv, "The Rending of Dionysos" (pp. 130 ff.).
[2] So at Magnesia on the Maeander. For the placing of this incident in the fifth century, see Farnell, *Cults*, v, 152.

orgies, and even overcame his opposition to putting on the dress and taking the attributes of a Bacchant for the purpose. Having thus got him thoroughly in his power, he led him forth unresisting to his doom, dazed and hypnotized by the Bacchic influence so that his vision of the familiar city became blurred and the god who accompanied him appeared in his bestial form. Arrived at the scene of the *orgia*, he was set high on a pine-tree where he could better be spied upon than spying. Detected by the maenads, he was pelted with stones, fir-branches and thyrsi, and finally brought down by the uprooting of the tree. The raving women gathered round and tore him in pieces, and his head was carried off in triumph by his own mother Agave under the delusion that it was a lion's.

That, owing to the survival of the *Bacchae* of Euripides, is the best-known of the resistance-myths. (It was also treated by Aeschylus in a play called *Pentheus*.) For the others we are not so well supplied with classical or earlier authorities, but the mythographer Apollodorus (? second century A.D.) quotes Hesiod as his authority for saying that it was refusal to accept the rites of Dionysos which was responsible for the madness of the daughters of Proitos, king of Argos. The wrath of Hera was another suggested reason (cited for example in a poem of Bacchylides), and their madness is mentioned by a number of writers (including Herodotus) without reference to its cause. In Apollodorus' account the madness took the recognized form of Dionysiac ecstasy: the women roamed over the whole Argive land and other parts of the Peloponnese, running through the solitary places with every sort of disorderliness. Other women joined them, abandoned their houses, destroyed their own children, and flocked to the desert.[1] In another part of his summary of Greek mythology, the same writer recounts that "having shown the Thebans that he was a god, Dionysos came to Argos, and there again, because they did not honour him, he drove the women mad, and they on the

[1] A particularly good illustration of the infectious nature of the madness, which plays so large a part in Dionysiac story (we need not press the parallel further than to say that it testifies to the reality of the phenomenon), is quoted by Frazer in his note on the passage of Apollodorus (Loeb ed., 1921, i, 147). A Malayan laid a complaint about the women of his settlement, stating that they "were frequently seized by a kind of madness . . . and that they ran off singing into the jungle, each woman by herself, and stopped there for several days and nights, finally returning almost naked, or with their clothes all torn to shreds. He said that the first outbreak of this kind occurred a few years ago, and that they were still frequent, one usually taking place every two or three months. They were started by one of the women, whereupon all the others followed suit." On ecstatic religious experience cf. Havelock Ellis, *Man and Woman* (Heinemann, 1934), 320 ff.

mountains devoured the flesh of the infants whom they carried at their breasts".[1]

The story of the daughters of Minyas at Orchomenos is similar. Dionysos had come to their city, and all the other women had yielded to him and taken to the hills and woods in the customary frenzy. Only the daughters of Minyas self-righteously remained at home, refusing to be seduced from their husbands and their household tasks. According to one version, Dionysos first appeared in the form of a girl to persuade them to join the others. As they persisted in their refusal, he began to work his spells. Visions of wild beasts filled the room, vine- and ivy-shoots began to twine themselves round the looms at which the girls were working, wine and milk dripped from the roof. Madness descended on the girls, they lusted after human flesh, drew lots and tore in pieces the child of Leukippe on whom the lot fell. This story emphasizes particularly that aspect of the worship which angered Pentheus and doubtless many other right-thinking Greek males, the seduction of the women from their domestic surroundings and their proper tasks. In Euripides they were taken "from their looms and shuttles". At Orchomenos (let us have it in Ovid's own smoothly polished lines):

parent matresque nurusque,
Telasque et calathos infectaque pensa relinquunt.

As for the daughters of Minyas, Ovid prepares us to feel some sympathy with the god by making them so demure as to border on the priggish.

Solae Minyeides intus
Intempestiva turbantes festa Minerva
Aut ducunt lanas, aut stamina pollice versant,
Aut haerent telae, famulasque laboribus urgent.
E quibus una levi deducens pollice filum,
"Dum cessant aliae commentaque sacra frequentant,
Nos quoque quas Pallas, melior dea, detinet" inquit,
"Utile opus manuum vario sermone levemus".[2]

[1] Apollod. ii, 2, 2; iii, 5, 2; cf. Hdt. ix, 34. For other references to the story, see Frazer, Loeb ed., i, 146, n. 2. Eustathius quotes three actual lines of Hesiod referring to the Proitides (Hes. fr. 29, Rzach).

[2] Ovid, *Met.* iv, 9 f., 32 ff. Other sources for the story are Antoninus Liberalis 10 (quoting earlier authors Korinna and Nikandros), Plutarch, *Qu. Graec.* xxxviii, 299e, Aelian, *Var. Hist.* iii, 42. In Plutarch the story is cited as the *aition* of the murderous proceedings at the Agrionia of Orchomenos which have been referred to above (p. 162).

A tale of Attica shows the motif of resistance to the victorious progress of Dionysos through Greece, and the consequent vengeance of the god, grafted on to other material which it could not altogether obliterate, so that the story takes a different turn. Ikarios, who was supposed to have lived in the time of the legendary king Pandion of Athens and given his name to the Attic deme of Ikaria, received Dionysos hospitably when he came to Athens. In return, Dionysos taught him the art of viticulture and revealed to him the blessings of wine. He travelled about the country to spread the new gift, but when he gave the wine to some peasants and they began to feel its effects, they thought themselves poisoned and killed him. His daughter Erigone, led to her father's grave by his faithful dog, hanged herself on a tree. Angered by these proceedings, Dionysos avenged himself in the usual way by driving the women of Attica mad, so that—in this case—they followed the example of Erigone and hanged themselves. In an attempt to get rid of the curse, a festival called *Aiora* ("Swinging") was founded in honour of Erigone, at which little images were hung swinging from trees. This is a fairly common rite, and Ikarios and Erigone were probably in the first place local deities, perhaps of vegetation. (The name "Erigone" means "Born in Spring".) The story of the introduction of the Dionysiac cult at Athens, with its customary trappings of some form of resistance followed by madness among the women, has been rather clumsily imposed upon them.[1]

Another tale concerned the introduction of the cult of Dionysos Melanaigis ("of the black goatskin") at Eleutherai on the northern borders of Attica. We know it only from the colourless little summary in the medieval compilation going by the name of *Suidas*, which has this entry under the word Melanaigis: "This is the reason for the introduction of Dionysos Melanaigis. The daughters of Eleuther, having seen a vision of Dionysos wearing a black goatskin, objected to it [or "found fault with it" ἐμέμψαντο]. He was angry with them and drove them mad. After this Eleuther was instructed by an oracle to honour Dionysos Melanaigis in order to stop their madness."

The story of Boutes and the women of Phthiotis must also be quoted for its resemblance to, and connexion with, that of

[1] The authorities for the tale seem to go back to the Alexandrian poet Eratosthenes. (PWK *Realenc.* ix, 973.) It is referred to in a papyrus fragment of Callimachus' *Aitia, Oxy. Pap.* 1362.

Lykurgos, but reference to the whole tale as told by Diodorus (it has not often been quoted in full) shows that the motive alleged is not the usual one of resistance to the cult, though this may have occurred in other versions which have not been preserved. Boutes and Lykurgos were brothers, sons of Boreas. Boutes, the younger, was detected in a plot against his brother, who told him to take ship with his fellow-conspirators and find another land to dwell in. He therefore gathered the other Thracians who had helped him, and occupied Naxos. Having no womenfolk, they sailed around the islands and ultimately to the mainland in search of wives. After landing in Thessaly, they came upon "the nurses of Dionysos" celebrating the *orgia* of the god in Achaia Phthiotis. At this point the story becomes in many respects a double of that of Lykurgos. Boutes and his followers rushed upon the women, whereat they cast away the sacred objects (τὰ ἱερά) and some fled to the sea, others to the mountain called Drios in whose neighbourhood they had been carrying out their rites. One, Koronis, was caught by Boutes and made his wife. She however summoned Dionysos to help her, and Boutes, driven mad by Dionysos, threw himself into a well and was killed.[1]

Perseus is also brought into connexion with these myths by the tradition that he not only opposed Dionysos in Argos but actually killed him. Dionysos had come thither from the islands of the Aegean with a band of women, who for this reason were known in Argive legend as the Sea-women. Perseus led the Argives in battle against them and slew many of the women, whose burial-place was shown at Argos in later times. Dionysos himself was buried at Delphi, or so said one account, linking the story with the general belief that the grave of Dionysos was in the temple of Apollo there. Perseus was also said, however, to have thrown him into the Lernean lake, which reminds us of the Argive rite of summoning him from the water (p. 162 above) and, like the title of Sea-women given to his followers, puts the story in the same circle of ritual mythology as the others. As Pausanias heard the tale at Argos, Dionysos was not killed, and after the war with Perseus laid aside his enmity and became greatly honoured by the Argives. His diving into a lake near Argos (Pausanias says it was the Alcyonian lake, which he visited himself) was an attempt to bring up Semele

[1] Diod. Sic. v, 50. The name Boutes of course means Ox-herd and recalls the ox-goad (βούπληξ) with which his brother Lykurgos chased the nurses of Dionysos in the *Iliad*.

from the underworld.[1] Perseus himself was not of course a Dionysiac figure like Pentheus or Lykurgos, and the story shows once again how the shifting tides of mythology may leave their wrack upon any outstanding hero, just as the myths may take different forms according to the practices current in particular localities.

The story of the death of Orpheus offers another example of a mixture of traditions. Most commonly, though not universally, he is described as having been killed by the women of Thrace, but the motive for the slaying is not always the same. According to the version in the *Bassarids* of Aeschylus, Orpheus incurred the anger of Dionysos by neglecting his worship for that of the sun, and the women, who were Dionysos' own followers the Bassarids, were sent against him by the god. They tore him in pieces and scattered his limbs—the customary treatment for the victim in a Bacchic sacrifice. Virgil follows this version in making the murder an act of ritual:

> Inter sacra deum nocturnique orgia Bacchi
> Discerptum late iuvenem sparsere per agros,

but his women need no divine instigation for the act. They were moved by their own indignation at the utter scorn for women and indifference to love which Orpheus displayed after the death of Eurydice. This natural feminine motive of pride or jealousy occurs elsewhere with variations, e.g. that he refused to initiate them into his mysteries, or that he enticed their husbands away from them.

The representations of his death on vase-paintings, which together with the references to Aeschylus' play provide our earliest evidence, do not show him being torn in pieces, but attacked with stones, spears, axes and other weapons. This may of course have preceded a *sparagmos*, as did the pelting of Pentheus in the *Bacchae*, and have been chosen by the painter as an easier and more suitable part of the proceedings for reproduction. The combination on the same vase of the death-scene and the picture of Orpheus charming Thracian men with his lyre does perhaps

[1] Paus. ii, 20, 3; 22, 1; 23, 8; 37, 5. The death of Dionysos in the fight is mentioned by St. Augustine, *Civ. Dei*, xviii, 12, and his drowning by Perseus in the Lernaean Lake by the scholiast on *Iliad*, xiv, 319. According to Eusebius (*Chron.* p. 168 Karst.) and Cyrillus (*c. Iul.* x, 341) the death of Dionysos at the hands of Perseus goes back to an unknown but probably Hellenistic poet Deinarchos. The motif of Perseus fighting the maenads has also been detected on sixth-century black-figured vases. (See Roscher, *Lexikon*, iii, 2016, and J. L. Catterall in PWK *Realenc.* xix, 987.)

suggest that the painter had in mind the motive of feminine jealousy rather than that of divine wrath.[1]

It is obvious that the stories which we have been considering, in so far as they concern Dionysos at all, are projections of the pattern of Dionysiac ritual. No attempt to see in them memories of historical opposition to the cult in Greece can deny this fundamental fact. The phenomena of god-inflicted *mania*, that is, *enthusiasmos*, and of *sparagmos*, are monotonously repeated. Even the idea of opposition, with which the stories regularly start, was probably inherent in the ritual and comes into the myths primarily from that source and only secondarily, if at all, from the fact of historical opposition to his cult in Greece. It expresses indeed a deep and abiding truth about human nature as well as something inherent in Dionysiac religion, a truth which underlies a tragedy like the *Bacchae* and gives it its permanent and universal validity. No man can submit without a struggle to the experience of having his distinctively human faculty of reason, and all that connects him with the normal world, overwhelmed and submerged by those animal elements which, normally dormant or at least in subjection, are released and made dominant by the irresistible surge of Dionysiac power. Every surrender to this power must have been preceded by opposition, which, at least among the Greeks, was sure to find imaginative expression in myth. The truth of this is more clearly seen now than in the past, with the natural consequence that the historical explanation of the myths is being abandoned.[2] As more positive evidence against it is quoted the fact that the scene of the opposition can even be laid in Thrace, as in the stories of Lykurgos and Orpheus, so that these stories at least are no evidence of opposition to the progress of the cult through Greece.[3]

Yet once we have granted that the framework of all the myths

[1] Authorities for the preceding paragraph, and illustrations of vase-paintings, will be found in my *Orpheus and Gr. Rel.* 32 ff.

[2] See for example Otto, *Dionysos*, p. 72, and M. Tierney, "Dionysos, the Dithyramb and Tragedy" (*Studies*, Sept. 1944, p. 339): "The ordinary explanation of these stories is that they reflect a historical resistance to the cult of Dionysos from Thrace. This explanation is however very improbable; it is much more likely that the idea of opposition, struggle, and catastrophe was an ancient component of the god's ritual, which represented him as taking violent possession of men's souls and bodies, sweeping them out of themselves, and driving them to act like madmen."

[3] I cannot follow the argument of those who assert that because Homer does not mention the native country of Lykurgos, therefore "it was Aeschylus who first made him a Thracian" (Tierney, o.c., p. 338, n. 2, cf. Otto, o.c., p. 57). Wherever his home is mentioned he is king of the Edonians in Thrace, and the onus of proof must lie the other way.

alike is largely aetiological, we need not suppose that the same source was responsible for every detail. In relating them we noticed that there were considerable differences in the stories of different localities, and one such difference strikes us as marking off the Thracian stories from those whose scene is Greece proper. In the Thracian stories, the worship of Dionysos is established. Someone opposes it, as it must have been periodically opposed everywhere, and either persecutes the maenads (Lykurgos) or is attacked by them at the instigation of the wrathful god (Orpheus). In either case the maenads, or Nurses of Dionysos, are there to play their part. Their ravings are as it were a familiar feature of the country, and the stories contain no hint that Dionysos might be a recent arrival and the women now for the first time initiated into his fearful ecstasies. Yet this is precisely the point of the stories told of Greek cities. It is the *introduction* of the cult that is opposed, and the madness of the women is a terrifyingly *new* phenomenon. Admittedly the myths can tell little or nothing that deserves the name of historical about the date or manner of the progress of Dionysos through Greece. Yet I venture to think that they would not have taken precisely the form they did were it not that (*a*) the introduction of the cult was sufficiently recent to be still remembered in the folk-memory of cities like Thebes, Orchomenos, Argos and Athens, and (*b*) it retained for the Greek mind something of its character as a terrifying incursion from the outside world. In one sense it must always and everywhere have had that character, namely that it is an incursion from the fathomless depths beyond the limits of sane and conscious human personality: but to the Greeks it was so in a literal sense also, an incursion out of the world of the *barbaroi* from which Hellenism, in the words of Herodotus, had divided itself off. For them the two went inevitably together, since sanity, self-consciousness and limit were the very qualities that distinguished the Greek mind from its surroundings. Those qualities and their particular view of what constituted feminine modesty and duty set the Greeks in sharp contrast to their barbarian neighbours of Thrace or Phrygia and make it certain that their opposition to the effeminate stranger from those regions (for so Pentheus called him) must have been a historical fact not to be explained away by any talk of aetiological myths. To the conservative Greek his acceptance was "a great reproach to the Hellenes".[1]

That is all that can be said here with profit on the historical

[1] ψόγος ἐς Ἕλληνας μέγας, Pentheus at *Bacchae*, 779.

side of the introduction of Dionysos into Greece.[1] Come he did, and the next question therefore is what effect he had upon the Greeks and they on him. Did they succeed in taming and hellenizing this wild spirit or did he leave his mark upon them? In particular, what contribution did his impact make to the Greek idea of the relations between man and god which we have declared to be the main object of our whole inquiry? No one acquainted with the tolerant Greek attitude will be surprised to learn that the result was a compromise, and that there is therefore a distinction to be drawn between the ideas associated with the original Thracian cult and those which were accepted by the Greeks after they had modified it to suit their more Olympian mentality.

The Dionysiac worshipper, at the height of his ecstasy, was one with his god. Divinity had entered into him, he was *entheos*, and the one name Bacchos covered both deity and devotee. Now I have remarked that divinity meant immortality, and there is no doubt that in Thracian religion both were believed to be attained together. The Thracian belief that they could become immortal was one which caused comment among the Greeks, to whom it evidently appeared as something strange and abnormal. Herodotus, in introducing into his history the Thracian tribe of the Getai, speaks of them as "the Getai who believe they are immortal". They owe their immortality to a god or spirit (*daimon*) of the country, Zalmoxis, and similarly Socrates, pretending to have a charm which will cure young Charmides of his headache, says: "I learned it abroad on a campaign, from one of the Thracian physicians of Zalmoxis, who are said to attain no less than immortality."[2] Since in this cult of Zalmoxis we have an example of a purely Thracian worship untouched by the Greeks, let us see what Herodotus has to say about the beliefs and practices which it involved. Here is his account:[3]

The manner of their immortality is as follows. They believe that they do not die, and that whoever of them is ready for death goes to one Zalmoxis, a daemon, the same who is also called by some of them

[1] Those interested should however compare the evidence cited by Jaeger that the rise of Dionysos into favour with the political authorities coincided with the rule of the tyrants, e.g. the displacement of the ancient hero Adrastos of Sikyon by Dionysos under Kleisthenes, the rise of Dionysiac festivals in Corinth under Periander, and in Athens under the Peisistratids (W. Jaeger, *Theol. of Early Gr. Phils.* (Oxford, 1947), p. 58).

[2] Hdt. iv, 93, *Γέται οἱ ἀθανατίζοντες*, Plato, *Charm.* 156d, *οἳ λέγονται καὶ ἀπαθανατίζειν.*

[3] iv, 94.

Gebeleizis. Every four years they choose one of their number by lot, and send him as an ambassador to Zalmoxis, instructing him about their particular needs on each occasion. The way that they send him is this. Certain of them are appointed to hold three spears, while others take the envoy to Zalmoxis by his hands and feet, and swinging him up on high cast him on to the spear-points. If he dies when he is impaled, they take it as a sign that the god is gracious; but if he does not die, they blame the messenger himself, saying that he is a bad man, and having rebuked this one they dispatch another. They give him his instructions while he is still alive.

Continuing, Herodotus describes, on the authority of the Greeks of the Hellespont and Black Sea regions, the Euhemeristic story according to which Zalmoxis was a human reformer who had learned the more refined habits of Ionian civilization through having lived on Samos as the slave of Pythagoras. Having won his freedom and amassed a fortune, he returned to his native Thrace, where, finding his compatriots given to evil and foolish ways of life, he decided that a belief in immortality would make them mend their ways. Accordingly he invited the leading citizens to a feast in a specially built banqueting hall, at which he announced that neither he nor his guests nor their descendants would die. Instead they would be transported to a land where they would live for ever amid all good things. After this he vanished from among the Thracians, having constructed a secret underground chamber where he lived for three years. The Thracians believed him dead and mourned him accordingly. In the fourth year he reappeared, and so what he had said about immortality came to be believed. Herodotus' conclusion about him is restrained but sceptical. "For my part," he says, "concerning Zalmoxis and his underground chamber I do not disbelieve nor am I over-inclined to believe, but I do hold that he must have lived many years before Pythagoras. Now whether there ever was a man called Zalmoxis, or whether he is a native daemon of the Getai, let us leave him."

In spite of its Euhemeristic elements, which are easily discounted,[1] the above passage provides a straightforward and very

[1] I am sorry if I seem to be cavalier in this dismissal of the humanity of Zalmoxis and his connexion with Pythagoras (which has most recently been maintained by E. L. Minar in *Early Pythagorean Politics* (Baltimore, 1942)), but I cannot believe in it. For the probable connexions of the Zalmoxis myth with Pythagoreanism, see the sensible remarks of A. Cameron in *The Pyth. Background of the Theory of Recollection* (Wisconsin, 1938), pp. 13 ff. As Cameron says, "The Thracians, we know, did not need Pythagoras to tell them about immortality or rebirth, or καταβάσεις to the underworld".

welcome account of purely Thracian faith and ritual. The belief in immortality is central, and the barbarous rite of human sacrifice shows in what a primitive stage of society such a belief could flourish. The reference to the feast with which Zalmoxis entertained the chiefs, and at which he announced the gift of immortality, is transparently aetiological, and clear evidence for what one would expect in any case to form a part of this religion, namely a sacramental meal.

This example from Herodotus, and the words addressed by Socrates to Charmides, illustrate the point that for the Greeks in general the Thracian belief in immortality was something strange and foreign. It is added by the writer as a distinguishing mark by which the people to whom he is referring will be instantly identified: "The Getai who immortalize themselves" and "the Thracian physicians of Zalmoxis—you know, those people who call themselves immortal". It is natural enough that it seemed a barbarous tenet to most of the Greeks, whom we know to have been brought up in the tradition of the aristocratic gods of Homer, with whom any infringement on their privileged position as the Immortals was a deadly sin and a courting of destruction. Yet the fact appears to present a problem, since by the time that Herodotus and Plato were writing, the religion of Dionysos, which contained all the essential features of Thracian religion as exemplified in the account of his brother-god Zalmoxis, had long been adopted in Greece, not only privately but as an official cult of the states. At the same time the contemporary religion of Thrace can still be spoken of as something foreign, and its central belief as one strange in Greek eyes. It is not however matter for great astonishment to one who is familiar with the Greek genius for transforming any elements which did not appeal to them in a religion which for other reasons they were tempted to adopt. In this they did not show themselves strikingly different from the rest of mankind. A living religion is a stone of many facets, any one of which can be turned to face the light while the gleam of the others is dulled by shadow: nor is the possessor necessarily conscious that the stone has turned in his hands.

We have already noticed the tradition that the Thraco-Phrygian god, when he first began to take Greece by storm, was stubbornly opposed by those in authority, and we can be sure that when, as in the fifth century, we find festivals of Dionysos in the state calendar of Athens, they have undergone a change of character in the meantime. Everyone knows that an occasion like the Great Dionysia, at which the plays of the tragedians were performed, and sacrifice was made in full sunlight before the whole city, had little in common with the typical nocturnal *orgia* which with the aid of Euripides have already been described in this chapter. Yet even among the officially recognized festivals there seems to have been a distinction. Thucydides speaks of "the more archaic Dionysia" which were celebrated in the spring month of Anthesterion at the sanctuary of Dionysos in the Marshes, and other evidence suggests both that more of the ancient licence was preserved on this occasion and that it had impressive connexions with the spirits of the dead. Rohde went so far as to say that in these "more archaic Dionysia" Dionysos appeared just as he was in primitive belief, as the "master of the souls", and there is much to support him.[1] This celebration lasted three days, and its fully official character is most strikingly demonstrated by the solemn marriage between the god and the wife of the King-Archon which formed a part of it. The magistrate (archon) who retained the title of King retained with it the religious functions which had belonged to the vanished monarchy. The law demanded that his wife should be a citizen and a virgin when he married her, yet this carefully chosen consort of the official religious leader of the city had to go through (by what exact procedure we are not told) an annual ceremony representing her marriage and corporal union with Dionysos. This took place, Aristotle tells us, in a building which used to be the residence of the King and was now called the *Bukolion* (Ox-stall). The dread appearance of Dionysos as the mighty Bull was not forgotten.[2] In this rite the political adoption of the god is seen to be complete. The winter festival of the Lenaea, at which in the second half of the fifth century works of the great comic poets were performed, was also under the direction of the King-Archon, which meant that it was regarded as among the most ancient of the city's cults. In his hands, says Aristotle, were

[1] *τὰ ἀρχαιότερα Διονύσια*, Thuc. ii, 15, 4, cf. Rohde, *Psyche* (Eng. trans. 1925), ch. ix, n. 11, p. 305. For full discussion of the evidence for the Anthesteria, as for other Dionysiac festivals, see Farnell, *Cults*, v, ch. 5.

[2] Arist. *Ath. Pol.* 3 *ὁ μὲν βασιλεὺς εἶχε τὸ νῦν καλούμενον βουκόλιον, πλησίον τοῦ Πρυτανείου (σημεῖον δέ· ἔτι καὶ νῦν γὰρ τῆς τοῦ βασιλέως γυναικὸς ἡ σύμμιξις ἐνταῦθα γίνεται τῷ Διονύσῳ καὶ ὁ γάμος)* (quoted by Farnell, *Cults*, v, ch. 5, n. 34e, p. 284; the other classical reference [Demosth.] *c. Neaer.* 75, is quoted ib., n. 69e, p. 299; see also ib., pp. 126, 135, 159 f., 217, 260, and PWK *Realenc.* i, 2373 f.). A. B. Cook (*Zeus*, i, 686), following Frazer, points out that the connexion of the marriage-ceremony with the Anthesteria is not certainly attested: it may have fallen at another date.

"all the ancestral observances", and Plato bears him out that "to him who has obtained the office of King have been assigned the most solemn and peculiarly ancestral of the ancient observances".[1] Its name, which must be connected with *lenai*, a synonym of maenads, points to an original connexion with orgiastic women, but by historical times this tradition had already disappeared. There were also in Attica rural Dionysiac festivals, such as the one celebrated by Dikaiopolis in the *Acharnians* of Aristophanes—occasions so far as one can see for communal drinking and village merrymaking, in which the phallic element was present—but these too have none of the passion and terror of the *enthusiasmos* experienced by those who gave themselves to Dionysos in the wild abandon of nocturnal mountain revels.

The authorities of the Greek states, then, did not accept the barbaric stranger without, in some cases at least, emptying his worship of its most characteristic content. Yet the original orgiastic worship was not entirely suppressed. One of the most remarkable instances of official recognition of the cult was the reconciliation effected between Dionysos and Apollo at Delphi, the greatest, and almost the only, Pan-Hellenic religious centre. Of this there will be something to say in the next chapter, but it is relevant to notice here that in the winter months, when Apollo ceded the shrine to Dionysos, the *oreibasia* was carried out in all its glory on the highest parts of Parnassos by an officially sanctioned band of maenads. Their festival was held every two years, and a troop of Attic women called Thyiades was sent from Athens to join the revels of their Delphic sisters.[2] Euripides was not describing a dead religion in the *Bacchae*, even though the days were past when the Dionysiac fury swept down upon the whole female population of a city and carried them off to the mountains in defiance of authority. A chorus in the *Antigone* gives a vivid picture of the scene above Delphi, when "Thou art seen in the smoky glare above the twin-crested rock, where rove the Korykian Bacchic nymphs", and Bacchos is summoned in the words: "Thou that leadest the dance of the fiery stars, watcher over the nocturnal cry, Zeus-born child, appear, Lord, with thine attendant Thyiads, who all night long in frenzied ecstasy dance thy dance, Iacchos our Master."[3]

We may conclude that in the state-cults, at Athens at least,

[1] Arist. *Ath. Pol.* 57; Plato, *Politicus*, 290e.
[2] Paus. x, 4, 2; 32, 5. Cf. Dodds, intro. to *Bacchae*, xi.
[3] Soph. *Ant.* 1125 ff

much of the original madness of Dionysiac worship was purged away, though Dionysos could never be pressed into the Olympian mould and the populace seem to have fastened on those aspects of him which linked him to their local rural saints or the rites of their "All Souls' Day" and similar observances to propitiate the spirits of the dead. Fertility-worship and the cult of souls belonged to that side of religion which had been driven underground by the predominance of the Homeric gods, but they remained, as they have always done, close to the heart of the people, and the acceptance of Dionysos gave them fresh encouragement. At the same time there remained here and there the wild nocturnal orgies, celebrated sometimes no doubt by private *thiasoi*, but sometimes, as we have seen, in a more officially recognized way. Their character was familiar to every Greek. Indeed there can scarcely have been a break in this less respectable, more fearful side of the worship from before the days of Euripides and Sophocles down to the time when Bacchic *thiasoi* were giving offence to the authorities of Rome, and had to be suppressed by the *Senatus Consultum de Bacchanalibus* in 187 B.C., or when in the first century B.C. Diodorus was writing: "This they say is the reason why in many of the Hellenic states Bacchic bands of women collect together every other year, and it is lawful for maidens to bear the thyrsus and join in the enthusiasm, worshipping the god with cries; and the women form groups to do sacrifice to the god and rave and hymn the presence of Dionysos, representing by their actions the legendary maenads who accompanied the god of old."[1]

With these facts in mind, let us return to the central question posed by the existence of two contrasting ideas in Greek religion, the one emphasizing the gulf between human and divine, mortal and immortal, and the other teaching that the aim of the religious life was to exchange mortality for immortality, to become god from man. Homeric religion we saw to be saturated with the first idea, and the Homeric notion of divine *phthonos* was inherited by later ages and is reflected in the pages of Herodotus and developed, rather than contradicted, in much of Greek tragedy. We have looked also at a different notion of divinity, the materialistic god who was a legacy from the first attempts at natural philosophy, though in this the philosophers struck a chord that was waiting to respond and helped to pave the way to a more spiritual and even mystical conception of the relations between man and god

[1] Diod. iv, 3, quoted Farnell, *Cults*, v, 297, n. 65.

than the Homeric creations could offer. Now we are met by Dionysos, a god whose history gives every reason to believe that he would be a powerful influence for the encouragement of a belief in immortality. In his own home he was the god of a people in whom that belief was firmly rooted. Did he also implant it in the minds of the more rational Greeks? At least he found in them an unpromising soil, and the way in which Greek writers refer to the Thracian belief as something foreign suggests that he did not succeed. This seems a credible enough consequence of the emasculation of his worship by the civil authorities in a state like Athens, but what of the nocturnal orgies which, with or without official sanction, were still carried on?

Clearly this is a difficult question to answer with certainty, and to avoid misunderstanding it should be said at once that Dionysiac worship was emphatically one of several influences which assisted some of the best minds in fifth- and fourth-century Greece towards a new conception of the human soul in which its immortality played an essential part. These however were rather theologians, or religious philosophers, than ordinary worshippers, and by no means whole-hearted participators in the untamed Thracian rites. Curious as it may seem, I would say that the promise of immortality contained in the wild Thracian rite remained latent so far as the ordinary worshipper in Greece was concerned. So foreign was the idea of equating man with god that the Greeks, although they might yield to the emotional temptations which Dionysos brought, did not at the same time absorb the central message of Thracian religion, that by communion with him they might become permanently and eternally immortal, exempt from death. They felt the exaltation of being snatched up into the personality of the god, and to experience this *enthusiasmos* they submitted to his intoxicating and ecstatic rites, but they seem to have believed that this possession by the god was only temporary. While it lasted there was nothing on earth to compare with it, but it left them as they were before, save that they were more deeply under the sway of the deity who from time to time could give them this incomparable experience. The *ekstasis* was temporary, as was emphasized by Socrates' remark in the *Ion* about the contrast between the Bacchae when they are "possessed" and when they are "in their minds", and as it receded they felt that the god had left them and that they were human—*thnetoi*—once more.

In this way, and to this extent, the Thracian belief in immortality by communion appears to have been watered down and hellenized even by the orgiastic worshippers of Dionysos in Greece. The conclusion, no doubt, is based on personal impressions, and may be thought to take too little account of the celebrations of *teletai* by private groups or clans, which find occasional mention in ancient records. But we know too little to be certain either of the character of these rites or of the beliefs behind them, nor is it likely that their influence was at all widespread. What we do know suggests that their worship had individual features, the result of local or family traditions. My suggestion is simply that in its ordinary form, without such modifications and before the speculations of theologians got to work on it, the religion of Dionysos did not offer to the Greeks what it had offered to his original worshippers outside Greece, because that was something too foreign to their notions of the proper relations between man and god. The effect of Homer and Hesiod was not so lightly to be undone. There is no mention of immortality or divinity for man in the *Bacchae* of Euripides. Had it figured prominently in the *orgia* of his own experience or knowledge, he would hardly have boggled at reproducing it, but from all the good gifts that the exultant Bacchae claim to receive from Dionysos, that of immortality is absent. It might be said that it was implicit in the idea of possession by the god, which itself receives no emphasis but must be inferred from the very name, *Bacche* or *Bacchos*, which his followers take to themselves. But as I have tried to point out, this possession was temporary, and it is noteworthy that not only is the union of mortal and divinity slurred over and the promise of immortality left out, but the *Bacchae* emphasizes perhaps more than any other play the Greek contrast between mortal and divine, and the proverbial wisdom of remembering one's mortality and not striving to set oneself up against a god. Such references are: "Appearing a god to mortals" (Dionysos in the prologue, line 42); "Born a mortal, the gods I hold not in scorn" (Kadmos, 199); "'Tis no wisdom to be clever and not think mortal thoughts" (Chorus, 395); "I would sacrifice to him rather than kick against the pricks in anger, a mortal against a god" (Dionysos to Pentheus, 794); "To be modest and reverence the gods I hold to be best and wisest for mortals" (messenger, 1150).

To preach obedience to Dionysos is natural, and would presumably have appealed to a Thracian who believed himself immortal, as much as to a Greek; but the purely Hellenic form in which the admonition is put, laying stress in every phrase on the gulf between mortal and god, shows that it was still beyond the strength of Dionysos to change the Greek outlook and substitute his own doctrines for those of him who, incongruous as it seems, was still in a real sense the Greeks' own Bible—Homer.

Chapter VII

APOLLO

THE more one looks at the ideas associated with the worship of Apollo, the stranger and more contradictory his character appears to be. This makes him difficult to write about, since when dwelling on one aspect the mind is haunted by the feeling that what is said should be instantly qualified, if not contradicted, by reference to another. Since however the subjection of one's statements to constant qualification leads only to confusion and that sensation of bafflement so familiar to all who seek to probe the Greek religious mind, it will be best to take a bolder line, a course which will not only be simpler, but probably take us nearer to the truth as well. For if at every step we were to qualify our account of one side of Apollo's nature with reference to certain other sides, we should not only invite confusion but should be treating as if they were equally important ideas which by no means deserved, in Greek eyes, the same general measure of respect and attention. We may, then, speak first of the most important and influential aspect of his religion, and only after that turn to aspects which were decidedly secondary.[1]

Under his most important and influential aspect may be included everything that connects him with law and order. Primarily he represented the Greek preference for "the intelligible, determinate, mensurable, as opposed to the fantastic, vague and shapeless".[2] His advice was "Know thyself" and "Nothing too much". Others of the precepts which were inscribed on the fabric of Apollo's temple at Delphi convey, especially in their original wording with its associations (impossible to capture in translation), better than anything else the spirit that he stood for:

[1] The reader may be reminded of the discussion of Apollo's origin in Ch. II, which must naturally be brought into close connexion with the present chapter. The account which follows owes much to that of Professor Nilsson in ch. 6 of his *Hist. of Gr. Rel.* and to his selection of ancient texts in *Die Religion der Griechen* (*Religionsgeschichtliches Lesebuch*, ed. A. Bertholet, no. 4, Tübingen, 1927).

[2] p. 152 above.

Curb thy spirit.
Observe the limit.
Hate hybris.
Keep a reverent tongue.
Fear authority.
Bow before the divine.
Glory not in strength.
Keep woman under rule.[1]

His connexion with law and order was not confined to vague maxims. All Greece looked towards him as both the giver and the interpreter of law. To the primitive mind all law is divine, and it was long before even the Greeks became too sophisticated to ask the gods to legislate for them. The word is appropriate, for it was primarily the sophists who undermined this religious conception of law by their intellectual probings into *physis* and *nomos*, nature with her eternal decrees and the merely man-made conventions by which, they claimed, the life of states and the relations between neighbours were regulated in contemporary Greece. Up to the time of their speculations in the middle of the fifth century, it was natural for Greek law-makers to seek divine authority for their laws. To learn the divine will they consulted the oracles, and above all the oracle of Apollo at Delphi. Thus many Greek states were represented as having got their constitutions from him, though in practice, as Farnell suggested, it may more frequently have been a question of simply obtaining his approval for a code already drawn up.[2] The most famous example of Apollo's activity as a law-giver is probably the constitution of Sparta which he was said to have laid down for their legendary ruler Lykurgos. Of this Tyrtaios sang:

For thus the lord of the silver bow, far-working Apollo, the golden-haired, gave response from his rich shrine: There shall govern the Council the Kings, honoured of the gods, to whose care is entrusted the lovely city of Sparta, and the Elders ripe in years, and after them the men of the people, giving obedience in turn to just decrees; and they shall speak fairly and act justly in all things, nor give any crooked counsel to this city. And upon the increase of the people shall follow

[1] θυμοῦ κράτει, πέρας ἐπιτέλει, ὕβριμ μείσει, εὔφημος γίνου, τὸ κρατοῦμ φοβοῦ, προσκύνει τὸ θεῖον, ἐπὶ ῥώμῃ μὴ καυχῶ, γυναικὸς ἄρχε. These are selected from the long list in Dittenberger, *Syll.*³ 1268, an inscription of the third century B.C. from Miletopolis in Mysia. The actual temple-inscriptions at Delphi have of course perished, but several lists of the precepts exist, for which see the full note of Dittenberger, l.c. Concerning the inscription here quoted he concludes: "ergo haec quoque sacra praecepta cum Delphico templo coniungi ut coniectu promptum ita antiquitatis testimonio confirmatum est".

[2] *Cults*, iv, 198. Xenophon's account suggests that this was so in the case of Lykurgos: ἐπήρετο τὸν θεὸν εἰ λῷον καὶ ἄμεινον εἴη τῇ Σπάρτῃ πειθομένῃ οἷς αὐτὸς ἔθηκε νόμοις (*Rep. Laced.* viii, 5). But Xenophon's is not the only account.

victory and strength. Thus did Phoibos make revelation to the city concerning these things.[1]

This sounds as if, to some minds at least, a fairly comprehensive plan of the peculiar Spartan form of constitution was obtained from the god himself. Herodotus, always ready to set down the more and the less mythical accounts of an event side by side, and leave his reader free to choose, has also described the experience of Lykurgos. "Lykurgos, a man of note among the Spartans, went to the oracle at Delphi, and as he entered the chamber, straightway the Pythia spoke as follows." There follow four lines of the oracle consisting entirely of compliments to Lykurgos, and Herodotus then goes on: "Some people say that in addition to this the Pythia also explained to him the constitution which is now established at Sparta, but according to the story of the Spartans themselves, Lykurgos brought these things from Crete."[2] Tyrtaios, of course, was himself a Spartan, and the difference in outlook between the two stories is a difference of period. The second version given by Herodotus was the work of the rationalists already active in the Greece of his day, for it rests on the real and observable similarity between the laws of Sparta and those of Crete. It is beginning to take its place beside the earlier account which gave credit for the constitution to Apollo, but it never entirely succeeded in replacing it. The *Laws* of Plato opens with a question addressed by the Athenian to Kleinias, a man of Crete: "To whom is the merit of instituting your laws ascribed? To a god, or to some man?" and the reply is unambiguous: "Why, to a god, sir, indubitably to a god: in our case to Zeus, in the case of Lacedaemon, to which our friend here belongs, I believe, according to their own story, to Apollo."[3] In spite of what Herodotus says, the divine origin of the Spartan constitution is still ascribed to "the story of the Spartans themselves". When, centuries later, Plutarch wrote the life of Lykurgos, he too made the Delphic oracle the author of his laws.

At Athens, the laws of Drako about murder and homicide seem to be modelled on Delphic ideas of *miasma* and its purification,[4] and the oracle also had a hand in the beginnings of Athenian democracy, according to Aristotle's statement that when Kleisthenes introduced his artificially constructed *phylae* to replace the old organization based on blood-relationship he called them after

[1] Tyrtaios (seventh century B.C.), fr. 3, Diehl.
[2] Hdt. i, 65.
[3] Trans. A. E. Taylor.
[4] On which cf. pp. 190 ff. below.

heroes whose names had been given to him in a response from the Pythia.[1] Herodotus tells of other cities who sought the oracle's advice in similar situations. For example, the people of Cyrene sent to Delphi to ask Apollo what sort of constitution would give them the happiest life. The god's reply instructed them to get a law-giver from Mantinea in Arcadia. They applied to the Mantineans, who sent them one of their leading citizens named Demonax, and this man reorganized the state.[2] Plato reminds his law-givers that all legislation on religious matters should be left to Apollo:

> What then, he said, is still left for us to do in the way of legislation?
>
> For us nothing, I replied, but for Apollo at Delphi there remain the greatest and finest and most important of legislative acts.
>
> What are these? he asked.
>
> The founding of temples, sacrifices, and other services to gods, demigods and heroes; also the burial of the dead and any observances which are necessary to propitiate the spirits of the other world. These matters we do not understand ourselves, and in founding our city we shall not, if we are wise, listen to anyone else nor ask anyone to expound them to us save the god of our country. For he is the national expositor who explains these things to all men from his seat at the navel of the earth.[3]

Apollo was the "national expositor" (*patrios exegetes*), and for his work of *exegesis* he made use of human instruments. Besides the oracle at Delphi he had ministers, themselves known as *exegetai*, through whom he gave advice both to states and to private citizens and was able to make his voice even better heard in the internal affairs of the independent cities of Greece. These *exegetai* are a curious institution, and an interesting example of the influence and methods of Delphi. Known to us from Athens, they probably existed in other cities as well, and at Sparta each of the Kings chose two "Pythians", described as *theopropoi* or prophets. They dined with the Kings at the public expense and interpreted the will of Delphi to the city. Their functions must have been similar to those of the Athenian *exegetai*, who were of two sorts, those named by the oracle (*πυθόχρηστοι*) and those elected by the Athenian people (*ὑπὸ τοῦ δήμου καθεσταμένοι*). The latter appear to have been chosen from one or two noble families who had a hereditary authority in certain matters of religious cult.[4]

[1] Arist. *Ath. Pol.* xxi, 6.

[2] Hdt. iv, 161.

[3] Plato, *Rep.* iv, 427b. Cf. also *Laws*, vi, 759c.

[4] *ἐξηγητὴς πυθόχρηστος*, Ditt. *Syll.* 697e, line 9; Suidas s.v. *ἐξηγητής*; *ἐξηγητὴς ἐξ Εὐπατριδῶν χειροτονητὸς ὑπὸ τοῦ δήμου διὰ βίου*, *IG* iii, 241 (PWK *Realenc.* vi, 1583). For the Spartan *Πύθιοι* see Hdt. vi, 57.

Plato recommends a method for the appointment of *exegetai* which allows for a final selection by the oracle at Delphi from a number of candidates nominated by popular vote.[1] In either case, though accounted the ministers of the Delphic god and his mouthpieces in the interpretation of civil and religious law, they not only resided in, but remained citizens of, their own city. This was no doubt necessary for their influence, in view of the indissoluble unity of the city and its religious cults, a mark of the communal origin of religion which Greek city-states retained throughout their history. This illustrates the difficulties which confronted the Delphic authorities if they ever had hopes of achieving a single Pan-Hellenic religion. In all probability such an idea would have been incomprehensible to them. Apollo preferred to gain his influence in the natural Greek way, not by supplanting the gods of the various states but by establishing himself as the one to whom all turned for advice on the best methods of worshipping the gods of their fathers. His responses usually took the form of upholding established local usage, the "ancestral custom" (πάτριος νόμος). "What worries me," says Euthydemos to Socrates in Xenophon's *Commentaria*, "is that so far as I can see no man can ever make sufficient return for the goodness of the gods." "Don't let that depress you," replies Socrates. "You know that the god of Delphi, whenever anyone asks him how he should show his gratitude to the gods, replies, 'According to the law of the city'."[2]

The duties ascribed to the *exegetai* include the giving of information on a variety of religious matters—temples, cult-procedure, sacrifices—but especially on the rules of purification to be followed in cases of homicide or any contact with it. An interesting illustration of this is the provision in Plato's *Laws* whereby if a man sell, without informing the purchaser, a slave who is a homicide (thus automatically bringing pollution into the purchaser's house), the purchaser shall have the right to return his purchase, and the vendor, as well as repaying the price threefold, "shall purify the dwelling of the purchaser as laid down by the *exegetai*".[3] Another interesting passage, from an Athenian law-court speech attributed to Demosthenes, shows the *exegetai* acting in the capacity of legal advisers to the private citizen. A brawl had taken place in which a woman had been killed. Says the speaker:

After the death of the woman, I betook myself to the *exegetai*, in order to find out what I ought to do, and I related to them all that had

[1] *Laws*, 759d. [2] Xen. *Mem.* iv, 3, 16. [3] *Laws* xi, 916c.

occurred, the arrival of these men, the kindness of the old woman, how I had received her in my house and how through refusing to give up the cup she met her death. When the *exegetai* had heard my story, they asked me whether I wanted only information from them or advice as well. I answered that I should like both, and they replied: Then we shall give you information about the legal position and practical advice as well.[1]

This they proceed to do in considerable detail.

These officials seem to have been employed in normal times for what might be called routine work. They were on the spot to be consulted when it was a matter of interpreting the law, or answering a question about the conduct of one of the official cults by pointing to or elucidating ancestral custom. In circumstances of exceptional difficulty or importance, Delphi itself was applied to, and the problem referred directly to the god in his own shrine. Such a crisis would be a national disaster like a plague, showing that the anger of the gods had been in some special way incurred and extraordinary expiation was therefore necessary. There was a story that during a time of plague the Athenians consulted the Pythian priestess to find out where, or against what deity, they had offended, and were reminded that they had been visited by a begging priest of the Great Mother of Phrygia and had either driven him out of the country or, according to another version, stoned him and cast him into the great pit called the *barathron*. They must therefore make amends to the goddess whose servant they had insulted. They built her a temple, and in this way the Oriental cult was first introduced into the Athenian city.[2] Another extraordinary occasion for which the advice of the *exegetai* was considered inadequate was the founding of a colony. The influence of the Delphic oracle on colonization was considerable.[3] As Professor Parke remarks, "To dispatch a body of citizens from their native land to settle as a community abroad was not solely a civil act: to the Greeks it involved a number of serious religious consequences". In particular, for the all-important question,

[1] [Demosth.] xlvii, 68.

[2] The story is known only from late sources (Julian, *Or.* v, 159, Spanhem; Suidas, s.vv. μητραγυρτής and βάραθρον = Schol. Aristoph. *Plut.* 431; Schol. Aeschin, iii, 187; Photius s.v. μητρῷον). These references are cited by Nilsson, *Gesch. Gr. Rel.*, vol. i (Munich, 1941), 687 n. 3, who strongly defends the antiquity of the story, and dates it, on archaeological evidence provided by the remains of the Metroon itself, at the end of the sixth or beginning of the fifth century B.C.

[3] Cf. H. W. Parke, *A History of the Delphic Oracle* (Blackwell, 1939), bk. I, chs. i and ii.

which was the god under whose protection the new community should be placed, recourse was had to Delphi itself. The patron-deity of Massilia (Marseilles) was the Ephesian Artemis, which perhaps seems curious until we learn that it was founded as a colony by the Phocaeans from the coast of Asia Minor, who when they set out had been advised by Delphi to take this goddess for their guide.

We see then that Apollo was first and foremost the patron of the legal or statutory aspect of religion. In his province were the rules for the founding and prosecution of official cults all over Greek lands. We notice also that his legislative functions extended outside the purely religious field into what we should regard as the domain of secular law. This was inevitable, since the line of demarcation between the secular and the religious was by no means so clearly marked for the Greeks as it is for us. Among his functions as legislator, there is one in particular which displays this double character, and deserves especial mention, partly because it was more than any other the special concern of Apollo, and partly also because it serves to connect his official aspect with other, more puzzling sides of his religion. It reveals the link which existed in the Greek mind, enabling it to see the whole complex of ideas as fittingly embodied in the character of this one great god. I refer to his authority in cases of homicide or murder.

Whatever were the prevailing views about the taking of human life—and important changes took place within the history of classical Greece—they always sought ratification in the sanction of Apollo. Thus in effect Apollo himself seemed to alter his views and adopt a more civilized attitude with the passing of the centuries. The progress is from the blood-feud or vendetta to the state regulation of trials for killing. According to the ideas of the first, the ghost of any man who had been killed by violence was hostile to his kin until vengeance had been taken on the killer. The earliest belief (surviving in the wilder parts of modern Greece) was that the unavenged victim was denied entrance to the world of shades, and that his soul was liable to re-animate the corpse and wreak a terrifying physical vengeance either on the murderer or on a kinsman who failed in his duty towards him.[1] Such a vendetta is an in-

[1] Cf. the interesting comparison of ancient and modern evidence in Lawson, *Mod. Gr. Folklore and Anc. Gr. Rel.* (Cambridge, 1910), ch. iv, sect. 4: "Revenants as Avengers of Blood".

heritance as much as land or goods, and a son had no choice but to pursue it. Until the wrath of the dead man had been appeased, his family lay under a pollution, a *miasma* that was almost physical. As soon as there were cities, this pollution might be held to affect the whole community. Thus while the exaction of vengeance remained the duty and privilege of the family, the state had, in its own interests, to make sure that this duty was performed. If the killer remained undiscovered, so that the possibility of a personal feud could not arise, it fell to the ruler of the city to pronounce a ban, or curse, on the man, whoever he might turn out to be, in the hope of thereby casting off the pollution. This seems to have been the early teaching of Delphi, and when the doctrine is invoked by Oedipus in Sophocles' play, it is the Delphic oracle which he quotes as the authority for his action. The ban which he pronounces on the unknown murderer of Laius runs as follows:

> I ban him, whosoever he be, from this land whose royal power and sceptre I wield. Let no one receive him or speak a word to him, nor give him part or lot in prayer and sacrifice to the gods, nor in the lustral water: but let every man thrust him from his doors, since he is to us a pollution [*miasma*]. So the oracle of the Pythian god has but now revealed to me.[1]

In his dealings with homicide, it was above all this question of *miasma*, or pollution, which concerned Apollo. As it was he who pronounced a city or an individual to lie under its cloud, so it was he who could grant the ritual purification which would set them free. With the parallel growth of moral enlightenment and the power of the state, the blood-feud was held more and more in check, and replaced step by step by ideas less inimical to political and humanitarian progress. The laws of Drako on homicide, which formed the most important and permanent part of his legislation and almost the only one about which we have trustworthy information, mark a stage of compromise between the claims of family and state, between the old superstition and the new enlightenment. The old view made no difference between intentional and accidental killing: in either case the blood of the dead man called equally for vengeance and the pollution of the killer was automatic. In Drako's code we hear for the first time of a distinction. Moral considerations are again introduced by the

[1] Soph. *O.T.* 236 ff. Cf. for this and what follows, F. E. Adcock in *C.A.H.* iv, 29–31. P. B. R. Forbes has an interesting article on "Law and Politics in the Oresteia" (*Class. Rev.* lxii (1948), 99 ff.), with not all of which I am in agreement.

differentiation between wanton attack and self-defence. The prosecution is expressly reserved for the family of the dead man, and if the murderer be judged guilty, it is to them that he is handed over for execution. But the trial takes place before a court of the city. In this way the claim of the dead man to demand vengeance from his family is still allowed, though the state comes between to ensure that justice is done. At Athens the suspected murderer could take sanctuary on the Areopagus, where he could swear to and plead his innocence before his accusers and the Council of the State. If he was acquitted, the avenging kin had to look elsewhere for the murderer.

The contrast between old and new is indelibly impressed on our minds by Aeschylus. He pleads for a higher cause than had been won by the stern laws of Drako. The court of the Areopagus had been founded to prevent mistakes, to ensure that the avengers killed no innocent man in error, thus leaving the spirit unappeased and the land doubly polluted. But when Orestes after killing his mother, the slayer of his father, has recourse to the Areopagus, where Apollo himself is his advocate, it is not on these grounds that his claim to mercy is based. He and none other did the deed. He declares it himself.[1] Nor can he claim that the killing was accidental, or that he had acted in self-defence. In this, which for the purposes of his play and his message Aeschylus has designated as "the first trial for shed blood", the occasion of the founding of the Areopagus and the basis of its future conduct, acquittal is secured on grounds more civilized than underlay the laws of Drako's time. The real lesson of the *Eumenides* is clearly that the old law of blood incessantly crying for more blood, which hitherto had been thought inescapable, must be superseded, and that Athens, mother of civilization, is the natural sponsor of the higher code. Converted by Athena, the avenging Furies change their nature and become the Well-disposed.

Thus with the advancement of civilization was the moral content of the laws on homicide deepened. But one thing remained throughout all change—the need for purification. A man who was proved to have killed in self-defence was protected from the avengers by the State. This meant, not that he was now considered to be in no need of purification, but that he was allowed to proceed to it. The *miasma* was an automatic consequence of the killing, and had nothing to do with its moral aspect. This was

[1] *Eum.* 588: ἔκτεινα, τούτου δ᾽οὔτις ἄρνησις πέλει.

shown by the passage just quoted from Plato's *Laws*.[1] The way in which any contact with death or the world of the dead was believed to infect with pollution is further illustrated by the curious practices employed in connexion with those who while away from home had been falsely reported dead, and for whom in consequence the due rites of mourning had been performed. The performance of these ceremonies had made them, from a religious point of view, dead, and their presence therefore would bring pollution like that of a *revenant* from the tomb. Hence they were not admitted to the ordinary privileges of companionship with the living until the taint of death had been removed. They had to be reborn, and the procedure adopted consisted accordingly in treating them as babies. They were washed and swaddled and a show was made of feeding them at the breast. In describing this custom Plutarch cites the case of a certain Aristinos who finding himself in this uncomfortable case sent, as one would expect, to Delphi to find out how he could be purified, and received instructions in this sense. There was even a special name, *hysteropotmoi*, for these people, whose condition Professor Rose aptly compares to that of a man in quarantine in the modern world.[2] It must also have been the sense of danger from the infection of death that made it seem necessary to conduct a regular trial of inanimate objects which had been its cause. At Athens there was a special court in the Prytaneion for cases of this nature, and the object, if found guilty, had to be cast beyond the boundaries of the state. Aristotle and Demosthenes vouch for the historicity of this procedure and Plato enjoins it in his imaginary city.[3]

These illustrations of the effects of death, and any contact with it, in ancient eyes, are intended to show how Apollo's original connexion with homicide explains also his continued authority and interest in it. Both alike proceed from his essential nature as the god of purification (*katharsis*).[4] From the story of Orestes, perhaps the most famous myth in all Greek literature, down to the misfortunes of the undistinguished Aristinos, examples of this could be multiplied. Special ceremonies were involved, which Apollo could prescribe and administer. For Aristinos' case they

[1] 916c. See p. 187 above.

[2] Plutarch, *Aet. Rom.* v, 266e. Cf. Parke *Hist. Delphic Oracle*, p. 371, Rose, *Prim. Cult. in Greece*, pp. 112 f., 199. Rose remarks on the similarity between the way these *hysteropotmoi* were regarded and the attitude to manslayers.

[3] Arist. *Ath. Pol.* 57; Dem. xxiii, 76; Plato, *Laws*, ix, 873d. Cf. Paus. i, xxviii, 11, and Frazer's note ad loc.

[4] On purification in general, cf. now L. Moulinier, *Le pur et l'impur dans la pensee des Grecs*, Paris, 1952.

were strange indeed. For Orestes, at least in the version of Aeschylus, the sacrifice of pigs was an important element. "The *miasma* of matricide *can* be purged away," cries Orestes, "for when it was fresh upon me it was driven out at the shrine of Phoibos with slaughter of pigs in cleansing rites."[1] Pigs were regularly sacrificed to the powers of the underworld. As the god who purifies from blood, Apollo looks downward, not upward to the bright Olympus to which he seems most naturally to belong. Beauty and light, sanity, limit and order are all represented in his character, and with that side of it we are familiar. Let us now turn to some of his less regarded aspects. As god of law he gave judgment in cases of homicide. His authority there revealed his character as giver, or withholder, of *katharsis*. If a slayer is to be purified, the nether powers must be appeased, including the soul of the dead, which, as we are now learning, was not relegated by everyone, as it was by the Homeric warriors, to a world of strengthless shades. Thus with the cathartic side of his nature are bound up some religious or superstitious ideas not easy to connect at first sight with the god or the people of "the intelligible, determinate, mensurable, as opposed to the fantastic, vague and shapeless".

The best approach to this side of Apollo is probably through certain strange servants of his, figures of legend who have no connexion with any other god, yet are the subjects of surprising stories, in which *ekstasis* plays a prominent part. Several of these may be mentioned, and it is perhaps worth quoting in full, exactly as it appears in the pages of Herodotus, the story of one who may be taken as typical. This is Aristeas of Prokonnesos (a town on an island in the Sea of Marmora), whom Herodotus introduces with the remark that he came to the land of the Issedones "possessed by Phoibos".[2]

And I will tell [he continues] the tale which I heard about him in Prokonnesos and Kyzikos. They say that Aristeas, who was in birth inferior to none of the citizens, entered a fuller's shop in Prokonnesos and there died; and the fuller closed his workshop and went away to report the matter to the relations of the dead man. And when the news had already been spread abroad through the city that Aristeas was

[1] Aesch. *Eum.* 281 ff. Cf. P. Amandry, *Eschyle et la purification d'Oreste*, *Rev. Arch*, 1938.

[2] φοιβόλαμπτος γενόμενος, Hdt. iv, 13. It will be remembered (pp. 77 f. above) that the Issedones, according to Aristeas, lived next to the one-eyed Arimaspi and at two removes from the Hyperboreans.

dead, a man of Kyzikos who had come from the town of Artake entered into controversy with those who said so, declaring that he had met him going towards Kyzikos and had spoken with him. While he was vehement in dispute, the relations of the dead man came to the fuller's shop with the things proper in order to take up the corpse for burial: and when the house was opened Aristeas was not found there either dead or alive. In the seventh year after this he appeared at Prokonnesos and composed those verses which are called by the Hellenes the *Arimaspeia*, and having composed them he disappeared a second time. So much is told by these cities; and what follows I know happened to the people of Metapontion in Italy 240 years after the second disappearance of Aristeas, as I found by putting together what I heard at Prokonnesos and at Metapontion. The Metapontines say that Aristeas himself appeared in their land and bade them set up an altar of Apollo and place by its side a statue bearing the name of Aristeas of Prokonnesos; for he told them that to their land alone of all the Italiotes Apollo had come, and he, who now was Aristeas, was accompanying him; but that when he accompanied the god, he was a raven. With these words, say the Metapontines, he disappeared, and they sent to Delphi and asked what the apparition of the man might be; and the Pythian prophetess bade them obey the apparition, saying that it would be better for them if they did so. They accepted the answer and performed the commands, and there stands a statue now bearing the name of Aristeas close by the altar of Apollo, and around it are laurel trees. The altar is in the market-place.

This story of a servant of Apollo's cult contains a number of interesting points. First comes the phenomenon of *ekstasis*, illustrated in its most literal form by Aristeas falling down as if dead and appearing at the same time somewhere else. This part of the story must have been founded on the belief, illustrated by Frazer[1] from uncivilized people all over the world, in the temporary separation of the soul from the body during sleep, illness or trance, during which it can be seen in visible form. The disappearance of the body (if it was in fact the body of Aristeas that visited the fuller, and not its psychic simulacrum alone) is not of course demanded by such simple tales of a soul's wandering from, and returning to, its material envelope. It may perhaps be an embellishment on the part of Herodotus' informants, and serve to remind us of the many hands that this story must have gone

[1] *G.B.: Taboo and the Perils of the Soul,* ch. 2, esp. pp. 50 ff., "Wandering Souls in Popular Tales".

through since the times of its primitive origin. In its primitive purity, the idea of the wandering soul is more exactly represented by the story of Hermotimos of Klazomenai to which we shall come shortly.

Secondly we have the hint of transmigration in the statement of Aristeas that he accompanied the god in the form of a raven.[1] This suggests a possible connecting thread with Pythagorean circles of doctrine, and Metapontion, where these miraculous events are supposed to have taken place, was an early centre of Pythagoreanism, being in fact the town to which Pythagoras is said to have fled when exiled from the nearby Kroton, and in which he died and was buried.

Apart from the nature of the beliefs involved, the story illustrates a third point, that the Apolline religion had its enthusiastic missionaries. The object of the sudden miraculous appearances of Aristeas in different towns is to spread the cult of the Delphic god, who, originally an immigrant, never became attached to any Greek city-state or group of states. He was always Pan-Hellenic and his ministers endeavoured to extend his influence as widely as possible. If *ekstasis* and transmigration make us think of Pythagorean and Orphic ideas, this too may remind us that Apollo was the chosen patron of Pythagoras and the one for whom Orpheus neglected the worship of Dionysos; for it was a characteristic of both Pythagorean philosophers and those who initiated in the name of Orpheus to overleap state boundaries and go from city to city to win their converts.

Other figures also emerge from the twilight between myth and history who combine an Apolline connexion with similarly primitive miraculous powers. Such was Abaris, who like Aristeas was mentioned by Pindar.[2] He came from the land of the Hyperboreans, the legendary servants of Apollo, lived without food, and travelled all over the world bearing the golden arrow, the symbol of the god, a wandering missionary like Aristeas.[3] Hermotimos of

[1] In the stories quoted by Frazer, the soul of a man is often seen to leave his mouth in the form of a living creature, sometimes a tiny man, sometimes a lizard or other animal, and frequently a bird. The story of Aristeas is brought into line with these by the version in Pliny's *Natural History*, according to which "Aristeae [animam reperimus] visam evolantem ex ore in Proconneso corvi effigie" (*N.H.* vii, 52, 174). These instances of the more primitive form of a story occurring only for us in the later authority set nice problems for the historian.

[2] See the passages from Harpokration and Origen quoted by Bowra as fragments 283 and 284 in the Oxford Text of Pindar.

[3] Hdt. iv, 36.

Klazomenai is one who was said by some late authorities to have been an earlier incarnation of Pythagoras himself. His soul could leave his body for many years at a time, which it spent in gathering prophetic lore. Once when it was thus engaged, his enemies set fire to his empty body, thus preventing the soul's return—a story which can be matched from India and China. Our sources of information on Hermotimos are all of post-Alexandrian date, with the exception of Aristotle, who in his summary of the achievements of previous philosophers mentions him in connexion with his fellow-citizen Anaxagoras. Anaxagoras' contribution to philosophy was the conception of Mind, as something distinct from body and constituting the force responsible for motion and order in the *kosmos*. "We know," writes Aristotle, "that Anaxagoras certainly adopted these views, but Hermotimos of Klazomenai is credited with expressing them earlier." The credit for having anticipated Anaxagoras' view must have been owed to these legendary powers of his, which emphasized both the possibility of separate existence for the soul and its superiority to the body. The soul of Hermotimos was evidently no feeble ghost or shadow of the body, but the philosophic part of him, in the Greek sense of seeking after wisdom and knowledge.[1]

Similar legends gathered about Epimenides of Crete, though there is no reason to doubt that he was a historical figure. According to one tradition, related by Plato, he prophesied to the Athenians, ten years before the Persian War, the discomfiture of the Persians. Aristotle however and later authorities speak of him being called in to purify the city from the pollution incurred by the bloodshed and sacrilege which had been involved in the suppression of Kylon's bid for tyranny, an event which occurred about a century earler.[2] It is not surprising that there should be some confusion about his date, for his age at death was variously given as 154, 157 and 299.[3] He is connected with the other figures by the story that he fell asleep in a cave for fifty-seven years, and

[1] Arist. *Metaph.* A, 984b, 15–20, quoted above in the Oxford translation of W. D. Ross. For other references to Hermotimos, see Rohde, *Psyche* (Eng. trans.), p. 331, n. 112, and for parallels to the story of burning his body, Frazer, *G.B.: Taboo and the Perils of the Soul*, 49 f.

[2] Plato, *Laws*, 642d, Arist. *Ath. Pol.* i. On the date of Kylon see F. E. Adcock's note in *C.A.H.* iv, 661.

[3] Diog. Laert. i, 111. As Sandys remarks (on *Ath. Pol.* i), we are saved from giving too much credence to the last figure by Epimenides himself; for it is given as the Cretan estimate, and Epimenides is the authority for the statement (quoted in the Epistle to Titus, i. 12) that the Cretans are always liars.

that his soul could leave his body at will. His chief activities were prophecy and purification.[1]

Epimenides is not explicitly connected with Apollo, and it may therefore seem inappropriate to include him here. His home was in Crete, and his connexions were rather with the god of that land, the Cretan Zeus, and his orgiastic cult. Plutarch epitomizes his knowledge of him thus: "He had the reputation of being dear to the gods and wise in divine matters with the wisdom won by *enthusiasmos* and mysteries, wherefore the men of his time called him the son of a nymph named Balte, and a New Kures."[2] The Greatest Kures, or leader of the Kuretes, was the God of Crete himself, and the name Kures was given to those who had been initiated into his mysteries.[3] Yet the two activities for which he was famous, *katharsis* and ecstatic prophecy, inevitably remind us of Apollo and his ministers, and the similarity must have been obvious to the ancients too. We find, indeed, that with the Pythagoreans, whose god was Apollo, Epimenides was a favourite figure, and we are scarcely surprised, but deeply interested, to note the existence of a tradition, mentioned several times by Pausanias, that after killing the Python Apollo himself was purified not, as the common story said, at Tempe, but in Crete by a Cretan called Karmanor.[4] For our study of Apollo, the interest of Epimenides lies in this, that he combines the activities which we are wont to ascribe to Apollo and his prophets with an allegiance to the god of Crete, whose nature we saw in an earlier chapter to be chthonian, and in all points a contrast to the Olympian inheritance from Homer. Apollo himself, primarily an Olympian of the Olympians, who in his prophecies claimed to be doing nothing but declare the will of his father Zeus, cannot be denied to have had a foothold in this other world as well.

No discussion of Apollo's ministers can close without giving more than a mere mention to Pythagoras. His name itself declares him to have been a servant or prophet of the Pythian. Men said that he was the son of Apollo, or even, in Kroton itself, that he was an actual epiphany of Apollo Hyperboreios. He worked miracles, and one of the few doctrines that can be ascribed to him with certainty is that of the transmigration of the soul. It was a con-

[1] The earliest extant references to him are in Plato and Aristotle. Besides passages already quoted, cf. especially Plato, *Laws*, 677d, Arist. *Rhet.* iii, 1418a23. For later reff. see *Psyche*, 331 f., notes 116 ff.

[2] Plut. *Solon*, xii. [3] Cf. pp. 42 ff. above. [4] Paus. ii, 7, 7; ii, 30, 3; x, 6, 3; x, 7, 2.

temporary, Xenophanes, who satirized him in the story that he once cried out to a man who was beating a dog: "Stop! Don't beat him! It's the soul of a friend of mine—I recognize his voice."[1]

In the teaching of Pythagoras are reflected all sides of Apolline religion, which, since he was certainly a historical human being, is part of the evidence for his greatness. Any good Greek could see in Apollo the preacher of "Nothing too much" and "Know thyself"; some revered him as the patron of primitive magicians like Aristeas or Abaris. But to see him steadily and whole was perhaps the unique achievement of Pythagoras. We have approached Pythagoras on the side of his miracle-working and belief in transmigration, which, though the latter doctrine was capable of infinite refinement in the mind of a Plato, link him primarily with the magicians. To see the other side we have only to consider that his whole philosophy is based on the exaltation of *peras*, limit, and shows above all things a passionate devotion to form and law. The universe is a *kosmos*, and philosophy is a necessity because only by understanding the order of the macrocosm can man hope to imitate it and implant a similar order in the microcosm, becoming *kosmios* or orderly in his soul. The impulse to this view came to Pythagoras largely from his discoveries in mathematics, its basis was the conviction that the real and comprehensible nature of things was to be found in proportion and number. Here mathematics combined with music, for much of his thought followed from observing that there was a mathematical ratio between the lengths of string required to produce different notes of the scale at a particular tension. That Apollo was god of the lyre is something that I have passed over only because it was too well known to need repeating, and here again is an obvious reason for Pythagoras to have given him his devotion. Finally Pythagoras was the founder of a religious brotherhood with a definite rule of life, whose aim was expressed in the word *katharsis*. It was a *katharsis* to be achieved partly by the observance of certain taboos of primitive aspect, partly also, as we have seen, by philosophy. In either case, the word and what it stood for were yet another essential link between the brotherhood and its divine patron.

This sketch of the Apolline religion has followed immediately on one of the Dionysiac, and we may take the opportunity in conclusion to consider what were the probable relations between

[1] Xenophanes, fr. 7, Diels.

the two. In his account of the god Zalmoxis, a form of the Thracian Dionysos, Herodotus mentioned the tradition that he had been a slave of Pythagoras. This linking of the names of Zalmoxis and Pythagoras is very natural when we consider that the Thracian god preached immortality and almost certainly transmigration. The Orphics also, from whom Pythagoras probably derived the religious side of his doctrine (in any case the two were identical, which is all that matters at this point), worshipped Dionysos as their chief god, though introducing many modifications of an Apolline character into the Thracian cult. At Delphi Dionysos was at home, in Plutarch's words, "no less than Apollo". The connexion was obviously close, and might lead one to the theory that Apollo was originally no more than the god of light and beauty and reason, of limit and "nothing too much", and that the ecstatic element in his religion was the outcome of his contact with Dionysos after the latter had made his victorious southward progress. This explanation has in fact been put forward to account for the frenzied prophecy of the Pythia. There are two kinds of prophecy, carefully distinguished by Plato.[1] One is the conscious art of the augur, who has learned how to interpret signs and omens, telling the will of the gods from the flight of birds or the entrails of a sacrificial victim. He remains perfectly self-possessed, but because of his acquired skill (*techne*) claims to be able to read what heaven has to say. The second is the prophecy of inspiration. When the prophet speaks he is not himself. He is wrought upon and changed in a manner sometimes terrifying to behold and exhausting to himself. He is possessed by the god and becomes for the time being only a mouthpiece for the utterance of the divine voice. The Pythian prophetess of Apollo was of this sort. She was a true mantic, giving voice in a state of possession. She was affected in the same way as the Cumaean Sibyl, another into whom Apollo entered, and although her condition might be described by reference to Greek authors, no better impression of it could be given than the lines of Virgil:

> Cui talia fanti
> ante fores subito non voltus, non color unus,
> non comptae mansere comae; sed pectus anhelum
> et rabie fera corda tument, maiorque videri
> nec mortale sonans, adflata est numine quando
> iam propiore dei.[2]

[1] *Phaedrus*, 244a–d. [2] *Aen.* vi, 46 ff.

Those who like to see in Apollo nothing but what is sane and human and moderate and "typically Hellenic" are inclined to account for this behaviour by the presence of Dionysos at Delphi. If Apollo succeeded to some extent in taming Dionysos, Dionysos in his turn imparted a measure of his ecstasy to the Pythia.[1] I would only suggest that the material which we have so far considered in this chapter makes it probable that the element of *ekstasis* was original in the worship of Apollo to a sufficient extent to make the hypothesis of borrowing in the case of the Pythia unnecessary. It was rather a feature of his religion which made easier the reconciliation with Dionysos that undoubtedly was effected. The stories of Aristeas, Abaris and Hermotimos bear all the marks of being early and purely Apolline legends. The *ekstasis* which they depict, the only possible link with Dionysos, is a universal primitive form of the phenomenon which might be found in the service of any great god. There is no hint of any orgiastic ritual, of inducing the *ekstasis* by "drum, dance or dramatic representation",[2] no hint indeed that the ordinary man could perform such feats at all. We hear nothing of communion with the god, of a worshipper becoming an Apollo as the votary of Dionysos became himself a Bacchos. Apollo imparts no *teletai*, no initiatory rites, either in these stories or elsewhere. These are differences which make it difficult to believe that the mantic *ekstasis* of Apolline religion was simply borrowed from that of the worshippers of Dionysos. Indeed, as has been pointed out before,[3] the Bacchae or maenads of Dionysos are nowhere credited with the gift of prophecy. The woman-priest who is also prophet, the Pythia or the Sibyl, appears only in connexion with Apollo. Yet *teletai* and

[1] So for example O. Kern in PWK *Realenc.* v, 1017. It was the view put forward by Rohde in *Psyche*.

[2] The absence of which, by the way, is noted by Norah Chadwick as a mark whereby European manticism is in general distinguished from that of Asia and Polynesia. The point is worth consideration, even though its application to our present subject may not be immediately clear. (N. K. Chadwick, *Poetry and Prophecy* (Cambridge, 1942), p. 59.)

[3] See K. Latte, "The Coming of the Pythia", in *Harvard Theol. Rev.* xxxiii (1940), pp. 9 ff. Latte concludes: "The Pythia was but the Greek form of a priesthood which from its very beginning belonged to the cult of Apollo", and "The Pythia came at the same time as Apollo himself, and the arrival of Dionysos, whatever its other consequences, brought about no revolution in the cult of Apollo". He traces this woman-priesthood, on excellent evidence, to Anatolia, where most modern opinion is inclined to see Apollo's original home. Note however that the Bacchae whom Dionysos brings to Greece are also "Asiatic women" from Phrygia or Lydia. The point serves to show still more clearly what close affinities there seem originally to have been, in spite of essential differences, between the cults of the two gods.

katharmoi go closely together, as the *Phaedrus* again reminds us,[1] and often fulfilled similar purposes. The ecstatic and cathartic sides of the cult of Apollo are not to be explained as mere borrowings, but rightly understood they help to make more comprehensible what has often been thought puzzling, his reconciliation with his brother-god of the vine, the torches, the tympanon and the Phrygian flute.

That the reconciliation took place is important. It had become clear to the Greeks that Dionysos had come to stay, whether they would or not. The Pentheuses of the land might regret it, but their efforts had been of no avail. More and more people were succumbing to the intoxication of his *orgia*, seeing no doubt that here was a type of religious experience which their own hitherto established cults had failed to offer. It was not simply that it was more emotional. It paved the way for a completely different conception of the relation between god and man. The Cretan "Zeus" in his own name and right had failed to do this. His identification with the Olympian had spelt his failure. The Greeks accepted the legend of Zeus' birth, in their large-hearted way they found a place for it in their mythology, but the Olympian was too firmly seated on his throne for the mystical conceptions, which originally lay behind it, to make any headway. But Dionysos had no Olympian tradition behind him. He was a god who made his worshippers even as himself, and he was nothing else. He conquered where the Cretan alone had failed.

Nevertheless, though admitting his conquest, the Greeks were not willing to accept him without making him conform as far as possible to their own ideas. Some of the ways in which they did this were indicated in the last chapter. In particular I suggested that they emptied his worship of its promise of immortality. Above all he had to be accorded a recognized and official position which would curb the wild irresponsibility that had marked his first entry into Greece and bring him as much as possible into line with the πάτριος νόμος, the ancestral tradition and conventions of the Greek people. And who was better qualified to do this than Apollo, the "national expositor" of these traditions? They did therefore the best that they could do: they gave Dionysos a place at Delphi.[2] Since he, like the Cretan Zeus, was of the type of god

[1] 244e.

[2] That this was the order of events, i.e. that Apollo was the earlier in possession of the shrine and took Dionysos under his wing, has not always been accepted. The opposite view, that Dionysos was there first and was displaced by Apollo, is maintained

who suffers death, his tomb was shown at Delphi.[1] On vases he may be seen clasping hands with Apollo across the trunk of the bay-tree.[2] The characters of the two gods seem to have become thoroughly mingled by the fifth century, if we may trust two fragments of Aeschylus and Euripides which are quoted without their context by Macrobius to prove this very point. The line of Aeschylus speaks of Apollo as "the ivied, the Bacchic, the prophet", and Euripides invokes "Lord Bacchos lover of the bay, Paean Apollo of the tuneful lyre".[3] We have heard already of the official band of the Thyiades, who roamed the heights of Parnassos in licensed orgies during the biennial festival which took place in the three winter months. For the whole of these months it was believed that Apollo was absent from his shrine, spending the time among his peculiar people the Hyperboreans. He had ceded it for the period to his fellow-god, by a kind of voluntary concession which reminds us of the way in which, according at least to Aeschylus, he himself had originally taken possession of it.[4] Plutarch, our most prolific source for the cult of Dionysos at Delphi, speaks of it as a place "in which Dionysos has no less share than Apollo".[5]

I would sum up this chapter in two parts: first, the character of Apollo in classical times, which it is my particular aim to elucidate; secondly, the more dubious question of his original nature and habitation, about which I would do no more than throw out a tentative suggestion for the consideration of those to whom origins and their problems make a stronger appeal. In

---

by Professor A. B. Cook (*Zeus*, ii, 233–67). I cannot here give a full discussion of the historical material, and must refer the interested reader to his arguments. Pickard-Cambridge (*Dith. Trag. and Com.* p. 9, n. 1) finds the view "hardly justified by the evidence", and Dodds accepts the opposite order (*Bacchae*, p. 103: "When Dionysos came to Greece he found there an established mantic god, Apollo, with whom it was difficult to compete"), which was also favoured by Wilamowitz (*Glaube*, ii, 74). I confess I find the priority of Dionysos difficult to swallow. For Dionysos at Delphi in general cf. P. Amandry, *La Mantique Apollinienne a Delphes* (Paris 1950), ch. 17.

[1] For authorities see Rohde, *Psyche* (Eng. trans.), p. 110, n. 32.

[2] Illustrated by Pickard-Cambridge, *Dith. Trag. and Com.* figs. 1 and 2.

[3] Macrobius, i, 18; Aesch. fr. 341: *ὁ κισσεὺς Ἀπόλλων, ὁ Βακχεύς, ὁ μάντις,* Eur. fr. 477: *δέσποτα φιλόδαφνε Βάκχε, παιὰν Ἄπολλον εὔλυρε.*

[4] Aesch. *Eum., ad init.* Euripides, *I.T.* 1259 ff. tells a different story!

[5] *De E* 388e, *ᾧ (sc. τῷ Διονύσῳ) τῶν Δελφῶν οὐδὲν ἧττον ἢ τῷ Ἀπόλλωνι μέτεστιν.* But the syncretistic atmosphere of late antiquity is such that even Plutarch's evidence must be used with caution. Cf. the sentence which Nilsson quotes from Dio Chrysostom: "Some tell us that Apollo, Helios and Dionysos are one and the same . . . *and generally reduce all the gods to a single force or power.*" (Dio. C. *Orat.* xxxi, ii; Nilsson, *Greek Piety* (Oxford, 1948), p. 117.)

the mind of the Greeks, I suggest that the central place is occupied by his jurisdiction over homicide. From here the threads lead in two opposite directions. Judgment upon killing is a legal matter. It reminds us of what I have called Apollo's primary aspect, his championship of law and order, his widespread legal activity embracing criminal, civil and constitutional codes, everything whether in religious or secular life that was brought under rules and regulations. In the same orbit are his famous maxims enjoining limit, moderation and obedience to authority, and condemning excess in all its forms. Here speaks the Olympian. But killing to the Greeks was more than a crime, to be dealt with by fines, imprisonment or death in the interests of peaceful living. In the other direction the threads lead first to the need for purification. Here too Apollo was the final authority. He understood the terrible *miasma* which was cast by any contact with the world of the dead. Men have always obtained comfort from the thought that the god to whom they pray for help and solace in a particular case has himself experienced the depths that the human sufferer must now explore.

> Christ leads us through no darker rooms
> Than he went through before,

and the woman who prays for easy delivery or who mourns the loss of a son will address the Virgin with a fairer hope because she too has known these pains and sorrows of motherhood. "Help me . . . for Thou too . . ." The pagan no less derived comfort from being able to pray in this way, and so it was believed that in his early days Apollo himself had killed, and though no moral stain attached to the slaying of the Python, had had like others to flee and seek the purification which ever afterwards he was to dispense at his own shrine. The need for purification, as we have seen, was bound up with dark superstitions about the power of the dead to return and visit with frightful plagues the guilty or neglectful living. *Katharmoi* and *teletai* are spoken of together by Plato as means of averting their curse, and *teletai*, as we know from the nature of the Eleusinian and other mysteries, were above all things a means of getting into touch with the spirits of the other world. They were in the gift of chthonian powers like Demeter, Pluto, Dionysos and him of Crete. In this way therefore Apollo's connexion with homicides points not to Olympus but to the chthonian depths, and he stands as a unique bridge between the two worlds.

As to his original nature and habitation, my tentative suggestion is simply this. I cannot believe that his mantic side, involving an *ekstasis* in which the ravings of the Pythia are brought into close connexion with the feats of seers like Aristeas and Hermotimos, is borrowed from any other god. It is an essential feature of Apollo and his peculiar ministers. I mentioned this in a previous chapter at the close of a section in which I had discussed various theories concerning his original habitation. If the findings of the present chapter have done anything to strengthen the case for it, they may be regarded as further encouragement for believing that he came to the Greeks from an original home in the north-east, perhaps Siberia. The encouragement lies in the resemblance between Apollo's particular form of mantic *ekstasis*, especially as it appears in connexion with figures like Aristeas and Hermotimos,[1] and the behaviour of the shamans of those regions, for details of which the curious may be referred to the excellent, short and readable work of Norah Chadwick, *Poetry and Prophecy*. This argument from the functions of Apollo accords well with his traditional association with the Hyperboreans, an association so strong that few scholars have felt it could be left out of account in any attempt to discover the original home of the god; for as we saw,[2] a careful examination of the geographical associations of that elusive tribe led not so much to Northern Europe, where some have seen them in the past, but rather to Northern Asia. If this is so however we must not on that account deny that he was at home in Anatolia also before the Greeks made his acquaintance. The evidence for this is too strong, and no doubt it was there that he acquired his female priests and prophetesses, who seem to have been an especial feature of the religion of Asia Minor.[3]

[1] Cf. K. Meuli in *Hermes* lxx (1936), 137 ff., for the possibility of a direct influence of shamanistic cultures through the lands of the Scyths and the Massagetae, and on the same point Nilsson, *Gesch. Gr. Rel.* i (1941), 584.

[2] pp. 79 f. above.

[3] Cf. the article of K. Latte referred to above (p. 200, n. 3) and remarks in the previous chapter on Dionysos.

Chapter VIII

HEAVEN AND EARTH

IN this chapter we shall once again come close to what I have called our main subject of inquiry, and shall do well to keep it consciously in mind. From the complexity of Greek religious thought we selected two conceptions of man's relation to god as particularly stimulating to our curiosity on account of the vivid contrast which they present.[1] These sharply opposed groups of ideas can be summed up as, on the one hand, the advocacy of "mortal thoughts for mortal men" on the grounds that men are essentially inferior to the gods, that the gods are jealous for the superior position which they hold in virtue of superior power and above all in virtue of their immortality, and that therefore any attempt to encroach upon the divine status and privileges can have no other result than a visitation of divine displeasure; and on the other hand, an awareness of a kinship, indeed an ultimate identity, between human and divine nature, with the corollary that this divine and immortal spark in the human breast should be cherished and purified from earthly taint until it emerges as from a chrysalis to spread its new-found wings. On the means whereby this was to be attained—whether by outward ceremonies, by purity of life, or by intellectual effort—opinions differed as much, perhaps, as they do to-day.

The existence of these two extreme views means, of course, that it was possible and inevitable for many other religious opinions to be held at the same time which inclined in a greater or less degree to one or the other. The complexity of religion, closely linked to the non-rational element without which it would not be religion, is something that must never be lost sight of. One of our aims as religious historians is to separate as far as possible the various threads interwoven in it, and account for the presence of each in the texture of the whole; and to pursue this metaphor, if we had to unravel a tangled skein of many-coloured wools, we should choose to start with two that were sharply distinguished, a black and a

[1] Ch. III above.

white, a red and a blue, and leave until a later stage, when a certain amount of thinning-out had already been done, the separation of those which only differed by the depth of a shade or two. That is the justification for the method employed here, which is not based on any belief that Greek religion is simple enough to be accounted for by two elements only.

With this qualification, I hope to show that the two religious ideas—immortality implying apotheosis, and mere submission to a higher power—arise in the spheres of what are nowadays commonly called chthonian and Olympian religion respectively. The suggestion is not new, but in the present state of classical studies it is perhaps in need of restatement and defence. First let us look more closely at the meanings of the terms chthonian and Olympian, for the first essential is to be sure that they correspond to notions genuinely Greek, and to understand as accurately as possible what these Greek notions were.

Better than the term "Olympian" would perhaps be "uranian". The gods which it includes are indeed those who dwelt on Olympus, but the characteristic which marks them off from the chthonians (Gr. *chthon* = earth) is that they belong not to earth but to heaven (Gr. *ouranos*), and as *ouranioi* as well as *Olympioi* they were worshipped by the Greeks. A single quotation will suffice to show that the distinction between heavenly and earthly divinities was in Greek eyes real and important. At the beginning of his plans for religious legislation in the *Laws*, Plato lays it down that each of the twelve months of the year is to be sacred to one of the twelve gods after whom, according to a previous enactment, the twelve tribes, into which he had divided the population, were to be named. He continues: "Moreover the cults of the earthly [*chthonioi*] gods and of those whom we should call the heavenly [*ouranioi*], and all that follow upon them, must not be confused, but must be kept apart." Arising from this principle he makes a law that all festivals of chthonian deities are to be confined to the twelfth month, which has Pluto as its patron god and will not contain any uranian festivals at all.[1]

The contrast between chthonian and Olympian then is the

[1] *Laws*, viii, 828c: *ἔτι δὲ καὶ τὸ τῶν χθονίων καὶ ὅσους αὖ θεοὺς οὐρανίους ἐπονομαστέον καὶ τὸ τῶν τούτοις ἑπομένων οὐ συμμεικτέον ἀλλὰ χωριστέον, ἐν τῷ τοῦ Πλούτωνος μηνὶ τῷ δωδεκάτῳ κατὰ τὸν νόμον ἀποδιδόντας.* One must of course allow for the philosopher's natural tendency to systematize, and A. D. Nock calls this "a theoretical hardening of the division of categories into a sharp contrast" (*Harv. Theol. Rev.* (1944), 164). Nevertheless Plato did not invent the distinction.

contrast between earthly and heavenly, since we may safely commit ourselves to the equation of the Olympians with those whom the Greeks called *ouranioi*. There is however more to be said before the terms are understood, and first of all a possible objection to be met. The Olympians are so called because they have their dwelling on Mount Olympus, a solid earthly mountain which was visible to every Greek just as it may be seen by any traveller in Greece to-day. Can we give the name heavenly to those who had their palace on its summit, and contrast them with a separate class of earthly gods? We need not be deterred. If Olympus was the abode of Zeus and the other uranian deities, that was precisely because it gave to the Greeks the impression, as it reared its ten thousand feet through and beyond the clouds, of being very loosely connected with the earth, and at its summit heavenly rather than earthly in its nature. It was only a natural development when in later writers it tended to float off the earth altogether, and the name came to be used as an equivalent of heaven.

This can be put more exactly. The Greek word which approaches most nearly to the English "heaven", with all its associations, is not *ouranos* but *aither*. A Greek of any period would agree that it was in the *aither*, if anywhere, that the gods dwelt, and that the *aither* itself was divine, the epithet with which Prometheus addresses it in one of the best-known passages in Greek literature.[1] In ordinary parlance the *aer* belongs, as much as the earth itself, to the region of corruption and decay and mortality. It is the sublunary atmosphere, the air that we breathe, fog, mist, cloud, even darkness—all these can be represented by the word *aer*. The root meaning of *aither*, on the other hand, is "blazing". To the popular mind this distinction was present and real, though popular thought is not free from confusion and does not deal in absolutes. We may remind ourselves here of the discussion in Chapter V, from which we learned that for two classes of people at least the distinction was not an absolute one. The monist philosopher does not believe in the existence of more than one real substance, and those therefore who made *aer* the self-moved material basis of the whole universe must of course have believed that the *aither* is no more than this same substance in its purest (and thus, let us remember, its most divine) form; and secondly the religious and philosophic teachers who held that the *aer* which we breathe is the soul or life-substance, and that this substance is identical with the

[1] Aesch. *P.V.* 88. Cf. also the examples given on p. 38 above.

world-soul, so that the soul of each individual man is "a small portion of the divine", clearly based their doctrines also on the ultimate identity of *aer* and *aither* and considered the one to be only a base and contaminated form of the other.

The distinction then was relative rather than absolute, but it remained as real as the distinction between dark and bright, and, I think we may say, between mortal and immortal. It remained also as a local distinction. Living in England, we might be pardoned for supposing that the soft atmosphere in which we move, at times thickening into mist or cloud or dissolving about us in rain, constituted the whole depth of the sky. Not so the Greek. In his climate it was possible to see beyond these impure vapours, and what he saw as he looked up into the dazzling vault of a clear Mediterranean sky was so striking that he felt as if he was seeing into something generically different from the air and vapours which hang around the earth. This it was which he named the brilliant, or blazing, element *aither*. To discover therefore whether the summit of Olympus pertained for the Greeks to earth or heaven, we have to decide (if the discovery is to have any significance) whether they regarded it as situated in the *aer* or the *aither*. The answer, beyond a doubt, is that it was in the *aither*. Zeus who holds court on Olympus is at the same time Ζεὺς αἰθέρι ναίων —the dweller in the *aither*. Professor A. B. Cook has pointed out how this belief was based on observation: "The ancients were much impressed by the fact that Olympus rears its crest above the rain-clouds."[1] The distinction between *aer* and *aither* arose from the difference in appearance between the air up to cloud level and the dazzling light beyond. The summit of Olympus is bathed in this pure, aetherial light whose presence betokens divinity.

Thus the Olympians, even if we take their name in the most literal sense, are of the heaven, heavenly. Yet while claiming to have established the right so to describe them, we must still be careful lest some of the associations attached to the English word should lead us astray. The distinction between *aer* and *aither* is genuinely Greek, and provides a clear line of demarcation between the earthly and the heavenly, but it should bring home to us at the same time how close together, in Greek eyes, the two are, and

[1] *Zeus*, i, 101. See also the photograph (ib., pl. ix) taken by Professor Wace, which shows the mountain girdled with a ring of clouds, through and beyond which the peaks easily push their way.

how thin is the line of demarcation. The dwelling-place of the heavenly gods is not "above the clear blue sky", it *is* the clear blue sky, and it may even be the top of an earthly mountain, since there are mountains high enough to reach from the impure atmosphere of mortality into the divine and immortal element above. Heaven and earth are parts of the same visible universe, and may even interpenetrate one another. One important result of this is that it made for easy intercourse between gods and men. It was a necessary arrangement in a period of religion naïve enough to conceive of gods as a kind of supermen, with physical bodies which moved from place to place. Man needs access to his divinity. No ordinary mortal derives much comfort from the spectacle of such gods as Epicurus depicted. And so long as the gods are the far from spiritual beings whom we find in Homer, the only sort of access possible is literal physical presence. Athena or Hermes must be able to stride or fly down from tall Olympus to the earth, to pass freely up and down between the regions of *aither* and of *aer*. This of course, with the cosmic geography of Homer, is easy enough. The later history of Greek religion, especially on its more philosophic side, shows as might be expected a development on two parallel lines: a growing spiritualization of the gods side by side with a widening of the gulf between heaven and earth. The need for contact remains, but if God is a spirit, there is not the same necessity for the journey between heaven and earth to be physically easy to perform.

The need for contact was often, and very properly, emphasized by Wilamowitz, but it led him to a further conclusion where it will not be so helpful to follow. The distinction between Olympian and chthonian, aetherial and sub-aetherial, or to put it more simply, between gods of the heaven and gods of the earth, is one which I hold to be fundamental for the understanding of Greek religion. We can never understand its complexities unless we have grasped the essential difference—for example—between the Zeus of Homer and the Zeus of Crete. If any doubt is still left about the reality and importance of this difference, it will I hope be dispelled when we have taken a closer look at the chthonians in the next chapter. Yet it is just this distinction which Wilamowitz would obliterate. I quote first from a reviewer's summary of his conclusions: "Their gods, even Zeus, are distinctly and definitely of the earth; a being, however wonderful, who did not come into contact with men, but stayed in a remote sky or elsewhere quite out of their reach, was not worshipped, though it might be theoretically granted that he was a *theos*."[1] The need for contact is here seen as an argument for saying that all Greek gods alike were of the earth; and so, to translate Wilamowitz himself: "The gods whom we have so far considered were active on the earth or up from out of the earth. This is equally true of Zeus, and moreover this is something which has not altered even when in Homer he himself is changed in nature, for he still lives on the mountain Olympus."[2] Naturally Wilamowitz is aware that the summit of Olympus is an aetherial region. Almost in the next sentence, still speaking of Zeus, he remarks: "Up there he lived, *αἰθέρι ναίων*." But the fact cannot have for him the significance which I suggest it ought to have if we are not to lose sight of a real distinction which was indeed a leading motif in the intricate pattern of Greek religion. The Zeus of Homer and the Zeus of Crete were deities of two different kinds, and the difference is not at all badly represented by saying that one was a deity of heaven and the other of earth. The Greeks would have understood and approved, owing to their keen appreciation of the difference between the regions of *aither* and the regions beneath, and their assignment of the home of Zeus on Olympus to the upper of these two cosmic divisions. That Wilamowitz attaches so little importance to this is all the more remarkable in that it is he who is responsible for drawing our attention to the meaning of *aither* for the Greeks in particularly striking and poetic language: "There is one natural phenomenon which we ourselves both can and must call by its Greek name, if we are going to enter properly into the feelings of the Greeks. That is the *aither*. . . . They must have looked up, when all overhead is filled with shimmering light, when, as Lord Byron somewhere says, none but God alone is to be seen in Heaven. That is a different element from the air, from the atmosphere, beyond which the eyes of us Northerners cannot penetrate, so that we must content ourselves with mere blue sky. It is therefore inadequate to render *aither* by 'air' or 'heaven'; often it is, as the etymology suggests, 'fire'."[3]

We need not, then, reduce the Olympians to earthly levels out of consideration for their accessibility. Recognition of the need for contact with mortals need not obliterate the distinction between

[1] H. J. Rose, review of *Der Glaube der Hellenen*, vol. i, in *Class. Rev.* xlv (1931), 174.
[2] *Der Glaube*, i, 224. [3] Ibid., 138.

earthly and heavenly, chthonian and uranian.[1] Nevertheless in emphasizing this need Wilamowitz has drawn attention to a further point which is of value in preventing us from being misled into un-Greek ways of thinking by a facile use of English terms. Once we admit the existence of two classes of gods worshipped by the Greeks, and call one class gods of the earth and the other gods of the heaven, the latter phrase might suggest the worship of the heavenly bodies, sun and stars, especially since such worship is common enough among other peoples. This however was foreign to the logical and practical temperament of the Greeks, and there are few traces of any genuine worship of the heavenly bodies so long as their religion retained its independence. Apollo or Poseidon or Hermes might come down and traffic with men, helping or punishing them, but anyone who used his eyes could

[1] A further source of confusion should perhaps be cleared up as far as the facts allow. The pre-Greek peoples of Greece worshipped gods as dwelling at or near the tops of mountains whom nevertheless they did not regard as heavenly. These gods belonged to the earth, as was frequently indicated by the belief that their habitation, though high in the mountains, was a cave. I regard them as identical with the chthonian spirits of fertility, and if, as there are good reasons for believing, they were supposed to send the fructifying rain from their lofty seats, I do not think that these peoples saw any incongruity in supposing them at the same time to have embodied the life of the crops which arose from this impregnation of Mother Earth. (Cf. pp. 49 f. above. The same youthful, virile figure was often thought of as at once consort and son of the Mother.) Kronos and the god of Crete, who were both in different ways displaced by the Hellenic Zeus, and others also were worshipped in this way in caves upon the mountains. Their worshippers lacked the lively imagination of the Greeks, and I am not therefore inclined to agree with the distinction which Kern draws between two classes of gods among these prehistoric folk, the powers of the earth who bless the crops and the gods on the mountain-tops who send the fertilizing rain. With this reservation I would draw attention to his account (*Rel. der Gr.* i, 42): "Neben der uralten Vorstellung, dass der Segen des Ackers von den göttlichen Mächten kommt, die in der Erdentiefe wohnen, stammt auch die andere schon aus vorgriechischer Zeit, dass auf den Höhen und Bergen ein Gott wohnen muss, der Sonnenschein und Regen, Wärme und Kälte, auch segnende Blitze zu richtiger Zeit von oben herabschickt. Gewiss hat es da nicht nur eine Gottheit gegeben, der diese Macht zugeschrieben wurde. Viele Berggötter hat der Kult des Hellenischen Zeus später abgelöst. . . . An eine Gleichsetzung von Höhe und Himmel ist aber in dieser alten Zeit kaum zu denken. Das der Berg zur Erde gehört, ist nicht vergessen. Darum wohnt auch der Höhengott in Kult und Sage in einer Höhle wie die kleinasiatische Bergmutter."

As Kern says, it is unlikely that at this early date there was any question of equating the mountain-tops with heaven (which is perhaps in favour of my theory that only one class of gods was involved). The facts are, then, that in prehistoric times there were mountain-gods in Greece who were also earth-gods and were often worshipped in caves, sometimes on rock-cut thrones in the open air. The place of these early gods Zeus, the god of the Hellenes, usurped. Hence he took over their ancient seats, but in his own nature, as chief god of the invaders, he was a god of the sky—*ouranios*. Then the distinction was made which assigns the mountain-tops to heaven, a distinction doubtless due to the keener wits and more lively imagination of Hellenic tribes.

see that the great visible deities, the sun and the stars, never left their exalted stations and had no contact or intercourse with the lower world. There was no point in offering cult to such unresponsive divinities. "There are also," wrote Wilamowitz, "in elemental nature certain great and mighty phenomena which reveal themselves directly to mankind as divine, and hence attain personality, but which nevertheless receive no cult, because they do not come down to men on earth, and so remain out of human reach."[1] Even the sun, which on account of its obvious influence upon human life has been accorded regular cult and prayer by other peoples, received little attention from the Greeks. Storms were sent or kept away by one of the Olympians, Zeus or Poseidon, and there was no general feeling that Helios himself might reveal or withdraw his presence in response to prayer or sacrifice. The moon also, whose waxing and waning and monthly disappearance gave her a greater interest for mankind, so that it was even believed that the Thessalian witches could draw her down out of the sky with their spells, was mainly a goddess of poetry and mythology to whom little or no worship was accorded by the people.[2]

There is, be it observed, no denial of the divinity of these phenomena. To call them visible or manifest deities is only to translate a Greek phrase for them, ἐπιφανεῖς θεοί. Such splendid and moreover eternal beings must be gods, but they are gods out of touch with men. They move to an instinctive awe, but they do not demand temples and sacrifices, for they do not come down to reward piety or avenge neglect. Of all the heavenly bodies, Helios is the one whom we should most naturally expect to be the object of cult, since he is at the same time the most glorious and the most active in influencing the rhythm of earthly life, and is in consequence the most frequently mentioned in Greek literature as a god. He is, it is true, regularly invoked as witness to an oath, for the reason, explicitly set forth in the formula of swearing, that in his daily journey from one side of heaven to the other, he "sees all and hears all"; but the evidence for sun-cults in Greece before the Hellenistic age is very small, and where they do occur they can usually be shown to be non-Greek in origin and claiming only a small local influence among the Greeks. The outstanding example is of course Rhodes, where the cult was a foreign one, and the surprising thing is, not that Helios was such a great god in Rhodes itself, but that, great as he

[1] *Der Glaube*, i, 253. [2] Ib., p. 257.

was, his cult did not spread from such an important centre to other parts of the Hellenic world.[1] This would assuredly have happened, as it did with the great patron deities of other places, if the cult had been at all sympathetic to the Hellenic mind.

More important than negative considerations based on the rarity of sun-cults in Greece is the fact that the Greeks themselves regarded worship of the heavenly bodies as a particular mark of the barbarians. In the *Peace* of Aristophanes, the hero Trygaios affects to disclose to Hermes a dastardly plot aimed at the Olympian gods on the part of "the Moon and that villain the Sun". They are betraying Greece to the barbarians. "What's the idea of that?" asks Hermes. "Why, it is because we Greeks sacrifice to *you* [i.e. Hermes and the others on Olympus], whereas the barbarians sacrifice to *them*. So it is natural that they should want to get us all out of the way, and then they will have the rites of the gods to themselves." Again, in Plato's *Cratylus* Socrates, to support a somewhat far-fetched derivation of the word *theos*, says: "It looks to me as if the earliest inhabitants of Greece believed only in those gods which in our own time are widely revered among the barbarians—sun and moon and earth and stars and heaven." We need not take his etymology nor his historical suggestion seriously, but it is noteworthy that for his own time he regards the worship of these beings as typically barbarian rather than Greek.[2]

To sum up this discussion, we started with a re-statement of our main problem, which is posed by the coexistence among the Greeks of two sharply opposed conceptions of the relations between gods and men. I suggested that light would be thrown on it by an investigation into what is meant by dividing the gods into two types, Olympian and chthonian, since these corresponded roughly to the two sorts of gods which were needed to explain the contrast: gods before whom men can only abase themselves, and gods, on the other hand, of whose divinity and immortality they themselves might hope to partake. Taking Olympians first, we found justification for calling them the heavenly gods, if we were sure what we did and what we did not mean by the term. What we did mean was gods who lived in the *aither*, and the justification for using the term was that the distinction between aetherial and subaetherial was as real to the Greeks as the distinction between heavenly and earthly is to us, and of great importance for their

[1] Cf. Nilsson in *Archiv für Religionswissenschaft*, xxx (1931), 141.
[2] *Peace*, 404 ff.; *Crat.* 397d.

religion. To the gods of the earth, of whose existence we have already become aware at several points in this book, we shall return in the next chapter. At this point it became necessary to enter a caveat that there was no gulf between the *aither* and the regions beneath it comparable to the gulf which has existed for many Christians between earth and heaven. Finally, what we did not mean by heavenly, when the term was used to describe the Olympians, was any reference to the worship of sun, moon and stars, since these awoke little in the Greek breast beyond a vague feeling of awe, and were rarely accorded cult. Star-worship, which entered increasingly into Greek religion from the fourth century B.C. onwards, was an un-Hellenic phenomenon and a mark of increasing cosmopolitanism.

In trying to decide whether, and in what sense, the Olympian gods can be described by the term "heavenly", we have been led to make many interesting remarks about their nature. But when all reservations and refinements are made, it will perhaps be better after all to drop the term and refer to them simply as Homeric. It was Homer who created the Olympians as such, and so long as their sway lasted, it was in the form given by Homer that they dominated men's imaginations. They were thus very definitely a product of the Hellenes, of the time "when the Hellenic had distinguished itself from the foreign stock".[1] This is something which it is well to note in passing, and perhaps return to again.

This same fact, that the heavenly dwellers on Olympus are the gods of Homer, relieves us of the task of proving the correspondence between their type of divinity and the mentality of "mortal thoughts for mortal men", for we have done this already. We have already seen how impossible it was to conceive of anything like human communion with the divine in connexion with the gods of Homer. Their relations with men are purely external, and approximate to those between two levels of aristocracy in a society with a basis of strictly observed caste. Each knows its place and keeps to it, and there is little more to be said about the duty of man to god.

Before turning from the Olympian to the chthonian side of religion, it would be well to interpose a word to prevent us from being made the victims of our own method. That method is one of analysis, of separating the various elements of a compound,

[1] Hdt. i, 60. Cf. Introduction.

and there is a danger of being led to think that, just as we can separate these elements and lay them side by side in our minds, so they had separate existence in actual fact at the time when they formed the components of the religion of living people. The result would be that so long as we continued to live in the world of our own clear-cut abstractions—Olympian and chthonian and the rest—all would seem more or less plain sailing; but as soon as we turned back from these to the facts of Greek belief as reflected in Greek literature, we should at once be confronted by a bland disregard of nice distinctions before which our neat and pigeon-holed system of classification would fall to the ground. The mind of an Athenian writer, and still more of an ordinary pious Athenian citizen, was an amalgam in which these various elements existed in fusion. The mixture was not a mechanical but a chemical one. It cannot be sifted out in any literal way, to find here a grain of *x* and there one of *y*. We can only, like the chemist, apply certain reagents whereby the presence of different constituents in the compound may be detected.

To leave our metaphors, the practical effect of these observations is this. Our classificatory methods might lead us to suppose, for example, that certain gods were heavenly and certain others earthly. We might tend to group them accordingly, putting, say, Zeus, Hermes, Apollo on one side of the line, and Pluto, Persephone, Dionysos on the other. Such an attempted marshalling would survive only so long as we cut ourselves off from the reality; for as soon as we reopened the Greek authors, we should be dismayed to find Zeus and Hermes both addressed as *chthonios*, and Apollo displaying certain traits of character which were sadly out of keeping with the Olympian of the *Iliad*. For each separate case there is a different explanation. For the three Olympians whom I have cited, it lies in earlier chapters of this book. We have seen how Zeus acquired a twofold character from the blending of a pre-Greek deity with the supreme god of the invading Greeks,[1] how Hermes' character as the guide of wayfarers, together with his presence on grave-mounds in the visible form of the herm, gave him the specific duty of conducting souls to the underworld and so made natural the addition of *chthonios* to his titles, and how

[1] Not that this explanation covers every mention of a chthonian Zeus. The universality of Zeus brought about the attachment of his name to a great variety of divinities. As Zeus *chthonios* he is perhaps most frequently occupying the role of his grim brother Pluto. Cf. Aesch. *Suppl.* 228 ff. (below, p. 217).

Apollo, through being the god of *katharsis*, had connexions both with the clear, Olympian world of law and order and also with darker notions of ghostly vengeance, of magic and of *ekstasis*.

In general terms, these complexities in the character of Greek gods are most frequently the result of a complex origin. Here our brief studies in the origins of some of the most important may come to mind and assist understanding. In many instances, though not all, it is possible to be rather more precise and say that the contradictions result from the imposition of Homeric ideas, and sometimes Homeric names, on the nature of a deity who existed before Homer. So great was the influence of Homer, and so vivid and comprehensible were the personalities which he gave to the gods, that these remained for centuries uppermost in the consciousness of Greece. But the gods existed before Homer, and it was inevitable that memories of their earlier nature should break through.

To conclude, there were, as it seems to us, many different types of religion in Greece, and some of these were related to the worship of particular gods, making it tempting at first sight to suppose that each god or set of gods stood for a different kind of religion—here the Olympians of Homer, there Dionysos, and there again Demeter and Kore. In fact however we must be prepared to find that the devotees of what we regard as opposing types of religion will invoke the same god to entirely different ends (the difference being sometimes, but not necessarily, marked by a change of epithet), and also that gods whom we had thought of as inspiring incompatible beliefs and aspirations are sometimes claimed as patrons together by one and the same band of worshippers. It can only lead to unreality if we try to discover order and reason in matters whose explanation is simply a calm unconsciousness of incongruity. It is, after all, unlikely that the future religious historian will find more consistency within the limits of any single religious denomination of to-day.

Chapter IX

THE CHTHONIOI

Yea, though he die, in Hades
The guilt of his ill deeds shall find him out.
There sits to judge our sins, as we are told,
Another Zeus, the dead's last arbiter.

Aeschylus, *Suppl.* 228

I. General

WE may now turn to the second of our religious worlds, the world of the *chthonioi*, spirits who live in the dark recesses of the earth (*chthon*). To us it seems indeed a different world, and though its separation from the gods above cannot have been so clearly marked in the minds of those whose religion found a place for both, it was sometimes at least regarded as such by the Greeks, and its denizens plainly distinguished from those of Olympus, even though they might bear the same names. As Danaos says in the passage quoted above, it is possible to meet another, a different Zeus, and with him religious ideas of a different order. Retribution for sin appears as something which awaits the ordinary man after death. Zeus *Katachthonios* ("beneath the earth") is once mentioned in the *Iliad* as the husband of Persephone. It is a name for Hades or Pluto, the brother of the Olympian, as in the passage of Aeschylus. Rhadamanthys is mentioned in the *Odyssey* as one of the dwellers in Elysium.[1] But neither is given the position of law-giver and judge among the dead which they hold in the mythology of the fifth century. The reference of Danaos to "Another Zeus", who punishes sinners in the next world, is one illustration of the fact that the chthonian powers stood for different religious conceptions from those associated with the Olympians, and that, with their distinctive characteristics, they had no significance for Homer.

That was an isolated instance, chosen almost at random, of the kind of ideas associated with the chthonians. We must now

[1] *Il.* ix, 457; *Od.* iv, 564.

attempt to formulate their character in more general terms. They are dwellers in the earth, and the earth does two services for men. By its fertility it provides them with the means of life, and it takes them into its bosom when they die. The *chthonioi* accordingly have two primary functions: they ensure the fertility of the land, and they preside over, or have some function or other connected with, the realm of the souls of the dead. It should perhaps be mentioned that Wilamowitz revived, or clung to, an old hypothesis that the true *chthonioi* were originally connected solely with the dead, and that their nature as fertility-gods is the result of a later fusion. Demeter, who represents the earth in her aspect as the bountiful mother of fruits, had originally nothing to do with the *chthonioi*, though later both these aspects of the earth became united. Whether or not this was the historical sequence of events, the contention is only of minor importance for the study of Greek religion from the time of Homer onwards. If the two functions were originally separate, then this was a case when the original state of belief disappeared altogether, and our present rule is only to take account of origins in so far as they throw light on the beliefs or practices of historical times.[1]

On the other hand Wilamowitz, as is usual with him, makes interesting points in the course of reaching his conclusion. In his latest statement[2] he has based his case on the original difference in meaning between the two Greek words for earth, *ge* and *chthon*. The earth only became *ge* when she had been wedded and made fruitful. *Chthon* with its derivatives refers in origin to the cold, dead depths and has nothing to do with fertility. It is the earth in which graves are dug, not furrows ploughed. The chorus in the *Choephoroi* invoke *Chthon* along with the tomb itself.[3] "If modern scholars, who talk so much about chthonian cults, think in this connexion of agriculture and all that goes along with Demeter in that sphere, they have not yet accustomed their ear to the overtones of Greek words." Yet even Wilamowitz admits that the question is one of origins, and that in the classical poets the two words mean the same. In spite of his warning, I think it is safe enough to side with Rohde in this matter, and adopt his conclusion: "This dual efficacy of the *chthonioi* is explained naturally enough by their nature as underground spirits. There is no reason

[1] In the present instance I may however be influenced also by my personal conviction that Wilamowitz is wrong.

[2] *Der Glaube*, i, 210 f.

[3] Line 723: ὦ πότνια χθὼν καὶ πότνια ἀκτὴ χώματος.

for supposing that their influence on the fertility of the fields was a later addition."[1] At any rate we may claim the right to determine the extension of our own technical terms if they have been so explained as to ensure that they do not mislead; and I intend to apply the name chthonian to all gods or spirits of the earth, whether their functions are concerned with agriculture or with the grave and the world beyond, or (as often) with both. Let our justification be this: if the Greeks could speak of Zeus Chthonios as another name for Hades, ruler of the dead, and Hesiod could advise the farmer to pray, for the sake of his crops, "to Chthonian Zeus and pure Demeter", then whatever may be the truth about his far-off origin, the Zeus Chthonios to the mind of the historical Greeks was in both cases the same.[2] One of the commonest names of the lord of the dead is that which derives from *plutos*, wealth, and marks him as the treasurer of the earth's rich abundance no less than the king of souls.

One natural result of the earthly nature of these spirits is that most of them were firmly attached to the soil of the locality in which they originated. They could not be so easily universalized as were the Olympians. These when they had passed through Homer's hands were the common property of the whole of Greece, but not so the chthonians. There are, in consequence, a great many of them. Some were scarcely heard of outside their own village or district, but, apart from other casual sources, the guide-book of the traveller and antiquarian Pausanias has preserved the names of many, and of some the details of their cult as well. Even in this sphere, the greater universalism of the all-pervading Olympians made itself felt, with the result that the name of Zeus Chthonios tended to appear everywhere; but the originally local character of the god might be betrayed by the survival of his name as a kind of epithet, or rather surname. Thus for example the local underworld spirits Amphiaraos of Thebes and Trophonios of Lebadeia in Boeotia are also referred to as Zeus Amphiaraos and Zeus Trophonios. For Trophonios this occurs on actual inscriptions at the site of his shrine.[3]

[1] *Psyche* (Eng. trans. 1925) ch. v, n. 1.

[2] Hesiod, *Works*, 465. Cf. the mention on an inscription of about 200 B.C. from Mykonos of a sacrifice ὑπὲρ καρπῶν Διὶ Χθονίῳ Γῇ Χθονίῃ (Dittenberger, *Syll.*[3] 1024, lines 25 f.). For the significance of Γῇ χθονίῃ cf. G. Vlastos, *Presoc. Theol. and Philos*, *Philos. Quart.* 1952, 108 f.

[3] For examples see Rohde, *Psyche*, ch. iii, nn. 18 and 19, and for further details about Trophonios below pp. 223 ff.

What should we call these beings: gods, heroes or what? So far I have used "spirits" as a wide and non-committal term in order not to prejudge the question. The *chthonioi* undoubtedly included both gods and heroes, and it is sometimes difficult to know which name is most appropriate to a particular individual. The question is a frequent source of learned controversy. Hero-worship, that is, the elevation of ancestors or other dead men to a semi-divine status with all the apparatus of prayer and cult, was widespread in Greece, and what other name could be given to them but *chthonioi*, since their habitation is beneath the earth? The dead kings, says Pindar, hear of the achievements of their descendants with "chthonian mind", or "soul beneath the earth". The invocation of the suppliant Danaids, in the strange land to which they have come, is: "O city, O land and bright water, O ye gods above, and reverend *chthonioi* who dwell in the tombs . . .!"[1] Equally certain is it that some of those called *chthonioi* were no souls of the departed, but examples of the spirits of fertility, invoked to bless the crops, whom we have met already and who spring up everywhere in agricultural communities at an early stage of religious development. In some cases the difference is obvious, but in others the discovery of the class to which a particular *chthonios*, or dweller in the earth, originally belonged, calls for careful investigation and may even elude the search altogether. Professor Rose has noted a few useful guiding principles, as for instance that the presence in the cult of taboos on food or wine and other such irrational practices usually betray the god of fertility.[2] Yet he and everyone else are agreed on the difficulty of the task. Even the details of the cult may do little to help, for to quote Farnell, who had studied hero-cults more deeply and to greater effect than most, "unfortunately there was always great resemblance between the ritual at a buried hero's tomb and that at the underground shrine of the earth-deity or daimon; therefore in certain cases it might be hard to determine whether the personage belonged to one or the other class; and in the shifting popular tradition the one could easily be transformed into the other".[3]

These words are of great importance. In the first place, they add strength to our decision to recognize as the one fundamental cleavage in Greek religion the line between the Olympians and

[1] Pindar, *Pyth.* v, 101 χθονίᾳ φρενί; Aesch. *Suppl.* 23 ff.
[2] *Modern Methods in Classical Mythology* (St. Andrews, 1930), pp. 22 ff.
[3] *Greek Hero-Cults and Ideas of Immortality* (Oxford, 1921), p. 239.

the chthonians. The forms of cult provide a valuable test. By this test we can detect no sharp line of cleavage within the *chthonioi* themselves, whereas it throws into high relief the contrast between them and the Olympians. Here are some typical differences, which I offer with the proviso (to forestall captious criticism) that strict logic and the absolute rule have no more place here than in other phenomena of Greek or any religion. We are speaking, as Aristotle would say, of what happens "either always or for the most part".[1]

i. Name for the act of sacrifice: θύειν for the Olympians, ἐναγίζειν for the chthonians.[2]

ii. Method: animal killed with throat upward for Olympians, downward for chthonians (so that blood may most easily soak into the earth).[3]

iii. Type of altar: for Olympians the high-built βωμός, for the chthonians a low altar called ἐσχάρα (hearth), or else no altar at all, but the sacrifice performed into a pit or trench (βόθρος). In either case the purpose is to make the offering immediately accessible to those beneath the earth.[4]

iv. Choice of victim: (*a*) Colour—for Olympians white, for chthonians black. So Odysseus to Teiresias in the *Odyssey*. There certainly seem to have been exceptions to this, but it is what the ancients themselves say, and must have expressed at least a preference.[5] (*b*) Species. The ram is the usual offering to the chthonians, also the pig, which had particular associations with sacrifices of expiation and purification, and was therefore the victim offered to Demeter in the Eleusinian mysteries.[6] The ox which was commonly offered to the Olympians was absent. It may be added that as well as animal victims "bloodless offerings", e.g. of honey or

[1] Cf. on this A. D. Nock, "The Cult of Heroes" (*Harv. Theol. Rev.* xxxvii (1944), 141 ff.).

[2] Cf. esp. Hdt. ii, 44 (referring to the unique double aspect of Herakles, as Olympian god and as hero): τῷ μὲν ὡς ἀθανάτῳ Ὀλυμπίῳ δὲ ἐπωνυμίην θύουσι, τῷ δὲ ἑτέρῳ ὡς ἥρωι ἐναγίζουσι.

[3] Ch. Picard in *Rev. de l'Hist. des Rel.* cxiv (1936), 157.

[4] *Od.* xi, 25 ff.; Ap. Rhod. iii, 1032 ff., for sacrifice ἐς βόθρον in the one case to the shades, in the other to Hekate. Archaeological evidence for sacrificial pits is plentiful. See P. Stengel, *Griechische Kultusaltertümer* (Munich, 3rd ed., 1920), p. 16, and for ἐσχάραι pp. 15 ff.

[5] Stengel, o.c., p. 151.

[6] Cf. p. 193 above, and Aristophanes, *Peace*, 374:

ἐς χοιρίδιον μοί νυν δάνεισον τρεῖς δραχμάς·
δεῖ γὰρ μυηθῆναι με πρὶν τεθνηκέναι.

the fruits of the earth, were commonly made to the powers of the earth.

v. Type of shrine: for Olympians the familiar classical temple, above ground and often on a height; for the chthonians a subterranean cave or *adyton*, which may or may not have represented a tomb.

vi. Time of day: sacrifice to the Olympians was performed in the morning sunshine, to the chthonians in the evening or at dead of night.[1]

vii. We may add, on the authority of Picard,[2] the gesture employed in prayer: the hand raised, palm upward, to the Olympians, and lowered with the palm downward to invoke the powers of the earth.

To fix the contrast in our minds, let us supplement this bare tabulation by a single connected account of the instructions given for a sacrifice to the dread underworld goddess Hekate. As we read it, we must keep before us the typical scene of sacrifice to an Olympian god, which is too familiar to need lengthy description. We shall not go far wrong if we recall the *Ode on a Grecian Urn*. The whole town has flocked out together in holiday mood and forms a procession in the bright morning sunshine. There is music and dancing while the victim, probably a pure white ox gaily garlanded, is led up to the shining marble temple with its altar before it. Priests and other participants are wearing white, and the whole scene has an air of festival. Set beside this the words of Medea to Jason, as she prepares him to enlist the help of the nether spirits in the task of sowing the dragon's teeth:

> Waiting for the mid-moment of the night's dividing, having washed thyself in the flood of the unwearied river, alone and apart and clad in sombre hue, dig thee a pit well-rounded. And within it slay a she-lamb, and lay it raw and whole on a pile which thou hast heaped together in the pit. Then pray to Hekate the sisterless, who is called Perseis, pouring from a cup the honey of the hive-bee. When thou hast thus mindfully propitiated the goddess, get thee away back from the pyre; and let neither thud of feet nor howl of dogs tempt thee to look back, lest thou bring all to nought and thyself return not to thy comrades in any seemly wise.[3]

[1] Stengel, o.c., p. 150.

[2] Ch. Picard, "Le geste de la prière funèraire en Grèce et en Étrurie", *Rev. Hist. Rel.* cxiv (1936), 137 ff.

[3] *Ap. Rhod.* iii, 1029 ff.

We have not yet however taken note of the most significant thing about Farnell's words, that is, the clue which they provide to our main problem, the question in what way, and in connexion with what cults, did the idea of immortality and apotheosis for man take root among the Greeks. To repeat his words: "In certain cases it might be hard to determine whether the personage belonged to one or the other class [earth-deity or buried hero]; *and in the shifting popular tradition the one could easily be transformed into the other*." A buried man could easily be transformed into a god! Here is something that Homer never taught. It is as well to have found this point made in Farnell, since we are here confessedly searching for the germs of a belief in immortality, and had I drawn the conclusion myself it might have been open to the suspicion of helping to grind an axe. Farnell in the context of his remark had no such object in view.[1]

In order to make more concrete the general impression that we have gained from Farnell's words, let us examine some individual examples of these underworld beings, choosing, so far as the evidence allows, first an earth-deity, then a hero, and then a doubtful case. As Farnell says, the one could easily be transformed into the other, and our criterion must be, so far as can be judged, the state from which they started.

II. The Earth-god: Trophonios

The only firm facts on which we can base our knowledge of Trophonios are those pertaining to his cult. His legends were not crystallized in epic poetry, and those that are told of him in scholia, grammarians and other late authorities are mutually contradictory, as well as containing elements of floating Märchen, or

[1] In considering the evidence for a cult of Agamemnon under the name Zeus-Agamemnon, A. B. Cook argues that the identification was original. "The hero was a Zeus all along, the local champion or king being as such the embodiment of the god." It is a survival of the old belief in the divinity of kings, attested also in Homer by Agamemnon's title ἄναξ ἀνδρῶν, which "is suggestive of a divine appellation", and by such heroic epithets as θεοειδής. It may be true that *originally* the chieftains were thought of as gods, but this does not mean that Homer taught the Greeks to believe in the divinity of man. Agamemnon is not called Zeus in Homer, and the epithets did not suggest divinity to the poet or to his audience as they do to the scholar. Their original significance, if that is what it was, was no longer understood, and we need not unsay what we have said already about the relations between men and gods in Homer. (A. B. Cook, *Class. Rev.* xvii (1903), 277; *Zeus*, i, 1070.)

folk-tales, such as attach themselves easily to any legendary figures. He was said to have been a master-builder who with his brother Agamedes was responsible for the building of an early temple of Apollo at Delphi, in recognition of which Apollo granted them the best reward—a painless death. This reward for service to Apollo was also that of Kleobis and Biton. The story was also told of how the two brothers, in building a treasury at Elis (or alternatively at Hyria near Aulis), made one of the stones removable, and by this means repeatedly entered the treasury and robbed it. At last Agamedes was caught in a trap which had been placed there, whereat Trophonios cut off his head, in order that he might not be recognized or tell tales, and fled to Lebadeia. This is a tale well-known to students of folk-lore as that of the Master Thief, and is told by Herodotus of the builder of the treasury of King Rhampsinitos in Egypt. An alternative story of the death of Trophonios tells that when he was in flight after his robberies the earth opened and swallowed him up at Lebadeia. It is obviously inconsistent with the story of Apollo's boon, and doubtless arose from the existence of the underground oracle of Trophonios at Lebadeia in classical times. Though not peculiar to him it tends to be associated with similar oracular figures like Amphiaraos of Thebes.

Direct references to Trophonios in classical literature say nothing of these legends, but refer only to the consultation of his oracle. It is mentioned by Herodotus as one of the many in Greece whose guidance was sought by Croesus as to the wisdom of attacking the Persians; in the *Ion* of Euripides, Xuthos consults Trophonios about his childlessness before proceeding to Delphi; and Aristophanes in the *Clouds* makes Strepsiades exclaim, before entering the school of Socrates, "Give me a honey-cake first, for I'm as frightened at going in as if it were the cave of Trophonios!"[1]

The fullest account of the oracle of Trophonios at Lebadeia is that of Pausanias, and we have his word that it is that of an eyewitness, for Pausanias claims to have consulted Trophonios himself and gone through all the hair-raising experiences which such consultation involved. It is therefore worth setting out in full. We may feel fairly confident that the procedure had not changed since the days of Euripides and Aristophanes. The only detail

[1] Authorities for the mythology of Trophonios are collected by Kroll in PWK, *Realenc.* 2nd series, vii, 678 ff. The reff. to the oracle mentioned in the text are Hdt. i, 46; Eur. *Ion*, 300, 393 f., 404; Ar. *Clouds*, 506 ff.

mentioned by them, namely the honey-cakes in Aristophanes, is repeated in Pausanias' account.

Trophonios, he says,[1] is a figure similar to Asklepios, for in the grotto of Herkyna in which are the sources of the river of that name (Herkyna is in fact the local river-nymph), "there are standing statues, with serpents coiled round their sceptres. One might guess them to be Asklepios and Hygieia, but they may also be Trophonios and Herkyna, for even the serpents they reckon to be sacred to Trophonios no less than to Asklepios. . . . The most celebrated things in the grove are a temple and statue of Trophonios. The latter, which is the work of Praxiteles, also resembles Asklepios." He then goes on:

As to the oracle, the procedure is as follows. When a man decides to go down to visit Trophonios, he is first of all lodged for a prescribed number of days in a building which is sacred to Agathos Daimon and Agathe Tyche [the Good Daimon and Good Fortune]. While living there he observes certain rules of purity, and in particular is allowed no warm baths: his bath is the river Herkyna. He gets plenty of meat from the sacrifices, for anyone who intends to make the descent sacrifices both to Trophonios himself and to the children of Trophonios, and also to Apollo and Kronos and Zeus surnamed *Basileus* [King] and Hera the Charioteer and Demeter whom they surname Europe and call the nurse of Trophonios. At each of the sacrifices a diviner is present who inspects the entrails of the victim, and having looked at them foretells to the man intending to descend whether Trophonios will receive him kindly and graciously. The entrails from the earlier sacrifices do not reveal the mind of Trophonios so clearly. But on the night on which a man is to go down, they sacrifice a ram into a trench, calling upon Agamedes. Though all the previous sacrifices may have been favourable, it goes for nothing if the entrails of this ram do not say the same thing; but if they too agree, then every man goes down with good hope. The method of descent is this. First of all, when night has fallen two boys of citizen families, aged about thirteen, bring him to the river Herkyna and there anoint him with olive oil and wash him. These boys are called Hermai, and it is they who wash the visitor to Trophonios and perform all needful services for him. After this he is brought by the priests, not straight to the oracle, but to springs of water which lie close to one another. Here he has to drink the water called Lethe, in order to achieve forgetfulness of all that he has hitherto thought of; and on top of it another water, the water of Mnemosyne, which gives him remembrance of what he sees when he has gone down. He next looks upon a statue which is said to be the work of Daidalos, and which

[1] Paus. ix, 39.

the priests reveal to none save those who intend to go down to the abode of Trophonios, and when he has seen this statue and worshipped it and prayed, he approaches the oracle, wearing a linen chiton girdled with ribbons, and shod with the native boots of the country.

The oracle is situated above the grove on the mountain-side. It lies in the middle of a circular floor of white marble, about equal in circumference to the smallest size of threshing-floor and raised to a height of slightly under three feet. On the floor are set spikes with circular rails joining them, both spikes and railings being of bronze, and there are gates made through the railings. Inside the enclosure there is an opening in the earth, not a natural chasm but an accurate and skilful piece of building. In shape this chamber is like an oven. Its breadth across the middle is to all appearances about six feet, and even its depth one would not estimate to be more than twelve. It is made without any means of descent to the bottom, but whenever a man goes down to visit Trophonios they bring a light, narrow ladder for him. When he has gone down, he finds an opening between the bottom and the masonry, whose breadth appeared to be two spans, and its height a span.[1] He lies down on the ground, and holding in his hand cakes kneaded with honey, he thrusts his feet into the opening and pushes forward himself, trying to get his knees inside the hole. The rest of his body is at once dragged in and follows his knees, just as a great and swift river would catch a man in its swirl and draw him under.[2] From this stage on, once men are inside the *adyton*, they are not all instructed of the future in the same way; some have heard, others have

[1] Liddell and Scott give the length of a *σπιθαμή* as seven and a half inches, though this estimate is omitted in the 9th ed. revised by Stuart Jones. One would hope for the sake of the visitor to Trophonios that it is an underestimate.

[2] Without suggesting that modern parallels have any historical value as "survivals", one may quote a remarkably similar phenomenon attested at the end of the nineteenth century. The value of such parallels lies in the added sense of reality which they give to what might otherwise seem the incredible stories of strange, remote people who lived two thousand years ago. In a book called *'Η 'Οδησσός*, published at Varna in 1894, J. Nicolaos gives an account of a Dervish *tekke*, formerly a Christian church, near Varna, containing a saint's tomb with healing powers. Extracts are quoted in translation by F. W. Hasluck in *Christianity and Islam under the Sultans* (Oxford, 1929), pp. 764 f., from which the following is taken. Near the tomb is a hole in the paved floor and the sufferer has to spend the night in the place (as in the incubation cures of the ancient world) and thrust the injured part into the hole. "One such sufferer, whose thigh was injured, relates that he stayed there all night with his foot thrust into the hole. . . . All night he felt his foot dragged downward by a violent force, and thought he would be sucked down altogether. To increase his alarm, he heard in the silence of the night a noise as of a man, or rather a spirit, trailing the slippers we have mentioned [a pair which always lay near the tomb and in another account are said to be the slippers of the saint himself] regularly over the paved floor of the church. . . . The noise continued till it was nearly morning. At last, thinking he was going to be sucked down altogether into the earth and making up his mind to hold out to the end, whatever might happen, he fell asleep at the hole about dawn."

seen as well. The way back is through the same opening, feet foremost.

They say that no one has died as the result of his descent, with the exception of one of the bodyguard of Demetrios, and as for him, he had not carried out any of the prescribed ritual at the sanctuary, nor did he go down to consult the god, but in the hope of getting gold and silver from the *adyton.*[1] . . . When a man has come up from the abode of Trophonios, the priests take him over again and set him on a seat called the seat of Mnemosyne, which is not far from the *adyton,* and while he is seated there they ask him of all that he has seen and learned. Then when they have heard it they put him in charge of his friends, who lift him up and carry him to the house of Agathe Tyche and Agathos Daimon where he lodged before, for he is still in the grip of fear and unaware of himself or of those around him. But later on his wits will return to him unimpaired, and in particular he will recover the power of laughter. I do not write from hearsay, for I have consulted Trophonios myself, as well as seeing others who have done so.

This detailed and sober first-hand account will suffice for our purposes. References to others will be found in Frazer's notes on the passage, which may also be consulted on any separate points not mentioned here. Pausanias' vivid narrative does not need much comment, and I wish only to draw attention to a few features which confirm the general impression that the visit was one to a local god of the underworld. It is interesting that the passage in Aristophanes refers not only to the honey-cakes but also to the extreme fright that is occasioned by the experience. In passing, we may remark that these scenes in the *Clouds* are full of suggestions that they are a parody of some descent to an underground oracle or initiation of the infernal gods, and when Strepsiades actually speaks of "going down" into the place (εἴσω καταβαίνων), one may suppose that the entrance to the "thinking-shop" of Socrates has been got up to resemble one of these underground oracular shrines.[2] The honey-cakes are to pacify the serpents which we

[1] Similarly in the modern parallel described by Nicolaos, the only person said to have died of the experience was a woman who tried to cheat the saint. "A woman of Varna, who did not believe what was reported of the healing power of the church, put her hand into the hole, pretending it was ailing, whereas in reality it was perfectly sound. She remained all night in the church alone . . . and had the same experience, that is to say, she was drawn down with irresistible force by the arm she had placed in the hole, and heard the noise of the spirit walking in the church with the slippers trailing over the floor. But in the morning, when she wanted to take her arm from the hole, they say she was totally unable to do so until a posse of villagers came and dragged it out by force. The woman herself was so frightened that she died a few days after."

[2] καταβαίνειν was also used of inquirers entering the shrine at Delphi (Parke, *History of the Delphic Oracle*, p. 28). Cf. below, p. 231 with n. 2.

know from other accounts to have been encountered by the visitor as he entered the *adyton*. Sacred serpents are one of the marks of a chthonian spirit, and honey-cakes are the regular offering. They were offered to Erechtheus, the guardian daemon of the Akropolis of Athens, who had the form of a serpent as had the chthonian god of Crete, Zeus who was called Meilichios, and Agathos Daimon in domestic worship. All seem to have some connexion with the earth and its fruits, which are aptly embodied in the snake who makes such sudden and mysterious appearances and disappearances through cracks in earth or rock.[1] We recall too the sacred serpents of Asklepios, which used to appear to the sufferer who sought an incubation cure. The effects of the fright are also vividly described by Pausanias, although he adds from his personal experience that the power of laughter does return after a time. It seems curious that he should think this worth recording, but the scholiast on the *Clouds* mentions it as a common belief that the man who went down to see Trophonios never laughed again. Indeed the thing had passed into a proverb, and of anyone with a preternaturally solemn mien it was said, "He has been to consult Trophonios".[2] Probably therefore the purpose of Pausanias in putting it in was to explode a popular fallacy.

We may notice also the observance of a preliminary regimen designed to ensure purity before the god can be approached, reminiscent as it is of the preparations for an invocation of Hekate described by Apollonius Rhodius, as well as of the preparatory sea-bathing of the neophytes at Eleusis and other instances all connected with the gods of the earth. Next there is the sacrifice of a ram into a pit or trench, said to be the most important of all the many sacrifices which have to be carried out. To this of course the most famous parallel is the sacrifice performed by Odysseus when he wished to call up the shade of Teiresias for the same purpose of learning the future, though it is also matched by the sacrifice to Hekate already quoted from Apollonius. To Homer Teiresias was a man and no god, and as we have observed, there is seldom any great difference between the ritual demanded by a hero and that demanded by an underworld god. Prophecy is however usually the function of the earth-spirit, although under

[1] For the serpent-guardian of the Akropolis, see Hdt. viii, 41, and for his original nature as a god, cf. Rohde, *Psyche* (Eng. trans.), pp. 98 f., Wilamowitz, *Der Glaube*, i, 118; for Zeus Meilichios and Agathos Daimon cf. Nilsson, *Gr. Pop. Rel.* pp. 69 f.

[2] εἰς Τροφωνίου μεμάντευται. Cf. Frazer's note on Paus. ix, 39, 13, and the story of Parmeniskos, Parke, *Hist. Delph. Oracle*, 423.

the influence of epic the shrine may be usurped by one of the heroes, or the original divine occupant, like Trophonios and Amphiaraos, may be transformed into a divinely favoured mortal of the heroic age.

The purpose of the visit is to learn the future. We have already noticed the two divisions of prophecy—"sane" prophecy or omen-reading and mad or inspired prophecy (*mantike*) involving actual possession by the god. The underground sanctuary of Trophonios was a *manteion*, and where this sort of prophecy is practised, it will usually be found that an earth-spirit is at the bottom of it. Gaia, the Earth herself, was "the first of prophets", and the best-known example of such an oracle of inspiration was Delphi, where it was universally acknowledged that Gaia had been the earliest occupant of the shrine. Before Apollo came on the scene, says Aeschylus, it had passed from her to her own daughter Themis and then to "another child of Chthon".[1] In this way among others chthonian cults introduce the notion of possession by the god, *enthusiasmos*, the god in us. Here is one door open for the ideas of immortality and divinity for man, which are a not unnatural extension of the entering in of the god to his representatives, as the god of Delphi entered and spoke through the Pythia. It is something closely related to the frenzy induced when the Bacchae were possessed by Bacchos, or the Kuretes by the Great Kuros.

The mention of the springs of Lethe and Mnemosyne is rendered particularly interesting by the survival of a striking parallel from a very genuine document of religious practice. In certain graves of Magna Graecia have been discovered thin plates of gold, buried with the dead and inscribed with verses containing instructions for his journey to the world below. The plates themselves are probably as early as the fourth century B.C., and the poems from which the scribbled lines are extracts were no doubt considerably older. On one of these plates (which is now in the British Museum) is written:

> Thou shalt find to the left of the house of Hades a spring, and by the side thereof standing a white cypress. To this spring approach not near. But thou shalt find another, from the lake of Memory [*Mnemosyne*] cold water flowing forth, and there are guardians before it.

In the few remaining lines, the soul is instructed to give an

[1] τὴν πρωτόμαντιν Γαῖαν κτλ, Aesch. *Eum.* 2.

account of himself to the guardians and ask them for a drink of the water of Mnemosyne, after which he will be able to join the blessed in their abodes.

I have dealt with these plates elsewhere, and shall have occasion to mention them again.[1] Here only one point need concern us, the presence of the fountains of Lethe and Mnemosyne in the landscape of the next world; for if the spring on the right, from which it is proper for the soul to drink when it is about to embark on a life of endless bliss, is the spring of Mnemosyne, that on the left, which it is warned to avoid, can hardly be other than the spring of Lethe. In Plato's description of the underworld, souls which were not completely pure and hence were destined for reincarnation in mortal bodies were made to drink a certain amount from this spring before being reborn.[2] The soul addressed on the gold plates is clearly regarded as one of the saved. Consequently it is instructed to avoid Lethe altogether, but to drink instead of Mnemosyne, after which, in the closing line of the extract, "among the other heroes thou shalt have lordship".

How, if at all, the procedure adopted by the visitor to Trophonios was thought to correspond to that enjoined on the souls of the dead, it would be difficult to say. One thing remains certain however, that in other accounts the two springs are not in the world of the living at all, but are encountered by the disembodied soul on its journey through the nether regions. It is one indication out of many that these oracular caves were believed to be actual entrances to the world of souls. Such local entrances were found in various parts of Greece, e.g. on the river Styx in Arcadia and at Cape Tainaron in the extreme south of the Peloponnese, and doubtless go back to a time before there was any universal realm of Hades at all. The two boys whom the visitor to Trophonios was given to attend him on the night of his descent were called Hermai, and must have been the representatives of Hermes *Psychopompos*, who conducted souls to the underworld. The same thing is probably suggested by the curiously complicated arrangement of spikes and circular railings (*obeloi* and *zonai*), with gates through them, laid out on the marble floor surrounding the entrance to the adyton. It suggests a maze, one use of which was to keep unwanted and possibly mischievous spirits in their place; for as all magicians know, even a system of lines traced on the ground

[1] pp. 321 f. below, and *Orpheus and Gr. Rel.*, pp. 171 ff.
[2] *Rep.* 620a.

can do this, provided the proper formalities have been carried out.[1]

To enter the sanctuary of Trophonios was then to visit the infernal regions. It was a "descent into Hades" as much as the legendary "descents" of Herakles, Theseus, Orpheus and other bold heroes. It was therefore no wonder that it was a terrifying exploit.[2]

Much in the foregoing description, as in the legends of Trophonios, may seem to suggest that the giver of the oracles was a buried man rather than a god, and his sanctuary a tomb. In a matter so much at the mercy of the "shifting popular tradition" it is indeed difficult to attain certainty, and Professor Cook sees him as originally a Frazerian deified king, "not only a dead man, but also a living god", but in the first place a man; and he would explain the "oven-like" shape of the sunken entrance to the adyton by the supposition that it was the *tholos* or beehive-tomb of an old Boeotian king.[3] Nevertheless I am inclined to follow the almost unanimous opinion of modern scholarship and suppose that he was originally a local spirit of fertility, and that he carries the suggestion of this in his name, with its echo of τρέφω and τροφή, "nourish" and "nourishment". The dual associations of the earth, as the provident nurturer of living creatures and the receiver of the dead, were not kept distinct in the Greek mind, and it need occasion no surprise if the dwelling of a chthonian god was equipped with all the adjuncts of an entrance to the realm of souls.

III. The Hero: Herakles

Before proceeding to my chosen example, it will be better to say a few words about the nature of hero-cults and the state of belief which gave rise to them. First comes the fact that the hero was a

[1] The literature of mazes and labyrinths is enormous. A conspectus of recent contributions will be found in A. B. Cook, *Zeus*, iii, 2 (1940), p. 1086. There are of course many theories about their original purpose, and the suggestion in the text must be regarded as a conjecture, though I should claim a certain probability for it.

[2] κατάβασις εἰς Ἅιδου was the title given to a number of poems on the subject. Cf. e.g. O. Kern, *Orphicorum Fragmenta* (Berlin, 1922), pp. 304 ff. The oracular shrine of Trophonios was called, according to some late authorities, Καταβάσιον (Cook, *Zeus*, ii, 2 (1925), p. 1075).

[3] *Zeus*, vol. ii, app. K, pp. 1073 ff.

man and not a god.[1] This does not mean that it is important whether as a matter of history he ever lived. Some heroes are historical, some are not. On many it would be difficult to pronounce. The important thing—the fact so far as religion is concerned—is the belief, and the belief about heroes is that they once were mortal men. Hero-worship rests on the belief that the dead have power in and from the grave. There could have been no cult without such a belief. No Greek would worship a spineless shade from whom neither good nor evil influence was to be expected; hence for those who practised hero-worship some at least of the dead were capable of a different sort of existence from that which was their common lot in the Homeric poems as "leaping shadows", "strengthless heads of corpses", who could do nothing but flit about ineffectually and utter thin cries.

The hero is still imagined as dwelling in his tomb. Hence of course the astonishing magnificence of tombs like the massive *tholoi* of Mycenae with their elaborately constructed domes which have lasted to this day, and hence the wealth and variety of treasure which was buried with the dead and has been found, for example, in the shaft graves of the same Mycenean civilization. Gold and silver cups and other vessels, jewellery and signets, swords and daggers, toilet articles for the ladies, all indicate that the dead were to live on in much the same regal state, and engage in the same occupations, that they had enjoyed in their earthly life. The belief in their continued vigour, and in the means necessary to ensure and sustain it, underwent many modifications in the course of Greek history. Changes of custom between burial and cremation, to mention one example, must, one would have thought, have entailed at least some change of ideas on this head. But in one form or another it persisted, and it certainly went back to a very early date. The tomb, whether it contain the body or only the ashes of the defunct, is his dwelling-place, and around the tomb his influence is felt. Consequently it is at the tomb that the cult must be observed if the spirit is to be propitiated by receiving the offerings of blood or wine as they soak into the earth. Great importance was therefore attached to the actual possession of the grave, and situations arose such as have not been unknown in Mediterranean lands even after their conversion to Christianity

[1] As I have tried to emphasize throughout, all wide generalizations about religious beliefs admit of exceptions. Cf. Nock, "Cult of Heroes" (*Harv. Theol. Rev.* (1944)), especially his remarks on the wide significance of the term ἥρως (162 ff.).

when the last resting-place of the remains of a saint have been concerned. It was said that after the Persian Wars the Athenians were advised by the Delphic oracle to recover the bones of Theseus from Skyros, where he had died, and that they were found and brought back by Kimon after he had taken the island in 469 B.C. A similar story was told of the Spartans, that after being consistently worsted in their war with the men of Tegea they sent to Delphi to know which god they ought to propitiate to ensure success. The oracle's answer was that they must recover the bones of Orestes, which at present lay in the territory of the Tegeans. This they were able to do by a trick, after which they soon got the upper hand in the war.[1] For this reason the growth of hero-cults in classical Greece was not unconnected with the rise of the city-state organization of society. Every city worth the name was ambitious to have its famous ancestor to help it fight its battles.

Let us however look more generally at this belief in the power of the dead to help the living. It would be difficult to find a more impressive example of it than the passionate invocation of the dead Agamemnon by his children in the *Choephoroi* of Aeschylus. The certainty that the dead can hear and save is shudderingly real. First we have Electra's prayer as she pours her libations over the tomb (lines 124 ff.):

Great herald of those above and below, Chthonian Hermes, aid me by proclaiming to the spirits beneath the earth that they hear my prayers, the spirits who keep watch over my ancestral home. . . . For myself, I pour my libation to a mortal shade, and 'tis my father I call, and say, Have pity on me, and kindle a light to shine upon this house, even my dear brother Orestes.[2] . . . I pray thee that by some fortune he may come hither, and do thou hearken to me, Father, and to myself grant a mind more modest than my mother's, and a hand more innocent. These prayers for ourselves, and for our enemies that there may arise one to avenge thee, Father, and thy slayers, as is just, die in their turn. In the midst of my prayer for blessings cast I this evil curse for them. Be thou the channel of blessings up from thy grave to us, aided by the gods, by Earth, and by victorious Justice.

[1] Plut. *Thes.* 36, Hdt. i, 67. The belief has a primitive ancestry. Cf. Lévy-Bruhl, *L'expérience Mystique* (Paris, 1938), 179: "certaines tribus bantou enterrent leur chef dans le plus grand secret: il ne faut pas que personne puisse indiquer, ni découvrir, ou le cadavre a été placé. Si des ennemis s'emparaient de ses os, en particulier de son crâne, le sort de la tribu serait entre leurs mains."

[2] The reading *φῶς ἄναψον ἐν δόμοις* is Wilamowitz's and Headlam's: *φῶς τ' ἄναψον* Schneidewin.

After Orestes' first cry to his father, the chorus break in with the significant words: "My son, the fire with greedy jaw devoureth not the spirit of him who has died; even in after time doth he show his anger", and at the end of the alternate prayers which follow, it would be an insensitive member of the audience who did not feel that there was now a third presence on the stage besides the living pair.[1]

OR. Father, I call thee! Hear thy children's cry. . . .
ALL. Come, dread spirit, to the light!
Help us! Against thine enemies we fight. . . .
OR. Father, in such unkingly fashion slain,
Make me the master of thine house, I pray thee!
EL. I crave a like boon, Father—to contrive
Aegisthos' death, and find a home and husband.
OR. Earth, send my sire to watch the fight with favour.
EL. Persephone, crown the end with beauteous triumph.
OR. Think of the bath whereby they slew thee, Father.
EL. Think of the fell device, the entangling net.
OR. Those unforged fetters that entrapped thee, Father.
EL. The cloak designed to shroud thee shamefully.
OR. Have not these taunts the power to wake thee, Father?
EL. Art thou not rearing up thy well-loved head?

So it goes on for some lines more, and ends with the triumphant affirmation of Orestes:

So, though thou didst die, thou art not dead.

It seemed worth while to quote at length from this scene, for it would be difficult to find a better example, not of a particular hero-cult, but of the state of belief which lay behind hero-cults and made them possible. True, it is no outpouring from the popular mind, but the finished product of one of the greatest of dramatists; but there can be no question of his having invented the whole setting and mood of the passage for dramatic purposes. It represented a procedure which was by no means strange or unfamiliar to his audience, and to which their hearts would naturally go out in response.

The dead have power. This power they might exert either for

[1] I have borrowed Mr. Sheppard's translation from the Cambridge acting edition of the play (Bowes and Bowes, 1933).

good or evil. Hence a city might found a hero-cult either in expectation of benefits to come, or to avert the effects of the dead man's wrath. Its origin, in technical terminology, was often apotropaic. So firm was the belief in the continuing influence of the dead that if a city suffered from a plague or other disaster, it was often thought that the cause must be neglect of some great man's spirit, and the oracle was consulted to find out who it was who was thus peremptorily demanding propitiation. In this way the dead of historical times might come to be venerated as heroes. Thus Kimon the Athenian died besieging Kition in Cyprus. His remains, says Plutarch, were brought back to Attica, "as is shown by the monuments which are still called Kimoneia". But the men of Kition also pay honour to "a sort of tomb of Kimon", that is, they presumably comfort themselves with the erroneous belief that the body is on their territory. The reason for their wanting to do this is that in a time of famine they were enjoined by the god "not to neglect Kimon but to worship and reverence him as a superior being". We may well suppose that the Homeric conception of the "strengthless dead" was a somewhat artificial construction only lightly imposed on the very different groundwork of popular religion. At the same time, Farnell is no doubt right in seeing in the Homeric poems a powerful influence for the spread of hero-cults in post-Homeric times; for epic is the narrative of the glorious deeds of heroic men of a bygone age. It kept alive the memory of great names, and must have "suggested many a name to forgotten graves". If there is contradiction here, it is of the sort which must be accepted as part and parcel of popular religious thought.

In turning to the chosen example of Herakles, it must be admitted from the start that he is not altogether typical. A character like Theseus or Orestes might illustrate more satisfactorily the regular marks, in cult and in personal character, by which a hero may be known. But we have noted some of these marks in the previous paragraphs, and the peculiarities of Herakles are such as to make his introduction especially suitable from the point of view of our main theme. There is, fortunately, no question about his being a hero. He may have *become* a god (that is one of the things which lend him interest in the present discussion), but the whole consensus of Greek belief indicates that he was first a man. Hero was his initial, god his final state. The evidence is plentiful, and easily available in Farnell's *Hero-Cults*. The opinion of classical writers, the types of legend associated with him, the forms of his cult all point in the same direction. Even his name, as Professor Rose, following Farnell, has noted, is of a type which plainly indicates belief in his humanity.[1] The sole instance to the contrary is one which by its very feebleness and contradictions tends only to support the general view. In talking of Egyptian religion, Herodotus makes out an elaborate and incredible list of parallels between the gods of Egypt and the gods of Greece, in which Herakles appears as one of the twelve gods of early Egypt. The aboriginal and primal Herakles was an ancient Egyptian god. But Herodotus adds that this is not Herakles the son of Amphitryon, who in his view was a real man, called after the god by his parents Amphitryon and Alkmena, who were of Egyptian origin.[2]

The earliest literary mention of him is of course in the *Iliad*, where his name occurs a few times. He is not one of the actors in the story itself, but already for those who speak of him a dead hero of past times, one such as Achilles or Agamemnon had become for the Greeks of the fifth century. Take for instance these words of Achilles himself, pondering on the fate that awaits him, as it awaits all heroes. Sons of god though they be, mortality is their lot.

> And I too shall meet my fate, at whatever time it pleases Zeus and the other immortal gods to accomplish it. Yea not even the mighty Herakles escaped death, dear as he was to the lord Zeus, the son of Kronos, but the common fate laid him low, and the grievous wrath of Hera. Even so shall I, if a like fate is laid up for me, lie low when my time comes to die.[3]

Like many another hero, he was a son of Zeus, but of a mortal mother Alkmena, whose labour in fact the jealous Hera was able for her own purposes to put off beyond the natural day.[4]

The *Odyssey* mentions Herakles in three places. In one, the story is told of how he killed Iphitos. In another he is referred to specifically as "a man of former times". Boasting of his skill with the bow, Odysseus professes his willingness to challenge any of the present generation. "But with men of former times would I not strive, neither with Herakles nor with Eurytos of Oechalia, who strove with the very gods in archery."[5] The third passage tells for the first time of the double tradition, of Herakles as man and Herakles as god. It occurs in the *Nekyia* or visit to the shades of the

[1] *Prim. Cult. in Greece* (Methuen, 1925), p. 97. Cf. Farnell, *H.C.*, p. 99.
[2] Hdt. ii, 43. [3] xviii, 115. [4] xix, 96 ff. [5] viii, 223.

eleventh book, and just as the *Odyssey* is likely to be a later work than the *Iliad*, so the *Nekyia* is commonly agreed to be one of the latest portions of the *Odyssey*. Whereas most of Homer confines its attention in the sphere of religion to the upper, Olympian world, in the eleventh book of the *Odyssey* we are plunged at once into the darkness of the chthonian world whose characteristics I have endeavoured to outline at the beginning of this chapter. I trust that my powers of description have been adequate to make the point that these two are indeed different worlds, and the inference seems legitimate that the society which produced the poet of the *Nekyia* was not the same aristocratic, worldly minded society in which the heroes of the *Iliad* had lived.

In his visit to the shades in this book, Odysseus sees many of the heroes of old, and among them Herakles, of whom he says: "After him I saw the mighty Herakles—that is, his wraith; but he himself among the immortal gods joys in the banquet, and has to wife Hebe of the fair ankles, the child of great Zeus and golden-sandalled Hera."[1] The other heroes too are of course mere shadows of their former selves, living a wretched, bloodless existence from which they are temporarily summoned and by drinking the blood of the sacrifice are given power to speak with Odysseus. But such as they are, they are all that remain of these once mighty men. Of Herakles alone is it said that the phantom is not all, that the real Herakles has been translated to the gods. Yet the wraith, the *eidolon* left behind, who is not the real Herakles, is able like the others to recognize Odysseus and speak to him, telling of the pains and labours that he was made to endure while a man on earth. This suggests that there has been an attempt here to put two stages of tradition together, to explain the new in terms of the old, and that it has not been entirely successful.

Hesiod, in a passage whose language recalls that of the *Nekyia*, tells in a straightforward manner the story of Herakles as the son of Alkmena who having accomplished grievous labours received as the final reward of his great deeds translation to Olympus, where he lives for ever beyond the reach of pain or old age and has a goddess, Hebe of the fair ankles, to wife.[2] He became a god, and an Olympian. This is not a question of confusion between hero and underworld-god, between the two classes of *chthonioi*, which we noticed earlier to be so much at the mercy of "shifting popular tradition". It is a unique case of a mortal who by his own super-

[1] xi, 601 ff. [2] *Theog.* 950 ff.

human efforts was raised to the plane of the upper gods. When in other writers Herakles is called god as well as hero, it is this that they have in mind, and where the same double character is indicated in cult, it is not because we may observe the always slight differences between the forms of cult offered to a hero and those offered to an earth-god. What we find is no less than a combination of Olympian with chthonian worship. Pindar designates him by the phrase "hero-god",[1] a remarkable one for his time, and Herodotus, trying to justify his fantastic theory of a double Herakles, the ancient Egyptian god and the human son of Alkmena, calls to witness the cult-practices of the Greeks. They are right, he says, to have established two types of shrine for Herakles, and to the one they sacrifice (θύουσι) as to an immortal, and call him Olympian, whereas to the other they make offerings (ἐναγίζουσι) as to a hero.[2] Pausanias records a similar double cult in Sikyon which persisted down to his own day. In the sacrifice which they perform at their shrine of Herakles, he writes, they observe the following custom. "They say that Phaistos came to Sikyon and found them making offerings (ἐναγίζοντας) to Herakles as to a hero. He did not think it right to do anything of this sort, but rather to sacrifice (θύειν) to him as a god. And to this day when the Sikyonians have slain a lamb and roasted the thighs on the altar (βωμός), they eat some of the meat as from a sacrifice and offer the rest (ἐναγίζουσι) as to a hero." [3]

We need not retell here the oft-told legendary exploits of Herakles, all of which suggest the superman rather than the god. Farnell divides them into three groups: the epic-historic legends, which include wars and conquests, raids and campaigns; the folklore-fantastic, in which he fights monsters, pursues the hind with the golden horns, goes to the farthest ends of the earth for magic apples, or descends to Hades; and the cultural, which show him as a civilizer, making roads and draining swamps. As Farnell, surely rightly, goes on to observe, no known Greek god has a mythic career at all resembling this; whereas it can easily be paralleled from among the heroes of Northern saga, Arthur, Sigurd or Rustum, or among those heroes of Christianity, the saints. Herakles is the hero of heroes, in whom the general characteristics of the class appear to an exceptional degree. His virility is boundless, and shows itself not only in feats of courage and strength but also in more Rabelaisian ways which made him

[1] *Nem.* iii, 22 ἥρως θεός. [2] Hdt. ii, 44. For ἐναγίζειν and θύειν see p. 221 above.
[3] Paus. ii. 10. 1.

an admirable figure for exploitation by the comic poets, in his Gargantuan appetite or his capacity for intercourse with fifty women in a single night. Of his strength it is enough to say that he outdid other heroes by wrestling successfully with Death himself, in order to save the wife of his friend Admetos. No other achieved this feat, and if one may put it so, most of the differences between him and the rest are due to his being more of a hero than them all. He was, for example, the only one to transcend completely the borders which divided the small communities of Greece. He was an exception to the rule that heroes were local and tied to a grave. So completely did he become the possession of the whole of Greece that no single city is recorded as having claimed to possess his tomb.

Most significant of all, he is the only hero to have pushed his way up among the Olympians, the sole bridge between earth and heaven, two worlds which were separated in the Greek mind by barriers not easy to surmount. Yet in this he is only showing in its most extreme form what the hero-cult in general stood for. It stood for a denial of the view which Homeric society sought to impose, that the dead were deprived of all strength and wit. In contrast to this it was rooted in the belief that the dead have power to work their will. This is at least a kind of immortality, and the logical conclusion of immortality is divinity, since to the Greek mind *athanatos* and *theos* were equivalents, and each implied the other. The translation of Herakles only shows us the belief in heroes carried to its logical conclusion. Nevertheless it is only in Herakles that we see the conclusion reached. Hence his unique importance. No particular hopes of personal blessedness for the dead were held out by a belief in their continued effectiveness such as lay behind the prayers of Orestes and Electra to the spirit of Agamemnon. The influence of epic, nourished by a certain strain of pessimism in the Greek outlook to which we may refer again, made this effectiveness more or less dependent on the attentions of the living and limited its purpose to the satisfaction of their needs or else to personal vengeance. In so far as hero-worship had progressed beyond this belief in the power of a dead ancestor to avenge his own death and succour his descendants, it was something reserved for the outstanding few, whether the canonization was offered to some legendary figure of the past or to a general or statesman of recent history. In both these respects the career of Herakles offered new hope to the ordinary man. To have achieved true immortality among the Olympian gods was obviously something different from the fate even of the other heroes; and in spite of his outstanding prowess, Herakles was felt to be, not more distant from, but actually nearer to the ordinary man than were the others. In his bluff good humour, his readiness to help a friend, his common sense and his keen delight in the plain man's pleasures, he showed himself a kindred spirit to the ordinary Greek, and perhaps especially to the ordinary Athenian as we see him in the pages of Aristophanes. It was this sort of man who took him as his patron, hailed him as Alexikakos, the Averter of Evil, and trusted to him for defence against all sorts of *Keres*, the malignant little demons who brought illness, death and other troubles on mankind. The Greeks took him to their hearts and into their homes, which some of them sought to protect by writing this charm over the door:

> The son of Zeus, the Conqueror dwells here,
> Herakles. Let no evil thing come near.[1]

In drawing a conclusion I prefer once again to quote the words of other authorities, who were not, as I am, engaged in seeking out the various ways in which the hope of immortality entered the Greek mind. I am in agreement here with both Farnell and Wilamowitz. Farnell says of Herakles:

"His record reveals an evolution of ideas interesting for the history of religion; and as for the Greek world he was the earliest and most salient example of the mortal achieving divinity through suffering and toil, his career could serve as a theme for the ethical teacher, and could quicken in the average man the hope of a blessed immortality. Therefore, in the Hellenistic age, when this hope was become a passion and a faith, we begin to find the image of Herakles set as a symbol on the grave-relief."[2] The idea of Herakles as a theme for the ethical teacher may seem slightly

1 *ὁ τοῦ Διὸς παῖς καλλίνικος Ἡρακλῆς*
ἐνθάδε κατοικεῖ· μηδὲν εἰσίτω κακόν.

Written over the door of a newly married man according to Diogenes Laertius (vi, 50). The lines have been found on a house-wall at Pompeii (Kaibel, *Epigr. Gr.* 1138: actually the interior wall of a shop or store, F. Buecheler in *Rh. Mus. N.F.* xii (1857), 247 f.), and the words *Ἡρακλῆς ἐνθάδε κατοικεῖ* "carelessly scrawled" on a well-cut rectilinear marble block in Thasos, in lettering which its publishers ascribe to the fourth or third century B.C. Of the block itself they say that it "may have formed part of the entry of a tomb or temple, less probably of a dwelling-house" (J. ff. Baker-Penoyre and M. N. Tod in *JHS* xxix (1909), 99).

2 *H.C.* 154.

shocking to the modern mind when it thinks of the gluttony, boastfulness and other characteristics attributed to him in popular cult-legends no less than by the comic poets. Yet such he was to the Greeks, and that as early as the fifth century. We have only to look at the allegory told of him by the moralist Prodikos, how when he grew to manhood and stood musing at the cross-roads whence lead the two paths of virtue and vice, two women appeared to him. The one, Virtue, was of noble mien, cleanly body, and modest eye, and clad in white. The other, "whom my friends call Happiness and my enemies Vice", was plump and soft, "so adorned as to appear redder and whiter than nature had made her", and clad in a manner to reveal her charms to the best advantage. Hastening to get in front of her rival, she paints to the hero in glowing colours the life of ease and pleasure that will be his if he will choose her path. Then Virtue speaks and tells of the great deeds that he can do and the great name that he can win if he will choose her path and act as the gods would have him. Nothing really worth while is to be achieved without labour, even food and drink and sleep are sweetest when they come after toil. Her followers are dear to the gods, beloved by their friends, and honoured by their country. No other choice is possible for the son of good parents, and this, not the primrose path of Vice, will in the end lead to the truest happiness.[1]

Wilamowitz sees in him a denial of the Homeric ethic, summed up in the word *aidos*, which exhorted all to keep their stations and show respect to those above them—the young to the old, slaves to masters, men to gods. Men are as nothing before the gods, mere leaves blown by the wind. We have quoted earlier the lines which draw this melancholy comparison, and may remind ourselves also of others, which say that man is weakest of all the creatures that breathe and move upon the earth. Against this may now be set the picture of Herakles starting as a mortal man and rising to a place among the gods by the might of his own unaided hands. His personal prowess gave him immortality and made him the apostle of human self-sufficiency.[2]

[1] Xenophon, *Mem.* ii, 1, 21 ff.

[2] Wilamowitz, *Glaube*, ii, 24 ff. Cf. Homer, *Od.* xviii, 130 f.

οὐδὲν ἀκιδνότερον γαῖα τρέφει ἀνθρώποιο
παντων ὅσσα τε γαῖαν ἔπι πνείει τε καὶ ἕρπει.

IV. God or Hero? Asklepios

It would be wrong to let our interest in these genuine and important figures of popular Greek religion be confined to proving a particular point. Let us remind ourselves nevertheless that one of our objects is to examine the similarities between the two classes of chthonian beings, divine and heroic, in order to test the rightness of the view that whereas a clear distinction was generally made between Olympian and chthonian, no such sharp cleavage can be detected among the chthonians themselves. The existence of beings of whom it is difficult to judge whether the Greeks originally thought of them as underworld gods or dead men of might would of course do much to confirm this supposition.

If asked to give, without much thought or sifting of evidence, our general impression of Herakles, we should reply without hesitation that we thought of him as a hero; and a closer look at ancient testimony confirms that impression as the right one. If we begin in the same way with Asklepios, then I think the impression given is rather that of a god. Asklepios, we should say, was the god of healing, not a great physician of the past; and we should be thinking of the manner of his cult in historical times at the great and famous shrine of Epidauros, of his acceptance at Athens in the late fifth century, of the *Plutos* of Aristophanes. Suppose however to test this vague impression we begin by noticing some of the passages in literature in which he is mentioned. In the *Iliad* his name occurs three times, but only for the sake of describing his sons, Machaon and Podaleirios, who are the physicians of the Greek army. In the Catalogue of the Ships they are described as "the two sons of Asklepios, those good physicians", and said to be lords of Trikka and other towns in Thessaly. Similarly when Menelaos is wounded, and Machaon has to be sent for, he is found among his warriors "who followed him from horse-rearing Trike". Here and in the eleventh book he is described as "son of the blameless physician Asklepios", and in the fourteenth book by the patronymic Asklepiades. He is a good fighter too, but when he himself is wounded the chief cause of distress is that, in the words of Idomeneus, "as a physician he is worth many others put together for cutting out arrows and spreading soothing medicines".[1] No more is said about Asklepios, and the natural inference would be that he was a human healer like his sons.

[1] *Il.* ii, 729 ff.; iv, 193 f.; xi, 517 f. and 514 f.

From fragments of the *Eoiai* of Hesiod it can be seen that he recounted the myth according to which Asklepios was the son of Apollo by a mortal mother, Koronis, who was later killed by her divine lover as she was on the point of marrying another mortal. Apollo saved the child whom she was carrying in her womb, and sent him to be brought up by the wise centaur Chiron, who taught him the medical art. In the pride of his skill he overstepped the limits proper to mortals by raising the dead to life, and in anger at this trespass on divine prerogatives Zeus slew him with a thunderbolt. Hesiod's version has been reconstructed in masterly fashion by Wilamowitz,[1] but in Pindar we have the whole story presented to us without recourse to intricate methods of research. It is important to notice the whole theme and purpose of the poem (the third Pythian ode) in which it occurs. Hieron, to whom the poem is addressed, has won victories with his horses, but he is ill. Pindar counsels him not to repine, for he is a mortal man, and to such the gods always give sorrow mixed with triumph, indeed they usually deal out two woes for every good. Unmixed success is not given to any, and would be a danger if it were. We must take pleasure in what we have and not anger heaven by seeking for more. This is the moral which is illustrated by the story of Asklepios among others. He, the hero (for so he is called) who could heal all sorts of diseases, was the son of Koronis, daughter of Phlegyas (eponymous hero of a real or mythical Thessalian tribe) who herself met an untimely fate for her folly in incurring the anger of a god. She planned another marriage, though she bore within her the pure seed of Apollo, and her fault is described as "craving for what she had not".[2] She belonged to that senseless sort of people who "scorning what lies at home reach out to things beyond, pursuing vain ends in idle hope". Apollo snatched his son from the pyre on which her body lay, and he was duly brought up by Cheiron and became skilled in all varieties of medicine and surgery. "But," as Pindar goes on in his sententious way, "even wisdom is the slave of gain. And him too gold seduced with glittering reward, shining in his hand, to bring back from death a man already slain. Then the son of Kronos cast with his hand through both their breasts, and robbed them of the breath of life, and the blazing thunderbolt crashed doom upon them." The moral is drawn at once. It is the necessity to

[1] "Isyllos von Epidauros", *Philolog. Unters.* ix (Berlin, 1886), 70 ff.

[2] Line 20: ἤρατο τῶν ἀπεόντων.

"think mortal thoughts" and not seek to rise above our human station. "We with our mortal minds must seek what is fitting at the hands of the gods, recognizing what is at our feet, to what portion we are born. Strive not, my soul, for an immortal life, but carry through the device that is in thy power."

The conclusion is inevitable that for Pindar Asklepios, like other heroes the son of a god and mortal mother, furnished an excellent example of a mortal man who forgot himself and was punished for competing with the gods, just as all of us would be courting disaster by comparable conduct. There is every reason to suppose that Aeschylus and Euripides thought the same. Blood once shed cannot be charmed back, say the chorus in the *Agamemnon*. "Did not Zeus for his own safety cut short the career of him who knew the art of bringing the dead to life?" The chorus of the *Alcestis* say much the same thing. There is no hope for Alcestis. Only the son of Phoibos, were he alive, could have helped her to come up from her dark abode within the gates of Hades. "For he could raise the dead, until he was laid low by the Zeus-hurled blow of the thunderbolt's flame."[1]

That is the poets' view of Asklepios, and the poets did much to mould the mind of classical Greece. It does not of course prevent us entirely from believing that he was originally a folk-deity who had become degraded in course of time to this lower stature. This, in the "shifting popular tradition" of which Farnell spoke, would be perfectly possible, and the "faded god hypothesis", as it is called, has explained other figures satisfactorily. In this case however we should have to assume a double shift, from god to man and back to god again, since he was certainly worshipped as *theos* in the fifth and later centuries. Even this is by no means impossible, but we should at least require some fairly convincing evidence of his original godhead before accepting it, and it may be doubted whether that is forthcoming. The view that he was originally a fertility-deity of the same nature as Trophonios was held by Rohde, and accepted without question by Otto Kern. The original place of his worship is taken to have been Trikka, the Thessalian town mentioned in Homer as the home of his sons. It is also mentioned in the fourth-century inscription of Isyllos from Epidauros, to which we shall come shortly, which says that there was an *adyton* of Asklepios there, to which men "went down".[2] It is certainly striking that Strabo speaks of a river called Lethaios

[1] Aesch. *Agam.* 1023; Eur. *Alc.* 122 ff. and cf. 3 f. [2] p. 250 below.

at Trikka, "by which Asklepios is said to have been born".[1] Yet we know no more, and these indications can scarcely be called decisive. The same may be said about the resemblance between Asklepios and Trophonios, which was noted by Pausanias. The existence of statues, one of which is definitely stated to be by Praxiteles, and neither of which need have been earlier than the fourth century, depicting the two figures as similar types, is hardly evidence of origin. No hint lingers of any connexion with vegetation. The etymology of the name Asklepios is obscure, but no one has seen in it such a hint as is given by names like Trophonios or Pluto. The concern of Asklepios was solely with healing, and this is a function shared by many heroes as well as gods. The arguments of Rohde are on this point so lacking in cogency that they can only confirm us in the view that there is no infallible criterion for distinguishing between the two classes of earth-denizens, heroes and gods. He writes: "For Homer and the poets he [Asklepios] is generally a great chieftain, a mortal who had learnt the art of healing from Cheiron. In religious cult he was generally set on a level with the upper gods. In reality he, too, is a local earth-dwelling deity from Thessaly, who from the earth dispenses, like so many earth-spirits, healing from the ills of the flesh and knowledge of the future. . . . Many peculiarities of the worship paid to him show clearly the original character of Asklepios as an ancient god living below the earth." Rohde goes on to admit that he lacks one essential characteristic of such a god, in not being bound to any one particular place. This he attributes to "an enterprising priesthood, wandering in company with the rest of their tribe", who "had taken with them this old-established worship of theirs, and spread it far and wide".[2] This enterprising priesthood is of course hypothetical, and when we turn to Rohde's note to find the evidence on which he bases his assertion that the original divine character of Asklepios is attested by many details of his worship, we find this:

"The chthonic character of Asklepios is shown specially by the

[1] Strabo, xiv, 647; Kern, *Rel. d. Gr.* ii. 305; i, 88. For the river of Lethe cf. pp. 229 f. above. For completeness one may add the address to Asklepios at the beginning of the fourth mime of Herondas as "Thou who rulest over Trikka and dwellest in sweet Kos and Epidauros". The lack of any further detail, and the date of Herondas (third century B.C.), mean that this passage can teach us nothing about origins. The site of the sanctuary at Trikka has not been excavated.

[2] *Psyche* (Eng. trans.), pp. 100 f. It should be noted that for the power of prophecy which he mentions Rohde quotes no authorities earlier than Apollodorus and Celsus. The statement that in cult Asklepios was equated with the *upper* gods is questionable.

fact that not only are snakes sacred and dedicated to him but that he himself was actually thought of as a snake. . . . The offer of a cock, too (as by Socrates before his departure to the underworld), points to the chthonic character of Asklepios, *for it was a sacrifice also made to heroes*." (My italics.) All the evidence, in fact, could be applied equally well to proving Asklepios a hero as to proving him a god. For the snake we may quote Farnell against Rohde: "this mysterious beast was equally the familiar of the buried hero and the nether-god".[1] All that Rohde is proving is that Asklepios was a *chthonios*, and this, in spite of the same authority's statement that he was "generally set on a level with the upper gods", is a fact that hardly stands in need of demonstration. Farnell's remark about the "shifting popular tradition" was made with reference to Asklepios, and the last word must be with him. There was always too much resemblance between the rites offered to a hero and those offered to a chthonian god for ritual to be of real help in assigning a being to one or the other class.[2]

There is little more to be said on this point, but let us look at a few more documents of the Asklepios-cult before we leave it.[3] Healing is his primary function, and he himself is first among healers. Many gods and heroes dabbled in cures, Apollo himself among the gods and Orpheus, Herakles and many others among the heroes. But the supremacy of Asklepios was unchallenged, and it was from him that guilds of human physicians regularly took their title. They called themselves Asklepiads, and would not have thought of tracing their descent from any other.[4]

Whether or not it is right to see in Thessalian Trikka the original home of Asklepios, Epidauros in the Argolid was in historic times the centre and heart of his worship. The place of pilgrimage, the Lourdes of Greece, was Epidauros, and from there branch sanctuaries were formed in other places. We are quite well informed about the bringing of the god to Athens, where he was introduced in 420 B.C., though a small sanctuary appears to have been in

[1] Farnell, *H.C.* 240. [2] Ib., 239.

[3] A full (though in the case of inscriptions necessarily selective) collection of the ancient testimony has now been made by E. J. and L. Edelstein in *Asclepius: a Collection and Interpretation of the Testimonies*, 2 vols. (Baltimore, 1945). The conclusion of the authors, though expressed with the hesitation which every cautious scholar must feel, is that Asklepios was originally a hero. He is more likely to have owed his godhead to the developments of his cult at Epidauros than to any supposed origin as an underworld god at Trikka.

[4] The term is used generically as early as Theognis (line 432 Diehl).

existence somewhat earlier at the harbour of Munychia.[1] This was a time when Athens was very much in the centre of the stage of history, and many of her most famous writers were alive. We may be surprised at the amount of credulity which seems to be displayed in the introduction of this new cult in what is often regarded as the great age of Athenian enlightenment and sophistication. It may well be that enlightenment and scepticism did not go so far as we sometimes think, and it is perhaps necessary to remind ourselves that the city was not only committed to the long war that was ultimately to lead to her eclipse, but had recently lived through the horrors of a plague in addition to those of the war. These are circumstances very favourable to an exhibition of superstition or the more credulous forms of religion.

The evidence for the event is the best possible, namely the actual contemporary inscription commemorating it, which has been unearthed on the southern slope of the Akropolis.[2] Mutilated though it is, it is worth many a lengthy account by some antiquarian of later centuries. It tells how the god arrived in the city from Epidauros during the celebration of the Eleusinia. He brought his sacred serpent with him on a car, and was met by a citizen called Telemachos, who seems to have been responsible for the introduction of the cult. "Together with him came Hygieia, and thus was this whole sanctuary founded." The event is then dated in customary fashion by the name of the archon for the year.

One of the most interesting traditions is that which assigns a prominent part in all this to the poet Sophocles. He was said to have been granted an epiphany of the god in his own house, and he composed a paean to him which continued to be sung for many years after his death. Our best authority is Plutarch, who in one passage says that Sophocles "rejoiced in the belief that he was entertaining Asklepios" and that he had an epiphany of him. In another: "There is a tradition that Sophocles even during his lifetime gave hospitality to Asklepios, a tradition in support of which there is much evidence still to be found." Among the evidence still existing in Plutarch's day one might think with Wilamowitz of an inscription on some altar set up by the poet in commemoration of his memorable experience, or with Kern of a lost part of the actual inscription in the temple recording the

[1] F. Robert, "Le Plutus d' Aristophane et l'Asclepiéion du Pirée", *Rév. de Philol.* lvii (1931), 132 ff. and for the excavations *Athen. Mittheil.* xvii (1892), 10.
[2] Dittenberger, *Sylloge*[3] 88.

founding of the Athenian cult. Fragments of a copy of the paean, dating from the second century A.D., have been found in the Asklepieion. They are the merest scraps, but one bears clear and complete the name of the poet, putting the authorship beyond doubt.[1]

Excavation at Epidauros and Athens has given us a wealth of information about the methods whereby cures were effected, bringing us into touch with the ordinary mind of ancient Greece in that fascinatingly direct way which is the peculiar gift of epigraphy. The inscriptions recording the cures do not go back beyond the second half of the fourth or beginning of the third century, but there is no reason for thinking that anything had changed since the days of Sophocles and Aristophanes. Nevertheless we can draw also on a source of more strictly classical date for our knowledge of what went on, none other indeed than Aristophanes himself. The *Plutos*, his last comedy (produced in 388), describes the procedure in some detail. This play tells how an old man called Chremylos, having lived justly all his life, is disturbed by the way in which the good things of the world seem to get into the hands of the wicked, while really deserving folk like himself and his friends end their days in poverty. The Delphic oracle puts him in touch with Plutos the god of wealth, and Plutos explains how such a state of things has come about. Zeus, out of a feeling of *phthonos*—jealousy, grudgingness—against mortals, has made him blind, so that in spite of his best efforts to visit only the deserving, he is apt to end up in the wrong house. Chremylos undertakes to get him cured of his blindness, and Plutos promises in return that Chremylos and his friends will be his beneficiaries in future, and the unjust will be left severely alone. Hardly a profound solution to the problem of evil, but more entertaining than this much-disparaged play is generally made out to be.

The method is to put the patient to sleep (to "lay him down" as the Greek word κατακλίνειν has it) in the precinct of the temple of Asklepios. What happened in the night is told through the mouth of Chremylos' slave, who acts the part of *angelos* afterwards. The priest told them all to go to sleep, but after covering up his head with his ragged cloak he kept an eye open through one of the holes and saw what was going on. He was first rewarded by the

[1] Plutarch *ne suaviter quidem* 1103b, *Numa*, ch. 4. For an excellent photograph of the stones bearing the fragments of the paean, see Kern, *Inscriptiones Graecae* (Bonn, 1913), p. 45.

sight of the priest going round all the altars and clearing off the offerings of food which had been made to the god during the day. Without wishing to read too much into a comedy, we may assume that bad behaviour and trickery on the part of the priests were not necessarily a hindrance to faith in the genuineness and divine origin of the cures. The Greeks took a realistic view of human nature, and were quite capable of holding that the two things could be kept apart. Later the god himself appeared, with his attendants Iaso and Panakeia, and when they came to Plutos the god first touched his head and wiped his eyes with a clean linen cloth. Then Panakeia wrapped his head and face in a red covering, and the god made a sign, whereat two huge snakes darted out of the temple, glided under the covering and (as the slave conjectured) licked his eyelids. After that Plutos got up with his sight restored.

The incubation in the temple-precinct is a regular and necessary part of the cure, which usually takes place as the result of a vision or dream experienced in sleep. Of historical cures, recorded on stone in the precincts at Epidauros or Athens, there are plenty to choose from. I shall quote a few examples in conclusion, but in approaching the epigraphical evidence let us first look at an Epidaurian inscription which forms one of the most striking and important documents of the Asklepios-cult and cannot well be omitted even in such a summary account as the present.

This long inscription, excavated by a Greek archaeologist, Kavvadias, and first published by him in 1885,[1] announces itself as a dedication to Apollo Maleatas and Asklepios by a certain Isyllos son of Socrates of Epidauros, and its date is the end of the fourth century B.C. After the simple statement of dedication, it consists of five separate poems. The first, which is in trochaic tetrameters, gives utterance to a weighty moral sentiment: that if a city trains up its citizens in the proper accomplishments of manhood, and punishes those who wander from the path of virtue, then it is not only acting rightly but also in its own best interests. It will be both "stronger" and "safer". This sentiment, explains Isyllos, who seems to have been himself a prominent citizen of good birth, he had vowed to set up in stone on condition that a law which he had to propose, and which seemed to him

[1] *Ephemeris Archaeologica* (1885), pp. 65 ff. Detailed treatment by Wilamowitz, *Isyllos von Epidauros, Philol. Unters.*, ix (Berlin, 1886). See also J. V. Powell, *Collectanea Alexandrina* (1925), 132–6.

designed in accordance with the maxim, was duly passed in the demos. He obtained his wish, "not without the gods", and is therefore fulfilling his vow.

The next part is in hexameters, and tells what the law of Isyllos was. A selection was to be made of all the finest men of the city, and those who have in their breasts the qualities of *arete* and *aidos* —manly virtue and reverence for authority—which are the bulwark of a state. These are to be formed into a procession in honour of the lord Phoibos and his son Asklepios the physician. With their hair long, clad in white garments, and bearing wreaths of bay for Apollo and olive-boughs for Asklepios, they make solemn procession, and pray for blessings on the city, health and *kalokagathia* and law-abidingness and peace and wealth. It is thus a law for the founding of a new festival for Apollo and Asklepios, but a festival with an aristocratic and eugenic purpose behind it. The morally and physically fittest are to be paraded before the eyes of all, and doubtless to the envy of all of like age who were not included.

Third comes a short section of five lines, forming two and a half elegiac couplets. Its purpose is to say something of the association at the same shrine of these two deities, Apollo surnamed Maleatas and Asklepios. The title of the former is derived from a man Malos, who makes his appearance as a local hero of Epidauros or its neighbourhood. The poem says:

> Malos was first to build an altar of Apollo Maleatas and adorned the precinct with sacrifices. And even in Trikka of Thessaly thou wouldst not attempt the descent to the nether shrine [*adyton*] of Asklepios without first offering sacrifice on the holy altar of Apollo Maleatas.

Until the discovery of this inscription, Trikka was little more than a name in a Homeric list. Now we have evidence that a cult of Asklepios existed there, with an *adyton* to which men descended.

The argument of the little poem seems clear, once we know that Malos is a native Epidaurian hero, and that we are told in the next section of the inscription. If Apollo Maleatas was so called after Malos, and the cult of Apollo Maleatas is to be found together with that of Asklepios at Trikka, then clearly the cult at Trikka is only an offshoot of that at Epidauros.[1] Whatever modern historians of religion may think, the Epidaurian is not going to stand any nonsense about Trikka having been Asklepios' original home.

[1] Recent excavations have shown that the cult of Maleatas at Epidauros is much more ancient than that of Asklepios (*Journ. Hell. Stud.* 1951, p. 241).

The fourth poetical section is prefaced by an explanatory piece of prose. It seems that Isyllos had written a lyric paean to Apollo and Asklepios, but was overcome with modesty and felt uncertain whether it would be acceptable. He therefore commissioned a friend called Astylaidas to go to Delphi for him and inquire of the oracle whether or not it would be a good thing for him to have his paean inscribed and set up. The oracle replied that it would be better for him both now and in the future, and thus reassured Isyllos gives us the paean.

In it we again have material of great interest, an Epidaurian version of the god's birth and genealogy. It agrees with Hesiod and Pindar, and the short Homeric hymn to Asklepios, that his mother's name was Koronis daughter of Phlegyas, but adds artlessly that Phlegyas was "dwelling in Epidauros as his fatherland". Phlegyas is the eponymous hero of a Thessalian tribe called the Phlegyai, and Isyllos is evidently appropriating for Epidauros as much of the old North Greek story as he can. This Phlegyas, says the poem, married the daughter of Malos who was husband of the Muse Erato. Their daughter was Koronis, though Isyllos says (perhaps aware that the name Koronis could only suggest northern associations) that her real name was Aigle, and that the name Koronis was added "on account of her beauty". Phoibos wooed her in the halls of Malos, and she bore Asklepios to him. The name Asklepios was given to him by Apollo after his mother Aigle. This essay in hieratic etymology is accepted as the genuine origin of the name by Wilamowitz, but not I think by anyone else.[1] After telling of his birth, the paean closes with shouts of greeting to the god and prayers for health of body and mind.

The fifth and last section returns to hexameters. It is addressed to Asklepios alone, and tells the story of a miraculous appearance of the god which turns out to have been an experience of the dedicator himself. Starting in the third person, it slips into the first.

This manifestation also of thy power didst thou accomplish, Asklepios, in those times when Philip led his army against Sparta, wishing to overthrow her royal power. To succour her came Asklepios from

[1] The first argument adduced by Wilamowitz is too good a sample of academic reasoning to miss. If an etymology is probable, there is of course no difficulty in defending it. If it is improbable, what then? The scholar is not at a loss for a moment. "This is *such* a bad etymology that *not even* a priesthood would have had the courage to propose it. *Therefore it must be genuine*." ("Das ist so selbst für eine hieratische etymologie zu stark. . . ." *Isyllos von Epidauros*, p. 91. He did not give up the opinion, though he found its consequences puzzling. Cf. *Glaube*, ii, 229.)

Epidauros, honouring the race of Herakles whom Zeus was wont to preserve from harm. At that time did he come when the child, the sick child came from Bousporos. Him as he journeyed didst thou meet, O Asklepios, gleaming in thy golden armour. And beholding thee the child stretched out his hand and addressed thee with suppliant voice: "I am come to seek thy gifts, O Asklepios the Healer. Have pity on me." And thou didst say to me clearly: "Have courage. In good time shall I come to thee—therefore remain here—so soon as I have warded off a harsh fate from the Lacedaemonians, because they observe faithfully the words of Phoibos, which Lykurgos when he had listened to the oracle laid down for the city." So was the god gone to Sparta; and my mind roused me to go and publish to the Lacedaemonians this miracle, all in order as it happened. I spoke, and they listened to the words of salvation, and thou, Asklepios, didst save them. Then did they call on all men to receive and entertain thee, proclaiming thee saviour of Lacedaemon of the wide dancing-floors.

This, O best of gods, has Isyllos dedicated unto thee, honouring thy divine power, Lord, as is just.

The experience of Isyllos must have reminded his readers of the way in which Pheidippides was accosted by Pan as he ran to Sparta before the battle of Marathon, and perhaps the existence of this famous precedent made the repetition of such an epiphany easier. Apparently he was coming from his native village in the territory of Epidauros (Bousporos is otherwise unknown) in order to get an illness cured at the sanctuary. He was only a boy at the time, and his boyhood coincided with Philip's invasion of the Peloponnese after the battle of Chaeronea. Unlike other cities of the Peninsula, Sparta had refused to receive him, and her safety was now threatened. To this boy Asklepios appeared, and announced that before he could attend to his own business at his shrine he must go to Sparta to save the city. The boy told his vision to the Spartans, and since in fact the city was saved, the credit was naturally given to the god.

The last section of the Isyllos-inscription reminds us of the god's chief function, the healing of disease, and may be allowed to lead on to the citation of a few examples of miraculous cures, taken from Epidaurian inscriptions, which we shall leave to speak for themselves as a conclusion to this account.[1]

(*a*) A man whose fingers were all paralysed but one came as a suppliant to the god. When he looked at the tablets in the precinct

[1] Dittenberger, *Sylloge*[3] 1168.

he did not believe in the cures, and scoffed at the inscriptions. But when he fell asleep he saw a vision. He thought he was playing dice beside the temple, and just as he was about to make a throw the god appeared to him and leaped on his hand, stretching the fingers out. As the god went away, he thought that he clenched his hand and then straightened out the fingers one after the other. When he had straightened them all, the god asked him whether he still disbelieved the inscriptions on the tablets about the sanctuary. He said no. "Then," said the god, "because you withheld belief before, though they were true, let Doubter [*Apistos*] be your name in future." And when day broke he went out cured.

(*b*) Ambrosia of Athens, blind in one eye. She came as a suppliant to the god, but as she went round the precinct she scoffed at some of the cures as incredible: it was impossible that the lame and the blind should become whole simply through seeing a dream. Then she went to sleep there and saw a vision. It seemed that the god stood over her and said that he would cure her, but that he required her to set up in the temple as payment a silver pig, in memory of her stupidity. When he had said this, he cut open her blind eye and poured in ointment. And when it was day she went out cured.

(*c*) Euphanes a boy of Epidauros. He went to sleep in the precinct suffering from stone. It seemed to him that the god stood over him and said: "What will you give me if I cure you?" The boy replied "Ten knuckle-bones". Then the god laughed and said he would cure him, and when it was day he went out whole.

Chapter X

HOPES AND FEARS OF THE ORDINARY MAN

I. Introductory: Literary Sources

THE gods or heroes whom we examined in the last chapter show a side of the Greek mind which is not prominently represented by interpreters of the classics. All that has been described was current thought and practice in the Athens with which we are familiar, Athens of the Peloponnesian War, when Pericles, Socrates, Sophocles, Euripides, Aristophanes and Thucydides were alive. The terrifying ritual at the *adyton* of Trophonios was familiar enough for a mere passing reference to it in the *Clouds* to be understood. The introduction of Asklepios in the city in 420 and the description of an incubation-cure in Aristophanes show clearly enough that we can trust the inscriptions of the third century as evidence of what went on in the Asklepieion at Athens a century earlier. The encouragement of scientific medicine which the name of Hippokrates has led us to connect with the Asklepieion of Kos seems in these records, to put it mildly, subordinate to the magical and wonder-working side, as indeed it doubtless was at Kos itself. There is nothing in the fourth mime of Herondas to suggest the contrary.[1] Yet the mentality which these phenomena reveal is not precisely that which we would put together from the great literature of the age. It is something else which must be remembered if our picture of the city's life is not to be one-sided. We think of it as the age which gave birth to the Sophistic movement, the age of Protagoras, Gorgias and Socrates, of the materialism of Anaxagoras and the atomists, of Euripides the Rationalist, and are accustomed to say that it was characterized by a growing scepticism and that religious beliefs were being challenged on every side. Let us now make two modifications in this generalization.

The first is that to study the Athens of the fifth and fourth centuries from the literary sources which alone are commonly

[1] Cf. esp. 90 f. ἔς τε τὴν τρώγλην
τὸν πελανὸν ἔνθες τοῦ δράκοντος εὐφήμως.

taken into account is to skim the intellectual cream off its surface. These are, in the nature of things, the sources on which we have chiefly to rely. It is not easy to get at the minds of ordinary people who lived over two thousand years ago. Their lives and thoughts are for the most part unrecorded, or recorded only in the transmuted form of the masterpieces of literary giants. But let us make use of what evidence we have, and note that if the revelations of the Asklepios-cult seem out of keeping with the outlook of fifth-century Athens as we had supposed it to be, that is probably because we had in mind only the outlook of a Euripides or a Protagoras. What the inscriptions tell of is the attitude of the man in the street. We cannot, it seems, absolve him from the Pauline charge of superstition. Even so, how civilized and above all how Greek he remains! What a world apart from the dark and stupid superstition of savagery! Notice how his god is not stirred, as others have been, to spiteful action by the incredulity of his visitors. On the contrary, it tickles his sense of humour. Where outside Greek civilization could such a god exist?

The second consideration is this. When we speak of a growing disbelief in the gods, the gods that we mean are the Olympian dynasty of Homer. These were beings unsuited by their very nature either to call forth or to satisfy the deepest religious feelings of men. Owing to the extraordinary and to some extent artificial canonization of the Homeric epics, they retained their influence, at least officially, for centuries after the decay of the peculiar society which had called them into being and to which alone they were relevant. With little permanent religious value in themselves, they were an anomaly serving mainly the secular purpose of uniting the city-state in allegiance to a common figure-head. The weakening of their hold was as much the sign of a revival of religious faith as of its decline. Side by side with the humanized Olympians, there had always existed chthonian spirits, whether heroes or local daemons, who must have remained far nearer the hearts of common people than any god of Homer could reach. Under the tyranny of Homer they were inconspicuous, and their worshippers were far less vocal than the poets who sang of the bright beauty of Olympus and its shining company. The undoubted emotion which stirred the breast of an Athenian at the name of Athena or the sight of her chryselephantine statue may best be understood by noting the identity of the names, as close as that of Britain and Britannia. It was a patriotic rather than a religious emotion. To attempt to divorce the two is doubtless an anachronism, but nevertheless to find the kind of thing which nowadays would go by the name of religious experience it is downwards rather than upwards that we must look.

When we speak, then, of an age in which the established beliefs were being called in question, our meaning is that the Homeric mythology was beginning to wear thin as a substitute for a satisfying religion. This, as we have said, did not mean the decline of religion. It was one of the signs of the decline of something else, namely the city-state, whose emblem and symbol the Homeric pantheon had come to be. It marked the failure of corporate spirit and the growth of that individualism which was associated with the close of the fifth century and came into its own in the fourth. When the conquests of Macedon had sealed the fate of the city-state, this individualism was a distinguishing mark of the new age. At the time of which we are speaking, the day of the underworld gods was only beginning. With their attractions of darkness and mystery, their communings between man and god and consequent hopes of immortality, they became the stay and prop of the individual bewildered by the cosmopolitanism of the new age, one of the most characteristic features of which is the flood of mystery-cults, some borrowed from the East but some indigenous, which swept over the whole Greek-speaking world.

We have now made an examination of the Olympian and chthonian types of religion. The Olympian taught of gods intensely personal, strong, wilful, possibly honest but by no means invariably so. Man entered into contracts with them because it was his only hope. If they broke the contracts he was angry, but could do nothing. Above all things he must remember his humbler station and keep his distance. It taught him too that all his hopes of happiness must lie in this life, since after it was over he would be nothing but a shadow. The chthonian cults brought us from this human, comprehensible and business-like atmosphere of daylight to gods who were surrounded with an air of mystery. They were approached at night, and often in the darkness of an underground cavern or pit. At these entrances to Hades they brought the worlds of the living and the dead together. They "possessed" prophets and made them their mouthpieces. Some of them possessed ordinary men too, who thus became *entheoi*, filled with the god, caught up into a new nature—an experience which contained within itself, latent or explicit, the promise of immortality. Men could put on the god in this way by eating him in a sacramental meal. This we have seen with at least two gods of the type, the Cretan Zeus and the Thracian Dionysos. To the same circle of religious belief, though in origin a different thing, belongs hero-worship, a flat denial of Homer's "strengthless dead". It rests on a belief that the dead have power. So naturally did this worship of the dead blend with that of the underworld spirits of fertility that we noted a difficulty in some cases in deciding whether a chthonian spirit was a hero, who among the general benefits which he dispensed in return for worship and sacrifice naturally enough included a blessing on the crops, or an underworld god for whom the enrichment of the fields and flocks was his original and essential function.

In the coexistence of these two types of religion lies the explanation of the paradox with which we started out,[1] the presence in contemporaneous Greek literature and thought of the two opposite points of view: the advice to "think mortal thoughts" and "strive not to become a god" on the one hand, and on the other the exhortations to "assimilate yourself to God" and "make yourself immortal as far as you can". What we have not yet done is to estimate the relative influence of these two views on the people of Greece in the classical age. To do this, it will be necessary to collect a little more of the evidence at our disposal for judging the beliefs of the ordinary man, as well as summing up such evidence as has come our way already. That will be the purpose of the rest of this chapter, with the proviso that we are not aiming at an exhaustive study of his mentality, but trying to answer a specific question: to what extent was his religious outlook really shaped by the theological and eschatological legacy of Homer, which may be said to have represented orthodoxy in so far as it formed the background of the official cults of the state of which he was a member, though not in the sense of fettering his judgment or damning any deviations as heresy? The account will be limited in another way too, that it will have in mind mainly the Athenian, and though much that is said about him would apply equally to the dweller in other Greek cities, it does not necessarily all hold good for every Greek alike.[2]

[1] Chapter III.

[2] These limitations are more excusable in view of the existence of Nilsson's excellent study of popular religion under the title of *Greek Popular Religion* (Columbia University Press, 1940), of which it was well said in the foreword by A. D. Nock: "In the extensive literature relating to ancient Greece, there is no work which serves the purposes of this volume."

Much of what we have already considered has thrown a real light on the popular mind. This applies with especial force to the Asklepios-inscriptions, the chthonian ritual of Trophonios and the companionable figure of Herakles discussed in the last chapter. In describing Dionysiac religion we also made some attempt to assess its influence over the ordinary citizen, and we may recall too the prestige of Delphi and especially the way in which, through the institution of local *exegetai*, it entered into the everyday life of state and individual. Moreover the great writers themselves, who sometimes seem lifted so far above the capacities of ordinary men, may, if interpreted with proper caution, be seen to reflect more than might be supposed of current views in the society in which they lived. No one would credit the average Athenian with the magnificent conception of deity presented by the Zeus of the *Agamemnon*, yet in the second play of the same trilogy the summons of the dead man from his tomb to aid the living may legitimately be used, as we have used it, to throw light on a phase of genuine popular belief. The poets may show themselves children of their age either by unconscious acquiescence in its faith and standards or by a conscious and polemical reaction from them. The religion of Homer, with its class-distinctions and elementary morality, is a mirror of the social conditions of his times. Xenophanes shows up no less the character and prevalence of Greek polytheism by his tirades against it. On the other hand when such a writer as Plato speaks of the gods, he usually utters views which were far indeed from being the common property of the Greek race. Yet he too, particularly in the religious institutions of the *Laws*, may teach us much about what may be called the routine of religion which was accepted by most of the citizens of Athens as a matter of course.

Among the great writers one, Aristophanes, stands out as a source for the opinions of the populace. Like every Greek poet he regarded himself as a teacher, but he had no lofty religious message like Aeschylus, nor like Pindar did he paint the aristocratic ideal of virtue under the patronage of kings and princes. His ideal was simply the sturdy, independent citizen of the Athenian democracy who fought its battles and supported it by the public spirit with which he attended the assembly and undertook public office. The decline of this spirit of loyalty and devotion to Athens was what he deplored, and in his plays we see it depicted and contrasted with the upstart types of the period after the death of Pericles, the selfish demagogue and the political *fainéant*. Citizens and slaves alike play prominent parts and are drawn from life. Dikaiopolis,[1] the hero of the *Acharnians*, is an excellent portrait of the best type of Athenian citizen in the Periclean age, whose degeneration was setting in at the time—four years after the death of Pericles—when the play was produced. There is a natural ring about his remarks, as in the opening scene when he sits lamenting the thin attendance at the *ekklesia*, which smacks of the real people. The religion that we are now seeking to understand is the religion of Dikaiopolis, and it is worth while therefore to sketch his character briefly. He is naturally inclined to peace, fond of good fellowship, full of practical common sense and robust, hard-hitting humour, the reverse of mystical in any sense of the word. He longs to exchange the commercial and litigious atmosphere of the city for the peace of his rural deme and its rustic festivals, yet is by no means uncritical of the present-day countryman, who is happy when some cheap and dishonest orator sings his praises and does not see that he is being bought and sold. Sociability is perhaps his strongest trait, in outlook he is deeply conservative, loyal to the state, to its old institutions and therefore as a matter of course to its gods. His conservatism saves him from spending much thought or imagination on those gods, and consequently he still has very much the Homeric idea of them: they are still the ruling class, and there is no more harm in having his joke at their expense than there would be in laughing at Pericles or Kleon under the democratic rule of Athens. The one is not treason, neither is the other blasphemy. It accords with his conservatism that Aeschylus is still his favourite tragic poet, but it may be doubted whether he appreciated the profundity of Aeschylean thought. What probably meant as much to him was the fact that Aeschylus fought at Marathon and Salamis.

[1] The word occurs as an ordinary adjective in Pindar (*Pyth.* viii, 22), where L. and S. translate it as "strict in public faith".

II. Sepulchral Inscriptions[1]

As sources for the beliefs of the ordinary man, the great writers must be used with care, according as they betray more or less in their account the distortion due to personal character and individual outlook. There is another source, more direct but unfortunately more fragmentary, namely inscriptions. In them we have contemporary records of people who may have been in no way noteworthy or memorable save in their own eyes and those of their relatives. We have already had recourse to them in forming an impression of the cult of Asklepios, and there are other ways in which they can assist the reconstruction of the mind of Dikaiopolis.

In speaking of epitaphs, one should no doubt bear in mind the salutary warning of Dr. Inge: "Inscriptions on tombstones, as we know, are not trustworthy evidence either for the character of the deceased or for the real beliefs of his surviving relations."[2] We will not therefore attach exaggerated weight to their pronouncements, but at least may allow ourselves to say this: if they express a positive assurance of immortality, there will always be the doubt whether this indicates genuine faith or mere lip-service to a conventional doctrine; if on the other hand (and this is what we find in Greece) their outlook on this matter is almost universally negative, it is more likely to represent the real attitude of the people concerned, since no motive of piety or priest-taught dogma can be at work. Greek epitaphs are well known to reflect an almost universal pessimism with regard to any life beyond the grave. Only the famous, or those who died gloriously, are assured of immortality, for the only kind of immortality possible is to live on in the memory of posterity. Simonides wrote of the Lacedaemonian dead at Plataea: "Having died they are not dead", but his meaning is no more than the next words show it to be: "For their valour by the glory which it brings raises them from above out of the house of Hades".[3] Of the Athenians he says that they enjoy

[1] See in general R. Lattimore, "Themes in Greek and Latin Epitaphs" (*Illinois Studies in Language and Literature*, xxviii (1942)).

[2] *The Philosophy of Plotinus* (Longmans, Green, 1918), pp. 51–2.

[3] *ἄσβεστον κλέος οἵδε φίλῃ περὶ πατρίδι θέντες*
κυάνεον θανατοῦ ἀμφεβάλοντο νέφος.
οὐ δὲ τέθνασι θανόντες, ἐπεί σφ' ἀρετὴ καθύπερθεν
κυδαίνουσ' ἀνάγει δώματος ἐξ Ἀΐδεω.

ἀγηράντῳ εὐλογίῃ; no ageless life, but only ageless glory is the reward of their sacrifice. Epitaphs which have survived on stone from the classical age tell the same tale; for example, "They have built themselves an immortal monument of valour".[1] These are from collective, publicly erected monuments, war memorials rather than epitaphs in the ordinary sense. Inscriptions on individual tombs, at least until the Hellenistic age, were customarily even more laconic. They would express no views at all, but simply record the name and parenthood of the dead, perhaps with the addition of the simple word "Farewell". Often they would be surmounted by reliefs of a simple and moving pathos. These showed the dead clasping hands with wife, husband or father in farewell, or reproduced some simple scene from the home life which he had now left for ever.

The epitaphs which speak of fame as the only form of immortality attainable by mortal man find their generalization in a literary parallel, the passage in Plato's *Symposium* in which Diotima explains to Socrates that longing for immortality is the mainspring of human action.[2] "All mortal nature," says the wise woman, "seeks to exist for ever and be immortal to the best of its powers." The only way in which it can achieve this, since it is not immortal in the exact sense, is by giving birth to other creatures like itself. In the child the parent sees its own life continuing, and this explains both the tremendous urge for sexual union and the pains and inconvenience to which all creatures, both animal and human, will submit, even leading sometimes to their own death, in order to ensure the survival and well-being of their offspring. "In this way every mortal creature is preserved, not by remaining always the same like divinity, but by leaving behind, when it grows old and departs, another young creature such as it was itself. By this device, Socrates, what is mortal has a share in immortality, both of the body and of every other attribute. No other way is possible." This fact, Diotima continues, is not only at the bottom of the sexual instinct but also of the instinct that makes men seek honour, again it may be at the price of their own death. "Think how consumed they are with love of fame, of laying the foundations of an immortal glory. For this they are prepared, even more than for the sake of children, to run all risks, spend their money, labour hard and suffer death. Think you that Alcestis would have died to save Admetos, or Achilles to avenge Patroklos, or your own

[1] *I.G.* 1^2 943. [2] 206 e ff.

Kodros to preserve his kingdom for his sons, except in the belief that an immortal memory of their own valour[1] would survive, the memory which we now preserve? Far from it. In my opinion all men are moved to action by the motive of an immortal reputation and good fame of this sort, and to a greater degree the better men they are; for it is immortality that they are in love with." From here Diotima goes on to describe the highest class, the thinkers, who, actuated by the same universal desire for immortality, achieve it by giving birth to children not of the body but of the soul. This is the motive which produces, for example, a great poem.

In this passage the distinctively Platonic doctrines of rebirth and genuine immortality are entirely absent. As so often, Plato has kept his own beliefs in the background where they are not necessary, and sometimes would be inappropriate, to a particular situation or train of thought. The teaching that Diotima evolves is a sublimation of what would be generally accepted as the limitations within which impermanent beings such as animals and men can speak of immortality. Where she speaks of honour, the resemblance to the soldiers' epitaphs leaves no doubt. The funeral oration of Pericles is full of the same assurances and no more.

I know of one, and only one, sepulchral inscription from the fifth century which expresses a different spirit and suggests that these limitations might be transcended. It is to be seen in the British Museum and refers to the Athenians who died fighting at Potidaea in 432 B.C. It contains the line:

αἰθὴρ μὲμ φσυχὰς ὑπεδέσχατο, σώ[ματα δὲ χθών].[2]

Aither received their souls; their bodies, Earth.

The language here is bound up with a whole complex of philosophical and semi-philosophical ideas which we have already touched on in Chapter V. The interesting thing is to find it not in a philosopher or a poet like Euripides, but on an inscription put up in stone for all to see and presumably to appreciate. Even if it was the work, as these inscriptions often were, of one of the great poets, the purpose for which it was intended must surely have limited him to the range of ideas which might be entered into by

[1] Compare the language here, *ἀθάνατον μνήμην ἀρετῆς*, with that of the epitaph quoted on the previous page: *ἀθάνατον μνῆμ' ἀρετῆς*.

[2] *I.G.* 1, 442, British Museum, *Guide to Select Greek and Latin Inscriptions* (1929), No. 9. In spite of the mutilation of the end of the line, the form of the first half leaves little doubt of what it was, especially when taken in conjunction with similar epitaphs of rather later date, for which see Rohde, *Psyche* (Eng. Trans.), p. 572, n. 135 to ch. xii, ii, and A. J. Festugière, *L'Idéal Religieux des Grecs* (Paris, 1932), 146 ff.

all. The notion as we find it in the philosophers and Euripides may be briefly recapitulated thus. *Aither* was the substance with which the heaven was filled, once one had passed beyond the reaches of the less pure atmosphere (*aer*) which lies immediately around the earth. In this upper region dwelt the gods, and the *aither* itself was spoken of as a divine substance. In fragments of Euripides it appears now as the home of Zeus, now as Zeus himself. It was also the substance of which the stars were made.[1]

In Chapter V we discussed the monist theory of Anaximenes and Diogenes of Apollonia according to which the primary stuff of everything was *aer*, which in its purest form was also the stuff of which the human soul was made. It is doubtful whether a clear-cut distinction between *aer* and *aither* as generically different substances was consistently maintained before the time of Aristotle. Certainly the monist philosophers must have held that *aither* was only their primal *aer* in its purest form. Nevertheless there was always felt to be a difference, and Anaxagoras is said to have likened the *aither* rather to fire. This must have seemed the more probable view, considering its derivation from *aithein*, to blaze, and the belief that it was the substance of the stars. What is certain is that there was a belief abroad in the fifth century that the soul was immortal and divine, based on the idea that it was composed of an imprisoned spark of the immortal *aither*, to which it would fly off on its release from the body at death. Euripides puts it in a strange way in the *Helena*: "The mind of the dead lives indeed no longer, yet retains an immortal power of thought, when it has plunged into the immortal *aither*." In another place he says: "But he who lately was blooming in the flesh is quenched like a falling star, having released his spirit [*pneuma*] to the *aither*." In the *Supplices* he provides an exact parallel to the Potidaean inscription: "Spirit to the *aither*, body to the earth."[2]

[1] Cf. above, pp. 207 f., 38.

[2] Eur. *Hel.* 1014 ff. ὁ νοῦς
τῶν κατθανόντων ζῇ μὲν οὔ, γνώμην δ'ἔχει
ἀθάνατον, εἰς ἀθάνατον αἰθέρ' ἐμπεσών.

fr. 971 Nauck ὁ δ'ἄρτι θάλλων σάρκα, διοπετὴς ὅπως
ἀστὴρ ἀπέσβη, πνεῦμ' ἀφεὶς πρὸς αἰθέρα.

Suppl. 533 f. πνεῦμα μὲν πρὸς αἰθέρα
τὸ σῶμα δ'ἐς γῆν.

These quotations suggest a curiously impersonal kind of immortality, nothing more than an absorption into the universal mind-stuff. To Euripides and the philosophers this was probably a reasonable and satisfying belief. The desire of the ordinary man to reconcile it with something more personal may have been behind the identification of souls with individual stars mentioned in the next paragraph.

Sometimes, if not always, the belief that the souls of the dead fly up to heaven was taken to mean that they actually turned into stars. In this connexion (if Euripides be disallowed as too much under the influence of philosophical speculation) we find the only other hint known to me that the belief was popular and widespread in the fifth century. In the *Peace* of Aristophanes, the hero Trygaios flies up to heaven on an enormous dung-beetle to persuade the gods to give back Peace to Greece. On his return from this adventurous journey, his slave eagerly questions him about what he has seen, and one of his questions is: "Isn't it true then what they say, that we become stars in the sky when we die?"[1]

When I spoke in an earlier chapter of the airy or aetherial nature of the soul as being a doctrine of the materialistic science of the fifth century, I pointed out that it only meant the reappearance in rational dress of an age-old popular belief. Where science and primitive belief are thus united in their conclusions, it would obviously be difficult to say which was responsible for the prevalence of a specific idea at this advanced stage of civilization. I think myself that if this particular idea was widespread in the fifth century, as perhaps the Potidaean epitaph shows, then its diffusion is most likely to have been due to the influence of popular science. It may well be the scientists themselves whom Aristophanes is parodying as he frequently does elsewhere. Euripides was certainly one of their followers, and if we are to be strict we must say that our epitaph remains, for its age, a solitary witness to the popular spread of the belief. I say "for its age", because numerous examples testify to a similar spirit in the Hellenistic and Graeco-Roman world. These I am deliberately leaving out of account, but their existence lends support to the view that the popularity of these opinions was growing in the earlier period too.[2]

[1] Ar. *Peace*, 832 ff.

[2] Cf. Rohde, *Psyche*, p. 541, of the epitaphs of the post-classical Greek world: "For many individuals the hope is expressed or the certainty announced that after death they will have their dwelling in the sky—in the shining *Aether*, among the stars. This belief in the elevation of the disembodied soul to the regions above the earth is so frequently repeated in various forms in this late period that we must suppose that among those who entertained precise conceptions of the things of the next world this was the most popular and widely held conviction." Among the many examples which Rohde cites in his note, the following, from an inscription, belongs to the fourth century B.C.: *Εὐρυμάχου ψυχὴν καὶ ὑπερφιάλους διανοίας αἰθὴρ ὑγρὸς ἔχει.* Festugière and Lattimore (opp. citt.), with a richer store of material to draw on than was available to Rohde, do not differ widely from him in their conclusions. It is of interest that Festugière feels justified in concluding from the epitaphs that the mystery-religions had little to do with the spread of beliefs in a future life among ordinary people (o.c. p. 143). Cf. the somewhat different view of Lattimore (o.c. p. 342).

III. The Social Side

Another department of ordinary life on which inscriptions have thrown a flood of light is the organization of clubs and societies in Greece. They appear to have been much more widely spread and influential in the lives of ordinary people than one would have dreamed from the scanty references to them in extant classical literature. The inscriptions so far found cover the period from the fourth century B.C. to the third century A.D. Thus they are all from a slightly later time than that which we are primarily considering, but there are just enough literary references to them to show that they were in existence earlier,[1] and there is circumstantial evidence to suggest that, for good reasons to which we shall come shortly, it was their prevalence rather than their character that altered with the passing of the city-states. That they were in keeping with the true Greek character no reader of Aristophanes can doubt.

Most of these societies had a religious side, and some were wholly religious. Dr. Tod, to whose fascinating study of the subject I owe all that is in this section, notes that "the earliest societies of which we have epigraphical record, those of the *orgeones*, are essentially religious in character, existing for the cult of some deity or hero and at first confined to citizens. Such a body of *orgeones* met in the fourth century in a little chapel on the western slope of the Acropolis", &c.[2] From the first, however, and to an increasing extent, the religious was combined with a social, and even an economic side. The comparison drawn by Tod with such modern societies as Freemasons, Druids, Oddfellows and Buffaloes is probably not wide of the mark. They were private organizations unconnected with the state, drawing up their own rules and supported by the subscriptions of members. The longest, most complete and most interesting of the inscriptions is that of a Dionysiac society at Athens in the second century A.D. In spite of its late date it is tempting to quote at length from it. From our previous acquaintance with Dikaiopolis we shall see that he has not changed much through the centuries. The society was called the Iobacchoi,

[1] e.g. Thuc. iii, 82; viii, 54.

[2] M. N. Tod, "Clubs and Societies in the Greek World", in *Sidelights on Greek History* (Blackwell, 1932), pp. 71 ff. See also W. S. Ferguson, "The Attic Orgeones", in *Harv. Theol. Rev.* xxxvii (1944), 61 ff.

and the inscription gives its statutes together with the minutes of the meeting at which it was decided to have the statutes revived and inscribed on stone. From the complete translation by Tod I take a few characteristic extracts:

No one may be an Iobacchos unless he first lodge with the priest the usual notice of candidature and be approved by a vote of the Iobacchoi as being clearly a worthy and suitable member of the Bacchic society. The entrance-fee shall be fifty denarii and a libation for one who is not the son of a member. . . . The Iobacchoi shall meet on the ninth of each month and on the anniversary of its foundation and on the festivals of Bacchos and on any extraordinary feast of the god, and each member shall take part in word or act or honourable deed, paying the fixed monthly contribution for the wine. If he fail to pay he shall be excluded from the gathering. . . .

When anyone has lodged his application and has been approved by vote, the priest shall hand him a letter stating that he is an Iobacchos, but not until he has first paid to the priest his entrance fee, and in the letter the priest shall cause to be entered the sums paid under one head or another. No one may either sing or create a disturbance or applaud at the gathering, but each shall say and act his allotted part with all good order and quietness under the direction of the priest or the arch-Bacchos. . . .

If anyone start a fight or be found acting disorderly or occupying the seat of another member or using insulting or abusive language to anyone . . [there follows a system of fines].

The priest shall perform the customary services at the meeting and the anniversary in proper style, and shall set before the meeting the drink-offering for the Return of Bacchos and pronounce the sermon, which Nikomachos the ex-priest inaugurated as an act of public spirit. And the arch-Bacchos shall offer the sacrifice to the god and shall set forth the drink-offering on each tenth day of the month Elaphebolion. And when portions are distributed, let them be taken by the priest, vice-priest, arch-Bacchos, treasurer, *bukolikos*, Dionysos, Kore, Palaimon, Aphrodite and Proteurythmos: and let these names be apportioned by lot among all the members.

And if any of the Iobacchoi receive any legacy or honour or appointment, he shall set before the Iobacchoi a drink-offering corresponding to the appointment. . . .

And if any Iobacchos die, a wreath shall be provided in his honour not exceeding five denarii in value, and a single jar of wine shall be set before those who have attended the funeral; but anyone who has not attended may not partake of the wine.

As Tod remarks, "A curious medley this—religion, drama,

good-fellowship, banqueting! Yet how many traits in this description and in other records of the ancient societies find their counterparts in the medieval guilds!" Let us add also, noting how practical and businesslike, social and this-worldly is the attitude of the Iobacchoi to their religion, how thoroughly in keeping with the fellow-citizens of Dikaiopolis!

Dr. Tod, after pointing out that although the existence of voluntary and unofficial associations can just be traced from an early date, yet it is not until the Hellenistic age that we find their development over the whole Greek world attested by scores and hundreds of inscriptions, goes on to remark that there was no doubt a good reason for this. It was not that the Greek character had changed, that this gregariousness and keen appreciation of social pleasures, in religion as in everything else, was a new feature in it. The explanation is rather that, as Tod puts it, "in the classical period the life of the citizen was closely and almost exclusively bound up with that of the state: the *polites* was a member of his *polis*, and he was little or nothing else besides. His social instincts were fully satisfied by the family, the phratry, the deme, the tribe, to which he belonged, as well as by the state itself; each of these had its own meetings, its festivals, its varied opportunities of enjoyment and good-fellowship. His religious aspirations were met, to a large extent though not wholly, by the worships connected with these bodies. And this satisfaction of social and religious cravings and ambitions left little or no room for the formation of voluntary societies."

One might note at this point that although there is evidence that as early as the legislation of Solon the legality of voluntary corporations was recognized and their regulations made binding on their members provided they were not contrary to the laws of the state,[1] yet in the only other literary references to them (those in Thucydides) they are in fact subversive organizations conspiring against the government. When the city-state was in its prime it was only the malcontents and misfits who felt the need of any form of association outside those officially provided by the state. "But" (for one cannot continue better than in Dr. Tod's own words) "in course of time the old simplicity gave way to a greater complexity of life. An increasing cosmopolitanism took the place of the old exclusiveness, while the growth of the empires of Macedon and of the successors of Alexander robbed Greece of her autonomy

[1] Tod, p. 72.

and sounded the death-knell of much that was characteristic of the city-state."

In the classical age, this mingling of the secular and religious sides of life which was so typical of the Greek and sometimes seems so alien to us, this indulgence in social gatherings with meat and drink and good fellowship all in the service of the gods, found its chief expression in the state-regulated worship of the chief gods of the city. There was no need of private societies. The great age of temple-building, and of the fine festivals which were celebrated in their expensively beautiful surroundings, seems to have been ushered in with the tyrants. Aristotle says that the tyrants erected great buildings in order to give employment to the people. They had been brought in on a wave of popular enthusiasm, which must be maintained if they were to retain their position. The building of temples and provision of magnificent festivals gave more than employment; it provided that element of *panem et circenses* so necessary to the continuance of a tyrant's popularity. The ceremonies of the cult were therefore accompanied (in Athens especially, whose outstanding wealth gave especial opportunity for this type of display) by sacrifices on an enormous scale. Hundreds of animals might be slaughtered, and the gods were by no means the only or even the chief participators in the resulting feast of roast meat. It was distributed among the people. As Nilsson observes: "The people feasted at the expense of the gods, and they soon learned the advantages of this kind of piety."[1]

To see the way in which the ordinary Greek took his religion we can look not only at the sacrifices and festivals of the separate states but also at the great *panegyreis* whose characteristic was that people flocked to them from more than one state. Some attained a Pan-Hellenic scope. In these great festivals, just as on a smaller scale in the proceedings of the private religious societies of the post-classical age, much goes on which seems to have little connexion with religion. At Olympia, the greatest of them all, attention is primarily concentrated on the games, and the homage of the people might seem to be almost exclusively reserved for the successful athletes. Nevertheless, as Nilsson rightly emphasizes, religion was the foundation, and if it is Olympia that we are considering, we must not forget "the great temples erected, the great sacrifices offered, and the many cults attended to by numerous

[1] *Gr. Pop. Rel.* 87.

priests".[1] If the combination causes any surprise to-day, that only brings out more clearly the difference between the most typical Greek attitude and our own. The Greek saw no incongruity. A feature of every *panegyris* was a fair. As Pythagoras—according to Aristotle—remarked, the crowd which assembled at Olympia was drawn by various motives. Some came simply to enjoy the spectacle, some to compete in the games, and others to buy and sell. Booths and tents were set up, not only for traders and cooks, but also, since the *panegyris* lasted several days, as temporary lodgings for the assembled multitude. The whole scene must have very much resembled that at Stourbridge or any other fair of medieval England.

In so far as the scene is a strange one, the contrast is not so much between ancient and modern as between the temperaments of North and South. Such things have disappeared from England since the Reformation, and the festivals of the Church have either become wholly pious in character or else completely secularized, turning from holy days into holidays. It was not in us to keep both sides together, and they have been divorced by the Protestant and Puritan tradition of England and much of northern Europe. The South wanted no Reformation. *Panegyreis* are still celebrated under the same name in Greece, and according to the statements of eye-witnesses very much in the same manner as of old. The occasion is still religious, though the gods have been replaced by the Panaghia (the Virgin) or one of the saints. This is remarked both by Nilsson and by J. C. Lawson, from whose book I take the following first-hand description:[2]

> But no foreigner, even though he were totally ignorant of the modern language, could chance upon one of the many festivals of the country without remarking that there, in humbler form, are re-enacted many of the scenes of ancient days. The *panegyria*, as they call these festivals —diminutives, both in name and in form, of the ancient *panegyreis*— present the same medley of religion, art, trading, athletics and amusement which constituted the Olympian games. The occasion is most commonly some saint's-day, and a church or a sacred spring (*aghiasma*) the centre of the gathering. Art is represented by the contests of local poets or wits in improvising topical or other verses, and occasionally there is present one of the old-fashioned rhapsodes, whose number is

[1] *Gr. Pop. Rel.* 99.

[2] *Mod. Gr. Folklore and Anc. Gr. Rel.* 34 f. Lawson was in Greece from 1898 to 1900. Cf. Nilsson, *Gr. Pop. Rel.* 100. Nilsson's whole section on *panegyreis* should be read.

fast diminishing, to recite to the accompaniment of a stringed instrument still called the *kithára* the glorious feats of some patriot-outlaw (*klephtes*) in defiance of the Turks. Then there are the pedlars and hucksters strolling to and fro or seated at their stalls, and ever crying their wares—fruit, sausages, confectionery of strange hues and stranger taste, beads, knives, cheap icons ranging in subject from likenesses of patron-saints to gaudy views of hell, and all manner of tinfoil trinkets representing ships, cattle and parts of the human body for dedication in the church. Then in some open space there will be a gathering of young men, running, wrestling, hurling the stone; yonder others, and with them the girls, indulge in the favourite recreation of Greece, those graceful dances, of which the best-known, the *syrtós*, and probably others too, are a legacy from dancers of old time. It is impossible to be a spectator of such scenes without recognizing that here, in embryonic form, are the festivals of which the famous gatherings of Olympia and Nemea, Delphi and the Isthmus, were the full development.

IV. Witchcraft and Curses

The superstition which was rampant in the Graeco-Roman world was by no means unknown in the Athens of an earlier date. Recent discoveries have put beyond doubt the prevalence, at least as early as the fourth century B.C., of superstitious practices which find occasional mention also in the literature of the times. If our previous remarks dealt with the social side of religion, these practices, we may say, reveal the anti-social side. In the *Republic* Plato condemns quack priests and prophets who get money out of rich men by claiming to have power to absolve them from their sins. Further, "if anyone wishes to injure an enemy, for a small fee they say they will bring harm on good or bad alike, bending the gods to serve their purposes by spells and curses [*katadesmoi*]".[1] In the *Laws* we find punishment prescribed for "those who in their contempt of mankind bewitch so many of the living by the pretence of evoking the dead and the promise of winning over the gods by the supposed sorceries of prayer, sacrifice, and incantations, and thus do their best for lucre to ruin individuals, whole families, and communities". Further indication of the methods employed is given in a later passage thus: Poisoners, says Plato, work in two ways. There are those who inflict physical harm by poisons of the normal sort, and "there is another form which works by art

[1] *Rep.* ii, 364c.

magic, incantations, and spells [*katadeseis*], as they are called, and breeds in the minds of the projectors the belief that they possess such powers of doing harm, in those of the victims the conviction that the authors of their suffering can verily bewitch them. . . . And it would be labour lost to try to bring conviction to minds beset with such suspicions of each other, to tell them, if they should perchance see a manikin of wax set up in a doorway, or at the cross-roads, or at the grave of a parent, to think nothing of such things, as nothing is known of them for certain."[1]

The practice of exercising sympathetic magic by means of a wax image is of course world-wide and too well known to need description. It is nevertheless worth noting that it was current in the cities of Plato's Greece. But of all the types of harmful magic mentioned by Plato the one whose popularity has been proved beyond doubt by epigraphical finds is that which he designates by the terms *katadesmoi* and *katadeseis*. These words, which literally mean "bindings", refer to curses which were scribbled on tablets, often, though not always, of lead, and left in tombs or buried in the ground where the spirits of the underworld, to whom they were commonly addressed, would be able to find and act on them. Sometimes the lead was first rolled up and tied round with wire, thus adding extra sympathetic force to the idea of "binding" contained in the curse. I quote first the earliest example so far known of one of these curses, though it is not on lead and does not contain the common reference to binding. It is referred to by Nilsson in his *Greek Popular Religion* and first published and illustrated by him in his *Geschichte der Griechischen Religion*, vol. i, which was published in Munich in 1941 and until recently has been difficult to come by in this country. The curse is inscribed on a broken piece of pottery of the early fourth or late fifth century, and reads simply: "I put quartan fever on Aristion to the death."[2] Of the lead tablets which have been found, the majority come from Attica itself and go back to the fourth century. As to the metal chosen, Nilsson warns against drawing far-reaching conclusions from this, pointing out that it was plentiful and easy to inscribe,

[1] *Laws*, x, 909b; xi, 933a (A. E. Taylor's translation).

[2] *Ἀριστίωνι ἐπιτίθημι τεταρταῖον ἐς Ἅιδα.* (*τεταρταίαν* in Nilsson's *Gesch. Gr. Rel.* is a slip.) The sherd is now in the National Museum at Copenhagen. Its place of origin is unknown, but Nilsson describes it as black-glaze of good Attic workmanship, and adds that although an exact dating is difficult it appears to be not later than the first half of the fourth century and possibly as early as the fifth. (*Gesch. Gr. Rel.* i, 758, cf. *Gr. Pop. Rel.* 114.)

and for this reason was also used for writing letters. He is arguing justifiably against the far-fetched hypothesis that its use is evidence for the introduction of Chaldaean astrological ideas into Athens in the fourth century. Nevertheless it is interesting to note that the choice was not purely prosaic, but served to further the magical purpose of the inscriptions. Its qualities are referred to in the texts as having sympathetic power, for example: "May his tongue and his soul become lead that he may not be able to speak or act, and pierce thou his tongue and his soul." At this point the writer would doubtless jab something through the lead as part of the magical procedure. Again: "As this lead is worthless and cold, so may he and his possessions be worthless and cold."

The same formulas are repeated over and over again, and the most characteristic word is *καταδέω*, I bind, that is, put a spell upon, from which these curses took the name given to them by Plato. Some tablets simply contain this word and a list of the people or objects cursed, for example: "I bind Dionysios the helmet-maker and his wife Artemis the worker in gold, their house, their workshop, their works and their life, and Kallippos.' Alternatively the verb may be *ἀνατίθημι*, I dedicate, followed by the name of one or more underworld deity—Hekate or Demeter or Hermes Chthonios—thus illustrating an interesting stage of mentality between pure superstition and religion. The element of automatic sympathy is obviously prominent, that kind of primitive natural law whereby if certain actions—the melting of a wax image, the jabbing of a piece of lead—were correctly performed with the proper incantations, certain results followed as surely as in a chemical experiment. At the same time personal gods are invoked and asked or constrained to ensure it. Here are two more examples which have a rather more varied and interesting content.

(*a*) From Knidos.

I consign to Demeter and Kore the man who has affirmed against me that I make deadly poisons for my husband. To Demeter let him go consumed with fire,[1] and in the presence of all his relatives confess his slander; and may he find no favour with Demeter and Kore, nor with the gods in Demeter's company. But for me may it be lawful and permitted to share a roof or have converse as I will. I consign also the man who has accused me in writing or ordered my accusation. May he not find favour with Demeter and Kore nor with the gods in Demeter's

[1] i.e. fever.

company, but may he go before Demeter consumed with fire, and all his family with him.

A favourite use for this potent weapon was to incapacitate one's adversaries in a lawsuit. Thus for example:

(*b*) From Athens, late fourth century.

I bind Theagenes in tongue and soul, and the speech that he is preparing. I bind also the hands and feet of Pyrrhias the cook, his tongue and his soul and the speech that he is preparing. . . . I bind also the tongue and soul of Pherekles, and the testimony that he brings in favour of Theagenes. . . . I bind also the tongue and soul of Lamprias and the speech which he is preparing, hands feet eyes and mouth. All this I bind, obliterate, bury, impale.[1] And whatever claims they may make either in the court or before the arbitrator, may these claims go for nothing in deed or in word.[2]

Before we condemn too easily the lack of enlightenment shown by the fellow-citizens of Dikaiopolis, we should remember how near to our own home and times these practices come. The following is from H. V. Morton's *In Search of Wales* (ch. iv, sect. 4), and I owe the reference to it to one of the audience at my lectures on Greek religion in Cambridge, whose name, unfortunately, I do not know.

I took one of these walks to a little place called Llanelian yn-Rhos, which in times past was one of the most feared names on the map of Wales. At the bottom of the hill is a depression in the earth which is all that is left of the cursing-well of St. Elian. [The author then explains how the well was originally a wishing-well, but in the course of time its character changed.] It was a very profitable well. . . . The most famous well-keeper was a man named John Evans, who died somewhere about 1850 or 1860. He made a good business out of it. The people who believed that they were cursed always paid more than those who did the cursing.

If a man wanted to curse someone, he would write the enemy's

[1] καταδῶ ἀφανίζω κατορύττω καταπατταλεύω. The words seem to work up to a grand climax of fury, which was doubtless intentional and increased the power of the curse. Cf. the description of savage sorcery by B. Malinowski in *Science, Religion and Reality* (London, 1926), pp. 66 f.: "The sorcerer has, as an essential part of the ritual performance, not merely to point the bone dart at his victim, but with an intense expression of fury and hatred he has to thrust it in the air, turn and twist it as if to bore it in the wound, then pull it back with a sudden jerk. Thus not only is the *act* of violence, of stabbing, reproduced, but the *passion* of violence has to be enacted."

[2] The examples in the text are taken from Dittenberger's *Sylloge*^{3}, nos. 1175, 1177, 1180, 1261. A considerable literature has grown up around the *katadesmoi*. The best conspectus is given by Nilsson, *Gesch. Gr. Rel.* i, 757, n. 2.

name on a piece of paper, put it in a piece of lead and tie it to a slate with the initials of the man who made the curse written on it. This was thrown into the well and the curse recited in a special way. . . . Of course, great care was taken to tell the parson who had been cursed! He came to pay for its removal! The well-keeper then read out two psalms to him, made him walk round the well three times and read the Scriptures. He took the curse in its leaden box from the well and gave it to the man who had been cursed. I have heard it said that sometimes whole farms were cursed at Ffynnon Elian. [1]

V. Ghosts

In speaking here of the belief in ghosts, I am thinking of the ghost-story in the modern sense, of which the most typical variety tells how the spirit of a dead man torments by his appearances the inhabitants of a house or some other locality because there is something that he wants done, and having accomplished his desire finds peace at last and therefore appears no more. Since we know how unhappy a dead man was believed to be in Greece if he either remained unburied or had died a violent death which had gone unavenged, there was clearly plenty of scope for stories of this kind. The ghost may be maleficent or merely imploring. In the *Iliad* the ghost of Patroklos appears to Achilles, to the latter's great astonishment, with the simple request: "Bury me as quickly as possible, and let me pass the gates of Hades." This belief in ghosts was strong enough in later Greece for Plato to be able to refer to and use it for the purposes of his own argument in the *Phaedo* (81c). Speaking of the souls of those who in their lifetime have been too much enslaved by the pleasures of the body, he argues that through these habits they have become contaminated with the earthy and corporeal, and therefore cannot immediately shake off these elements at death. "Such a soul is weighed down," he continues, "and dragged back to the visible world . . . and haunts, it is said, the graves and tombs, in the neighbourhood of which shadowy forms of souls have in fact been seen. They are the phantoms which such souls present, souls which were impure at their release and still partake of the visible. That is the reason

[1] Quoted with Mr. Morton's kind permission. The practice of throwing *defixiones* into the water goes back to Roman times in Britain. See No. 44 of the inscriptions from Bath in the Victoria County History of Somerset. (I owe this reference to Mr. J. H. Croon.)

why they are seen." No doubt those who claimed to have seen them offered a very different reason for the apparition from Plato's, but he is referring to a popular belief, and the churchyard-ghost of more recent times evidently has a classical ancestry.

Nilsson remarks[1] that actual parallels to the modern type of ghost do not appear in literature until the Roman period, and as evidence for their existence in earlier times points to the mischievous actions of certain heroes. Our passage from Plato perhaps shows even better what was going on in the popular mind, and surely one may class as a ghost-story the tale of Periander's wife in Herodotus. It possesses other features which add to its interest, notably the reference to necromancy, and it is true that this particular ghost appeared at the summons of her widower. These things give the story a Greek flavour but do not rob it of its title as a ghost-story. Periander the tyrant of Corinth sent to the *nekyomanteion* (oracle of the dead) at the river Acheron to make an inquiry on some matter concerned with a deposit of money. His dead wife Melissa appeared and refused to divulge anything about the money's whereabouts, giving as her reason that she was cold, as she had no clothes. The clothes which were buried with her were no use to her as they had not been burned.[2] Periander took prompt action. He issued a proclamation that all the women of Corinth were to go out to the temple of Hera. Imagining that this must be for a festival they all put on their best clothes, but he had armed men waiting for them, and having stripped the finery from free women and serving girls alike took it all to a pit, where it was burned with prayers to Melissa.[3]

Plato in his summary of religious law, mentioned in an earlier chapter,[4] included "the observances which we must adopt in order to propitiate the inhabitants of the other world". What sort of rites these were it is now easy to imagine, and Plato may also

[1] *Gr. Pop. Rel.* 112.

[2] This would prevent them from acquiring a spirit-existence and so joining her in the spirit-world to which she had gone after her own cremation. Lucian tells a similar story of how a husband who was very fond of his wife took great care to burn her clothes after her death in order that she might have the use of them. Nevertheless she appeared to him a week later and asked for the second of her golden sandals. It had been underneath the chest and overlooked, and so not burned with the rest. (Lucian, *Philopseudes*, 27, cf. Tylor, *Primitive Culture*, i, 491.)

[3] Hdt. v, 92. I have deliberately chosen a tale of the more popular sort, but the awful appearance of the ghost of Clytemnestra, wandering because her body is unburied and dishonoured, to the Erinyes in the *Eumenides* of Aeschylus, will also occur to everyone.

[4] *Rep.* iv, 427b, p. 186 above.

have been thinking of such a public act as that at the close of the Spring festival of Dionysos, the Anthesteria, at Athens. One of the last acts was to recite the formula "Begone ye Keres, it is no longer Anthesteria". The Byzantine lexicographer Photius adds the explanation: "Said in the belief that during the Anthesteria souls [*psychai*] go to and fro through the city."[1] *Psyche* is a neutral word, which might be used by a man with his own, possibly immortal, soul in mind as well as of a ghost. A *ker* is specifically a ghost in the malignant sense of the ghost-story. A *ker* could send blindness or madness or death. In poetry the word can be used in a metaphorically abstract sense, as when Euripides speaks of "casting a black *ker* upon his eyes",[2] and *ker* can be coupled with Erinys.

I made a distinction just now between a man's idea of his own immortal soul and his belief in ghosts. This is I think justified in any age. If asked whether the English people believe in the immortality of the soul, it would hardly be natural to reply: "Yes indeed—I know plenty of people who are absolutely terrified of ghosts." Our hopes of a personal immortality, linked with the notion of some sort of a heaven, are not connected in our minds with the belief in ghosts,[3] however inescapable may be the logic of the conclusion that the latter must imply some form of survival after death. Our present aim is to find out which religious attitude was foremost in the mind of the ordinary Greek, the Homeric legacy of mortal thoughts for mortal men or the hopes of immortality and assimilation to the divine which might have reached him from a number of sources. In my own mind there is no doubt that the victory went to the Homeric conception. A more spiritual view of man, death and the gods (I use the adjective advisedly; the Homeric outlook was distinctively *corporeal*) remained exceptional until the end of the fifth century at least. This conclusion may seem surprising after the attention bestowed on the chthonian cults in the last chapter, and especially after the remark that it was to them rather than to Homer that we must look for anything which would be recognized as religious experience to-day. The sway of Homer's marvellous literary creations over Greek religious thought was certainly artificial, and indeed a hindrance to the development of a real and inward religion, but it was nevertheless

[1] Photius s.v. *θύραζε Κᾶρες* (Quoted Farnell, *Cults*, v, 319, n. 124 l.) Cf. also the views of L. Moulinier, *Le pur et l'impur* (1952), 112 ff.

[2] *Phoen.* 950.

[3] I am not of course taking into account the manifestations claimed by modern spiritualism, since whether they be genuine or not, we know of nothing comparable in classical Greece.

a fact. Yet lest some should be troubled by an apparent inconsistency, it seemed necessary to refer explicitly to the religious limitations of a belief in ghosts, and it is still incumbent on us to make clear, as far as possible, how it was that the chthonian side of religion, popular and widespread as some of its manifestations were, failed nevertheless to undermine entirely the authority of Homer until assisted in the fourth century by all the political, social and psychological consequences of the fall of the city-states and the growth of large and unwieldy empires in their place.

VI. Modifications of Homeric Ideas: Eleusis

We have seen that unless the dead are properly buried (or in Homeric times cremated, and their ashes interred), they are cut off from the world of shades, and show their discontent by pestering their relations until the necessary ceremonies have been carried out. A murdered man is in the same unhappy state until his death has been avenged, and while this remains undone he has great power for harm among those whose duty it is. It is also possible for the kindred of a dead person to go to his tomb either to invoke his aid in some great enterprise, like Orestes and Electra in the tragedy of Aeschylus, or, like Periander and many others, to learn the future, or some hidden fact of present or past, by making use of the prophetic powers with which the dead were credited. A necessary part of such invocations was the pouring of a libation or the performance of a sacrifice, at which the wine or the blood was made to soak into the ground of the tomb. These dark communings with the dead were on the whole alien to the world of Homer, yet behind the outpouring of wine or blood was the belief that the spirit had not of itself or in its own nature the strength to answer the prayer, but that this was actually provided by the life-giving offerings themselves. For this belief the Greeks referred to Homer, and it is indeed not quite consistent with the ideas of the powerful and vengeful dead which they had inherited from other, older sources. When Odysseus visits the entrance to Hades in the eleventh book of the *Odyssey*, the souls which come up are unable to recognize or speak to him until they have drunk the blood of the ram which he has poured into the trench. It does not matter if the scenes in this book represent a later stratum of tradition than the main body of the Homeric poems, which, it is often claimed, would not have admitted the idea of such goings-on at all. In the first place, they were Homer to the Greek of the fifth century as much as was the oldest portion of the *Iliad*, and I do not wish to go further than to say that it was always the desire of the Greek, out of his innate respect for tradition, to find authority somewhere in Homer for his actions or beliefs.[1] In the second place, the need for the blood to give animation and intelligence to the shades is a sign that, even if in this book the poet has drawn on sources alien to the old Achaean tradition, he has taken care to Homerize his story and make it conform to the Achaean outlook. According to this, as we have seen, the dead are normally senseless, strengthless shades. The poet of the *Nekyia* does not deny this. He merely allows them a temporary revival brought about by the most material and Homeric of means. What they lack is the blood of earthly life and vigour, and this is given to them to drink. The soul of Teiresias himself is expressly said to be a unique exception. I have mentioned how, in the *Iliad*, the ghost of Patroklos appeared to Achilles, to ask him for a proper funeral which would enable it to join its brother-shades. "He was marvellously like himself to look at", said Achilles afterwards, and as the ghost, with a thin shriek, vanished like smoke beneath the earth, eluding his attempts to embrace it, he exclaimed with an ejaculation of astonishment: "True it is, then, that even in the house of Hades there exists a soul and a wraith, but there are no *phrenes* in it at all!"[2] *Phrenes* is a word which is sometimes to be translated "heart", as when a man feels grief at his *phrenes*, and sometimes "mind", as when one is said to know something, or to conceive an idea, in the *phrenes*. It is however a definite physical organ, and in the *Iliad* it is still thought of as such even when considered as the seat of the passions or the reason. It is in fact the midriff. Since the soul of Patroklos has made quite a long speech, setting forth its needs with clarity and good sense, Achilles cannot mean

[1] I see that this procedure has the support of Nilsson. Cf. *Hist. Gr. Rel.* (Oxford, 1935), p. 135: "Homer exercised an enormous influence upon the religious development of later times . . . and this influence was exercised by the Homeric poems as a completed whole, not while they were in process of formation. Hence the justification from the point of view of the history of religion for treating Homer in the main as an undivided whole, not forgetting the discrepancies which exist but whose history cannot be sufficiently illuminated."

[2] *Il.* xxiii, 101 ff. ταφὼν δ'ἀνόρουσεν 'Αχιλλεὺς
χερσί τε συμπλάταγησεν, ἔπος δ'ὀλόφυδρον ἔειπεν·
ὢ πόποι, ἦ ῥά τίς ἐστι καὶ εἰν 'Αΐδαο δόμοισι
ψυχὴ καὶ εἴδωλον, ἄταρ φρένες οὐκ ἔνι πάμπαν.

to say that it has no mind or wits. If we are to look for consistency in these matters, and attempt to reconcile this passage with others where the souls of the dead are said to be witless as well as strengthless (and it is by no means certain that we should), we may perhaps attribute it to his having not yet passed, as he says himself, beyond the river Acheron. Whatever the explanation, the feature which strikes Achilles is the absence of a bodily organ which may be most expressively rendered by the vulgar English expression "guts". After death the soul drags on indeed a bare existence, but has nothing that could be called immortality, for its separation from the body dooms it to an existence which is the negation of all that, in the opinion of the survivors, makes life worth living. Uniting this with more primitive notions, which could not be permanently suppressed, of ghosts that were powerful and active, the poet of the *Nekyia* thinks it reasonable, since flesh and blood is what the spirits lack, to suppose that by imbibing blood they might regain their powers. The later Greek could imagine it in the same way, with the least possible disrespect to the authority of Homer.

The point that I wish to make is simply this. There must have been a blend of many different ideas, from different sources, behind the funeral customs, tendance of graves and fear of the dead in classical times, but the Homeric view was still uppermost in men's minds. The impulse of the Greek was always λόγον δίδοναι, to account for his actions to his reason as far as possible, and the reasonable thing for him was to see what he did in the light of Homer. The notion that the dead were powerful for good or harm belonged to an age far more primitive than Homer's. It must have prevailed on Greek soil for hundreds of years before the Homeric poems existed. Yet owing to what one might almost call the accident of Homer's greatness, all these primitive conceptions were overlaid and pushed beneath the surface. That was what had happened to the religion of Dikaiopolis. Homer dominated and overshadowed it. Darker and more primitive conceptions lingered at the back of his mind, far more deep-rooted than anything that Homer taught and ready to burst out as soon as history brought about a weakening of the barrier which Homer had placed in their way; but in the age of which we are speaking, they were never in the forefront.

Hence it is that most Greeks were obsessed by the necessity of thinking mortal thoughts, remembering the barrier between human and divine, and not striving after immortality. Religious conservatism made them continue thinking in terms of a society of robust and aristocratic warriors although that society might be long dead and have little resemblance to their own. This conservatism[1] is in all ages more evident in religion than in most other departments of human life, and the old heroes who, owing to its effects, were still dominating the minds of Greece were not interested in immortality. Bodily strength and vitality seemed to them such glorious things that even if the soul continued to exist, its separation from the body must mean that it had lost all that was worth living for.

This, then, is how we must see the mind of the Athenian citizen, a mirror of conflicting ideas which, like a great many of ourselves, he had not separated or analysed at all clearly. Homer had given him his gods, and taught him his relation to them, and uppermost in his mind was the feeling that it was not for him to question the voice of tradition. Nevertheless for at least two reasons he was not content to remain exactly in the position to which Homer had assigned him. In the first place he no longer lived the life of a Homeric hero. His conservatism—in modern jargon the time-lag—preserved the authority of Homer, but in reality Homer's religion was something highly specialized which had little relevance to the conditions and needs of the fifth century. Mycenean kings may have had no use for an immortality designed to compensate for the unhappiness of this world and redress the balance of its injustice, but that is not the normal human attitude, and fifth-century Athens was nearer to normality. Aspirations arose again which are native to the human spirit and need no religious creed to implant them. The orator Hypereides was reflecting a universal human sentiment when he said: "But if there is a conscious life in the realm of Hades, and divine care, it is reasonable to expect that those who died defending the honour of their country's gods should meet with the loving-kindness of the divine power after death."[2] It is not the sentiment of the official epitaphs written by a Simonides—they kept closer to the ancestral heroic tradition—but still less is it the result of influence from Orphic or any other mystical doctrine. It is ordinary human sentiment, for as the writer says, "It is reasonable to believe . . ."

[1] Often referred to nowadays as the "time-lag", though this expression, apart from being uglier, scarcely makes the meaning so immediately clear.

[2] Stobaeus iv, 134 Meineke. Cf. Farnell, *Hero-Cults*, p. 392.

Similarly old Kephalos at the beginning of the *Republic* says that a man is apt to take no notice of all the talk about rewards and punishments in the next world so long as he is in full possession of health and strength, but as he gets older hopes and fears assail him and he finds himself taking them more seriously. This is something universal.

There we have one reason why the influence of Homer in religious matters was tempered in the mind of the ordinary Greek, that Homer's religion, for all the beauty, joy and strength which it contained, was artificial, and natural human aspirations were once more demanding satisfaction. Another is that, as we have seen, the material for their satisfaction lay at hand. A second challenge to Homer is to be found in the existence everywhere of cults which go back far earlier than his poems and are once more coming out of the twilight to which his authority had relegated them. These cults taught of a relation between men and gods very different from the Homeric. Their development illustrates the interaction of the two, and the way in which Homeric ideas had come to dominate the older, local religions of the soil. As always in this book, it is ideas rather than rites that I am trying to understand.

The most important and influential cult of this sort was the Eleusinian mysteries, and this is the point at which it seemed best to introduce it. Considering its outstanding position, not only at Athens but throughout the whole of Greece, it may have caused surprise that the earlier account of chthonian cults contained no mention of it. The reason was that I was concerned first of all to bring out the nature of chthonian cults as such, and make clear the points on which they differed from Olympian religion. Since the object was to point a contrast, it was best achieved by a description of those cults which had received least official recognition from powerful city-states and consequently remained least contaminated by the pervasive atmosphere of Homer and Olympus. Trophonios gave us an example of a purely chthonian cult of simple people, which had indeed achieved such fame that it was resorted to by individuals from over a wide area, but had never come under the aegis of one of the greater cities. The cult at Eleusis was adopted by the greatest of all as a part of her official religion, and inevitably underwent a certain amount of *Gleichschaltung* in consequence. To point the contrast, therefore, Eleusis would not have served so well. It is all the better as an illustration of the present point, that once a cult had been attracted into the orbit of a great city-state, it was possible, not to suppress or forbid it, but in more or less subtle ways to modify the assumptions underlying its background of myth and belief so as to gloss over its real origin and make it appear not incompatible with a natural development of Homeric ideas.

The cult of Demeter at Eleusis was not brought to Greece by any tribe of invading Hellenes. It belonged to the original inhabitants, as is suggested sufficiently clearly by its nature and confirmed by archaeological evidence. Excavation on the site has revealed a continuity of occupation from Mycenean times, and the *telesterion*, where the final rites were performed, was actually built over the ruins of the *megaron* of some Mycenean lord. This reminds us of how Athena had her temple on the site of the palace of the prehistoric overlords of the Akropolis at Athens.[1] The fact that in historical times the management of the cult was in the hands of a single family or clan, the Eumolpidai, may preserve the memory of an origin in the family rites of the local chief and his relations. The *telesterion* itself is a curious building, not a temple but a large rectangular assembly-hall with a stepped auditorium at one end, to which the nearest parallels are found in so-called "theatres" at Knossos and Phaistos in Crete. That the cult took its origin from Crete is extremely likely, and agrees with the opinion of the Greeks themselves. Describing the generations of the gods in the *Theogony*, Hesiod says that the birth of Plutos the god of wealth was the result of the union of Demeter with Iasion "in the rich land of Crete". In the Homeric Hymn to Demeter, a rich store of purely Eleusinian mythology (for it dates from before the time when the little town came under the sway of Athens), Demeter, in grief for her daughter Persephone who has been snatched away by Hades, leaves the company of the gods and wanders over the earth in search of her. She comes to Eleusis in the likeness of an old woman and is questioned by the daughters of its king Keleos. "My name is Dois," she replies, "and I have come from Crete over the broad back of the sea, not of my own will, but pirates took me by force." One should not perhaps pay too much attention to the statements of god or man in any poem in the Homeric tradition, when they are in disguise and trying to conceal their real origin. Caution is enjoined by the

[1] p. 106 above. Plans of the *telesterion* and of the building discovered below it, which is dated to the transitional period between middle and late Helladic, are reproduced by Nilsson in *Gesch. Gr. Rel.* i (1941), 318, 319. Cf. ib., 445.

memory that Odysseus, in the marvellous impromptu story which he invents for Athena's benefit when first landed on Ithaca, also pitches on Crete as his notional homeland. Nevertheless we are not quite in the world of the *Odyssey* here. The indication, such as it is, is in harmony with the theogonical information of Hesiod, and although for the purposes of the story Demeter is in disguise, the name which she gives herself is probably in fact another of her titles and not an invented human name.[1]

The cult at Eleusis has always been recognized, in ancient as in modern times, to have been an agricultural one. When Demeter in wrath and grief at the rape of her daughter neglects her wonted occupation, the result is a cessation of the fruits of the earth. No seed sprouts, in vain the oxen drag the crooked ploughs over the fields, in vain the seed-corn is scattered over the land, and the race of men wellnigh perishes of famine. After Zeus has intervened, and persuaded Demeter to agree to the arrangement whereby Persephone is to spend a third of the year below the earth and two-thirds in the upper world with her mother, the first result is that Demeter once more sends up the crops on the deep-soiled ploughlands, and the whole broad earth is heavy once more with leaves and flowers.

Demeter is the earth-goddess,[2] and her cult is devoted primarily

[1] What *exactly* the name was, is uncertain. The ms. reading in line 122 is Δώς, but is unmetrical. Passow's correction Δωσώ was accepted by Allen in the Oxford text of 1912. Allen and Halliday (*Homeric Hymns*[2], Oxford 1936) leave the ms. reading obelized. Whatever it be, it is probably connected with the root of "giving", unless indeed Fontein's suggestion is correct and it is actually a corruption of Δηώ, an alternative name of Demeter which is common enough and has occurred earlier in the Hymn itself (line 47). See also reff. in Kern, *Rel. der Griech.* I, 143, n. 5. Evidence for the Cretan origin of the Eleusinia is conveniently summarized by Persson, *Religion of Greece in Prehistoric Times* (1942), 149.

[2] Nilsson insists (*Gr. Pop. Rel.*, p. 51) that Demeter is not a goddess of the earth, or of vegetation in general, but solely of the corn, and holds indeed that this is the key to the understanding of the cult of her and her daughter. "Philologists disagree as to whether the syllable *de-* signifies 'earth' or 'corn'. The cult is decisive." After a careful reading of his arguments (also in *Gesch. Gr. Rel.* i, 443), I am not convinced that this is necessary, and on the whole it seems unlikely that one has to decide between these two as alternatives. The deification of the fertile earth was a familiar conception to the Greeks (cf. pp. 54 ff. above), and it is unlikely that a clear distinction such as that suggested by Nilsson was consistently present to their minds. No doubt Demeter at Eleusis was thought of pre-eminently as the giver of the corn, not however because she was nothing else but because that was her most important function. This impression is strengthened by the knowledge that she is likely to have been in origin a local manifestation of the primeval goddess of the land (rechristened by the Greeks with the title " mother " in their own language), for as we have seen many times already, such evidence as we have concerning the religion of the pre-Greek peoples of the Aegean basin suggests the widespread worship of a goddess who was regarded as the mother of all life, vegetable and animal. Cf. also Farnell, *Cults*, iii, 32.

to securing the fertility of the land. Her daughter, who represents the life of the crops, must spend a third of the year—the time when the fields are empty and barren—beneath the earth, an idea probably suggested, as Nilsson (following Cornford) says, by the fact that after harvest and threshing-time corn was stored by the Greeks underground in great jars or in subterranean chambers, whence it was brought up at the time of sowing and the seed-corn taken out and scattered over the earth's surface. In the Greek mind the two functions of the earth, as receiving the seed which is later to spring up in new and fertile life, and as the home of departed souls, were always connected.[1] Pluton, "the rich", was the same as Hades the lord of the dead. The daughter of Demeter was his consort, known perhaps especially as Persephone when her dread function as queen of the dead was in question, and as Kore, the Maiden, in her capacity as daughter of Demeter representing the young life of the crops.

Out of this association there arose at Eleusis the belief that Demeter had in her gift not only the fertility of the land but immortality for the human soul. Did the minds of her worshippers work in the same way as that of the Evangelist: "Except a corn of wheat fall into the ground and die, it abideth alone: but if it die, it bringeth forth much fruit", and of St. Paul: "That which thou sowest is not quickened, except it die"?[2] Did they draw the analogy that just as the dried-up grain by being buried in the earth sprang into new life, so when the dead are buried they may find a source of new life too? It is rash to dogmatize about the processes of thought of unselfconscious people, and we may rest content with the known fact that the goddess of fertility was also for them the giver of immortality. To receive it, men underwent, as at other shrines of the nether powers, preliminary rites of purification, followed by an initiation which must have meant, at least according to all analogy, a raising of the initiated mortal to the divine estate.

Most of these features could be matched from other local chthonian shrines; but for this little centre of typically Aegean fertility-cult was reserved a unique fate. The town of Eleusis lay in Attica, only about twelve miles by road from Athens, and this accident of situation changed its history. It was united with its greater neighbour, and so found its mysteries first taken under her protection, and later, owing to the predominance of Athenian

[1] pp. 218 f. above.

[2] John xii, 24, 1 Cor. i, 15, 36.

culture in Greece, raised to a position of Pan-Hellenic importance.[1] Athens gave full official status to the mysteries, which were put under the charge of the King-Archon and a body of overseers (ἐπιμεληταί) of whom two were chosen from each of the priestly Eleusinian clans of the Eumolpidai and Kerykes and two from the whole Athenian people.[2] A branch sanctuary, the *Eleusinion*, was built close under the Akropolis, where sacrifices were offered to Pluto and at the beginning of the great mysteries certain "sacred objects" from Eleusis were deposited, to be carried out again in the procession a few days later. So completely did Athens appropriate the mysteries that she found no difficulty in speaking of them as a purely Athenian institution, and thus they were made to serve, in the sort of way that is only too familiar to-day, the ends of her nationalist propaganda. On the strength of her control of the Eleusinian mysteries, it was claimed that the two greatest gifts of the gods to man—the arts of agriculture which first made possible a civilized life on earth, and the promise of a better life after death—had been revealed by heaven solely to the Athenians, and only through their generosity imparted to the rest of mankind. The Greeks still lived close enough to agricultural pursuits, and to the memory of a time before they were known, to realize their far-reaching significance. As Benjamin Rogers wrote: "Earth, with her corn and wine and oil, was to the Hellenic mind emphatically a civilizer of men. Her attractions drew them from the nomad state of wandering hunters; they became under her influence settled and agricultural peoples; she taught them the joys of

[1] Exactly when Eleusis was incorporated with Athens, the evidence does not seem sufficiently decisive to say, but it was probably before the end of the seventh century. If, as seems certain from internal evidence, the Homeric Hymn to Demeter was composed before the incorporation, this cannot have taken place much earlier. Wilamowitz even says that the vocabulary and style of the hymn place it beyond doubt in the sixth century (*Glaube*, ii, 47). Nilsson simply says that because it precedes the incorporation therefore it belongs more probably to the end of the seventh than to the beginning of the sixth (*Gesch. Gr. Rel.* i, 620). Farnell wished (on grounds not in themselves entirely cogent) to relegate the incorporation to "the prehistoric or at least the dawn of the historic period of Attica" (*Cults*, iii, 154), and therefore denied that the lack of any allusion to Athens in the Hymn need imply that Eleusis was not yet Athenian at the date of its composition. But the exuberant pride of the Athenians in the possession of the mysteries (shortly to be referred to in the text) makes it most unlikely that they would have sanctioned such an omission.

The best discussion of the subject for English readers is in Allen and Halliday's *Homeric Hymns* (2nd ed. 1936), 111 ff. The editors favour the view that the Hymn was composed in the latter half of the seventh century and shortly before the Athenian conquest of Eleusis.

[2] Aristotle, *Ath. Pol.* 57 *init.*, [Lysias] *in Andoc.* 4, Demosth. *in Meid.* 171.

HOME. To her and her life-sustaining produce was ascribed the institution of social laws, the rights of property, the laws of wedlock and the family."[1] All this, and heaven too, was now presented to the Greek world as not so much the gift of the gods as the gift of Athenian enlightenment. Isokrates, the spokesman of Athens in the fourth century, puts it in these words: "In the first place, then, the primary need of human nature was provided by our city. Yes, even though the tale be now well worn, yet it is right that it should be repeated here. Demeter arrived in our land, during her wanderings after the rape of Kore, and showed the goodwill that she bore to our ancestors by means of those blessings which it is not possible for any but the initiated to hear. Two gifts she gave, the greatest of all gifts: on the one hand the fruits of the field, which have been the instrument whereby mankind is raised above the life of beasts, and on the other hand initiation, participation in which gives sweeter hopes concerning the end of life and all eternity. But our city was so true a friend not only to god but to man that having these great blessings in her possession she did not grudge them to others, but gave freely of what she had received."[2] According to Xenophon's account of the speech of Kallias to the Spartans, advocating peace between Athens and Sparta in the year 371, he made use of the same claim to support his point. Kallias, it may be noted, was of the priestly family of the Kerykes and held the office of Daduchos at the mysteries. "We ought never to raise our hands against each other," said he, "for we are told that Triptolemos our ancestor revealed the secret rites of Demeter and Kore first of all to Herakles your national hero and the Dioskuroi your fellow-citizens, and made a gift of the seed of Demeter's fruit to the Peloponnese before all other lands. It cannot be right therefore, either for you to march out to destroy the crops of those from whom you received the gift of seed, nor for us to deny full abundance of food to those to whom we gave it."[3]

Kallias knew what he was talking about, and the theme is not confined to isolated outbursts of rhetoric by individual orators. An inscription of later date (117 B.C.), of which one copy was set up in the Athenian treasury at Delphi and another on the Akropolis of Athens, records a decree of the Amphictyonic Council conferring certain privileges and exemptions on the Athenian guild of

[1] B. B. Rogers, translation of Arist. *Thesm.* (London, 1911), intro. p. x.
[2] *Paneg.* 28.
[3] Xen. *Hell.* vi, 3, 6.

Dionysiac artists (i.e. actors). It uses language like this. The Athenian people "converted men from the life of beasts to civilization, and contributed to their mutual association by being first to impart the mysteries, and by their means proclaiming to all that the greatest good among men is mutual commerce and good faith. She imparted also what the gods had given concerning human laws and education; and likewise the gift of the fruits of the earth, though she had received it for herself alone, yet she granted the use of it to be common to all the Greeks."[1] The patriotism which breathes through much of the *Frogs* of Aristophanes, as through most of his plays, is perhaps to be seen not least in his choice of the mystics in Elysium for his chorus, which serves as a reminder of the surpassing gifts of this now wholly Athenian cult. In passing, we may note that the above quotations give the best answer to the question so frequently asked, whether the mysteries had any moral side, and if so, how it was conceived. The kind of connexion which the Athenians saw between their agricultural cult and moral obligations appears clearly in the Delphic inscription, and these form the best commentary on the words with which the blessed initiates close a chorus in the *Frogs*, and which seem to reflect the precision of a formula: "We who have been initiated and conduct ourselves righteously towards foreigners and private citizens."[2] Consideration for others and good faith in dealing with them are the first requirements of communal life, and to be able to live in communities is one of the gifts of Demeter to men.

This appropriation of the mysteries by Athens led of necessity to changes, or rather additions, of ritual, and also, as I believe, to a change of attitude in regard to the beliefs behind it. Since the mysteries are undoubtedly a part of the religion of the ordinary citizen, it is worth pausing to run briefly over some of the main features. It may be said at the outset that the obligation of secrecy applied only to the final rite of Beholding (*Epopteia*), which formed the climax to a procedure lasting a number of days. It does not stand in the way of our knowledge of the preliminary processions, purificatory ceremonies and so forth, which led up to the climax.

Not only new rites, but a new god, arose from the connexion of the mysteries with Athens. This was Iacchos. To cover the dis-

[1] Dittenberger, *Syll.*[3] 704e. [2] Lines 457 ff.

tance from Athens to Eleusis a procession was formed and passed along what came to be known as the Sacred Way between the two towns with dancing, singing and joyful shouts of "Iache, iache!" From this, by the personification which came so readily to the Greek mind, arose the idea of a god of the joyful cry, and who was he likely to be but Dionysos, himself the patron of wild dancing and already known as "Euios" from the ecstatic cry "Euoi" that was uttered by his impassioned worshippers? The cry was now regarded as an invocation to Iacchos, and Iacchos identified with Dionysos, with whose dress and attributes his image was adorned. This image, as well as the sacred emblems from the *Eleusinion*, was borne from his temple to the gathering-point of the procession in the market-place, and thence carried the whole way to Eleusis, like the saint and relics of many a Mediterranean procession to-day. The invocation of Iacchos has a prominent place in the *Frogs*, as also has another incident which offered obvious scope for the parodist, namely a proclamation that was made before the start of the procession bidding all stand aside who were impure, unprepared by the proper preliminary rites or in any other way unfitted to take part. One of these preliminary rites was purification by bathing in the sea, for which all candidates for initiation went down to the coast close to Athens on an appointed day. The procession took more than one day to cover the twelve miles of road, for it had to halt for all sorts of performances by the way. Later Greek writers mention dances, sacrifices, libations and hymns. The way was lined with the shrines of gods and heroes, each of whom must have his due. Thus torchlight played its part in adding to the atmosphere of excitement. At a certain bridge across the river Kephissos, a curious practice was observed that must have far antedated the days of the procession and been incorporated in it. As the procession arrived, one of its number sitting on the bridge, and answered possibly by the others, hurled abuse and curses, as one authority says, "at the most distinguished of the citizens". This "bridgery" (*gephyrismos*), as the often obscene jesting and cursing came to be called from the scene of its enactment, was not confined to the Eleusinian procession nor to the Kephissos bridge. Pointless as it sounds, there are parallels from Mediterranean custom to suggest that it had a practical aim, being considered effective in averting the evil eye.

We need not waste time in speculating on the nature of the

final spectacle in the actual *telesterion* at Eleusis. This it was that admitted a man to the highest grade of initiation, that of *Epoptes*, Beholder. Of these last solemn rites it was not permitted to speak. "A great awe of the gods holds back the voice", as the Homeric Hymn puts it, and a chorus of Sophocles says that a golden key is laid upon the tongue of mortals by the Eumolpid priests.[1] The secret was well kept. Christian writers, in their attacks on pagan ceremonies, have claimed to know and to reveal it, but we may well be chary of accepting their late and hostile accounts as evidence for what went on at Eleusis in the fifth or fourth century B.C. We know however that it consisted of a revelation or spectacle, even if there is doubt as to the precise nature of the things revealed. All evidence leads to the conclusion that the effect was achieved by immediate action upon the senses. The initiate was *shown* things, and convinced of his salvation by the evidence of his own eyes. The climax was called the beholding and the chief officiating priest the hierophant, which means literally a showman of holy things. He was not a teacher. As Aristotle said, the initiate was not required to learn anything, but rather after suitable preparation to undergo an experience and be put in a certain state.[2] One can scarcely speak of anything so definite as doctrine in connexion with Eleusis. The root idea was more akin to magic, whose efficacy depends on the thoroughness of the preparatory measures and the punctilious correctness with which certain prescribed actions are carried out. Clearly also a large part was played by the emotional state which had been induced by the series of preliminary actions leading to the ultimate revelation set, as it appears, in a scene of contrasts between darkness and the dazzling light of hundreds of torches. It may be doubted however whether Dikaiopolis and his friends were so easily overawed as some. The Athenian loved a show, and had no wish to water down the impressive and spectacular elements of the mysteries; indeed he added to them. But one cannot help feeling that it remained to him primarily a show, with certain desirable consequences. "Worshipful daughter of Demeter, what a grand smell of roast pork!" is how the slave Xanthias interrupts the solemn invocation of Iacchos, and Dionysos' only rebuke is, "Well, keep quiet and you may get a bit of the offal". Another reference to the pre-

[1] Hom. Hymn Dem. 479, Soph. *O.C.* 1052.

[2] Fr. 15 Rose: τοὺς τελουμένους οὐ μαθεῖν τι δεῖν ἀλλὰ παθεῖν καὶ διατεθῆναι, δηλονότι γενομένους ἐπιτηδείους.

liminary sacrifice of pigs also illustrates the severely practical mentality of the Athenian. Trygaios, the Athenian farmer who is the hero of the *Peace*, is told by Hermes that he has committed a crime against the gods for which the only possible punishment is death, and replies imperturbably: "Then lend me three drachmas to buy a pig—I must get initiated before I die."[1]

The emphasis on ritual action, and lack of positive teaching, meant that on the doctrinal side (I use the word for want of a better) the mysteries lay open to any influences which the passage of time, and the changing character of the worshippers, might bring to bear; and what we have seen of the ordinary Athenian prepares us to expect a modification. How did he conceive that after-life to which initiation entitled him, steeped as he was in the Homeric heritage which declared that the dead must necessarily drag on a miserable semi-existence in dank and mouldering gloom? I believe that he saw it—illogically it may be—as a development, not a contradiction, of the ideas in the Homeric poems. The mysteries did become a part of his religion, but failed to undermine the respect for Homer with which every true Greek grew up as part of his mental equipment.

In the *Odyssey*, Menelaos tells how the sea-god Proteus prophesied for him a blissful immortality:[2]

> But as for thee, Menelaos nursling of the gods, it is not ordained that in horse-rearing Argos thou shalt die and meet thy fate. Nay, to the Elysian plain and the farthest borders of the earth shall the immortals send thee, where dwells fair-haired Rhadamanthys, where life is easiest for men. No snow is there, nor heavy storm, nor rain ever, but always Okeanos sends forth the breezes of clear-breathing Zephyr to bring refreshment to men. Thither shall they send thee because thou hast Helen to wife and art in their eyes son-in-law of Zeus.

Homer then, the Greeks could say, was not ignorant of Elysium where men could live for ever under the perfect conditions of a paradise. Most probably it is not an Achaean notion in origin, but belonged to the pre-Greek peoples of the land. Certain indications suggest this, notably the automatic association of it with Rhadamanthys, the *-nth* suffix of whose name betrays it at once as pre-Greek.[3] Nevertheless the epic poet has welded it into his scheme

[1] Arist. *Frogs*, 337 ff., *Peace*, 374 f.

[2] iv, 561 ff.

[3] See further L. Malten, "Elysion und Rhadamanthys" in *Arch. Jahrb.* xxviii (1913), 35 ff., P. Capelle, "Elysium und Inseln der Seligen" in *Archiv f. Religionswiss.* xxv (1927), 245 ff., and xxvi, 17 ff., Nilsson, *Min.-Myc. Rel.*, pp. 540 ff., and *Gesch. Gr. Rel.* i, 302 f.

of things, and has done so without disturbing his general picture of the miserable lot of the dead. Deprived of the body, the soul could only exist as a pale image of it, without wit or strength. Menelaos therefore is not to die at all, but to be transported alive to a far distant corner of the earth's surface where he will live on for ever in his present state. The reason for this exemption is his adoption into the family of the gods, the only true immortals, through his marriage to Helen. For the ordinary man, who knew that he must die, this held out no hope of a life beyond the grave. Even the son-in-law of Zeus could not expect that. If he is granted eternal life, it is by avoiding death altogether. The paradise is an earthly paradise.

At the same time, Homer did bequeath to later Greece the conception of an Elysium where certain privileged persons might enjoy eternal bliss. The difference between being wafted there instead of dying and being wafted there after death was only important to Homeric society in which the manly qualities of bodily strength counted for so much. It is likely to seem an over-refinement to the ordinary man of a later age who is longing for some hint of a promise that death is not the end of everything that matters. After the passing of the epic age the idea of Elysium is more likely to return to what, if its pre-Greek origin may be accepted, was probably its original function. So when the Athenians, and under their leadership the whole of Greece, took over Eleusis, they fused the old idea of immortality, connected with the cult of Demeter and her daughter, with Homer's teaching about Elysium. The thin, barely conscious existence of the Homeric shade remained the lot of the ordinary man after death.[1] Now however the ordinary man was the uninitiated, and Elysium was removed from the surface of the earth, and made into a part of the realm of the dead, and its privileges reserved, not for the relatives-by-marriage of Zeus, but for the initiated. And initiation (as the Athenians, proud of their generosity, lost no opportunity to point out) was open to everyone who was not a *barbaros*, be he free Greek or slave.[2] The situation of the blessed mystics is made quite plain in the *Frogs*. Dionysos and Xanthias have descended to Hades. They have crossed the Acheron in Charon's ferry-boat and passed the place where dead sinners lie in eternal discomfort.

[1] It is noticeable how even such an out-and-out mystic as Empedocles retains Homeric language to describe the souls of the "ignorant": *καπνοῖο δίκην ἀρθέντες ἀπέπταν* (fr. 2. line 4, Diels).

[2] On the question of the admission of slaves see Farnell, Cults iii, pp. 155 f.

Only then do they suddenly emerge from the place of "mud and darkness" to where a light shines like the light above. Here they become aware of the sound of flutes and meet the mystics, who are disporting themselves in flowery groves and meadows full of roses. "For us alone", they sing, "does the joyous sunlight shine, we who have been initiated and conduct ourselves righteously." It is the Homeric Elysium transferred to a part of the realm of shades.

Moreover there was no need to give up altogether the idea, found in Homer, that kinship with the gods was the real qualification for a blessed immortality. The original belief of the Eleusinian religion, as of its Cretan forebears and its Thracian relations, must have been in an immortality dependent on some form of union with the divine. One form of this union was rebirth, or adoption, as son of the divinity. The two ideas are not separate, for in human families in Greece the solemn adoption of a child was represented as rebirth from the womb of his new mother.[1] Later writers speak of those initiated in certain mysteries (not the Eleusinian) as "reborn", and this phrase was also applied to adopted children. Some have held that the final ceremony at Eleusis actually contained a rite symbolically enacting the rebirth of the initiate from the womb of Demeter. This, though possible, must be held to be not proven. Yet considering the primarily agrarian nature of the cult, it is difficult not to suppose that at some point the analogy between cereal and human life was drawn. The promise of immortality must have been connected in the minds of the worshippers with the fact that the dead grain achieves rebirth by being restored to the womb of Mother Earth. Whatever the ritual symbolism employed, it need not be doubted that the initiate considered himself to have been adopted by Demeter. The cumulative evidence from other mysteries is strong, and there is one passage where the belief seems to be applied unmistakably to the Eleusinian, though its date must be admitted to be somewhat late. In the dialogue *Axiochos*, attributed to Plato but certainly not by him,[2] Socrates is telling Axiochos that he has nothing to fear, but everything to hope, from death. After a glowing description of the abodes of the blessed, he continues: "There the initiated have a special place of honour, and there too the holy ceremonies are

[1] Where no other ref. is given, the evidence for this paragraph will be found in Rohde, *Psyche* (Eng. trans.), app. xi, pp. 601 ff. Not all that Rohde says there is beyond objection, and I shall try only to make use of that which is.

[2] P. Souilhé, the Budé editor, concludes that it was probably written in the first century B.C.

performed. You therefore will surely be the first to share the privilege, being as you are a kinsman of the gods. Dionysos also and Herakles and those who went down with them to Hades are said to have been first initiated here [i.e. at Athens], and to have drawn courage for their journey from the goddess of Eleusis." To be a kinsman (γεννήτης) of the gods did not always imply initiation, but might be used only to indicate that a man was a full citizen and member of one of the "phratries".[1] Here however the encouragement to Axiochos is obviously given on the ground of his initiation, and the two are the same.[2]

The bond thus imagined between man and divinity may seem to our analytic minds very different from that which the epic poet conceived to exist between Menelaos and Zeus. That however is because we do not believe in the one or the other. The thought that they were being adopted into the family of the gods must have seemed equally satisfactory to those whose minds were saturated with Homeric tradition and those who had a feeling for the less prosaic ideas of the original mystery.

By way of conclusion, I append translations of three passages in which the poets of Greece have expressed the central idea of the mysteries, the contrast between the blessed lot of him who has experienced them and the unfortunate mortal who has not. It is noticeable that all three describe the central, essential act as a revelation, a *seeing*. That is all that we can know about it for certain, but it is enough to dispose at least of certain classes of wild conjectures about its nature. First comes, of course, the Homeric Hymn itself, in which we read (lines 480 ff.):

> Happy that one of mortal men who has seen these things. But he who has not fulfilled the sacred rites, nor had any part in them, never when his time has come enjoys a like fate down in the world of mouldering darkness.

Sophocles, in a passage quoted by Plutarch (fr. 753 Nauck), wrote:

> Thrice blessed are those mortals who see these mysteries before departing to Hades; for they alone have true life there. All that is evil besets the rest.

There is no need to see any reference to infernal torments in the last sentence. For the Greek brought up on Homer, the miserable

[1] Farnell, *Cults*, iv, 154.

[2] Cf. however the views of F. R. Walton, *Kinsman of the Gods?*, *Class. Philol.* 1953, 24 ff.

shadow-existence led by the ordinary soul "in the mouldering darkness" was quite bad enough to merit this language. Finally, Pindar speaks of the inner meaning of the mysteries in a passage which is consistent with the supposition that this solemn secret was revealed through the agrarian core of the cult, that the death of the grain and its mysterious upspringing into new life from the bosom of Mother Earth was used as an image and a promise of human rebirth. Clement of Alexandria quotes the lines, which, he says, refer to "the mysteries at Eleusis" (Pindar, fr. 137 Schneider, 121 O.C.T.):

Blessed is he who goes beneath the earth having seen these things.
He knows the end of life, and he knows its god-given beginning.

VII. Summary and Recapitulation. Rohde's Thesis and Later Modifications

This section will necessarily contain a certain amount of repetition of previous matter, but its insertion seemed advisable before we go on to discuss the Orphic writers, who (on the view which will be taken here) constructed an elaborate theological system deliberately evolved from existing elements of belief. Some recapitulation and a few additional observations are needed if the description of the situation, before their dogmatic intellects got to work on it, is to be sufficient for our purposes.

The effect of previous sections has been to show that religion in Greece existed long before the Homeric poems. It had the gods of Homer imposed on it—one is sometimes tempted to add, accidentally—and its subsequent history may not unfairly be described as the struggle of religion, as the word is understood by most people to-day, to free itself from this incubus. Nevertheless the struggle was for centuries an unequal one, so that Herodotus could say with truth in the fifth century that Homer and Hesiod had given the Greeks their gods. On the reasons for this I have nothing to add to what I have already said. Prominent among them appear to have been the natural conservatism and this-worldliness of the Greek, and particularly the Athenian, character, and the growth and nature of city-state government. Whatever the reasons, that is the contention that we are upholding, and it is worth pointing out that it rests upon a thesis which was put forward some fifty-five years ago, the thesis of Erwin Rohde's great book *Psyche*.[1]

The theme of the book is that Homer constitutes an artificial break in the continuity of Greek religion. Mystic and orgiastic cults, and what has in general been described here under the heading of chthonian, are almost entirely absent from Homer. Consequently it seemed not unreasonable when the studies of archaeology and anthropology were still in their infancy, to call these non-Homeric phenomena *post*-Homeric. This however began to appear in the highest degree unlikely as soon as the results of anthropological research were brought into relation with classical literature, and Rohde showed up the absurdity of supposing that religious rites and ideas which belong to an early stage of culture all over the world were unknown in Greece until the post-Homeric period. Examples of these phenomena are magical practices, rites of purification, the cult of the dead, and orgiastic rites of communion with, or absorption of, the god. A general survey of religious history makes the conclusion inevitable that these things must far antedate the Homeric poems.

For the purpose of contrasting them with Homer, two features of the chthonian cults are especially to be noted. First, it is they which contain the germs of later mystical religion, which has no ancestry in Homer. Secondly, they have only a local importance. In so far as they are directed towards gods, these gods are closely attached to the soil, and so each village or district has its own. But chthonian cults, as we have seen, are only partly of gods. Partly they are cults of the human dead. The effect in this case is that there was in the beginning no universal realm of the dead. The dead of a particular locality went beneath the earth and stayed in the region where they died. Hence the multiplicity of what were later known as entrances to Hades all over Greece. Lebadeia in Boeotia, the river Styx in Arcadia, Cape Tainaron the southernmost point of Greece—these and many other places were described as entrances to the lower world in an age when that world had become universalized and was imagined as a single whole.[2] Homer, writing as a poet, and for the warrior chieftains of a roving, fighting people, ignored both aspects of these cults. Their darkness and mystery and earthiness, their sense of the kinship of man with all the other creatures of the earth and with the spirits of

[1] First published 1894, translated from 8th edn. by W. B. Hillis (Kegan Paul, 1925).

[2] For lists of these entrances to the underworld, see PWK *Realenc.* x, 2383 ff., Roscher *Lex.* vi, 51 ff.

earth themselves, he expunged in favour of the bright daylight of Olympus and the clear and comprehensible individuality of its inhabitants. Their multiplicity and chaos he reduced to a system, giving universal sway to a handful of great gods living together in the organized relationships of the family. Similarly he wrote as if there were one universal place of shades ruled over by a single king, Hades the brother of Zeus. The way in which the three regions of sky, sea and earth were neatly parcelled out between the three brothers is typical of the epic poet's methods.

The thesis is obviously agreeable to common sense. Rohde moreover, with a healthy suspicion of the method of comparison and analogy when unsupported by positive internal evidence,[1] confirmed it by pointing to traces in Homer himself of the other side of religion, sufficient to show that it existed even for him, though he belonged to an age for which its meaning was largely lost. The outstanding example is the funeral of Patroklos. Rohde pointed out, and modern research has confirmed, that the elaborate sacrifices, including human sacrifices, which are described as being performed at his pyre, are not consistent with the simple explanation of them given by the poet. Achilles, in his wrath and grief at the death of his friend, puts his hands upon the dead man's breast and cries: "All am I now performing which aforetime I vowed: to drag Hector hither and give him as a raw feast to the dogs, and to slit the throats of twelve noble sons of the Trojans before thy pyre, because of my anger at thy death." Achilles' reason, in the poet's eyes, seems to be little more than the relief of his own feelings, and when in the following night the ghost of Patroklos appears to make its request, it does not seem to stand in need of anything of the sort. It asks only for a quick burial, because until the body is buried, the *psyche* is denied entrance to Hades, and must wander forlornly outside. That is all. It is a shade of the usual Homeric type, an *eidolon* or pale bodiless image of the living man. Having said its say to Achilles, "it vanished

[1] Cf. especially the remarks on p. 11 (Eng. trans.): "It is not from the comparison of religious beliefs and their development among kindred nations, nor even from the study of apparently primitive ideas and usages in the religious life of the Greeks themselves of later times, that we are to seek the truth about the religious customs of that remote period which is obscured for us by the intervening mass of the Homeric poems. Comparative studies of this kind are valuable in their way, but must only be used to give further support to the insight derived from less easily misleading methods of inquiry. For us the only completely satisfactory source of information about pre-Homeric times is Homer himself."

like smoke beneath the earth, uttering a thin shriek".[1] It is a different belief about the soul that demands the slaughter, that is, the sending to the other world in the dead man's company, of horses, dogs and slaves, and the offering of jars of honey and oil. The poet is relating a traditional story of which he does not understand the meaning, of which indeed he does not altogether approve. "Twelve noble sons of the great-hearted Trojans did he slay with the bronze, yea evil were the deeds that he devised in his mind." Having carried out these "evil deeds", he repeats what he had said before: "Now am I accomplishing all that I vowed before. Twelve noble sons of the great-hearted Trojans is the fire devouring together with thee, and Hector son of Priam shall I never give to be burned on the pyre, but to the dogs." Whatever vow Achilles may have made was certainly not exacted from him by the ghost of his friend, whose simple request hardly seemed to call for such a holocaust: "Bury me as quickly as possible, and let me pass the gates of Hades." All that Homer seems to see in the performance is a desire on the part of Achilles to do honour to the dead man's memory and to vent his anger on the slayer and his kin.

We know that the original reason for the burning, together with a dead man's body, of his possessions, domestic animals and slaves, was to give him the use of them in the next world, where he was imagined as following the same pursuits, and experiencing the same needs, as he had in this life. How far the poet had departed from these early and popular beliefs[2] is well illustrated by the lament of Andromache for Hector:

> Thee now lying by the beaked ships, far from thy parents, the slippery worms will eat, when the dogs have had their fill. Naked shalt thou be, for all the garments of thine that lie in thy halls, so fair and fine, the work of women's hands. All these of a truth shall I make to blaze in the devouring fire—no use to thee, for thou shalt not lie in them, but that thou mayst have honour from the men and women of Troy.[3]

The *Works and Days* of Hesiod furnishes an interesting piece of corroborative detail for the general thesis that Homer makes an artificial break in the continuity of Greek religious tradition. It appears in the account of the successive ages of the world.[4] By

[1] *Il.*.xxiii, 20 ff., 65 ff. Cf. p. 278 above.

[2] For which cf. the stories of Periander's wife and that told in Lucian's *Philopseudes*, p. 275 above.

[3] *Il.* xxii, *fin.*, Nilsson, *Hist. Gr. Rel.* (1925), p. 137. Professor Onians suggests a different interpretation (*Origins of European Thought*, Cambridge, 1951, p. 259, n. 8).

[4] *W. and D.* 109 ff. The view taken of the passage here is not quite that of Rohde (pp. 66 ff.)

leaving one out, we get a consistently ordered series, each age having a particular metal assigned to it and representing a steady degeneration from the perfect golden age in the beginning down to the evil age of iron which is Hesiod's own. First came the golden race of men, who lived like gods a life free from care and sorrow. The second race, of silver, was much inferior. These men were strong, but misused their strength, and Zeus caused the earth to swallow them. Third came the bronze race, who spent their whole time in war until they perished by each other's hands. The last race is the race of iron. Their lot is one of toil and woe, and the poet bemoans the fact that he was born among them.

The golden race is at the beginning, the iron at the end, and one would naturally suppose that the intention of the poet was to depict the steady process of degeneration reproduced above. But in fact it was only made to seem a steady process by omitting one of the ages. Between the third age of bronze and the last age of iron—that is, in the generations immediately preceding the poet's own—came the age of the Heroes, to which no metal is assigned. These are they, he says, who fought at Thebes and Troy. This race was "juster and better" than its predecessor, a race of *hemitheoi*, half-gods, and though some of them died, some were settled by Zeus at the ends of the earth, in the Islands of the Blest. These are none other than the heroes of the epic cycle. Traditional chronology made the poet put them later than the more wholly mythical ages of gold, silver and bronze, yet their appearance here destroys the continuity of his scheme and shows them up for the interlopers that they are.

While speaking of Hesiod, we may add (since it belongs to this rather rambling section to gather up some odds and ends omitted hitherto) a note on his own contribution to our knowledge of beliefs in the after-life. In describing the fate of the men of the Golden Age, the rural Boeotian shows acquaintance with a natural and primitive belief which had been obscured and suppressed in the Homeric period. His words are (*W. and D.* 121):

"But since even this race was swallowed up by the earth, they are become good spirits [δαίμονες ἐσθλοί] by the will of great Zeus, roaming the earth, the guardians of mortal men, who keep watch on the meting out of justice and on evil deeds, going up and down over the land clad in mist, givers of wealth."

Here is a belief in spirits who had once been men, and had died, but who though separated from the body were yet powerful to protect the deserving and avenge injustice. It may well be that some of those whom the poet has in mind, some of these perfect men who lived so long ago, many generations before the heroic age of Homer, are in origin not heroes at all, but underworld spirits, daemons of fertility. Their character as wealth-givers (πλουτοδόται) suggests the possibility, and in a matter so much at the mercy of the "shifting popular tradition" we cannot be sure. But for Hesiod they are men, and their death has been no bar to their continued influence on the affairs of those who come after them. In contrast to this, what he says of the fate of the men of the Heroic Age follows Homer exactly (161 ff.):

> And these too did wicked war and the dread battle-cry destroy, some at seven-gated Thebes, the land of Kadmos, fighting for the flocks of Oedipus, and some were brought in ships across the great gulf of the sea to Troy, for the sake of fair-haired Helen. There indeed the final doom of death enfolded *some*, but to *others* father Zeus the son of Kronos gave a life and a dwelling-place apart from mortals, settling them at the ends of the earth. And they live there with carefree hearts, in the Islands of the Blest beside deep-eddying Ocean, happy heroes, for whom the fertile earth bears its joyous fruit three times a year.

The dead are dismissed: no more is to be heard of them. But for some a blessed life was reserved by allowing them to continue on the surface of the earth, still in the body, without dying. As Paley said long ago in his note on the passage: "This refers primarily to the legend about Menelaos."[1]

Rohde's views may have been modified in points of detail, but his general thesis, so far as we have here outlined it, has only been substantiated by more recent work.[2] As a historical explanation of the fact which he had demonstrated, that the religious ideas of the Homeric poems constitute a break in the continuity of Greek religious tradition, which later gradually returned to a type of belief and cult prevailing in Greece at an earlier epoch, Rohde

[1] Cf. pp. 290 f. above. For an interesting illustration of the way in which the two different types of belief about the dead could be mingled in the fifth century, see the opening of the myth at the end of Plato's *Gorgias* (523a ff.). With a few characteristic modifications, the double tradition is used by Socrates to point his own moral.

[2] I do not wish here to go into Professor Jaeger's strictures on what Rohde says about the Homeric conception of the soul (*Theology of the Early Greek Philosophers* (Oxford, 1947), pp. 73 ff.). These should certainly be read. Jaeger draws some interesting and useful distinctions, together with others which perhaps attribute too clear-thinking a character to the religious mind of the times of which he is speaking. His critical account of the later work of W. F. Otto and Ernst Bickel should be noted.

premised that the epics arose in a colonial area. They were the product of Greeks living uprooted from their ancient homes on the coast of Asia Minor. The change of habitat brought a break in tradition, and old customs fell into oblivion, or changed their significance, which survived in their original forms in the motherland. This applied particularly to the cult of dead ancestors, which was essentially local. "Remembrance of the great ones of the past might survive transplantation, but not their religious worship, which could only be offered at the one spot where their bodies lay buried."[1]

Since Rohde's time, further studies of Mycenean Greece, particularly those of Professor M. P. Nilsson, based on a greater wealth of excavated material, have made it impossible to doubt that the life of Homer's heroes displays many features of the life lived by kings of the Mycenean age on the mainland. It was here, among mainland Greek traditions, that the epics must have arisen of which the *Iliad* and the *Odyssey* are the fine and final flowering. Nilsson has discussed the evidence for this in many of his writings.[2] Here it will be convenient simply to quote his conclusion as given in a lecture delivered at Cambridge and Manchester in 1936: "Archaeology and linguistics agree in proving that some elements in Homer go back into the Mycenean age, i.e. that Homer is the last outcome of epics which arose and were sung in the truly heroic age of great wars and sea expeditions to which the imposing ruins of the Mycenean fortresses in Greece, and some historical information from the East, testify."

To that extent Rohde's attempt at a historical explanation of the religious facts must be modified. But in the same lecture Nilsson made it equally clear that it was only modification, not contradiction, that was required. In Mycenean Greece a vast amount of wealth was expended in providing magnificent tombs for the dead and furnishing them with rich and costly gifts. The treasures of these tombs have been among the most spectacular finds of modern times, and the tombs themselves form the grandest of existing Mycenean monuments. In the absence of any direct evidence save the archaeological, it is of course extremely difficult to know the beliefs which lay behind this funereal pomp and lavishness. The natural inference is that here is a genuine religious cult of the dead, with all that that implies of belief in their continued power and influence. The coexistence of such

[1] *Psyche*, pp. 27 f.

[2] See especially *Homer and Mycenae* (Methuen, 1933).

cult and belief with the same practice of lavish offerings could be matched from elsewhere. Nevertheless we have seen that in the *Iliad*, where a very different belief about the nature of the dead appears to have been the rule, the same display of wealth in their honour is occasionally to be found, though its motive, as the words of Andromache make clear, is not now to benefit the dead in any material sense, but only to do honour to their memory. Perhaps therefore among the rich ruling classes of the Mycenean fortress-towns the motive was already the same. Thus Nilsson suggests: "It is no wonder that among the nobility the honorific motive of funeral customs was put into the foreground to such an extent as to obliterate the religious sense they once had. If we consider the luxury of the Mycenean tomb-buildings and tomb-furniture we may perhaps think that such was the case in that age already, although old cult-customs were not forgotten." Moreover he continues: "Further when epics were transferred to a colonial country and there remodelled and reshaped, I am very willing to believe that the fact that in this country no old tombs existed and the cult of the ancestors was cut off added to the emphasizing of the honorific side of funeral customs to such a degree that their religious meaning was quite forgotten and the dead were believed to be mere shadows."

Thus the old explanation is not given up, but finds its place alongside the modifications which further excavation and study have rendered necessary. Epic tradition is something which lasts for hundreds of years. In the *Iliad* we have the fruits of such tradition gathered up and crystallized into one magnificent poem, possibly by the genius of one man. The elements from which the poet wrought this work belong to different periods, and side by side with memories of the heroic age in which they began to take shape are the newer traditions of the colonizing Ionians among and for whom he composed the song of the Wrath of Achilles.

A point which has been made much of since Rohde's time, and especially in the work of Nilsson, is that the broadest divisions in Greek religion have a racial basis. It is of course no recent discovery that the historical Greeks represented a fusion between a Mediterranean people and a race of invaders from North or East: but recent years have added something to our knowledge of how, when and where this fusion took place. Much remains, and will probably always remain, uncertain, but the problem has been approached from all sides—by philologists working on the distribution of dialects or discovering that the percentage of non-Greek words in the Greek language was higher than had originally been supposed; by archaeologists sifting material remains and studying in them the relations between Minoan, Mycenean and later Greek civilizations; by religious historians and by ethnologists—and their efforts have not been entirely fruitless. Professor Nilsson has shown a genius for synthesis in producing from the results in these divers fields a picture of the early age of Greece which, at least in its broad outlines, is unlikely to be seriously challenged. This picture may be seen in *Homer and Mycenae*, from which I quote one sentence (p. 80): "The great antitheses in Greek religion are of a racial character, the emotional and mystical forms of religion being of pre-Greek origin."[1]

The elucidation of the emotional and mystical forms of Greek religion, their contrast with the religion of the Olympians, the interaction of the two and their respective contributions to the whole religious outlook of the Greeks, have been a leitmotiv of this book. I referred at the outset (pp. 28 f.) to the importance of racial considerations, and it is natural to return to them at the close. I suggested (p. 31) that although the contrast between Greek and pre-Greek elements in the population might account for much, it was an explanation which must be used with caution and would not necessarily cover every case. Having quoted that explanation in its most downright form, I should like in conclusion to suggest two modifications, or ways in which the recommended caution may be exercised.

First, in explaining a religious attitude it is more helpful to look at the circumstances in which its representatives lived, and the class in society to which they belonged, than to their race. Naturally the two may coincide, and must inevitably coincide when the society under consideration is one in which one race has in comparatively recent times overrun and subdued another. The ruling and wealthy class is of one race, the servants and tillers of the soil are of another. But if we are seeking causes, it is to the contrast between the lives that they lead, rather than to a contrast of racial characteristics, that the differences between their religious

[1] Nilsson is referring here to an expression of opinion in his own earlier work, *Min.-Myc. Rel.* (p. 559), but he repeats it without essential qualification.

outlook and habits is primarily to be assigned. The one class lives in palaces. For all menial or unpleasant tasks it commands the services of the other. It has precious metals and skilled craftsmen at its disposal. It has leisure to develope a cult of beauty and of that athletic and warlike prowess which has brought it to its present enviable position. Moreover by the fact of having recently invaded the land in which they are now settled, these people are already cut off from the ancestral cults of fertility which no doubt existed among their own race as among others.

The race which they have conquered, on the other hand, must now live a life of toil, subjection and longing. The idea of justice, for which their souls cry out, is likely to find a place in their religion. Their present miseries make them place their hopes in a better hereafter, a reversal of the attitude of their rulers, for whom the present holds such pleasures that they look upon any form of future life as little as possible, and only, if they must contemplate it, with feelings of loathing. Moreover in satisfying these aspirations the subject race has means to hand, for it is bound to the soil, and consequently has preserved alive what is lost to its conquerors, a multitude of cults of the gods or daemons of fertility. These spirits are very close to their worshippers. They dwell in the earth of their own fields, the earth in which they themselves will lie at death, and it is in the worship of these spirits that we have found the germs of mystical religion with its belief in some form of communion between god and man.

In the second place it is necessary to remind ourselves that we still know little of the history of the incursions of Greek-speaking peoples into Greece. The period when they first began to come, the question, that is, to which of the successive periods of civilization revealed by the archaeological discoveries (which are the sole evidence) must be assigned the first appearance of Greek tribes, is by no means settled. Probably most archaeologists would put it in the Middle Helladic period, say 2000–1800 B.C. Yet the state of our knowledge is still such that an extremely competent but cautious-minded scholar could write in 1935 (and would probably repeat it to-day): "There is nothing in the archaeological evidence nor in the tradition to establish as certain, or even as probable, the view that there was any invasion, between, say, 3000 and 1100 B.C., which radically affected culture, though there may have been less important wars and invasions, by alien or kindred peoples."[1]

If then we may accept, as I should be prepared to do, Nilsson's well-attested view that in writing of his Achaeans Homer was describing in the main the society of the Mycenean kings of which we possess such striking material remains, we must admit that we know little of the racial composition of their predecessors in Greece. The probability (I should say the certainty) is that they were almost the last of a series of waves of Greek tribes which had been penetrating the peninsula, either by conquest or by peaceful infiltration, for many hundreds of years. The language of the country had probably for centuries been Greek. Yet their Greek-speaking subjects may have seemed to them entirely foreign and may indeed have been largely assimilated in character and physical type, and perhaps wholly in religion, to the original inhabitants of the country.

To sum up, our second point gives reason for accepting only with certain reservations the view that the contrasting types of religion in Greece are to be explained by assuming that one type belonged to the Greeks as such, the northern invading peoples, and the other exclusively to the autochthonous inhabitants of the Aegean basin. Yet this view contains, if not all the truth, at least some of it, and if the necessary reservations and admissions of ignorance seem to detract from its value as an explanation, our first point comes to our aid: for our first point suggests that even if the racial facts are true, where religion is in question a better explanation is provided by social than by ethnical considerations.

[1] A. W. Gomme in *European Civilization* (ed. Eyre), i (Oxford, 1935), 536. Professor Gomme's scepticism perhaps goes too far, but is a healthy corrective. After giving a very necessary emphasis to the scantiness of the evidence, composed of (*a*) archaeological finds and (*b*) later tradition, on which our knowledge of these matters rests, he says, for instance: "It is unscientific to divide Greek civilization, and in particular Greek religion, into two elements and label the one Indo-European, Hellenic, late, the other non-Indo-European, non-Hellenic, Aegean, corresponding to the two (as though there could be only two) racial elements in the country; still more, to say when the former was introduced, or even that it is later than the other. . . . There had been an Indo-European conquest of Greece, but of quite uncertain date."

Appendix to Chapter X

I append a rough enumeration of the most important ideas relating to the fate of the dead which we have so far considered, and which may be expected to have played their part in forming the probably hazy notions of the ordinary Greek of the fifth century. The part played by each in the mind of any individual would vary, as it does to-day, according to temperament.

1. HOMER. *Rule*: Shadow existence regarded with abhorrence by the living. He also knows of *translation without death*—not an exception to the rule because soul and body remain united. Qualification for this is nobility of birth. Such men have no special power over, or interest in, the living, therefore no cult.

Apparent exception: The sacrifices accorded to the dead Patroklos. Significance of this as a custom surviving when its original motive has been lost.

2. HESIOD. (pp. 298 f.) (*a*) Knows of *daimones* who are for him the souls of the dead of a past age, retaining power and influence over the living. Evidence for a primitive belief almost lost in Homer, but surviving in a secluded agricultural district. (*b*) He also has the purely poetic idea of translation to the Islands of the Blest. (*b*) is derived from Homer, (*a*) from popular cult.

3. STORIES OF TRANSLATION BENEATH THE EARTH. These are very different from the Homeric translation to Elysium, because the translated were *local* (not ἐς πείρατα γαίης) and accessible to the living, therefore received cult and prayers. Some at least of the heroes of these stories were probably ancient earth-deities transformed by epic into heroes. Examples are Trophonios of Lebadeia (above, pp. 223 ff.) and Amphiaraos of Thebes (for whom see, in classical literature, Eur. *Suppl.* 925 ff.).

4. HEROES. (pp. 231 ff.) Souls which remained powerful after death had separated them from body. A form of ancestor-worship only accorded to persons of special distinction. Heroes are helpers or avengers of the living (cf. Aesch. *Cho.* and stories of national heroes), but their own happiness is hardly in question. This cannot have contributed much to the origins of a belief in a

blessed immortality for all souls by virtue of the actualization of their own higher nature.

5. CULT OF SOULS IN GENERAL. Denied by Homeric religion, but older than it and only temporarily suppressed by it. (Cf., e.g., the Anthesteria formula, p. 276 above.)

6. ELEUSIS. (pp. 281 ff.) Initiation (open to all) promised *better* future life to those who underwent it. Future existence was presupposed, only its quality affected. Absence of exclusiveness, intolerant demands or other-worldliness. On the whole it did not do much to undermine the widespread Hellenic belief in a gulf between gods and men which it was *hybris* to attempt to bridge.

7. DIONYSOS, a comparative newcomer, brought *true mysticism* into Greek religion. (Ch. VI.) The ordinary Greek mentality was inclined to empty his worship of the promise of immortality which it logically carried, but could not do so for ever. It tended to an amalgamation with that of APOLLO, which itself probably contained already the germs of a mystical conception of the relation between men and gods (Ch. VII). Apollo contributed his own elements of *ekstasis*, ecstatic prophecy, and *katharsis*.

Chapter XI

THE ORPHICS

INTRODUCTORY NOTE

The question of the existence of something called Orphism, and, if it exists, its nature, is one of the most hotly disputed in the field of Greek religion. In the past it has been approached with a lack of critical sense which has now brought its inevitable reaction, illustrated by the angry remark of Wilamowitz: "Die Modernen reden so entsetzlich viel von Orphikern." In 1935 I published a detailed study of the subject under the title of *Orpheus and Greek Religion*. Since then scholarship has not stood still, and apart from articles (among which may be especially mentioned for its general interest M. P. Nilsson's "Early Orphism and Kindred Religious Movements" in *Harv. Theol. Rev.* xxviii (1935), 181 ff.), we have seen one full-length book by a scholar of wide learning and critical judgment; that is, I. M. Linforth's *The Arts of Orpheus* (California Univ. Press and Cambridge U. P., 1941). The reader may also be referred to the work of P. Boyancé in *Le Culte des Muses chez les Philosophes Grecs* (Paris, 1937), Part I. On the whole, while accepting correction on a number of points of detail, I am inclined to retain the same general view of the subject which I took earlier. Such inferences as I drew from our fragmentary material, as to the existence of a particular synthesis made by people teaching in the name of Orpheus, still seem to me to be largely legitimate, and in so far as criticism has taken an even more sceptical turn it induces a horrid fear that the pendulum, having swung to an opposite extreme, may swing again and land us once more in the state of things of which Wilamowitz so justly complained. The reality of this danger seems to me apparent already in conversation with other classical scholars.

It is clearly in the interests of the readers of this book to avoid academic controversy as far as possible. The object of these introductory words is not to strike a controversial note, but simply to prepare the reader for two things: (*a*) that whatever is said here about the Orphics must be regarded as one person's view which would not necessarily find universal acceptance, (*b*) that a certain change of approach in this chapter is inevitable. It will not be possible to proceed straight to a descriptive account, taking the evidence as we come to it, without first making clear the method of inquiry which has been followed and the nature of the evidence at our disposal.

I. Method

WE have now made a brief résumé of some of the most important elements in Greek religion of which the average fifth-century Athenian may be supposed to have been aware, and between which he might make his choice, with no restriction save that imposed by his own character and predilections. We must beware however of assuming that there was in his mind any question of choice, of an "either—or". He must pay homage to the gods and take part in their feasts and sacrifices. But a new god might easily be adopted by the tolerant Greek, and an old god take on new characteristics. Apollo's character developed remarkably during his tenure of the Delphic shrine. Dionysos stood for a very different conception of religion from that associated with the Olympian Zeus. Yet if the temperament of a particular citizen inclined him to devote himself particularly to the Delphic religion or the Dionysiac, or to follow Homer in an unquestioning conservatism, whichever way his conscience led him there was no occasion for heart-searchings and dramatic revulsion of feelings. He would show his preference for one without denying the others. Intolerance between them was out of the question, however much to the modern mind the different gods may seem to stand for different types of religious experience.

One consequence of this is that we can only fall into error if we are always looking for logic or consistency in Greek religion. To do so is natural now that it has become a subject of study and research, but a very little reflection should save us from the mistake. It would not be hard in fact to find similar inconsistencies among those of us who attend the same church to-day, although we share a common basis of doctrine to a far greater extent than did the Greeks. Indeed the word religion could go out of use if it stood for something that could be entirely accounted for by rational and consistent thought, since all that it represents could be expressed by other terms—philosophy, ethics or metaphysics. If religion is anything, it is an experience which transcends thought.

Yet there will always be some, within the ranks of the believers, whom a more rational temperament leads to account by their reason for as much as they can, without thereby denying the mystery which must always lie behind. The religion of a Dr. Inge will show more internal consistency than that of the majority of churchgoers. In Greece also there were those who looked on the confusion, whose haphazard growth had been the result of anything but philosophic thought, and with the minds of religious philosophers sought to form a synthesis which should at the same time present a coherent system of doctrine and practice and give satisfaction to certain deep spiritual longings. This is how I see the Orphic writers, and for this reason I have left them until we have already made ourselves acquainted with some of the different conceptions which overlaid and overlapped each other in the minds of the Greeks, like geological strata in a place where some ancient upheaval of the earth's surface has disturbed the neat symmetry of their chronological order. They are the given material on which, as a conscious religious reformer, the Orphic writer worked.

The words Orphism and Orphics are familiar to many, but few could give an account of what they signify. They find frequent mention in works on Greek or comparative religion, but their meaning has seldom been investigated with sufficient attention to method and a proper use of material, and the whole subject has been brought into well-merited discredit. For a full discussion of the evidence, the reader who is sufficiently interested in the matter for its own sake may be referred to the works mentioned at the beginning of this chapter. For our present purposes, a brief outline must suffice, enough, let up hope, to allay the feelings of exasperation which have been roused so often in readers of Greek literature by the vague references of commentators to "Orphic influence". I shall try, first, to give some grounds for believing that the expression "Orphic religion" has meaning, and secondly to indicate what that meaning is. The evidence is scanty, and inference must play its part. I shall try to employ it soberly, without pretending that everyone would agree with all the conclusions reached, or that the truth can ever be fully known.

First, then, as to method. Everyone has noticed that there is a certain common body of doctrine, largely eschatological, to be observed in various writings of the sixth to the fourth centuries B.C. Empedocles, some of the great myths of Plato, certain passages of Pindar and the gold plates from South Italian graves[1] are the most outstanding examples. The resemblance extends sufficiently into details to be striking, even though it may not do to press for

[1] Cf. pp. 321 f. below.

unity on a precise point like the number of incarnations necessary to secure apotheosis. Clearly none of these writers was inventing the main scheme; they were relying on a common source. This, incidentally, takes away much of the force of something that is often claimed, namely that when a quotation from a poem of "Orpheus" in a Neoplatonist or other writer of a later generation reflects the same doctrines, it is simply a borrowing from Empedocles, or whomever it most resembles. We may grant that the form of the poem owes something to Empedocles—it is this verbal character of the imitation, where it exists, that gives the critics at first sight such an indisputable case—but the thought did not come in the first place from him, since it was not from Empedocles that Pindar took his eschatological passages, nor yet Plato nor the writer of the verses which were copied on to the gold plates. There was some other source common to all.

It next occurs to us that, granted this, the common source may be no compact body of doctrine which one can isolate at all, still less dignify with the label "Orphic", but simply a floating mass of popular belief which was the inheritance of every Greek. It would be caught up by some and ignored by others according as it did or did not appeal either to their religious consciousness (as articles of faith) or to their aesthetic sense (as material for poetry). Certainly a belief in transmigration, which is the central doctrine, is not confined to any particular sect or country. Against this we may point, first, to the strikingly detailed nature of some of the resemblances, arguing not merely a vague mass of popular tradition as the common source, but a system deliberately constructed *out of* popular tradition to convey a particular message (which is not the same thing, although a large part of its material may be the same);[1] second, to the existence of one obvious written system which could have been responsible, namely the Orphic writings. It cannot be denied that a body of writings under the name of Orpheus was well known to the classical authors, and that their subjects seem to fit them well enough to play this role. Plato speaks of a mass of books attributed to Orpheus and Musaios (usually referred to as a son or disciple of Orpheus), whose subject is purification and the after-life. He also quotes hexameters, mainly theogonical, as being "of Orpheus". In Euripides, the follower of Orpheus and of the ascetic life is the respecter of

[1] I am aware that the subjective must enter largely into the evaluation of these resemblances. For examples of them see, e.g., *Orph. and Gr. Rel.* pp. 175 ff.

"many writings". Aristotle, though he did not believe in a historical Orpheus, knew of theories of the soul contained in "the so-called Orphic verses". Euripides, Aristophanes, and the author of the speech against Aristogeiton know Orpheus as the author of *teletai*, for the double definition of which we may perhaps follow the *Etymologicum Magnum*: "A sacrifice of a mystical character; but Chrysippos says that it is right to give the name *teletai* to accounts of divine matters."[1]

We now look at the passages in Plato referred expressly to Orpheus or his followers,[2] and find that they contain references to an ascetic way of life, to the assertion that the body is the prison or the tomb[3] of the soul, salvation by initiation, bliss for the just and punishment for the unjust, and related ideas. These are our anchors. Having found them, we notice their context. We may even, without relinquishing our caution, allow ourselves to connect a passage in another dialogue which speaks of the same doctrines, although in this second instance Orpheus is not mentioned. For instance, if the idea of the soul being something incarcerated in the body as in a prison or tomb[3] is Orphic in the *Cratylus*, it is scarcely rash to attribute it to the same source when it occurs in the *Phaedo* (62b) and the *Gorgias* (493a). In the former it is ascribed by Plato to "a secret *logos*", and in the latter to "a clever mythologist, perhaps some Sicilian or Italian", thus turning our minds to the country of the gold plates with their eschatological verses, as well as of several reputed authors of Orphic poems. From

[1] Plato, *Rep.* 364e, *Crat.* 402b, *Phileb.* 66c, Eur. *Hipp.* 954, Aristotle, *de an.* 410b28, Aristophanes, *Frogs*, 1032, [Dem.] *in Aristog.* 25, 11. Other passages could be quoted.

[2] *οἱ ἀμφὶ Ὀρφέα*. Cf. the expressions *οἱ ἀμφὶ Πρωταγόραν, οἱ περὶ Ἡράκλειτον*, to denote the schools or followers of Protagoras and Herakleitos (*Theaet.* 170c, *Crat.* 440c).

[3] Linforth (*Arts*, p. 147) has objected, following Wilamowitz, that in the *Cratylus* passage the only interpretation of *σῶμα* attributed to the Orphics is that which derives it from *σῴζω* and equates it with *δεσμωτήριον*, prison. The derivation from *σῆμα* is ascribed vaguely to "certain persons" (*τινες*). This is true, but the objection would have more force if there were any substantial difference between the two expressions. In fact they are only two equally natural metaphors to express the same doctrine, that the soul is alien to the body, which hinders and represses it, and longs to be set free. Death is not, as is commonly thought, a calamity, but a release of the soul (as from prison) or the beginning of its true life (like a rising from the tomb). If *σῶμα-σῆμα* is a Pythagorean phrase, as Wilamowitz with good reason claimed, this only goes to confirm the impossibility of separating Orphism from the religious beliefs of the Pythagoreans. Cf. *Orph. and Gr. Rel.*, pp. 216 ff., and below, pp. 316 f.

In *Phaedo*, 62b it might be argued that *φρουρά* has its other sense of "guard-duty", but this is unlikely. It probably implies incarceration, as in *Gorgias*, 525a. Cicero paraphrased the passage: "nec tamen illa vincula carceris ruperit, sed . . . a deo evocatus atque emissus exierit" (*Tusc.* i, 30, 74), and Olympiodorus equated the word with *δεσμός* (Kern, *Orph. Fr.* 220, p. 238).

these other passages we may learn a little more about the same doctrines. This method would be much more dangerous if we could not assume from the outset that there was a body of Orphic writings known to Plato, containing of course (and this cannot be too often emphasized) ingredients culled from here and there, but nevertheless an elaborate and in some degree sophisticated attempt to form a coherent picture of the divine ordering of the universe and the position and fate of man. Fortunately this need not be doubted, and what obviously hangs together with the passages attributed to Orpheus or his followers may be taken as Orphic. I have omitted the use of Neoplatonic commentators, because they are so obviously and rightly open to suspicion, but may not even they be occasionally allowed to help? For instance, when Plato quotes a slightly distorted hexameter line in which the true initiate of Bacchos is distinguished from the mere acolyte, and refers it to "those skilled in the mysteries", and Olympiodorus cites this as an example of the fact that Plato "is full of echoes of the writings of Orpheus", it would surely be hypercritical to doubt the commentator's word.[1]

Having decided in this way on the unquestionably Orphic passages in Plato, we form from them as coherent and complete an account as we can. There are many gaps, which must not be bridged out of the imagination. We then collate this account with those in other writers which seem to be similar, of which Empedocles provides the chief. If the resemblances are sufficient to warrant the assumption of a common source (as I believe they are), the account of Empedocles may be used to supplement that of Plato and bring us yet nearer to a conception of what the original doctrine of the Orphic poems may have been. I need not emphasize the delicacy of this work, nor the pitfalls to which it may expose us. Neither Plato nor Empedocles was "an Orphic". Each was using the poems for his own purposes, and all that he wrote was moulded by his own philosophical aims. If I may anticipate, the conclusion that I reach is that they were drawing on poems which had worked out an elaborate and consistent scheme of purgatory, paradise and final apotheosis, and the variations in their own accounts were due to the requirements of the original philosophical genius of each.

[1] *Phaedo*, 69c, Olympiod. *in Phaed.* 70c (Kern, *Orph. Fr.* 224).

II. Why Orpheus?

Plato introduces an Orphic doctrine with the words: "They who tell it are those among priestly men and women who make it their business to be able to give an account of [or reasons for] what they undertake."[1] That is the first general characteristic to be noticed about these people. Their aim was "to account for their actions". To accomplish this aim they wrote religious books. Being anxious, as Plato says, to give an account of their religion, they became the authors of sacred *logoi*. Our earliest hint that this was a practice of the Orphics is the well-known passage of Herodotus (ii, 81) in which, after mentioning certain ritual prohibitions which he has noticed among the Egyptians, he remarks that they are in agreement with Orphic and Bacchic doctrine, "though in fact they are Egyptian and Pythagorean". "There is", he adds, "a sacred *logos* about them." References to these *logoi* occur several times in Plato, and often show from their content that they are the work of teachers of the same doctrines. A good example is in the seventh letter: "We must ever maintain a real belief in the ancient and sacred *logoi*, which proclaim that our soul is immortal, and has judges, and pays full requital for its deeds, as soon as a man has left the body behind."[2] These *logoi* must have been a "Bible" in a very real sense. In comparison with them, the Homeric epics are not sacred literature. They are narrative poems, mirroring, as good narrative must, the state of a whole society, including of course its religion. But they are not didactic, and didactic is the essence of a *hieros logos*. Yet it is the epics, and not these *logoi*, which have come to be called "the Bible of the Greeks". And this is right, for by an irony of history it was more than any other single factor the Homeric poems that shaped the religion of the ordinary man. He acknowledged no other, for the *hieroi logoi* completely failed to capture his imagination. The Greek genius was not dogmatic. The Orphics were dogmatists, and they remained exceptional. They were running counter to the spirit of their age by trying to inculcate a book-religion, whose tenets (though they might originally have been drawn from who knows what sources of popular tradition) were set and hardened in the mould of a mass of religious poetry. Since

[1] ὅσοις μεμέληκε περὶ ὧν μεταχειρίζονται λόγον οἵοις τ' εἶναι δίδοναι (*Meno*, 81a).
[2] *Ep.* vii, 335a. Cf. *Phaedo*, 69c, 70c, *Laws*, 715e.

these books were supposed, not in all probability to have been written by Orpheus, but to have been inspired by him, it was a religion bestowed by authority that his followers were asked to accept.

It is usual to draw a distinction between Orpheus and the Orphics, between the character and legends of the great singer himself and the religious movement which borrowed the authority of his name. This is of course necessary. Orpheus appears in legend as a prehistoric dweller in Thrace, the representative of a generation older than Homer. We cannot imagine that the Orphic religion was of great antiquity or that it arose in Thrace. It belonged to the climate of thought of the sixth century, as a brief account of its doctrines will I hope make clear; and only two places can put in a strong claim to have been its original home—Athens, the home of Onomakritos, which claimed to have had the mysteries of Orpheus revealed to her, and South Italy, the home of Pythagoreanism and of writers of Orphic poems.[1]

Nevertheless it can scarcely be wrong, having made that point clear, to take Orpheus himself as the starting-point for a discussion of those who were known to Plato and others as his followers. It can scarcely be that the two have nothing in common, and it is pertinent to ask the question: Why was Orpheus chosen as the patron of the movement? Let us look first of all at those legends which seem to be his own and do not implicate him in the activities of sixth-century mystics. It may be that they will suggest a possible answer.

Most prominent is his connexion with Apollo, whom in many ways he resembled. The musical skill by which he is known to everyone—which has inspired generations of European poets—goes back to the earliest records of antiquity. Beyond two words of Ibykos, the earliest known literary references to him must be those of Aeschylus and Pindar. Aeschylus in the *Agamemnon* refers to him as the man who charmed all nature with his song. His music reminds us at once of the lyre-god, and Pindar, to whom he is "the lyre-player, father of lays", makes Apollo his patron.[2] The resemblance is closer than is sometimes thought. The picture of the wild beasts gathering round in docile fashion to listen to the

[1] *Orph. and Gr. Rel.*, pp. 46, 217.

[2] *Agam.* 1630, Pindar, *Pyth.* iv, 177: ἐξ Ἀπόλλωνος δὲ φορμιγκτὰς ἀοιδᾶν πατὴρ ἔμολεν, εὐαίνητος Ὀρφεύς.

music suggests Orpheus to us, and the passage in Euripides where Apollo is the centre of a similar scene is not, I think, often quoted: "About thee were gathering, for the joy of thy song, the dappled lynxes, and the tawny troop of lions left their glen upon Othrys, and danced around thy lyre, O Phoibos."[1] The music of Orpheus, like Apollo's, is the calm, soothing note of the lyre. He has nothing to do with the wild din of Phrygian flutes and cymbals.

This devotion to Apollo, and aversion from Dionysos, finds early illustration in the plot of Aeschylus' lost play the *Bassarids*. In this play, we are told, Orpheus worshipped the sun, whom he identified with Apollo, and, living in Thrace, he used to ascend its mountain Pangaion each morning in order to greet him at his rising. This angered Dionysos, who sent the Bassarids, a troop of maenads, to tear him in pieces.[2]

The story may seem at first sight to fall into line with the whole class of legends which tell of opposition to Dionysos on the part of a Hellene and of the appropriate vengeance taken by the god. Such were the stories of Pentheus of Thebes or the women of Argos.[3] But these stories, where a Hellene is the protagonist, reflect the progress of Dionysos through Greece. The resistance offered is to his invasion of their country, and the scene is Thebes, Argos, Orchomenos, Attica. The legend of Orpheus puts beyond doubt the strange circumstance that he was a Hellene living in Thrace, offering opposition to Dionysos in his own native land. His whole character, his calm and civilized air, his resemblance to, and championship of, the Hellenic Apollo and his opposition to the Thracian religion make it impossible that he should have been imagined as a barbarian. Yet he lives in Thrace. It is Pangaion that he climbs to worship Apollo. Vase paintings of the fifth century, which are among our earliest evidence for Orpheus, show the same state of affairs. Orpheus is playing his lyre to an audience of men, and although they are wearing obvious Thracian dress, Orpheus himself is clothed as a Greek. The cloaks and peaked caps of the Thracians serve to emphasize both the Greekness of the player and the foreignness of his surroundings.[4] Later writers admittedly speak freely of him as "the Thracian", and so, once or twice, does Euripides. But it is fair to say that the earlier the evidence the more it lays stress on his being a Hellene and a

[1] *Alc.* 578 ff. [2] Kern, *Orph. Fr.*, p. 33. [3] Discussed above, pp. 165 ff.

[4] The reference is particularly to the red-figured Attic vase in Berlin, illustrated in *Orph. and Gr. Rel.*, pl. 6.

worshipper of Apollo; and since he was adopted, probably in the sixth century, by men who took Dionysos for their god, though they modified his worship profoundly, this, coupled with the fact that, barbarian or Hellene, his home was in Thrace, was sufficient to make it natural for later tradition to refer to him simply as a Thracian.

The early tradition of Orpheus as a kind of Hellenic missionary in Thrace certainly singles him out from the common run of mythological figures. So does the alternative tradition about his death, that the women of Thrace murdered him on their own account, without the instigation of Dionysos, being moved by jealousy because he excluded them from his rites (another typically Hellenic trait!) and enticed their husbands away from them. Whether these peculiarities are sufficient to warrant the conclusion that he was a historical figure, I gladly leave for others to decide. At present it is his religious connexions that interest us, and these show, I think, that his adoption by the Orphic sectaries was due to something more than a vague feeling of reverence for a great name of antiquity. There were elements in his character which warranted it.

Sixth-century religious and philosophic thought (as distinct from popular religion) was dominated by one central problem, the problem of the One and the Many. This appeared in two forms, one referring to the macrocosm, the other to the microcosm. In its first form it was the problem of the Milesian natural philosophers, who asked: "What is the relation between the manifold variety of the world in which we live and the one primary substance out of which, as we are convinced, it must in the first place have arisen?" In its second form it was the problem of the religious minds of the age. Their question was: "What is the relation of each individual man to the divine, to which we feel we are akin, and how can we best realize and actualize the potential unity which underlies the two?"[1]

The Ionians had little interest in the aspirations of the religious mind. The Orphics were not interested in the origin of the cosmos except in so far as it explained the relations between man and god, and were content with a purely mythical explanation. Pythagoras,

[1] The two sides find a meeting-point in the "air" theories of a philosopher like Diogenes of Apollonia, according to which the soul of man, consisting as it does of air, is *μικρὸν μόριον τοῦ θεοῦ*. These speculations were of great use to the religious thinkers, as is explained in Chapter V.

with his amazing breadth of outlook, endeavoured to embrace both, and to construct a system, involving both thought and conduct, which should at the same time provide a rational explanation of the paradox of the universe and satisfy the religious craving for union with the divine. That is the relation between them, and since all these movements arose roughly simultaneously, since moreover we have to rely for much of our information about them on testimony of at least slightly later date, it can scarcely be profitable to inquire further into the details of which of them borrowed from the other.

At present it is the religious teachers who concern us. It was obvious that the problem of the One and the Many in their own sphere, that is, the problem of the union of human and divine, was not going to be solved by the average man's conception of religion, with its dependence on Homeric tradition. Among existing forms of religion, the best hope of a solution seemed to be offered by the Dionysiac, in which by means of ecstasy and frenzy the puny, individual human soul felt itself lifted out of its loneliness so that at the height of its passionate experience it could call itself Bacchos, one with the god by whom it was inspired. Yet the *orgia* of Dionysos, as they were practised in Greece, fell short of the ideal which these religious reformers had set themselves. As I have tried to show, they failed to break through the resistance of the Hellenic mind and demonstrate that the human soul was potentially divine and immortal and could be made so actually for all eternity. The Greeks, with their mentality of θνητὰ φρονεῖν—mortal thoughts for mortals—sought nothing further from the ritual than a temporarily uplifting experience. For the Orphic, on the other hand, this belief in the latent divinity and immortality of the human soul was central.

In the second place, the Orphic might believe in possession by the god, and communion with him, as a means of attaining salvation, but he did not regard them as enough. He laid great stress on the importance of purity, holding indeed that it was necessary not only on certain specified occasions (as the Eleusinian initiates purified themselves at the festival before initiation), but throughout life. Orphic *katharsis* was an elaborate system of rules which had to be observed continually. It was nothing less than a καθαρὸς βίος, a pure life, which they demanded.

These then were the two things that the Orphic wished to preach: (*a*) a belief in the essential immortality and divinity of the human soul, (*b*) the necessity for constant ritual purity if that immortality were not to be forfeited. The first was to be found in the religion of the original Thracian Dionysos, the second in that of Apollo.

It would be impossible to say with any assurance how much of the character of Orpheus has accrued to him as the result of his adoption by these sectarians. The legends that I have mentioned have, in my opinion, all the appearance of being older than that adoption, but whatever may have been their origin, I should claim that there is an essential connexion between the character and legends of Orpheus and the character of the Orphic religion, and that the legends do throw light upon the aims of his followers. For Orpheus, according to our earliest evidence, is the Hellene in Thrace, messenger of the spirit of Apollo in the land of the wild worshippers of Zalmoxis, "who believe themselves to be immortal". Their religion he tried to modify by introducing the worship of Apollo, and in the attempt he met his death. The story throws light upon the Orphic religion because that is exactly what, in its main features, it stood for, a blend of the Thracian belief in immortality with Apolline ideas of *katharsis*. From the one it took *ekstasis*, enthusiasm and a deep spiritual hope; from the other a formalizing influence, an almost legal atmosphere of rules and regulations. The fusion would have been unnatural and difficult were it not that, as has been pointed out earlier in this book, *ekstasis* in one of its forms was already at home among the servants of Apollo.

III. Outline of Orphic Doctrine

Having claimed the not undisputed right to assume the existence of an Orphic system, and indicated its general aims, we are left with the task of giving an outline of its main tenets. This may be done briefly if it is done without the full discussion of the evidence which is available elsewhere, and that is all that can be attempted here. The important thing to bear in mind is that its achievement was one of synthesis, in which many existing elements of religion were combined into a somewhat different whole. Of these elements the two chief were those just mentioned. Others may be recognized as we proceed, since we are already familiar with so much of the background against which its authors worked.

First should come the theogony, but it must be prefaced with the caution that our knowledge of it depends almost entirely on authors of post-Aristotelian date, of whom the majority are Neoplatonists. Their evidence therefore has to be accepted with the greatest caution. The most persuasive argument for believing that their quotations from Orphic poems are in the main genuine (that is, the same in content as those which were already known to Plato) is that they seem to reflect the climate of thought of the sixth and fifth centuries B.C. rather than that of the writers who quote them, and who frequently have in their comments to twist their meaning in the most unnatural ways to make them fit their own philosophical outlook.[1] The poems are dominated by the problem of the One and the Many, in what seems to me its classical form. Much of the theogonical material is borrowed from Hesiod, and there are tags of Homer as well, but where they are original it is that problem that has occasioned their departure from the main stream of Greek tradition.

The first great god is Eros, also called by the Orphics Phanes, a figure who is clearly parodied by Aristophanes in the *Birds*.[2] He springs from the primal Egg which had been fashioned in the *aither* by Time, a conception foreign to the Hesiodic theogony. As Love, he is the principle of generation, by whom the other gods and the whole world are created. The world created by Phanes is not however the present one, for a curious episode follows whereby Zeus, who as every good Greek knew is the ruler of this world, swallows Phanes and his whole creation with him, and creates the world anew. This fantastic story is a mythological counterpart to the speculations of the natural philosophers about the production of the manifold world out of unity. In his mythological apparatus the Orphic invented as little as possible, for the incident of the swallowing is matched by many stories, notably by the way in which, according to Hesiod, Zeus swallowed his wife Metis before the miraculous birth of Athena. Yet through these crude folk-tales a new idea is set forth, the idea that the god who rules the world is also its creator.

The central part of the theogony is that which accounts for the origin of mankind, for on this depends the hope of salvation. The story is familiar. Less familiar is the fact that it is not attested by any writer earlier than Clement of Alexandria. It is the story of the killing of Dionysos by the Titans, the old giants who were the enemies of the gods of Zeus' generation. They gave toys to

[1] Cf. *Orph. and Gr. Rel.* 74 ff.

[2] Lines 693 ff.; *Orph. and Gr. Rel.* 92, 95 f.

the infant god, and while his attention was thus distracted set on him, killed him and feasted on his flesh. Zeus hurled a thunderbolt to burn them up, and from the soot arose the race of men. We are therefore a compound of divine and earthly nature (the Titans were sons of Ge), and it is our duty to cultivate the Dionysiac and suppress the Titanic element in our nature. The heart of Dionysos was saved by Athena. She brought it to Zeus, and from it he caused Dionysos to be reborn. According to Pausanias, this story was the work of Onomakritos, a dealer in oracles and religious lore who lived in the Athens of the Pisistratids. Pausanias says at least: "Onomakritos took the name of the Titans from Homer and founded *orgia* of Dionysos, making the Titans into the authors of Dionysos' sufferings."[1] Although it is only known in its entirety from later sources, there is one reference in Plato to the "Titanic nature" of humankind, which is most plausibly explained by supposing that the story was known to him. He uses it as an equivalent of "the old Adam" in describing the progressive degeneration of a community, whose members show a rebellious spirit first against their parents and elders, then against the laws, and finally against all decency and the gods themselves, "displaying", as he says, "the old Titanic nature as it is called".[2]

To realize our divinity we must then cherish and cultivate the Dionysiac and purge away the evil Titanic elements in our nature. This was done in the first place by participation in *teletai* or *katharmoi*, rites of initiation or communion and of purification, whose exact nature we do not know; and in the second place by living what Plato calls an "Orphic life", in which certain rules of purity are observed. Plato is referring to the tradition of a remote past when no man tasted the flesh of living creatures, and animal sacrifice to the gods was unknown. Life then, he says, was of the sort called Orphic. This abstention from meat is the most widely attested of the Orphic injunctions, being attributed to Orpheus by Euripides and Aristophanes as well as by Plato. It is based on the belief in transmigration, for as is argued by Empedocles—a passionate believer in the Orphic life—the animal that

[1] Paus. viii, 37, 3. But cautious minds may be referred to Linforth's remarks in *The Arts of Orpheus*, pp. 350 ff.

[2] *Laws*, 701c. Another almost certain reference to the myth (though the Titans are not mentioned) was pointed out by H. J. Rose in the fragment of Pindar quoted by Plato in the *Meno* 81b–c. (See *Greek Poetry and Life* (Oxford, 1936), pp. 79 ff.) Rose has replied to Linforth's criticism of his interpretation (*Arts of Orpheus*, p. 348) in *Harvard Theol. Rev.* xxxvi (1943).

you slaughter and eat may contain the soul of your nearest relative. From the passage of Herodotus already mentioned we learn another rule observed by the Orphics, for the custom of the Egyptians which he notes as being in accord with Orphic practice is that no woollen article is to be brought into their holy places or buried with them.

From references in Plato the conclusion may be drawn that the Orphic life was intended to include moral uprightness, though it is obvious that many minds felt only the need for mechanical ritual and that there were priests who were not above trading upon their superstitious fears. One has only to think of the misuse of Orphic literature by unscrupulous quacks which is denounced in the second book of the *Republic*, or of Theophrastus' description of the superstitious man and his recourse to the *Orpheotelestai*. In the same passage of the *Republic*, explaining from what unworthy motives righteousness or justice is commonly pursued, Adeimantos condemns religious teachers who, he says, hold out the bribe of a happy immortality to the good and threaten eternal punishment to the bad, so that men turn to goodness not for its own sake, but in fear or hope for their own future state. The poets whom he mentions in this connexion are not only Homer and Hesiod, who speak occasionally in the manner of some of the Psalms about the abundance of flocks, corn and fruit which accrues to the righteous man in this life, but also Orphic writers who promise him rewards in the next world. The point of Adeimantos' argument would be lost if the posthumous rewards and punishments which they announce had reference only to ritual purity, and the existence of the Orphic life saves them therefore from the jibe which Diogenes the Cynic is said to have cast at the mysteries of Eleusis, that according to their teaching a thief would have a better lot after death than a hero like Epameinondas, simply because he had been initiated. Nevertheless we must not rate this too high. The very distinction between ritual purity and moral righteousness, which we draw so naturally, would probably not have been easily grasped by the Orphic or by any other Greek.[1]

The eschatology of the Orphic presents a complicated system of dogma, which may be partly reconstructed by a comparison of accounts or references in Plato, Empedocles and Pindar. We are also greatly helped by the discovery, already referred to, of certain

[1] This point is developed in *Orph. and Gr. Rel.*, p. 200.

thin plates of gold, inscribed with religious verses, in graves of South Italy and Crete. The inscriptions record fragments of an eschatological system closely resembling that described in Plato's myths, and in them we have actual hexameter verses, fragments of the sacred literature which served as a source for the philosophers and poets whom we know, and which has disappeared with so little trace. The date of the plates themselves makes it certain that the books from which the verses were taken must have been at least as early as the fifth century. Their value lies not so much in the contribution which such fragments can make towards the reconstruction of the system as a whole, but in the fact that they give us the actual expression of the mystic's own hope, his own cry of exultation. We see it as it was, not transmuted by the literary genius of Plato or Pindar but scribbled out in crabbed Greek and buried with the dead man, for the very practical purpose of helping and comforting him on his journey to the next world.[1]

Judging from these various sources, the Orphic beliefs seem to have been somewhat as follows. At death our souls go to Hades, the road to which, as Socrates says in the myths of the *Phaedo* and *Gorgias*, is not simple but forked. Similarly in the *Republic* we learn that the just are allowed to take the road to the right whereas the unjust are sent to the left. This is strikingly matched by the verses on the gold plates, in which the soul is greeted with the words: "Hail, hail to thee journeying the right-hand road, to holy meadows and groves of Persephone." It is also given the following instructions: "Thou shalt find to the left of the house of Hades a spring, and by the side of it standing a white cypress. To this spring approach not near. But thou shalt find another, from the lake of Memory cold water flowing forth, and there are guardians before it. Say, 'I am a child of Earth and starry Heaven. This ye know yourselves. But I am parched with thirst and I perish. Give me quickly the cold water flowing forth from the lake of Memory.' And of themselves they will give thee to drink of the holy spring, and thereafter among the other heroes thou shalt have lordship." In Plato's myth of Er, all souls destined for reincarnation are made to drink a certain amount of the water of Lethe to make them forget their experiences in the other world. Those who are wise avoid drinking too much, but this is difficult, since they have just come through the stifling heat of the barren

[1] For the gold plates see *Orph. and Gr. Rel.*, pp. 171 ff., where references to earlier literature will be found.

plain of Lethe. Naturally the soul of the Orphic is considered to have achieved its final incarnation, and will return no more to a body. Consequently it must avoid drinking of Lethe altogether. As it is made to say, "I have flown out of the sorrowful weary circle".

The whole process of the "weary circle" was something like this. A soul dies and is judged, and according to its deserts is assigned to a place of punishment or happiness. Whichever it is, the sojourn there is temporary. After a lapse of time which together with its previous earthly life completes a period of a thousand years, it is prepared for another life on earth. At this point in Plato's account occurs the episode of the choice of life. It is difficult to be certain how far this comes from his Orphic source, but probably the fact of choice was there, since the Orphic writers seem to have laid stress on personal responsibility, as in the doctrine that our impurity is inherited yet we ourselves can purge it. Then after drinking of Lethe, the soul is reborn in a mortal body, either human or animal. For the ordinary mortal it seems to have been necessary to complete the circle ten times before salvation could be hoped for. He who chose a righteous, which we may feel justified in calling an Orphic, life three times in succession probably had a special dispensation whereby he could make his escape without further trial. Plato mentions this in an Orphic setting in the *Phaedrus*, and although he arouses suspicion by conferring the dispensation on philosophers, it is mentioned also by Pindar and was therefore probably a feature of their common Orphic source. Besides these two classes there is a third, that of the sinners who are considered by the infernal judges to be incurable. These are consigned eternally to Tartarus to serve as a warning to others. They are the traditional offenders of the epic poems, legendary figures like Tantalos, Sisyphos and Tityos, and if they occurred in the Orphic writings their presence was doubtless due to an unwillingness on the part of the author to deny the authority of Homer.

Elysium, or the Islands of the Blest, though already placed by Plato not on but above the earth, is according to this doctrine only a temporary resting-place, where those who have lived a good life may enjoy the happiness that they have earned for the rest of the thousand-year cycle. At the end of it they must return to the meadow of judgment to be reborn in a mortal body and carry on the allotted circle of reincarnations. It should even be regarded as a testing-place, for Plato says that the period of happiness, without the discipline of suffering, may seduce a soul into being careless in its choice of the next earthly life. Where then does the soul go when it has finally shaken off the fetters that bind it to the earth, escaped from the grievous wheel, and in the words of the gold plates, attained its longed-for crown?

This question is naturally bound up with what the Orphics believed to be the essential nature of the soul, and here I think they added to their complex scheme an element borrowed from that part of popular belief which was being stimulated by the scientific speculation of the day. Aristotle, a good and refreshingly early authority, attributes to "the verses called Orphic" the doctrine that "the soul comes into us from the whole as we breathe, borne by the winds."[1] The Orphics, then, seem to have agreed with Anaximenes and others of the monist philosophers that our souls are composed of *aer*, at least at the time when they enter our bodies. We have seen something already of the ramifications of this belief, how *aer* might be considered as the less pure form of *aither*, or *aither* as *aer* completely purified from the taint of earthy matter. We have heard Euripides speaking of the immortal mind (*gnome*) of a man plunging into the immortal *aither*. If the soul which is due to be born or reborn into a mortal body, because it has not yet completed its cycle of purification, is said to be airy in its nature, it is likely that the completely purified soul will be thought of as aetherial, and this is what I believe to have been the culmination of the Orphic hope. He will travel beyond the lower and less pure regions of *aer* to the bright heavenly *aither*, like to like, the divine to the divine.

The eschatology of the sixth book of Virgil's *Aeneid* is often said to derive from Orphic sources, and a closer investigation of the term Orphic gives every reason for thinking the view justified. A passage in this book illustrates the two points: first the distinction between Elysium as a temporary resting-place or purgatory and a yet higher sphere as the final home of the completely purified soul; secondly the definition of these two stages as the stage of *aer* and the stage of *aither* respectively.

> Quisque suos patimur manes, exinde per amplum
> Mittimur Elysium, et pauci laeta arva tenemus
> Donec longa dies, *perfecto temporis orbe*,

[1] *de An.* i, 5, 410b27. Hicks renders τὸ ὅλον by "space". This paragraph should be read in conjunction with what is said in ch. v.

Concretam exemit labem, purumque relinquit
Aetherium sensum, atque aurai simplicis ignem.
Has omnes, *ubi mille rotam volvere per annos*,
Lethaeum ad fluvium deus evocat agmine magno,
Scilicet immemores supera ut convexa revisant
Rursus et incipiant *in corpora velle reverti.*

So Anchises to Aeneas, who has found him in the Elysian fields. A little later the place where they are talking is described as follows:

Sic tota passim regione vagantur
Aeris in campis latis, atque omnia lustrant.[1]

That was the final hope—to become one with the divine mind which is at the same time the fiery *aither*, at once the encompasser and the orderer of the universe. To it the soul is by nature akin, but sin, especially the sin of shedding blood, has cut it off, a fallen daemon as Empedocles describes himself, to be enclosed in the body which to the Orphic is nothing but a prison or a tomb. If it has knowledge and courage to work off the impurity which clings to it in the body, and afterwards as a result of its contact with the body, that will be its reward, and the judges of the underworld will greet it with the cry: "Happy and blessed one, thou art become god instead of mortal."

To avoid misunderstanding, two points about Orphism must be constantly borne in mind. First, the search for concrete phenomena like Orphic myths and Orphic rites is bound to lead to disappointment as it has often done in the past. The Orphic writer, like every Greek, was a conservative, and contentedly eclectic in his matter. This need not blind us to the singleness and originality of the thought behind it, nor to the achievement of welding the different elements into a single system. Attention should not be primarily concentrated on the myth of Phanes or the sufferings of Dionysos, but on ideas such as the disregard of the barriers of clan and state, the theories of a creator and of the divine origin of mankind.

Secondly, we are dealing with an artificially constructed doctrine embodied in sacred writings, *hieroi logoi*. All the evidence points to its having been in origin the product of a few individual

[1] *Aen.* vi, 743 ff., 886 f.

minds active over a limited period of time.[1] Thus any argument implying that Orphism was a primitive form of religion is condemned to error from the outset. Of course it caught up pre-existing myths and practices which contained primitive elements, but it transformed their significance. To speak of the origin of these myths or rites as if it were synonymous with the origin of Orphism has led to much confusion of thought. Otto Gruppe long ago led the way to the conclusion that Orphism by its nature belongs to the movement of sixth-century Greek thought, and his convincing arguments have yet to be refuted.

IV. "Orphic Influence." Was Orphism a Religion of the Lower Classes?

Finally there is the question of the extent of Orphic influence on Greek thought and literature in general. This is not the place to argue in detail whether Orphic influence is to be detected in this or that writer or circle of society. But since it is something with which the reader of the classics is certain to be confronted, even an expression of opinion may be of value, especially when it follows on an exposition of what the Orphic doctrine is likely to have been, which gives us the right to attach a certain value to one or two *a priori* judgments.

It should have emerged from our account that this was a religion which ran counter to the most typical and most cherished of Greek ideas. It was not a religion of moderation, nor one which taught men to be mindful of their mortality. On the contrary, it asserted that all men had divinity within them, and that they should strive their hardest to throw off everything else and emerge as wholly divine and immortal. It was not likely that this would be taken kindly by a people whose mentality had shown itself capable of emptying the Dionysiac religion of its original promise of immortality, speaking of his compatriots with a sort of wonder as those "who are said to do no less than make themselves immortal", and of interpreting the mysteries of Eleusis in the terminology of Homer. The conclusion that I would suggest is that the

[1] Internally, there is strong evidence in its elaboration and (considering that we only see it through a number of different distorting mirrors) consistency; externally, there are the names of Onomakritos and other Orphic writers known to tradition, and the fact that the tradition is localized, in S. Italy or Athens.

Orphics were a small band of religious devotees, with what was to most Greeks, philosophers and laymen alike, an unusual and original message to deliver. Much of their language and a few of their ideas occasionally caught the fancy of poet or philosopher, but in general the gospel which they preached with such enthusiasm and confidence—the cry "God am I, mortal no longer!"—was a cry in the wilderness, because it was a gospel for which the age was not yet ready. It may have been based on the simple idea of union with the divine, and consequent immortality, with which common people had comforted themselves from time immemorial, and which in one of its forms was raised to an enormous popularity by the mysteries of Eleusis. But there was much more to it than that, and as we know, that side of the Greek nature had been repressed by the extraordinary hegemony exercised by the Homeric poems. There were simpler and pleasanter ways than the Orphic of attaining the feeling of ecstatic union. To "pay honour to the vapours of wordy volumes" (in Euripides' words) is not a characteristic of the ordinary man. Besides the performance of a possibly inspiring ritual, the Orphic was bound to the acceptance of irksome rules in his daily life. Besides accepting a strange and complex mythology he must understand its significance, its implications of primal impurity and individual salvation by the path of self-denial. Those who invoked the name of Orpheus without accepting these consequences were mere quacks, unlikely to earn respect from the average sane and intelligent citizens of Athens.

Furthermore, until the break-up of the city-state structure of society, the Greeks had little or no conception of personal religion. Religion was run by the state in its own interests. The citizen must do his duty by it out of loyalty, as he would by any other of the state's institutions, but he was not expected to do more. Apart from any question of duty, this was the sort of religion that at the time he most appreciated and enjoyed. As a householder he also had his private Hermes and Apollo, and would see that they received the appropriate prayers and offerings. This might affect the prosperity of the family as of the state. All this however had nothing to do with what we mean by his soul. The Orphic was an individualist. His attention was concentrated on the soul, with its long series of incarnations, and his object was to save it. The purifications and abstentions which he enjoined had this entirely self-centred end in view. Being thus an influence undermining rather than supporting the life of the state, Orphism deserved in Greek eyes the name of superstition rather than religion.

On the view taken here, Orphism was not especially a religion of the lower, unprivileged classes. That conclusion is based primarily on its dogmatism and its complexity. The religion approved by the state provided an easy and comprehensible world, in which the gods required certain attentions to be paid to them, and when these duties had been discharged a man's time was his own. The gods had had their due, and might be expected to play their part in return. The search for a reason must not be carried too far. Later religious history has shown that the passive acceptance of dogma is by no means abhorrent to the ordinary man. Someone else does the thinking, and he is happy to take what he is told upon authority. On the other hand the words of a few priests crying out *against* the established tradition are not likely to have this sort of appeal. Yet even if we limit our contention, and assert that, though the dogmatic nature of Orphism did not necessarily preclude its acceptance by the popular mind, yet it does make it impossible that its original creation could have been the work of the lower classes, there is still another side to be heard. The opposite view is held, namely that if Orphism shows itself running counter to the main stream of Greek religion, the difference is between an aristocratic belief (that inherited from the Achaean nobles and therefore appealing most strongly to the upper classes) and a belief that had its origin among the poor and unprivileged. We must step warily here, for we are in danger of appearing to commit one of the greatest crimes in the eyes of modern historians by neglecting the social factor in the formation of religion.

In favour of the origin of Orphism from the lower classes, three arguments in particular have been put forward.[1] To go into them will be more than a matter of mere academic controversy, for the discussion should throw light, not so much on the religion of the Orphics (which is a minor matter), but on the character of the Hellenic mind, which it is very much our business to elucidate. Each of them raises a point of great interest. I shall follow the

[1] By H. J. Rose in his review of *Orph. and Gr. Rel.*, *C.R.* xlix (1935), 69. Professor Rose will I hope forgive me for using his brief criticisms, to which I have given considerable thought, as a peg on which to hang a discussion of wider matters as well.

example of Plato in making them into a *trikymia*, meeting first the two smaller waves and afterwards the largest and most formidable.

First comes the seemingly conscious rivalry with Homer. Homer was the spokesman of the aristocratic Achaeans. His religion was one of race, in which the thing that tells is blood. Kings rule by divine right because the blood of gods is in their veins. The pride of an aristocratic Athenian family was based on its claim that it could trace its descent to a semi-divine ancestor, taken from Homer. Clearly then a religion of the lower classes, should such a thing arise in antagonism to what already existed, would first of all have to break the authority of Homer. Those therefore who see this character in Orphism point to the fact that Orpheus was held up as the superior of Homer both in age and inspiration. He was the son of a Muse. He sailed with the Argonauts, the companion of Herakles and other heroes. His date was in the heroic age of which Homer sang, rather than the later age in which Homer himself lived.

This is true, but hardly justifies the inference drawn from it. The evidence tends rather to the conclusion, as this book has tried to bring out, that even the most ordinary and undistinguished sections of the population acquiesced to a remarkable degree in the legacy of Homer and the state religion founded upon it. To some of the best spirits of the age it was certainly failing to give satisfaction, and considering the poverty of the epic in religious ideas it is not surprising that there were those who wished to supplant it. It was conceivable to do so from other motives than material poverty and lack of privilege. But whatever the religion was, if it were expressly setting itself up against Homer (a thing unthinkable to most Greeks) it would be necessary for it to establish a hearing by demonstrating that its prophet possessed an authority at least equally venerable. Moreover, as far as the Orphics are concerned, we have already seen in the second section of this chapter other reasons why they chose to consider themselves inspired by Orpheus, which have nothing to do with any attempt to rival Homer.

The second wave consists of an interesting historical argument. There is evidence for the patronage of Orphic writers by Peisistratos and his family at Athens. Onomakritos is the most frequently cited, the most undoubtedly historical, and the only known Athenian writer of these books, and according to Herodotus was a great favourite of the tyrant and his sons. This, it is urged, was in accordance with the normal policy of tyrants, who regularly favoured the poorer and less privileged sections of the population. That this was a part of their policy is as true as that Onomakritos enjoyed the favour of the Peisistratid court; but whether there is any causal connexion between the two facts still awaits demonstration. The court of a tyrant was not composed exclusively of down-and-outs, and the onus of proof still lies the other way. We need not be confined to such negative criticism. If we must suggest another reason for the tyrants' patronage of Onomakritos, to replace the suggested one of showing favour to the lower classes, the pages of Herodotus surely provide it. Let us look at his story. The Peisistratids are at Susa persuading the Great King to invade Greece.

They had gone up there taking with them Onomakritos, an Athenian teller of oracles and the editor of the oracles of Musaios, having first patched up their quarrel with him. For he had been banished from Athens by Hipparchos the son of Peisistratos, having been caught in the act of interpolating into the verses of Musaios an oracle to the effect that the islands lying beside Lemnos would disappear beneath the sea. For this Hipparchos banished him, though previously he had shown him every mark of friendship. Now however he went up to Susa with them, and when they came into the presence of the Great King, and the Peisistratids had spun a solemn story about him, he expounded the oracles. If there was among them one which boded trouble for the Persians, of that he said nothing, but picked out for recitation all those most favourable to the enterprise.[1]

This story suggests that the motive of the Peisistratids in retaining Onomakritos at their court was not connected with their general policy of conciliating the lower classes. It was a most useful thing for a tyrant to have a tame and not too scrupulous reciter of oracles who could be relied on to interpret the will of heaven in the sense desired on any particular occasion, and no further motive need be sought.

The third wave of argument consists of reference to the other-worldly character of the Orphic message. Its kernel was its eschatology, its picture of another world in which the wrongs of this one might be redressed and eternal bliss awaited the good. Here we meet the argument from social conditions in its simplest and most *a priori* form. Those who look with longing to an after-

[1] Hdt. vii, 6.

life, where the wicked find judgment and the good are always happy, are likely to be among those who are discontented with their present lot. The prosperous, who enjoy a position of acknowledged authority over the wills of others, do not waste their time in eschatological musings.

So runs the argument, and once again there is much truth in its premisses. We have said already that the reason why the surviving part of a dead Homeric hero was such a poor weak thing was simply that his body meant so much to him and he could not conceive the point of an existence in separation from it. Different times brought different ideas. I quoted Hypereides on the reasonableness of expecting that those who died gloriously would find something good awaiting them after death. The characters of Aristophanes refer to the dead as "the blessed", which suggests a very different belief about them from the Homeric. Plato is full of passages which indicate a similar attitude and yet are obviously no more than a reflection of existing belief. There are the words of Kephalos about "the tales told of those in Hades, how the man who has done wrong here must pay the penalty there". There are Socrates' words in the *Phaedo*: "I am of good hope that there is something for the dead, and, as has been said from of old, something much better for the good than for the bad." Socrates wants to prove it, and therein he shows his difference from the rest. The belief itself was abroad already.

Expressions like these are surely in themselves sufficient indication of the attitude of those who, in the changed conditions of Greece, are no longer living a happy life and turn their eyes to the hope of a reversal of fortune after death. But these are not the Orphics. The Orphics took up these *mythoi* about rewards and punishments in Hades, and wove them into their poems. But it is impossible to believe that their system itself, with its quasi-philosophical (one might call it theosophical) elaboration, was the work of an ordinary poor and unprivileged Greek. It must for one thing have been the product of a considerable amount of leisure, and there are also more definite objections arising out of the content of the scheme itself. If one were a member of the poor and oppressed classes, indulging in eschatological dreams simply from motives of wish-fulfilment, the doctrine of transmigration and the sorrowful wheel of births would scarcely seem satisfactory. That kind of man may accept eagerly what there is every evidence that he did accept, a belief that when we die we are immediately given our deserts. That is not Orphism, though it is one piece of the material out of which Orphism was constructed.

The main hypothesis itself, that other-worldly interests belong most naturally to the poor and oppressed, is by no means universally borne out by experience. Our own age and others have seen plenty of instances to the contrary, which show that hypochondria can concern itself with the spiritual no less than the physical state, and in either manifestation is likely to be an indulgence mainly afforded by the rich. The mystery-religions, like those of Isis and Osiris, which flooded the West in the time of the Roman Empire, drew many of their devotees from the idle and privileged. Noble Roman ladies were among the addicts, and Apuleius was born of a wealthy and aristocratic family. In our own day, though the Salvation Army may appeal to the poor, theosophy is apt to be a pastime of the leisured classes.

Chapter XII

PLATO AND ARISTOTLE

THROUGHOUT the greater part of this book, our quest has been an understanding of the mind of the majority. This was not undertaken in the spirit of a sentence which I remember once reading in the *Cambridge Companion to Shakespeare Studies*, that "for the serious student of any period, the average is more important than the conspicuous exception". If that were true, our prospects as serious students of classical Greece would not be bright, since for all the great work that has been done to assist our comprehension of the average man of Greece 2,500 years ago, we shall always inevitably know more about the conspicuous exceptions, as they doubtless were, whose magnificent works have come down to us. In so far as our inquiry was directed to the average, this was done, as I stated at the outset, in the hope of enlarging our appreciation and understanding of the leading spirits in literature and philosophy. To remind ourselves of this, and as a relief from the difficulty and uncertainty that have beset much of our path hitherto, let us conclude with a glance—it can be no more—at the two greatest philosophers of our period, the period before the conquests of Alexander submerged the idea of the city-state in that of "the inhabited world", and Hellenism became a missionary culture, thinned out and mingled with the vast lump of which it was henceforth to be the leaven.

I. Plato

Plato's dialogues are a unique compound of philosophy, religion and poetry. They are moreover in dramatic form, and the subtle characterization of the speakers is sometimes not the least of the author's aims. Their value lies in the direct impression which they make upon the reader, and I have never found it easy or profitable to go out to meet them with sharp logical weapons and cut them into neat parcels of philosophical theory or religious doctrine. Yet one thought is perhaps better than none, if we remember how inadequate and partial it must be, and one thought occurs to me as having some continuity with our theme and therefore worth consideration here.

It will be obvious that much of what I have described as typical of the Greeks in religion depended for its survival on the existence of the city-state organization of society. It was not so much that they made the Church subordinate to the State as that they had only a state and no church. The only people who might have liked to give them one, with its own priesthood separate from the officials of the state, were the Orphics, and they had no use for them. The inclusion of religion in the corporate life made possible by the small city-state meant that, as we have seen, personal religion was something almost unknown in Greece. The compact nature of society had a very wide effect, for its ability to give to so many of the community the opportunity for an active and satisfying life prevented the overflow of those individual religious yearnings and fears which are never far beneath the surface. To be convinced of this we have only to look beyond and see what a flood of other-world religion was let loose on Greek lands once the restraining influence of the city-state was gone. Many features of Hellenistic religion can be traced to an origin in the earlier Greece. But whereas up to the fourth century they have to be searched for in holes and corners, in the later period they set the tone and dominate the minds of high and low.

Now Philip and Alexander, by sealing the doom of the city-states, only completed in drastic fashion a process of decline which had been going on for a considerable time. This compact unit had long been subject to attack on both its political and its religious sides. The attack had taken a variety of forms. Natural philosophy, mysticism and the sophistic movement, aided, from the middle of the fifth century onwards, by the disruptive effects of inter-state warfare, had all in their different ways contributed to loosen the foundations of the established traditions. The first said that the gods could not possibly exist in the form in which the city had inherited them from Homer; the second, that a man's religion might concern his own individual soul and not his duty to the state; and the third suggested that the laws of the city had after all no divine sanction: they had been made by man and might as easily be unmade.

These various currents of thought had already been having their effect for some time when Plato wrote. Since he was among other things a practical political thinker, who had renounced an active political career only to devote his life to the consideration of political ideas, he was committed to one of two courses. Either he must join with the disruptive forces, consign the city-state with all its institutions and convictions to the past, and out of the different elements that had brought about its downfall build up a new society and a new religion to take its place; or else he must use all his powers to uphold the city-state, refuting its opponents when they were wrong, and using them only to add strength to its framework when they were right and represented an element whose lack was a weakness in the existing order. In any case the two sides, political and religious, must go together. No real reform of religious faith and life could take place without a corresponding reform in the structure of the state. All this was clear to Plato, and he threw the whole of his forces on the side of Hellenism and the city-state. The writing of the *Republic* in the prime of his life, and his return to the same subject at the end of it with the *Laws*, show that he was true to the same ideal throughout, the ideal of a reformed society based on the purification and strengthening, not on the abolition, of the city-state. Among the ruling classes in Plato's *Republic* the individual is to be subordinated to the common weal with what appears to our eyes an excessive relentlessness. The taking away from these, the most valuable citizens of the state, of property and family life, the communal supervision of their children, the distribution of duties and privileges according to an almost inexorable system of class-distinctions—all this seems shocking to our eyes. One of the listeners in the dialogue itself is moved to remark that those who in the new order are to be the masters of the state do not seem destined for a particularly happy life, since they will have no houses or lands or other possessions but live as if they were a garrison of mercenaries—without even drawing a mercenary's pay, as Socrates points out to make his friend's criticism even stronger than it was. The only reply given is: "Our aim in founding the city was not to give especial happiness to one class, but as far as possible to the city as a whole." The measures proposed were the logical conclusion of the city-state, and Plato saw that it had no chance of survival unless it were pushed to its logical conclusion and deprived of the individual vagaries which, in the circumstances of the time, only gave room for the operation of the destructive forces already at work within it.[1] Only if it preserved a homogeneity, or rather a harmony as Plato would put it, based on the acceptance by each citizen of an allocation of function according to character and capacity, could it hope for salvation. The saint of Platonism is Socrates, who sat in prison awaiting death while his friends devised a plan for his escape, and replied to them in words like these: "Do you think a city can go on existing, and avoid being turned upside-down, if its judgments are to have no force but are to be made null and void by private individuals?"[2]

How then did Plato deal with the three main movements of thought, natural philosophy, the teaching of the sophists, and mysticism, which threatened the continued existence of the idea of the city-state and its religion? That is the question which I propose as the subject of our necessarily limited discussion. In the work of the natural philosophers, by which I mean here the Milesian school and its successors, his all-embracing mind felt a much keener interest than had his master Socrates. Yet so far as their effect on human conduct was concerned, the objection made by Socrates was valid for Plato also. They had been content to raise the question of matter, and considered that the explanation of the universe lay in finding out what it was made of. The question of a first cause was solved (or as Aristotle not quite fairly put it, "lazily shelved") by assuming a power of self-motion in the world-stuff itself. When this conception became no longer tenable, and Anaxagoras therefore assumed a moving cause separate from matter to which he gave the name of "mind", his predominantly physical interests caused him to ignore the philosophical implications of his own statement and "drag in" this mind, as a purely mechanical cause, only when at a loss for another explanation. So at least it seemed to Plato and to his pupil Aristotle. Now Plato had learned from the Pythagoreans that the essential nature of anything lay not in its matter but in its form. If matter is the essence, then there is no real difference between a lump of marble forming part of the flank of Mount Pentelikos and a finished statue from the hand of Pheidias. Similarly in the

[1] Worse was to follow in the *Laws*. Compare the horrifying passage 942a–b quoted by Professor Dodds in his valuable paper "Plato and the Irrational", *J.H.S.* lxv (1945), 20, n. 33.

[2] *Rep.* iv. *init.*, *Crito*, 50b.

natural world, according to an Ionian monist philosopher, there can be no essential difference between a tankful of water and the delicate organism of a racehorse or a human being. Since both are formed of the same ultimate matter, the cause of their difference lies elsewhere, and it is there, said Plato, in the principle of organization by which the matter has been differentiated, that the true philosopher will look for his explanation.

Plato had also learned, especially from Socrates, to equate form with function. A horse and a man differ in the organization of their matter, and it is important to understand these differences of organization, from obvious external facts like the difference between four legs and two, to the internal arrangements of muscles, organs, brain and so forth. These however are but the necessary preconditions for an even more essential difference, namely that horse and man can *do different things.* The horse can run faster and further without tiring. The man can reason. Since the physical arrangements are necessary to the performance of these typical functions, it seemed right to many Greek thinkers, as it seems right to many to-day, to describe them as the *cause* of the functions. This, said Socrates, as he sat in prison on the day of his execution discussing these matters with his friends, is as if one should say that the reason why I am sitting here is that my body is composed of bones and muscles, that the bones are solid and separated by joints, that the muscles are capable of an increase and decrease of tension, and cover the bones together with the flesh and skin which hold them together; that, therefore, when the bones are raised in their sockets, the relaxation and contraction of the muscles makes it possible for me to bend my limbs—and so on and so forth. It is true that without this arrangement of bone and muscle I could not sit here, but that does not make them into the explanation or reason of *why* I am sitting here, which is that my sense of what is right has made me decide to await in quietness whatever fate the state of Athens chooses to decree for me. If it were not so, I assure you these bones and muscles would have been carrying me off at full speed to Megara or Boeotia!

The cause, then, of any object or any natural event is not to be sought in what preceded it but in what lies before it, the end or purpose at which it aims. That is not difficult to admit where human activity is concerned, but to suppose that the cause of all the creatures of nature is to be sought in the same direction, in the function which each is intended to perform, involves a belief in a supreme organizing mind behind the universe. This was Plato's belief, and in this he differed from the natural philosophers. To see further where this belief led him, we will consider how he dealt with the second class of thinkers, the so-called Sophists.

It has often been pointed out that the Sophists did not constitute a particular philosophical school. They were rather a profession, for the name *sophistes*, "Practitioner of wisdom", which hitherto had had none but the most honourable connotation, came to be applied about the middle of the fifth century to a new class of itinerant teachers. An unprecedented hunger for rational guidance in practical affairs was arising at this time out of impatience with the natural philosophers and a growing doubt of the validity of traditional religious teaching. Speculation about the nature of reality had culminated in the opposite extremes of Eleaticism and atomism, the one declaring that all motion was illusion and the real world nothing but an immovable plenum, the other that the only realities were atoms and void and all perceptible qualities merely subjective. If either school were right, then the real nature of things was something utterly remote from the world in which, as it seems to common sense, we have to live our daily lives, and the ordinary man was quick to draw the conclusion that natural philosophy was of very little consequence to him. Before we blame him, we must remember the absence, first, of any experimental proof of their assertions, and secondly of any form of applied science. The physicist of to-day tells me equally that the desk which seems so solid under my typewriter is in fact a whirling maelstrom containing more empty space than solid matter. Yet I cannot turn my back on him and say that in that case its reality is of no consequence to me, since I do not experience it in that way. We are only too dismally aware of the practical impact which atomic science may have upon our lives. The Greek could and did turn his back. The apparent blind alley to which the physicists of his day had brought him was one of the reasons for the general shift in interest at this time from physical speculation to human affairs. Seizing the opportunity which this situation offered, the Sophists filled a real need and made a living at the same time.

Without making the mistake of regarding these men as a single school, we can yet point to certain common features of their teaching. One was its essentially practical nature. They described it as the inculcation of *arete*, a word which is commonly translated "virtue", but means rather "efficiency". A correspondence course in business methods, had such a thing been called for in Greece, would certainly have been conducted by a Sophist. In the setting of Athenian democracy (and Athens was the most profitable place for the exercise of their talents) the road to success lay not through business acumen but through political and rhetorical skill, and those subjects therefore were at the head of the sophistic curriculum.

Besides this community of aim and method, they shared something which may be more properly called a philosophical attitude. This was a common scepticism, a mistrust of the possibility of absolute knowledge, which was the natural result of the impasse to which, as it seemed, natural philosophy had led. Hitherto it had been assumed without question that our senses brought us into some touch with reality. Now however Parmenides had denied this on the ground that the senses show us motion, which his deductive reasoning had proved to be unreal; and the atomists had taught that taste, sight and hearing are alike deceptive, for the atoms, which alone are real, have none of these secondary qualities at all. Moreover the ordinary man, like the philosopher, based his knowledge on the faith that there is an underlying stability in the world. That faith had been rudely shaken. Parmenides only offered unity and stability at the price of disbelieving in all that the ordinary man regarded as real. In atomism there is no unity underlying the bewildering multiplicity of phenomena; there is only an infinite many. Philosophy had set out to find stability by proving that the world is at bottom one. It could not have failed more conspicuously.

Hitherto there had been no philosophy of human conduct. The province of philosophy had been the world of nature, and moral and political precept had been left to the poets, who in Greece were regarded, in the words of Aristophanes, as "the schoolmasters of grown men". In order to understand the attitude of Socrates, Plato and Aristotle it is important to be aware of this point, that moral and political philosophy first arose in Greece (and so in Europe) in an atmosphere of scepticism. The life-blood of philosophy is controversy. Any new development is in part a reaction from the previous generation, and it was this scepticism which Socrates and his successors made it their life-work to combat. Expounding his atomic theory, Demokritos had said that the physical sensations of sweet and bitter, hot and cold, were only conventional terms. They did not correspond to anything real and permanent. That explained why what seemed sweet to me might seem bitter to you, or why the same water might seem warm to one of my hands and cold to the other. It was all a matter of the temporary arrangement of the atoms in our bodies and their reaction to the equally temporary combination in the so-called sensible object. The transference to the field of morals was only too easy, and was first made about this time. Later tradition attributed it to an Athenian named Archelaos, a pupil of Anaxagoras. If hot and cold, sweet and bitter, have no existence in nature but are simply a matter of how we feel at the time, then, he argued, must we not suppose that justice and injustice, right and wrong, have an equally subjective and unreal existence? There can be in nature no absolute principles governing the relations between man and man. It is all a question of how you look at it. Fastening on ideas like this, the Sophists undermined the basis of morals by denying the existence of any absolute standards of conduct.[1]

In a similar way they attacked the immutable basis of law, which had hitherto been regarded as divine in origin. As we have seen, the earliest makers of constitutions, like Lykurgos the legendary founder of Sparta, were believed to have been inspired by Apollo, and it was still customary for lawgivers to apply to his oracle at Delphi and get its advice, or at least its sanction, for their plans. This religious foundation for the laws was now being undermined not only by the atheistical trend of natural philosophy, which the Sophists welcomed, but also by external circumstances such as the increasing contact of the Greeks with foreign peoples and the great body of contemporary lawmaking connected with the foundation of colonies. The first taught them, as is illustrated abundantly in the history of Herodotus, the fundamental differences which might exist between the laws and customs of different peoples living in different climes. As for the second, it was difficult to believe that constitutions came from heaven when one's own friends, or still worse one's political enemies, were on the commission which drew them up. Protagoras, one of the greatest of the Sophists and a fellow-citizen of Demokritos, was himself on the commission appointed in 443 B.C. to draft a constitution for the new Athenian colony of Thurii in South Italy. It is not sur-

[1] Archelaos, Diels-Kranz *Vors.*[5] II, 44 f. Cf. Antiphon fr. 44, ib. p. 346.

prising that he became the first promulgator of a kind of social-contract theory of the origin of law. According to him, men were early driven to band themselves together in communities for reasons of self-protection and the advancement of their standard of living, and social life was found to be impossible if they continued to allow the standards of the jungle to prevail. Hence by painful experience they learned the necessity of laws and conventions whereby the stronger pledge themselves not to attack the weaker simply because they are the stronger. Protagoras emphasized the necessity for this social contract. Other more radical teachers repudiated it, and maintained the natural right of the stronger to have his way and to dominate the mediocre herd. Different conclusions might be drawn, but the premisses were the same for all. All alike based their views on the complete absence of absolute values and standards, whether based on theological considerations or not. All human action was regarded by the Sophists as based on experience alone and dictated by expediency. Right and wrong, wisdom, justice and goodness were high-sounding names and no more. To Plato these premisses were anathema. Whatever conclusions might be drawn from them, they represented in themselves a fundamentally misguided and harmful outlook on the world and human life.

Somehow stability must be restored to the world. Only thus could we discover any standards to guide our conduct, and only thus could we rescue the antecedent possibility of scientific knowledge. Plato had a passionate faith in the existence of both, and in the contemporary state of thought the two were inevitably linked together as one single question. Moral and political anarchy had been the direct outcome of scepticism about the possibility of knowledge. In seeking a solution, Plato was concerned to take account of the often conflicting views of previous thinkers, some of whom made a deep impression on him, and above all to vindicate the convictions of his friend and master Socrates. Other philosophers who seem to have assisted him to his conclusions are Herakleitos, Parmenides and the Pythagoreans.

Herakleitos and his followers maintained that everything in the world of space and time was continually flowing, as they put it. Change never ceased to operate for a moment, and nothing was the same for two instants together. Consequently knowledge of this world is impossible, since one cannot be said to know something which is different one moment from what it was the moment before. Knowledge demands a stable object to be known. Parmenides had argued that there is such a stable reality, which can be discovered only through the thought of the mind working altogether apart from the senses. The object of knowledge must be immutable and eternal, exempt from time and change, whereas the senses only bring us into contact with the mutable and perishable.

Both these schools of thought affected Plato in his task of defending the teaching of Socrates, which may be summed up as a plea for the formulation and use of general definitions. That however needs a little expansion. Socrates' aim was not scientific but moral. He wished to convert men to a better way of living, but as he said, "efficiency in living [*arete*] means knowledge". Life is an art or craft, as much as shoemaking, and the shoemaker will be no good unless he has from the start a clear and detailed knowledge of what he is setting out to do. He must have a pattern in his mind, that is, he must first of all understand what a shoe is, must be able to define a shoe; and to be of any use, the definition must include as its most important element a statement of the function which the shoe has to perform. Shape, style, material and tools all depend on that. In the crafts this is understood, but it should be applied to moral conduct also. In the confusion of ethical thought which was a mark of his time, it seemed to Socrates particularly mischievous that men's talk was interlarded with a variety of general terms descriptive of ethical notions—justice, temperance, courage and so forth—but that no one whom he questioned seemed able to say what these terms meant. Perhaps in the light of sophistic teaching it ought to be supposed that they had no universal and permanent significance. If so, men should stop using them. If on the other hand, as appeared to be assumed, they have a meaning which is the same each time a word is used, men ought to be prepared to say what it is. It is impossible to talk about acting wisely, justly or well without knowing what wisdom, justice and goodness are. If, as Socrates suspected, different people using the same words mean different things, they are talking at cross-purposes and only confusion can result. The confusion will be at once intellectual and moral, and this double side of the problem was what Socrates wished to express by his dictum that virtue is knowledge. So clear and steadfast were his own mind and character that it seemed to him self-evident that if men could be brought to see the truth they would automatically choose the right when they knew what it was. Hence his second famous saying, that no one does wrong willingly.

The required knowledge is obtained in two stages, referred to by Aristotle when he says that Socrates can claim credit for two things, inductive argument and general definition. The logical terms do not sound as if they had much connexion with morals, but to him the connexion was vital. The first stage is to collect instances to which it is agreed that the name "just" (if justice is the quarry) can be applied. Then the collected examples of just actions are examined to discover in them some common quality, or nexus of qualities, by virtue of which they bear that name. This constitutes their essence as just acts. It is in fact, abstracted from the accidental features of time and circumstance which belong to each just act individually, the definition of justice. The fault that Socrates found with the victims of his tireless questioning was that they were satisfied with performing the first stage, mentioning a few scattered instances, and saying "This and that are justice". The type is summed up in Euthyphro who when asked for a definition of piety replied, "Piety is what I am doing now". To another Socrates said, "I only asked you for one thing, virtue, but you have given me a whole swarm of virtues". You must see, he said, that even if there are many and various examples of right action, they must all have one common character by reason of which they are called right. If not, the word is meaningless and should go out of use.

To get from the swarm of virtues to the one thing, virtue, was the aim of the importunate cross-examination which made him so unpopular. It looks like an exercise in logic, but was in fact the only way in which it seemed to him possible to combat the subversive moral effects of much of the sophistic teaching. Those who, in answer to the question "What is piety?" reply "What I am doing now" are the same who will say that the only rule of conduct is to decide on the spur of the moment what is most advantageous. Of rules in the accepted sense, that is, universally applicable principles, there are none. Intellectual idleness led directly to moral anarchy.

In all probability the simple zeal of Socrates did not lead him further than this. It was a position bound to arouse further questioning in the lively and sceptical minds of contemporary Greece. With this questioning the more universal mind of Plato, metaphysically as well as ethically inclined, was pre-eminently suited to deal. The particular question which imperatively demanded an answer was what sort of reality was to be attributed to the entities—justice, wisdom or courage—which Socrates had told us to define. To say that we must not be content with grouping individual actions but go on to discover the real nature of the justice or courage which lies behind them is to make a large assumption, the assumption that such a thing as justice or courage or virtue does exist apart from the acts in which it is manifested. In more modern terms, what is the ontological status of these universal notions? Is there such a thing as absolute justice or is it merely an abstraction of the mind? A number of people have acted in different times and circumstances in a way which we call just. But none of these separate actions is claimed to be identical with the perfect justice whose definition is to be sought. All are thought to be only imperfect approximations to it. Yet what after all can be said to exist except the individual actions? And if nothing else exists over and above them, what we are trying to define is a mere will-o'-the-wisp.

To this problem Plato brought among other things the lessons of his meditations on Herakleitos and Parmenides. Since for him a sceptical answer was unthinkable, he did the only thing possible. He maintained that the objects of knowledge, the things which could be defined, did exist, but were not to be identified with any objects or actions in the perceptible world. Their existence was in an ideal world outside space and time. These are the famous Platonic "Ideas", so called by a transliteration of the Greek word *idea* which Plato used, and which meant form or pattern. To us the word suggests what has no existence outside our own minds, whereas to him the *ideai* alone had full, complete and independent existence. In another way, however, the English word will help us to understand what it was to which he attributed this perfect and independent existence. We say that we have an "idea" of goodness or equality, which enables us to mean the same thing when we talk of good wine or a good cricketer, equal triangles and equal chances, although there may seem to be little shared in common between wine and cricketers, triangles and chances. If there is not some common ground of meaning when the same epithet is applied to different objects, then communication between man and man must be given up as impossible. This common ground we call the idea or conception of goodness or equality. So did Plato. But, he would add, it is just these things which you call merely ideas or general conceptions in our minds which we must believe to be absolute entities with an existence independent of our minds and out of reach of time or change. Otherwise knowledge is an idle dream and its objects are fantasies.

We must suppose then an ideal world containing eternal and perfect prototypes of the natural world. Whatever of quasi-existence our changing world possesses, it owes to an imperfect participation in the full and perfect existence of the other. To explain the relationship between the two, Plato has recourse to metaphor, as Aristotle was quick to point out in criticism. It could hardly be otherwise. Sometimes he speaks of the ideal world as the model or pattern of the other, which imitates it as far as material things can, sometimes of a sharing or participation of the one in the existence of the other. His favourite word to describe the relationship is one which suggests that between an actor's interpretation of a part and the part as it was conceived by the author of the play. We have come to the doctrine, as Plato did, by way of Socrates. Consequently we have met first the Ideas of moral and intellectual concepts. But Plato widened it to include mathematical concepts and natural species. We only recognize individual horses as members of a single species, and have a concept which enables us to use and define the general term "horse", because in the non-material world there is laid up an absolute ideal of horse, of whose being the individual horses in this world imperfectly and transitorily partake.

From this part of Plato's answer to scepticism and sophistic, we begin to get a glimmering also of what his attitude will be to the third of the movements of thought which we have noted, the mystical view of Orphics and Pythagoreans. This will become even clearer as we go on to ask the question how we become aware of the Ideas, and then to look at the theology which Plato put forward in answer to the sophistic assertion, based again on the findings of the atomic philosophers, that the universe and all that occurs in it are due not to intelligence but to chance. After that we will turn directly to the consideration of the place which the mystics have in his scheme, but first these other two parts of his answer to the sceptics must find their place.

Given, then, the existence of a perfect and timeless pattern-world as the cause of whatever reality may be attributed to the phenomena of this in which we live, how and when (it may be asked) did we make the acquaintance of its eternal forms, so that we can as it were refer to them in order to identify the creatures that we see, or recognize as partaking of the Good any good action that we see performed? Here Plato developed and confirmed, in the light of Pythagorean and Orphic doctrine, another side of Socrates' teaching. The exhortation of Socrates to seek knowledge and improve one's life by self-questioning was put in a particular form. He urged men by these means to "tend their souls". This was to his contemporaries a novel and somewhat embarrassing suggestion which itself called for elaboration and defence.[1] Most Greeks were matter of fact in outlook, with both feet firmly planted on the ground. The soul (*psyche*) was not a thing in which they were greatly interested. Many were still under the sway of the primitive notions, shaped by Homer, that it was a kind of breath or vapour which animated the body but in turn was dependent on the body for its effectiveness. At death the body perished, and the *psyche*, left as it were homeless, slipped out "like smoke" into a pale and shadowy existence without mind or strength. Perhaps (as Socrates on the day of his own death mischievously accused his friends of believing) it was particularly dangerous to die when a high wind was blowing, for it might catch up the *psyche* and scatter it to the four corners of the earth! Even for those who through the Eleusinian mysteries, or the "tales told of those in Hades", hoped for something better after death, it was probably a new and astonishing thing to be told that the *psyche* was the seat of the moral and intellectual faculties and of far greater importance than the body.

In support of this conviction of his master's, Plato affirmed that the soul is indeed to be cherished as the most important part of us, for it belongs in essence to the eternal world and not the transitory. It has had many lives, and before and between them, when out of the body, has had glimpses of the reality beyond. Death is not an evil for it, but a release from imprisonment in the body enabling it to fly back to the world of Ideas with which it had converse before its life on earth. Immediately before incarnation it has drunk the waters of Lethe (which perhaps in Plato's mind was no more than an allegorical expression of the actual effect of contamination by the clogging matter of the body), and forgotten all or most of its knowledge of that other world; but in perceiving through the senses, which are now its only instruments, the im-

[1] See the interesting paper of John Burnet, "The Socratic Doctrine of the Soul", in *Essays and Addresses* (Chatto and Windus, 1929).

perfect approximations here below, it is dimly reminded of the full and perfect knowledge which it once had. All knowledge acquired in this world is in fact recollection, and once set on the way by sense-perception, the philosopher will ignore the body as far as possible and subdue its desires, in order to set free the soul (that is, for Plato, the mind) and allow it to rise above the world of sense and regain its awareness of the perfect forms. Philosophy is "a preparation for death", in that it fits the soul to stay permanently in the world of the Ideas instead of being condemned to return once more to the limitations of a mortal frame.

Obviously we can give here no complete outline of Plato's philosophy, and there is a danger that a partial view may be misleading. Lest, therefore, what has been said should suggest a picture of him as sitting with his eyes ever fixed on another world, let us remind ourselves of the sense of duty which he inculcates, for example, in the allegory of the Cave. The philosopher, who has succeeded in leaving the shadow-play of the cavern for the real world in the sunlight outside, will, he says, inevitably be impelled to return and tell his former fellow-prisoners of the truth which he has learned. Such men in fact must form the ruling class of the Platonic Republic. To govern adequately, its rulers must attain a wisdom that is almost divine, for if they are to direct the state towards the good they must know the truth and not merely its shadow. That is to say, they must recover the knowledge of the perfect Idea of which all the goodness in this world is but a pale, unsteady reflection. That is the object of the long and rigorous discipline which they have to undergo before they are adjudged fit to rule. A preliminary education up to seventeen or eighteen is to be followed by three years of physical and military training. There follow ten years of advanced mathematics, leading to five more years of study in the highest branches of philosophy. Some elimination takes place at each stage, and those finally selected are ready for subordinate posts at the age of thirty-five. Political power will then be for these philosophers a burden rather than a temptation, but they will shoulder it for the good of the community. It is another indication that the ruling class in the Platonic state will be by no means the most fortunate.

The most devastating attack levelled by the Sophists at the moral laws which were the cement of the city-state's life was one which transcended the sphere of ethics and based itself on a view of the constitution of the whole universe. Here also they professed to see their favourite antithesis between law and nature. There was no law in nature because cosmologies of the type of atomism left no room for any cosmic force save chance. The main points of the attack are these, as given by Plato in the tenth book of the *Laws*. All the most important things in the world are the products of nature, which one might also call chance, as it is a purely inanimate and unreasoning force. The world itself, the course of the seasons, animals, plants and inanimate nature are in the first place the result of fortuitous combinations of matter. Later came art or design, a more insignificant force of purely human origin, and created a few shadows with little reality about them. Law, and the beliefs that go with it, are the products of this secondary force, and are opposed to nature. The fairness of law is different from the fairness of nature. Justice is purely a creation of law and has no existence in nature. The gods themselves are products of human artifice. They have no existence in nature, but are created according to a convention which differs from place to place. The "life according to nature", which this doctrine upheld, consists in getting the better of others and not being their slaves through stupid adherence to any law or convention. Clearly therefore, to complete the case against these opponents, Plato needed not only an ethic and a doctrine of the human soul, but a more complete metaphysic and a theology.

His reply was that undoubtedly a "life according to nature" was the proper end and aim of man, but that their mistake lay in supposing that there was any antithesis between nature on the one hand and art or design on the other. Nature and art, he said, are the same thing. Design is prior both in importance and in time to chance, since it came first and all the universe is the unfolding of a plan. Consequently to make any distinction between the life according to nature and the life according to law, and to try to exalt one at the expense of the other, is simply to talk nonsense. Art and law are the products of intelligence, and intelligence is the highest manifestation of nature. Here is a metaphysic which, if it could be proved, was obviously going to have far-reaching effects on ethical theories as well.

The young men infected by these pernicious doctrines have, says Plato, inverted the proper order of causation. They suppose the first cause to have been a random movement of matter without life, out of which life arose as a secondary manifestation. This is impossible. Life must have been there first, and is the primary cause of the movements of matter. The proof starts from an analysis of motion, which is first classified in ten divisions.[1] These divisions are then brought under two main heads, spontaneous and communicated. We are seeking the first cause of all motion whatsoever, and this obviously cannot be anything whose motion is communicated to it from outside. It must be something which has the origin of motion in itself, and so can communicate it to everything else. Do we know of anything in our experience to which the definition "self-mover" can be applied? Yes, says Plato, we can think of one thing and one thing only, namely *psyche*, the life-principle. Whether motion is eternal, or as some would have it, all things were at first stationary, self-motion must be primary, and the only self-moved entity is soul. Soul therefore is the oldest of all things and the primary efficient cause of everything.

If soul is prior to matter and the cause of its movements, then the attributes of soul must be prior to material attributes. Mind and will are attributes of soul, and are therefore prior to such material attributes as size and strength. To unite in the one thing, *psyche*, the attributes of life as self-mover and as the moral and intellectual force was for Plato a lesson from Socrates. Yet it did no more than clarify, develope and make explicit a tendency that had been observable in Greek philosophy from the beginning. The Ionians got round the problem of the origin of motion by the assumption that their primary world-stuff moved itself, that is, it was alive. Aristotle explains the statement attributed to Thales that "all things are full of gods" as meaning that "soul is mingled in the whole".[2] As a Platonist he may have read something of his own ideas into the bare statement, but there is no doubt that Anaximander and Anaximenes thought it right to call the stuff of the world "God". It is wrong to call these men materialists, a word which is applied to-day to those who, being well aware of the distinction between matter and spirit, deny the separate existence of the latter. The Ionians belong to a stage of thought before the distinction was consciously formulated. In Herakleitos we see an interesting intermediate stage. Matter and spirit, united in one

[1] It is important to remember that the Greek word for motion (κίνησις) includes not only locomotion but every process of change, whether of quality or quantity, and the birth and dissolution of all natural objects, including (for those who believed that it had a beginning in time) the universe itself.

[2] *de Anima*, i, 5, 411a7.

substance by the Ionians without any misgivings, begin to tug and strain at the bonds which unite them. The philosopher finds that he cannot satisfactorily explain things by causes that are purely material, yet has not become fully conscious of the difficulty, and the need to separate the two. Hence he assigns to a quasi-material substance more and more of the attributes which, in the more fully developed thought of Plato, are taken from matter and considered wholly incorporeal. Herakleitos gives to his first principle the name of fire. Besides being the only material basis of the universe, it is the governing and ordering principle within it, and as we read his fragments it becomes plain that we are intended to identify it with the *logos* or *gnome* and regard it as something intelligent and rational. The concept of rational fire is scarcely one with which philosophy could rest content, and it is not long before Anaxagoras appears with his doctrine of a Mind which not only knows everything and orders everything, but "is mingled with no single thing, but exists alone and by itself". Now that mind and matter were separated, the way was open for the atomist to affirm that dead matter was the only reality, thus attributing all things to chance and occasioning the atheistical theories which aroused Plato's opposition.[1]

In this argument Plato is only concerned to establish his point that the first cause of the workings of the universe is intelligent and moral. He shows no interest in deciding whether there be one god or many, nor by what means the supreme soul initiates in matter the motion of which it is the cause. The existence of evil, and of irregular motion, means perhaps that there are depraved souls at work as well as a good one. But the good and rational soul is in control. This is argued from the fact that the principal motions, those which take place on a cosmic scale such as the revolutions of the stars and sun, the production of night and day

[1] In writing this historical paragraph I confess that I have had in mind the extraordinary statement of Professor Farrington that "the identification of a 'motion that moves itself' with the life principle (*psyche*) was an empty phrase; an analysis that identified the motion of the heavenly bodies with the motion of a living animal was so superficial as to be beneath contempt; the ascribing to the 'motion that moves itself' all the rich connotations of the Greek word *psyche* was a gross logical error springing from a total failure to understand the historical development of language and its symbolic function". (*Science and Politics in the Ancient World* (Allen and Unwin, 1939), pp. 105 f.) From the confusion that would identify self-motion with the *psyche*, Professor Farrington regards the Ionians as having been quite free. The recent study of Werner Jaeger, *The Theology of the Early Greek Philosophers* (Oxford, 1947), is a valuable corrective to this sort of talk.

and the seasons, exhibit an order and regularity which suggest that they are governed by intelligence and not by madness. The good soul then is in supreme control, and that for Plato is the important thing. He is not troubled further, any more than another Greek would be, by the question of polytheism or monotheism. He shows a similar lack of dogmatism about its method of working, suggesting several possible methods whereby soul might initiate movement in matter and ending with the conclusion: "This at any rate is certain, that by one or other of these means it is soul that controls all things."

We have spoken of two of the three currents of thought with which, as we said at the beginning, Plato as the champion of the city-state had got to reckon. They were not wholly separate, since the subversive moral and political doctrines of the Sophists were the natural outcome of the atheistical trend of natural philosophy, and they made great use of its conclusions. The mystical teaching of the Orphics and Pythagoreans was in a different category. In itself it offered no better support to the city-state and its religion than did the Sophists. Yet the pages of Plato are so permeated by it that its later influence may be said to be due rather to the vitality of Platonism than to any vitality which the Orphic poems, or even the religious teaching of Pythagoras, was likely to achieve unaided. In Plato the upholder of the divinity of law, the *malleus Sophistarum*, it is not hard to see the champion of the old Hellenism and the customs and religion of the state. But what of his attitude to the mystics? The truth is that in defending, under the intellectual conditions of his time, the old religious sanction for law he had had to evolve a religion of far deeper content than that of any existing state. We have seen how the struggle to uphold the validity of knowledge, with its corollary of the existence of a real and stable object to be known, had led him on to the vision of a transcendental world of which the human soul has had knowledge when out of the body and will have more perfect knowledge hereafter. It was inevitable that in all this the mystics should become his allies rather than his opponents.

It may be admitted from the start that their doctrines had for him an appeal that was as much emotional as intellectual. He was fascinated by them, and though they might contain much that was blameworthy and more that was best dealt with by a kindly irony, he also saw in them a truly inspired description of what he himself was utterly convinced was true, though reason unaided could never prove it. That is, the potential divinity and immortality of the human soul. In all probability he accepted their eschatological doctrines with little substantial change, except the transformation which they underwent in being newly set forth by a master of imaginative prose, and which has conferred on them an immortality greater, perhaps, than their deserts. Plato was however no pious simpleton, and in the rest of their system he makes some subtle, not to say sly, changes, at the same time altering their application. It is noteworthy that one of the most elaborate eschatological myths, that of the *Gorgias*, comes at the end of Socrates' defence of *nomos*, obedience to the traditions of the state and of accepted morality, against the so-called *physis* ("nature") upheld by Kallikles in his exaltation of the superman. It forms the climax of the defence, and its moral is that even if the individualist may get the best of this life, yet it will be the worse for him in the long run. This application would doubtless have surprised the originators of the eschatological dogmas which Plato employs.

The precepts of the mystics must always be harnessed to the service of philosophy. In his treatment of the other parts of Orphic doctrine there are many touches of irony which show how clearly he had grasped in his own mind the limitations of these people as an influence for right. He had no use for the Orphic life with its mechanical conception of purity. A pure life was certainly the ideal, if it carried with it an understanding of what true purity meant. He uses the language of the mysteries, but with his own modifications. The pure become "the pure in *psyche*", and we know what an intellectual flavour was attached to this word by the disciple of Socrates. The *Phaedo* is full of illustrations, for instance:

SOCRATES: And so I shall set forth cheerfully on the journey that is appointed me to-day, and so may every man who thinks that his mind [διάνοια] is prepared and purified.

SIMMIAS: That is quite true.

SOCRATES: And does not the purification consist, as we have said, in separating the soul [ψυχή] from the body, as far as is possible, and in accustoming her to collect and rally herself from the body on every side, and to dwell alone by herself as much as she can both now and hereafter, released from the bondage of the body?

SIMMIAS: Yes, certainly.

SOCRATES: Is not what we call death a release and separation of the soul from the body?

SIMMIAS: Undoubtedly.

SOCRATES: And the true philosopher, we hold, is alone in his constant desire to set his soul free? His study is simply the release and separation of the soul from the body, is it not?[1]

Similarly at the end of a passage in which he has praised the organizers of *teletai* for teaching that the uninitiated and impure will suffer torments after death and the initiated and pure will dwell with gods, he adds that doubtless they were speaking in riddles. "In my opinion the latter class means those who have rightly studied philosophy."[2]

II. ARISTOTLE

It is inevitable that the philosophical and religious ideas of Aristotle should show traces of mental conflict. His mind was in many ways a contrast to Plato's. Its hallmark was a robust common sense which refused to believe that this world was anything but fully real. Philosophy, as it appeared to him, was an attempt to explain the natural world, and if it could not do so, or could only explain it by the introduction of another pattern-world, devoid of the characteristically natural property of motion and constructed (or so it seemed) out of the imagination, then it must be considered to have failed. That was Aristotle's attitude in his maturity. Yet he was the friend and pupil of Plato for twenty years from the age of seventeen. As a young man he accepted the whole Platonic philosophy—the doctrine of Ideas, the immortality and transmigration of the soul, and the view of earthly knowledge as a gradual recollection of knowledge from another world. So deeply did it impress him that he could think of no better subject for his own first essay in philosophical writing than a dialogue on the immortality of the soul closely modelled on the *Phaedo*. The friendship between the two men was only broken by Plato's death. If he felt compelled, as an independent thinker, to give up the mystical doctrines of the Ideas and the kinship of the soul with the things beyond, there were parts of the legacy which never left him. Fundamentally he remained on the side of Plato and Socrates, and their opponents were his. As

[1] *Phaedo*, 67b–d, trans. F. J. Church.

[2] Ib., 69c. In tempering the religion of *teletai* with philosophy, and in particular with mathematics, Plato was of course following in the footsteps of Pythagoras.

Cornford put it: "For all his reaction towards the standpoint of common sense and empirical fact, Aristotle could never cease to be a Platonist. His thought, no less than Plato's, is governed by the idea of aspiration, inherited by his master from Socrates—the idea that the true cause or explanation of things is to be sought, not in the beginning, but in the end."[1] In other words, the question that both can and must be answered by philosophy is the question "Why?" To answer the question "How?" is not enough.

Here as with Plato we are under the necessity of adopting a strict principle of selection. Aristotle was an encyclopaedic writer and a natural scientist of high achievement, and much of his philosophy has little or no connexion with our subject. For the purpose of outlining briefly his contribution to religious thought, let us define this as dealing with the question of the existence, nature and function of a god or gods, and the relation to him of the natural world and in particular of the human soul. To understand his views on these matters it will however be necessary to make clear two interrelated conceptions which underlie all his philosophical work. These are (*a*) the conception of immanent form, (*b*) the conception of potentiality.

Together with the teleological point of view, Aristotle had naturally inherited from Plato and Socrates a sense of the supreme importance of form, which is the same thing expressed in a different way. To understand a given object so as to be able to define it, it was necessary to know not only the matter *out of which* it was made, the initial state from which it had developed. This was a secondary consideration, since the original matter was something shared by that object with other things which had developed differently, whereas the aim of definition was to lay bare the characteristics which *distinguished* it from other things. The definition then must describe the form *into which* it had grown. In that, according to Plato and Aristotle, lay its essence. In this question of whether the essence of things is to be sought in the "out-of-which" or the "into-which", we are introduced to a fundamental cleavage of outlook which exists in the present world as much as in the ancient, and among laymen as well as philosophers. Knowing as we now do that man has evolved from much lower types of life, it is natural for some to say that he is "after all nothing but" an ape, or even a piece of protoplasm, which has

[1] *Before and after Socrates* (Cambridge, 1932), 89 f.

happened to take a certain direction. They define with reference to his past. To others his essence lies in the qualities which now distinguish him from the lower forms of life to which he may once have belonged. They see it not in what he has left behind, but in what he now is and even in what he is capable of becoming. The ultimate reason for the choice is probably not rational, and it is notoriously difficult if not impossible for the one set of people to convince the other by argument. The first-mentioned set cannot have any religion, in the sense in which the word has been used in this book.[1]

Here, then, was Aristotle's problem. He was a Platonist, first, in being the enemy of the sceptic. He entered on his work in the belief that knowledge was possible. He was also a Platonist in acknowledging the supremacy of form as that in things which must be understood if the philosopher was to make good his claim to explain them. But he rejected the Platonic explanation which demanded the belief in a transcendent world of changeless and eternal forms in whose being the transient phenomena of our experience have some sort of share. He saw no evidence for the existence of such forms, and considered that even if they existed they could not serve as causes in any way which we can understand or express save by deserting rational thought for the language of poetry and metaphor. Nature is always changing. Aristotle went so far as to define nature as an internal principle of, or impulse towards, change and motion. To leave that out of account is to omit the one thing above all others which calls for explanation, yet it is precisely at this point that the theory of Ideas breaks down and takes refuge in figurative language.

Thus the fight against scepticism must be taken up again, and the problem faced afresh: how bring within the compass of rationally acquired knowledge a world of unstable phenomena, always changing, this one passing away and a new one coming into being, never the same for two instants together? Aristotle's answer is contained in the two concepts which I have already mentioned as underlying all his special investigations.

(*a*) *Immanent form.* Granted, said Aristotle, that at a first view

[1] The statement that Marxism is a religion is one designed to bring into the light certain aspects of it which are undoubtedly real, and has served a valuable purpose in showing them up. But it needs its own explanation, and cannot stand without important reservations.

the world seems to be in constant flux and to offer no fixed truths such as alone can be the objects of philosophic knowledge, yet the investigator can, by a process of thought, analyse this flux and find that there are underlying it certain basic principles or causal factors (*archai*) which do not change. These are not a set of substances existing apart in Platonic remoteness, but they are capable of being thought of separately. Though they are not changeable, the creatures of nature change by reason of the presence or absence of the *archai* in them. Such *archai* are the objects of the philosopher's search.

In asking what these *archai* are, it is essential to remember Aristotle's initial common sense postulate that only the individual sensible object has separate existence. For its sake the whole investigation is being carried out—this man, this horse, this house. To understand this individual as far as it is understandable, we must grasp certain things about it—the class to which it belongs, the internal structure which logically it must be supposed to have. This question of structure involves talking about its logical constituents separately, but must not mislead us into thinking of them as if they existed separately, which they never do. We must picture the philosopher examining the things he sees around him in an attempt to abstract, by means of logical analysis, certain common principles which exist (they are not inventions of our own minds), but exist only combined in the concrete objects. They can nevertheless be regarded separately by a mental process, and, so seen, will explain the nature of the concrete object itself.

In this way, each separately existing object in the sensible world is resolvable into a compound, the Greek word for which, *syntheton*, is for Aristotle synonymous with such an individual object. It consists at any given moment of a substratum (*hypokeimenon*), also called its matter (*hyle*), informed by, or possessed of, a certain form or quality (*eidos*). Since perceptible things change, and change was conceived of by the ancients as taking place between two opposites or extremes (e.g. in colour from black to white, in temperature from hot to cold and vice versa), Aristotle made use of the term which had been employed by the earliest Greek thinkers and called the forms also "the opposites". The reason why his predecessors had found the problem of change so baffling, he said, was that they had argued as if it demanded assent to the supposition that these opposite qualities could change into one another. They confused the statement "this hot thing has become cold" with the statement "heat has become coldness". Such a violation of the law of contradiction is impossible, hence the need to postulate the substratum, which is in itself (though of course it never exists naked and alone) quite qualitiless.[1] Given this substratum, one can explain an act of change—e.g. cooling, fading or death—by saying, not that heat, darkness in colour, or life have changed into their opposites cold, lightness, death, but that the heat, darkness or life have left the concrete object and been replaced in it by something else. The distinction had been already made by Plato, who speaks in the *Phaedo* (103b) of the confusion of thought resulting from an identification of "the things which possess the opposites" with the opposites themselves. Aristotle's solution differed however in this essential respect, that whereas Plato had imagined the forms as existing apart and by themselves, at the same time as they in some mysterious way "entered into" the concrete things which were called by their names, for Aristotle they were always in some physical body.

(*b*) *Potentiality* (Dynamis). Here it must be said of the Platonic and Aristotelian teleology that it demanded the actual existence of the *telos*, that is, the end or aim at which the activity of the natural world is directed. There is more in it than the idea of ordered progress towards a final state. Ordered progress is a perfectly possible conception without the assumption that the perfection, or goal, to which it is directed already exists,[2] but the Platonist does not think in that way. In Aristotle's words: "Where there is a better there must be a best", or as we might put it to-day, comparisons are meaningless unless there is an absolute standard to which they may be referred. You cannot speak of progress at all, or indeed know whether things are going forwards or backwards, unless your scale of values is other than purely relative: and it must be relative unless there exists somewhere a perfection by which they can be judged, according as they fall short of it by less or more. To avoid obscurity, it will be better to state explicitly at this point that the *telos* of Aristotle's world is its god, who is the only pure form existing apart from matter (*hyle*) and therefore apart from body. He is not the form *of* anything in the world, so

[1] It is therefore important not to confuse matter in the Aristotelian sense (ὕλη) with its modern meaning of corporeal substance, the Greek for which is σῶμα.

[2] It is for example the conception favoured by Julian Huxley in *Essays of a Biologist* (London, 1923) and elsewhere. He expresses the difference as that between *evolutionary* and *emergent* progress.

we are not brought back to the separate specific forms of Platonic idealism, which seemed to Aristotle a kind of useless replicas of perceptible things. The characteristics of this being we must leave for the moment, and continue in the world of sense. In this world every newly conceived creature has before it an example of perfection within its own species, that is, its parent. The perfection is not of course absolute, but the term may be used comprehensibly, if loosely, to signify the relationship of the adult creature to the embryo or immature, just as the term "perfect insect" is used by entomologists of a butterfly to distinguish it from the egg, larva or pupa. It is the "nature" of the infant animal or plant to strive to realize its own specific form, as exemplified in the parent, whose previous existence is a necessity (as efficient, formal and final causes in one) if the birth and subsequent development of the new member of the species is to take place. Had the world been created in time, the hen would, in Aristotle's philosophy, have come before the egg. He held however that it has existed eternally, and its existence is ensured by the eternal and absolute perfection of the pure form, God. Having no matter, he has in him no possibility of change. Moreover, just as the individual infant creature requires a parent, that is, an instance of perfection in the circumscribed and relative sphere of the species, so the whole world collectively demands the existence of an absolute perfection for its continued maintenance. By realizing as adequately as it can its own specific form, every creature may be said to be progressing by its proper and natural method as near as is possible for it to the nature of God.

Natural organisms possess an innate tendency to develop in this direction. That accounts in general terms for the process whereby an acorn grows into an oak or an embryo into a man. It is the definition of natural objects that they "contain within themselves a principle of motion and rest", and nature (*physis*) herself is defined as "the principle and cause of motion and rest to those things . . . in which she inheres primarily".

This whole-hearted acceptance of the idea of development,[1]

[1] To avoid misunderstanding, it is necessary to state that the Aristotelian idea of progress in nature does not imply any theory of evolution in the Darwinian sense. Not only his general theory of motion, but also a number of statements in his biological works make one wonder that he did not stumble on such a theory, but he did not. The immutability of species, like the eternity of the world, is for him an accepted fact. The progress of which he speaks is only that of the individual from birth to maturity, within the limits of its specific form.

and hence of motion, in nature, laid Aristotle under the obligation of answering those who, like Parmenides, had denied the possibility of motion. The dilemma of Parmenides was as much as anything a result of the immaturity of logic and language in his day, and the way of escape from it had already been pointed out by Plato. As Aristotle paraphrased it, it ran as follows: There is no such thing as becoming, since neither will that which *is* become (for it already is), nor can anything come to be out of what is not. Plato had already shown that this dilemma depends for its effectiveness on the inability to realize that the verb "to be" is used with two quite different meanings, i.e. to exist ("before Abraham was, I am") and to have a certain quality (to be white, hot, &c.). Building on Plato's foundation, Aristotle introduced as his solution the twofold concept of being as either potential or actual, a distinction so constantly used to-day that it is difficult to remember how much thought was needed to prepare the way for it.

The old antithesis between "what is" and "what is not" does not, he said, represent the true position. Certainly where nothing at all exists, there never can be anything. No Greek would deny the dictum *ex nihilo nihil*, and that was one of the reasons why he held the world to be eternal. That however is not the situation we have to deal with. An embryo "is not" a man. This simply means that it does not at present possess the form of a man. The statement does not imply non-existence, but rather the positive fact that here is a piece of matter of such a nature that it is possible for it to become a man. In other words it is potentially a man. In Aristotle's own words:

> The matter which changes must have the potentiality of both states. Since being is thus twofold, everything that undergoes change passes from being potentially to being actually, e.g. from potential whiteness to actual whiteness, and similarly with growth and decay: so that not only is it possible for something to come to be out of what is not—only "incidentally" not—but it is also true that everything comes to be out of what is, i.e. of what is potentially, though it is not in actuality.[1]

The phrase translated "incidentally" means literally in virtue of a concomitant, or accident, that is, a quality which is contrasted with what is natural or essential to a thing, because it may equally well be present or absent. Individual sensible objects had, as we saw, to be regarded as compounded of a substratum qualified at any given moment by an attribute which lies somewhere on the

[1] *Metaph.* 1069b14 ff.

scale between two opposite extremes. The opposites might each have a name (as heat and cold, life and death). On the other hand language, following thought which in particular instances regards one as having an especially positive character and the other simply as its negative, might provide no separate name for the second of the pair save what described it as the negative of the other (e.g. order and disorder, in Greek *taxis* and *ataxia*). This phenomenon of language leads Aristotle to speak sometimes not of two opposite forms, but of a form and its *steresis*, which literally means no more than the deprivation or absence of the form. Since however nothing can exist in an absolutely formless state, *steresis* had a positive content too, and this is not without its importance in Aristotle's philosophy. When he says that a thing is characterized by the *steresis* of a certain form, he means that it consists of matter plus the potentiality of realizing that form. Its nature is so far developed already as to determine what its proper function should be. Thus the function of an eye is to see. In Aristotelian terms, it has not fully realized its form and actuality unless it is seeing. If then an eye is blind, it is characterized by the *steresis* of sight. The statement cannot properly be applied to the leaf of a plant, though that does not see any more than the blind eye, because it is not its nature to see. If on the other hand a plant is grown in the dark so that its leaves are white, they are rightly said to be characterized by the *steresis* of greenness, which it is their nature to attain. It is another illustration of how Aristotelian philosophy, like the Platonic, is dominated by the teleological point of view. Form is essence, or the true nature of a thing, and the full possession of form is equivalent to the proper performance of function.

The two conceptions here described—(*a*) immanent form and (*b*) the notion of potential and actual being—are closely interrelated. The view of natural creatures as progressing from the potential to the actual cannot be separated in the mind from the analysis of things taken as they stand at any given point of time, which reveals the necessity for an indeterminate substratum capable of being informed to different degrees by qualities which in themselves are untransformable. The one might be compared to an instantaneous x-ray photograph. The other is a dynamic explanation of the process. Since however it seemed to Aristotle that the phenomena primarily demanding explanation were motion and change, it is the dynamic view of nature given by the concepts of *dynamis* and *energeia* which dominates the system and is of most use to its inventor in formulating his theories in every branch of knowledge.[1]

We can now approach the question of the Aristotelian god and his relation to the world. Plato in his old age had defined god as soul and soul as self-mover. Aristotle started from that point, but could not rest there, since the conception did not satisfy his conscientious rationalism. His god was not an initial postulate, but the final step in a chain of reasoning. His theory of motion was worked out first, and according to that theory a self-mover was an impossibility. One or two points about it remain to be made clear, and although they may seem remote from what we are accustomed to regard as theology, a knowledge of them is essential to an understanding of the peculiar nature of the Aristotelian deity.

Everything depends on this, that for every act of motion there must be an external cause.[2] We know that the *physis* of things consists of an innate tendency to, or capacity for, movement, change and development in a certain direction, and is therefore also referred to as *dynamis*. It may be called a power of response to the right stimulus, but is not the complete explanation of the change which takes place. An external cause is necessary as well, without which the *physis* in things will remain dormant. Over against a matter, possessed of a certain *dynamis*, there must be something to act as efficient cause (in its capacity of initiating the motion), formal cause (for in natural generation the initiative can only come from a member of the same species to which the new creature will belong) and final cause (as representing the goal to which the development of the new creature will be directed). In more concrete terms, for anything to come into being and grow up, there must already exist a perfect member of the same kind to be its cause. You cannot have a child without human parents, or a seed that has not dropped from a mature plant.

[1] The English word "potentiality" has a less active sense than the Greek *dynamis*, and represents only one side of it. Often it should rather be rendered by "potency" or "power". It is synonymous with "nature" (*physis*) in the sense in which Aristotle defines that word as an internal source of motion or change.

[2] It is convenient to use the single word motion for the Greek *kinesis*, but it is more than ever necessary to remember the width of its application. It includes generation, growth in size, and every form of qualitative alteration, as well as locomotion.

Motion in the wide philosophical sense is defined as the unfinished process of actualization of the movable, that is, of a potency. The point that there can be no motion without an external moving cause is translated into the same terms of act and potency thus: "What is actually *x* comes to be out of what is potentially *x* through the agency of what is actually *x*", or again: "The mover already exists in actuality, e.g. that which heats is hot, and in general that which generates already possesses the form."[1]

We have then these two statements: (*a*) that motion is the *incomplete* actualization of a potency, or in other words that what is undergoing an act of *genesis* or change cannot already be in full possession of the form which it is tending to acquire; (*b*) that the agent of the change *must* be already in possession of that form. Taken together, the two statements mean that *nothing can move itself*. In order to do so it would, in Aristotle's terminology, have to be both actual and potential at the same time with respect to the same act of change. In other words, since potential and actual are relative terms, it would have to be at the same time in two different stages of actuality, which is impossible.

This condition is satisfied in each separate act of natural production within the physical world: the internal *dynamis* or *physis* of a creature enables it to grow on specific lines once it is started, but it is started from outside. But it must be satisfied also for the universe as a whole. There must be a cause external to it, and since its framework is everlasting the cause must be eternal. Nothing within the universe is completely free from matter and motion, nothing is perfect. A perfect being is demanded, the "best" by which all the "better" and "worse" in the world are assessed, a first cause of motion to which all the causes of motion within the world ultimately owe their being. This cause it will be which keeps in motion the wheeling heavenly bodies, on whose regularity depends the due succession of night and day, summer and winter, and therefore ultimately the life of all living things on earth.[2] Plato had seen this cause in the life-principle itself, which

[1] *Phys.* viii, 257b8: *ἔστι δ' ἡ κίνησις ἐντελέχεια τοῦ κινητοῦ ἀτελής· τὸ δὲ κινοῦν ἤδη ἐνεργείᾳ ἐστιν, οἷον θερμαίνει τὸ θερμόν, καὶ ὅλως γεννᾷ τὸ ἔχον τὸ εἶδος*; *Metaph.* Z. 1049b24: *ἀεὶ γὰρ ἐκ τοῦ δυνάμει ὄντος γίγνεται τὸ ἐνεργείᾳ ὂν ὑπὸ ἐνεργείᾳ ὄντος.*

[2] The stars, it should be said, contain matter, but matter of a finer kind than any in the sublunary world, and hence subject to one sort of motion only, namely change of place. From other forms—generation and destruction or qualitative change—they are free. Thus it is that the main framework of the universe is everlasting

imparted life and motion to others because able in the first place to move itself and requiring no higher cause. To Aristotle this conception of a self-mover had become impossible, and the first cause is therefore a being capable of imparting motion without being subject to any form of motion itself.

We thus arrive at the conception of God as the Unmoved Mover. From this conception his other attributes follow. He is perfect, for whatever is imperfect is subject to motion, having in it a *physis* urging it towards complete form or actuality. He is eternal, which is only another way of stating that he is unmoved and unalterable. He is incorporeal. Nothing that is connected with body, or matter in our sense of the word (*soma*), can be unmoved or eternal, for it must be a *syntheton*, compounded of matter (*hyle*) and form; and *hyle* can always change. Only the *eide* are unchanging. A man as he grows from babyhood becomes more and more fully possessed of the form of man, so that we can say of the adult, in contrast with the child, that he has realized the form. But the form can never be fully realized in the individual. There has not been and cannot be a perfect man, nor, therefore, an everlasting man. The fact that on earth the form is always realized in matter precludes it. If God is perfect, eternal and unchanging, he has no body.

We cannot name the attributes of Aristotle's god without using the terms fundamental to his philosophy—matter and form, potency and act. That is why the explanation of them was a necessary preliminary. Using these terms, we see that it follows, if God is to be free from motion, that he must be pure actuality (*energeia* in Greek). None of him exists only potentially or could ever so exist. Aristotle expresses this as forcibly as possible by saying, not that he exists in actuality but that he is actuality. God is pure *energeia*. What then is meant by *energeia*?

For Socrates, Plato and Aristotle the essence of things is in form rather than matter because form subserves function. What matters is the performance of function.[1] The acquisition of form, then, as a static condition or structure, although in comparison with the unformed matter it represents completion and fulfilment, is not yet the highest stage of being for anything. It is the final stage of preparation. The fulfilment of its being comes not merely in the possession of the proper faculties but in the exercise of them. This is *energeia*. Whereas *kinesis* (motion) is the arduous process of

[1] Cf. p. 337 above.

acquiring actuality, *energeia* is the unimpeded flow of activity which is possible once actuality has been acquired. A mass of metal is potentially a machine. When the machine is built it already has its proper *eidos*. But only when it is running is it in full actuality, only then does it in the strict sense exist in *energeia*. As pure actuality therefore God, though exempt from "motion" (*kinesis*), is eternally active with an activity that brings no fatigue but is for ever enjoyable.

Thus the conception of God as unmoved (or unchanging) and as pure form, unsatisfactory as it remains, for several reasons, to the religious mind, is not quite so cold and static as it appears at first sight. The essential quality of God is life, the best of all lives lived eternally without fatigue. It is indeed extraordinary how through the staccato jottings (for they cannot be otherwise described) in which the attributes of God are set down in book *Lambda* of the *Metaphysics*, Aristotle succeeds in expressing, and even communicating, a sense of warmth and enthusiasm. He even seems anxious to concede all the attributes popularly associated with divinity which are not inconsistent with his premisses, though never forgetting that he is a philosopher and that his deity must be one worthy of philosophers, which for him means rational thinkers. God, he says, lives a life which is comparable to the best life which men can enjoy for a short time. In men the element of matter or unrealized potentiality soon mars its enjoyment with fatigue, but God being all activity cannot feel fatigue.

Of what then does his activity consist? He is engaged in eternal thought. In one of the lapidary phrases which are our rare compensation for possessing only the notebooks of Aristotle and not his published works, he sums up the philosopher's creed: ἡ γὰρ νοῦ ἐνέργεια ζωή—the highest and truest activity of life is the exercise of the mind. *Nous* is life in its highest manifestation. It is not the same as *syllogismos*, the process of reasoning things out step by step. That is a *kinesis*, a progress from potentiality to actuality which the imperfect minds of human beings have to go through if they are ever to be rewarded, as they may be after sufficient well-directed effort, by the sudden flashing glimpse of the whole truth which is attained by unadulterated *nous*. God, as we know, goes through no processes. He is pure mind, which can contemplate in a single instant, and does so eternally, the whole realm of true being.

It is a splendid thought, but unfortunately we have not finished with the philosophic conscience. "The whole realm of true being"—yes, but of what does this realm consist? God, says Aristotle, must clearly think only of what is highest and best. We cannot suppose him to expend his thought on any chance object. That is a slightly rhetorical consideration, but there are more strictly philosophical objections to any contemplation by God of the lower orders of nature. It would be difficult to maintain the initial postulate on which all his nature depends—his freedom from *kinesis*—if we tried to imagine any way in which he might be supposed to think of creatures which are themselves subject to *kinesis*. God's thought therefore is not of the world or of anything in it, but simply and solely of himself, the only pure and active being untainted with matter and potentiality. "He thinks himself, therefore, if his thought is of the best, and his thought is a thought of thought." Thus the most important question, from a human point of view, remains unanswered: What is God's relation to the world, and in what way is he its cause?

The answer to this, as to most questions in Aristotle, is to be found by applying the few fundamental principles of his philosophy. Indeed, though we may dislike the conclusions to which it led him, it is impossible not to admire his consistency. According to his philosophy, there are four aspects of natural causation: material, efficient, formal and final. In any act of change there must be a matter to be acted on, a moving cause to start the process, a form or mould to which the matter is being fitted and an end at which the process is directed. Yet although these four factors must be present for an act of change to take place, they are normally manifested in only two separately existing entities. On one side is the material, endowed with *physis*, the same thing as *dynamis* or the capacity for development, and on the other the external cause which calls this latent power into activity. In natural generation this cause—i.e. the parent—includes the other three aspects in itself. It can only be the efficient cause which calls the new creature into being because it represents (relatively but adequately in comparison with the embryo) the form which the new creature is to attain and the goal to which its growth is directed. It is efficient, formal and final cause in one. Moreover once the initial efficient act, the begetting, has taken place, the parent need theoretically take no interest in the offspring, whose internal *physis* will assure its continued development provided the perfect members of the species only exist to provide the model for its growth.[1]

It is thus with God and the world. The only difference is that here there is no initial act of creation in time, because Aristotle believes that the world was never created but is coeval with time itself. This does not remove the necessity for a first cause, for it is fundamental to Aristotle's philosophy that all *physis* and *dynamis* would remain sunk in inactivity were it not for the existence of an external goal of perfection towards which its activity can be directed. In this case, however, the existence of that perfection suffices. God, wrapped in eternal self-contemplation and indifferent to the world, nevertheless calls forth by his presence the latent powers of nature, which strive in their various ways to achieve form and carry out their proper functions in imitation of the one supreme and eternal active being. God does not go out to the world, but the world cannot help going out to him. That is their relationship, summed up in another pregnant phrase: κινεῖ ὡς ἐρώμενον—God moves as a beloved moves the lover. He is the supreme object of desire; and of thought too, adds Aristotle, for to desire the truly good, as opposed to the merely apparent good, is to mingle one's desire with reason. Besides, desire and thought are two examples, and the only examples, of ways in which a thing or person can move without being moved. A person who is loved by another may be the cause of a whole series of mental and physical actions on his part without even being aware of his existence. In approaching the ultimate mystery (he would never have called it that), Aristotle like Plato describes it by an analogy. Plato explained all movement in the universe by something familiar to everyone, the life-force; Aristotle by an equally undeniable fact of experience, the psychological phenomenon of desire. Cornford spoke of "the idea of aspiration" as a common feature of the philosophies of Socrates, Plato and Aristotle. *Eros* is a conception by no means foreign to Plato's thought, but it is in Aristotle that "the philosophy of aspiration" finds its culmination.

The question of the position of man is not a simple one. Like everything else in nature, he has a function to perform, and like everything else he is a compound of matter and form. But he is a compound of a peculiar kind, and his function is correspondingly

[1] Parent for Aristotle, in the sense of efficient-formal-final cause, means male parent. He believed that the function of the female was only to provide the matter.

complex. Having a material nature he shares much in common with the other animals. Bodily needs constrain him and he is subject to fatigue so that his activity on the highest level can only be intermittent. But on the side of form he possesses something which makes him unique among natural creatures. He possesses reason. Pure reason is the only characteristic that can be ascribed to God, and it may be said therefore that the highest and best part of man's nature is identical with the nature of God. This Aristotle states explicitly when at the end of his treatise on human conduct he allows himself to leave the lower spheres of moral and political life and expatiate for a moment on the highest and noblest activity which is open to man.[1]

> If then *nous* [mind in its highest manifestation] is divine in comparison with the human being, the life of *nous* must be divine in comparison with human life. But we must not follow the advice of those who tell us to "think human thoughts being human", or mortal thoughts because we are mortal. No, let us be immortal as far as we can and do everything possible to live according to the highest that is in us. Even though it be but a small part, yet in power and in worth it far exceeds everything else. Moreover it is this which may be thought actually to *be* each one of us, since it is the ruling and better part; and it would be absurd to choose not one's own life but the life of something else. This is in agreement with what we have said previously: what is proper to each thing is naturally the best and pleasantest for it. So therefore is the life of mind for man, since mind in the fullest sense *is* man.[1]

Even in the severest of Greek philosophers the old religious antithesis is echoed. Must man, being mortal, be mindful of his mortality and think only mortal thoughts, or should he strive to cast it off and make divinity and immortality his aim? And the severest of Greek philosophers, the champion of reason, the denouncer of myth, replies: "Man's highest nature is identical with God's. Cultivate it, and emulate the immortal."

The philosopher may, for short periods, attain this supreme intellectual experience of union with the divine. Most men never reach it, and even for the philosopher the activity of contemplation cannot be continuous and at all times he must live a life on the physical plane among his fellows. A community is necessary for the good life, and this brings with it the need for moral virtue and for laws. Man, that unique compound, is "by nature a political animal", and even the philosopher, the most withdrawn of men,

[1] *Eth. Nic.* x, 1177b30.

cannot pursue his researches if his bodily existence is passed in an ill-organized community of bad men. Aristotle therefore divides human virtue into two sorts, moral and intellectual, and devotes the greater part of a considerable treatise to the former. Its study was necessary for practical ends, but the whole subject is clearly for Aristotle a descent into the Cave, a temporary turning of the back upon the search for truth which is philosophy. This is apparent not only from his almost lyrical outburst in praise of pure thought at the end of the work, but from constant reminders during the course of it that since he is dealing with the contingent it is no use aiming at truth or knowledge. These are strangers to the realm of the contingent, and the only possibility is to give some practical rules which, having been arrived at empirically, will probably work. Now that the virtues no longer form, as they did for Plato, the content of a changeless ideal world, no other alternative was left. The following extracts illustrate his approach to the subject of ethics:

> It is the duty of an educated man to aim at accuracy in each branch of inquiry only as far as the nature of the subject allows it. To demand logical demonstration from an orator would be no more appropriate than to admit the art of persuasion in mathematics.
>
> We must remember what we said before, and not strive after exactness indiscriminately in everything, but only with reference to the subject-matter and to the extent that is proper to the inquiry. A builder and a geometrician do not look for the same degree of straightness in a line. The one seeks it only in so far as it is useful to his work, but the other tries to discover its essence and the sort of thing it is; for he is a contemplator of the truth.
>
> The present inquiry does not aim at knowledge [*theoria*] as our others did. Its purpose is not to know what virtue is, but to make ourselves good.
>
> In the field of conduct the aim is not to contemplate or to know, but to act.[1]

It is not hard to see how this split between knowledge and conduct, this denial of "virtue is knowledge" in a man who was still in so many things the spiritual heir of Socrates, sprang directly from the renunciation of the Platonic Ideas.

One final question. What were Aristotle's beliefs about the prospect of immortality, which seems to be hinted at in his deifica-

[1] *Eth. Nic.* 1094b23, 1098a26, 1103b26, 1179b1.

tion of *nous* and identification of it with the highest faculty of man? It is difficult to know exactly, since there is little in his writings that has a bearing on the subject. From this very circumstance, and from his consuming scientific curiosity about the natural world, we may legitimately infer that it did not greatly interest him. On a strict interpretation of his psychology, any survival of the soul after the dissolution of the body would appear to be impossible. Man like other natural objects is a unity, and his components of form and matter are not separable save in thought. To ask for a general definition of soul is not very helpful, since it can only be understood in its varied manifestations (e.g. movement, sense-perception, thought). If however one must attempt such a general definition, it can only be that soul is the form of an organic body.[1] Thus any belief in the transmigration of souls he explicitly and vigorously rebuts, and with it, as it would seem, any suggestion that the soul might survive in separation from the body. Body and soul are one thing. It follows, he says, from the fact that soul is the form or actuality of a living body that "the question whether soul and body are one is no more legitimate than the question whether the wax and the impression of the seal are one, or in general whether the matter of a thing is one with the thing of which it is the matter."

This seems conclusive. Nevertheless he appears to have held, as the passage at the end of the *Ethics* would suggest, that *nous*, the highest manifestation of the reasoning faculty, was of a different order from the other vital principles, and to have left open the possibility that it might be a separate substance existing in its own right and survive the death of the body and of the faculties of nutrition, sensation and mere "putting two and two together" (*syllogismos*), which belong to man as a composite creature. We cannot hope to understand Aristotle's inmost thoughts about the nature of *nous*, for he has nowhere set them down in the writings that survive. But side by side with the hints in the *Ethics* we may put a passage like this from the *De anima*:

> Concerning *nous*, or the faculty of active thought [τῆς θεωρητικῆς δυνάμεως], we have as yet no evidence. It appears to be a generically different manifestation of soul, which alone is capable of separation, as the eternal from the perishable. The other parts of soul have been clearly demonstrated not to be capable of separate existence as some

[1] Cf. *De an.* 412b4: εἰ δή τι κοινὸν ἐπὶ πάσης ψυχῆς δεῖ λέγειν.

have maintained them to be, though they are of course different in definition.[1]

He nowhere goes further than this,[2] which however, taken in conjunction with the conclusion of the *Ethics*, leaves no doubt of his belief that in the possession of *nous* man has something which is not shared by other forms of life. Since moreover he shares it with the eternal unmoved first cause of the universe, Aristotle probably believed that in man too it was eternal and need not share the fate of the rest of the soul. Probably the reward of the philosopher was the absorption of his mind into the one eternal incorporeal Mind. More than this he certainly does not say, nor can we say it for him. The tenor of his thought is better seen in those things which his philosophy excludes. The description of the thinking part of us in *De anima*, iii, 4 and 5, makes it clear that there can be no survival of individual personality, and no room therefore for an Orphic or Platonic eschatology of rewards and punishments, nor, as I have noted, for a cycle of reincarnations. The doctrine of form and matter has the last word.

[1] *De an.* ii, 413b24 ff.

[2] The distinction between active and passive reason, which is thrown out in what appears to be a hastily written note in *De an.* iii, 5, is too obscure and disputed to lend any assistance in the question of immortality.

Appendix to Chapter XII

The rash attempt to set out in a few pages such parts of Aristotle's philosophical system as have a bearing on religion could not be made without leaving loose ends. The system was a remarkably coherent one; consequently, the fact that large parts of it have been omitted altogether means that certain questions have been left unanswered which arise naturally out of what has been included. Two in particular occur to me as likely to trouble the intellectually curious. They are (i) the problem of our knowledge of individuals, and (ii) the apparent pathetic fallacy involved in the doctrine that God moves the world as the object of love. I give here a brief note on each.

(i) *Knowledge of the individual*

For Aristotle the individual alone, the τόδε τι or σύνθετον, has full separate existence. (p. 356 above.) The individual, as he says in the *Categories*, is substance in the primary sense. Specific and generic forms are secondary substances, because they exist only in the individuals and not independently. The primary purpose of the philosopher therefore must be to understand the individual. If he seeks to define the specific form, it is with that in mind. I said in the foregoing chapter that it is form, not matter, which distinguishes, say, a horse from a man. This is true, but only means that formal classification enables us to distinguish one whole species from another. Definition can only be by genus and differentiae, and can go no further than the *infima species*. The difference between one individual and another within the same species still eludes us. It is a difference of matter—not of course of pure matter, which *ex hypothesi* is undifferentiated, but of matter so little informed that its differentiae escape the classificatory methods of the scientist. Aristotle's interests were primarily biological and zoological, and it was natural therefore that he should adopt the classificatory methods which are still the basis of those sciences. He insists that they should be followed as rigorously as possible. It is no use trying to define a thing by reference to its genus alone, or to any group or species that is unnecessarily large. Nevertheless the difference between the two twin dachshunds Fido and Bruno can never be stated scientifically, but only by the evasive phrase that they differ in their matter, or as Aristotle also puts it, they are formally one but numerically two.

How then, and by what right, do we first make the generalizations on which depends the method of definition by genus and differentiae? From our earliest years our senses make us aware of an infinite multitude and variety of objects, no two exactly alike and all differing in various degrees. How do we sort them out and begin to become aware of the forms that are in them? I put it in this way because for Aristotle the forms, though no longer existing separately, retain something of the substantiality which was an inheritance from Plato, and to define them was not to impose an order on nature out of our own heads, but to discover a structure that was already there. How and by what right (to put it in another way which was also Aristotle's) do we make inductive judgments?

Doubtless he did not solve the problem. (Has it been solved yet?) But he was aware of it, and since our account of him so far suggests that he was not, it behoves us to make amends. His awareness is shown by such a passage as the following from the *Metaphysics* (B.999a24 ff.):

> Connected with this is a difficulty which is the most obstinate of all, and the most in need of examination, and to this difficulty the argument has now brought us. If nothing exists apart from individuals, and the individuals are infinite in number, how is it possible to have knowledge of an infinite number of things? For it is in so far as they form a unity, and possess some universal attribute, that we know all the things of which we have knowledge.

This takes us to the root of Aristotle's epistemology, which is most clearly set forth in a passage of the *Posterior Analytics* (B.99b 35 ff.), justly described by Ross as a "magnificent account of the unbroken development from sense to reason". If anyone has read so far, he is probably sufficiently interested to read Aristotle's own account, and the reference is enough. Briefly however it may be said that all knowledge begins from sensation. Some creatures are also gifted with memory (defined as the persistence of the sense-impression in the *psyche*), others again with *logos*, the faculty of systematizing the remembered impressions. In man, the instruments of thought are two: *episteme*, which is knowledge acquired by reasoning from premisses, and *nous*, the highest category of mind, which is a kind of intuition. Because man is endowed with a mind, sensation itself is not only of the individual but at the same time in a rudimentary way of the specific form.[1] "What is perceived is the individual, yet perception is also of the universal, e.g. of man, not simply of Kallikles *a* man." When we have seen thousands of men, of whom memory has enabled us to retain the impressions, a consciousness of the universal concept *man* begins to take shape in our minds. Thus the first beginnings of knowledge are acquired through sensation by induction, and the inductive leap from the mass of particulars to the general concept is made possible by the faculty of *nous* which is lacking in the lower animals. When we have clearly grasped the first or lowest universals, *nous* treats them in their turn as individuals and forms higher generalizations until the *summa genera* are reached. We can then proceed by the scientific methods of *episteme*, that is, by syllogistic or deductive reasoning.[2]

(ii) *The "desire" of nature to imitate God*

The objection that the doctrine κινεῖ ὡς ἐρώμενον involves a pathetic fallacy goes back to Theophrastus, who said that if that is so, ἔμψυχα ἂν εἴη τὰ κινούμενα. Does Aristotle illegitimately extend to the whole of nature an attribute which can only properly belong to animate and sentient beings? In this connexion I wish only to draw attention to one or two passages in his biological works which suggest that if he erred, it was due not to a flight from reality into the poetic metaphor of which he was so critical in Plato, but to a view of nature that was implanted, or at least confirmed, by his observations as the first scientific natural historian. The phrase ὡς ἐρώμενον is admittedly a simile, but it attempts to express the conviction that it is at bottom the same impulse, for which no name exists, that manifests itself in the higher animals as desire or conscious aspiration, and in the lower orders

[1] It is important here to remember Aristotle's insistence on the unity of the *psyche*. We do not perceive with one part of us and think with another. In sensation the *psyche* works through bodily organs, but the *psyche* that receives the sensations is the same as that which carries on the activity of thought.

[2] Cf. Ross, *Aristotle* (Methuen, 4th ed. 1945), p. 55, for a fuller account.

Language and thought are so inseparable that it is extremely difficult, thinking in English, to understand exactly what a word like νοῦς meant to a Greek, and how he was influenced by the history of its ordinary usage. With its verb νοέω it seems to have combined the ideas of suddenly becoming aware of something, and of grasping it in its entirety, of sensation and of thought, in a way which our somewhat different minds find it difficult to follow, but which may none the less correspond to something real. Sainte-Beuve's remark on its use in Homer is both true and important: "Homère dit νοέω, je vois, je conçois. Voir et concevoir, c'est la même chose, ce n'est plus la sensation, c'est déjà la pensée, la perception." With the last sentence, compare Aristotle's καὶ γὰρ αἰσθάνεται μὲν τὸ καθ' ἕκαστον, ἡ δ' αἴσθησις τοῦ καθόλου ἐστίν.

of nature as what he called *dynamis* or *physis*. In all alike we see this impulse towards the realization of form, and the reason why it must not be regarded as something generically different in man, mollusc and mushroom is that there are no hard and fast lines in nature. That the *scala naturae* is a smoothly ascending slope, not a ladder with separate rungs, was something which as a practical zoologist he had observed. I may be told that it has something in common with the old idea of the kinship of all nature which goes back to the Pythagoreans and can doubtless be traced to an origin in primitive tribal beliefs.[1] No scientist ancient or modern is entirely free from the "groundwork of current conceptions"[2] which are the common property of his age and country. Yet how far Aristotle had travelled from the irrational or *a priori* conceptions of earlier Greeks is shown, I think, by the passages which I have chosen to illustrate this point.

Part. anim. 681a12 ff. (trans. of A. L. Peck):

The ascidians differ very little in their nature from plants, but they are more akin to animals than the sponges are, which are completely plants. Nature passes in a continuous gradation from lifeless things to animals, and on the way there are living beings which are not actually animals, with the result that one class is so close to the next that the difference seems infinitesimal.

Hist. anim. 588b4 ff.:[3]

Thus nature advances little by little from the inanimate to animals, in such a way that owing to the continuity it is impossible to tell to which class the intermediate creatures and those on the borderline belong. After the class of inanimate things comes first the class of plants, and within this class one member differs from another in the degree to which they seem to possess life. The whole class appears living as compared to inanimate matter, but lifeless in comparison with animals. Moreover the gradation from plants to animals is continuous, as has been pointed out before.

A little earlier (588a18) he has said:

In most of the other animals can be discerned traces of the psychical modes which attain their clearest differentiation in man.

The remarks in the foregoing chapter dealt of necessity with the more speculative side of Aristotle. It is as well to be reminded that he was among other things the first great observer of nature.

[1] Cf. pp. 11 f. above.

[2] Cf. F. M. Cornford, *The Laws of Motion in Ancient Thought* (Inaugural Lecture, Cambridge, 1931), p. 12.

[3] If, as is now commonly thought, this book of the *H. A.* is Theophrastean, I do not think there is a difference here between the teaching of master and pupil. (See Regenbogen in PWK *Realenc. Suppl.* vii, 1433).

GENERAL INDEX

INDEX OF GREEK WORDS

Many Greek words will be found in Latin characters in the General Index. The following occur in Greek characters.